THE GRAND INCENDIARY

The Dial Press

NEW YORK
1973

THE GRAND INCENDIARY

A Biography of
SAMUEL ADAMS
By Paul Lewis, pseud of

Gerson, Noel Bertram

Library of Congress Cataloging in Publication Data

The grand incendiary.

Bibliography: p.
1. Adams, Samuel, 1722–1803. 2. United
States—History—Revolution—Causes. I. Title.
E302.6.A2G47   973.3'092'4 [B]   73–6723

For Anne and Bill

Foreword

On the rare occasions when Samuel Adams found the time to feel sorry for himself, he complained to Elizabeth Wells Adams, his loving second wife, that he was unknown to the world, an anonymous manipulator of men, events and nations. As usual, he exaggerated, but he could not help it, for the twisting of the truth and the magnification of reality had become chronic.

In his own day he was many things to many people. His Harvard College classmates called him the Last of the Puritans because, under the influence of his almost fanatically religious mother, he did not drink, smoke, use snuff or "consort with the wenches who frequented the Boston waterfront." Time and experience, opportunity and temptation changed him, and forty years later he was known to the more sophisticated John Hancock as a modern Nero, a man who could drink more rum toddies, yet remain sober, than anyone else in the new United States, no mean achievement in an era when every gentleman was expected to hold his liquor.

Until he reached the age of forty-two, his fellow citizens were forced to agree with his relatives that he was a miserable failure, and for more than a decade he had been the laughingstock of Massachusetts Bay, the most inept tax collector in the history of the colony. Then he sniffed the most precious of perfumes, the scent of freedom, and everything was changed.

The British considered him a reincarnation of Machiavelli, a cunning insurrectionist who distorted the truth for his own evil ends, a liar and perpetrator of vile mischief. The principal Crown representative in Massachusetts Bay on the eve of the American War of Independence, General Sir Thomas Gage, rightly called him "the most dangerous man in the New World" and put a price on his head.

By that time the Boston masses worshipped him and were willing to follow wherever he led, although the aristocrats—members of his own class—were not yet willing to think of him as anything but a radical and a rabble-rouser. The leaders of other colonies may have been the first to recognize his genius, and eventually their views became widespread: for fifteen years he was rightly regarded as the first citizen of the United States, his stature greater than that of such giants as Benjamin Franklin and George Washington. Gradually the whole world came to know his worth and could measure his contributions to American independence. He was the architect who inspired liberty, and men of talent being in short supply, he necessarily served as his own best operative. It was he who implanted the seed of freedom in the American people, nurtured and fertilized it, then protected the young plant in the hour of the new nation's greatest peril, rallying leaders and the people alike to the cause he believed sacred.

Sam Adams was a living paradox, knew it and enjoyed it, for one of his many gifts was his ability to understand himself. Unlike such leaders of revolution as Bolívar and Lenin, he was no philosopher, and he was a man of peace who lacked the military talents of an Alexander the Great or Napoleon Bonaparte. He had no training for the herculean tasks he performed, awakening the American people to a craving for liberty, uniting them for the struggle, then guiding them on the tortuous path. He was forced to rely on his own instincts, which were unerring, and his own intellect, which was far greater than even the most admiring of his contemporaries credited him with possessing.

By the time the long march through the wilderness to the Promised Land of freedom came to its successful end, Adams's modesty and the emergence of other, more readily recognizable heroes sent him plummeting once again into relative obscurity. Perhaps his vanity was less pronounced than that of colleagues who demanded greater ego fulfillment. Certainly he was more cynical than any of them, wiser in the ways of men and indifferent to the fame he regarded as ephemeral. For whatever the reason, he retired from the front ranks when the military heroes and more aggressive politicians and statesmen moved into the limelight, and stayed there.

Sam Adams has remained in the shadows from the latter years of the eighteenth century to the present, his renown obscured for two hundred years by the brilliance of Washington, Hamilton, Jefferson, Franklin and a host of others. Patrick Henry, the great Virginian whose feelings were similar to those of Adams, has fared better at the hands of posterity. But that does not make Samuel Adams less of a genius; it does not detract from his accomplishments nor diminish his real stature.

His goal was the creation of an independent, democratic nation, and when that end was achieved, he was content. Until the end of his days he remained as indifferent to fame as he was to money, and he died as he had lived, a poor man.

He is the least known of America's Founding Fathers, although he was one of the greatest of them. This book has been written in the hope that, in some small measure, it will help restore him to the high place in the esteem of Americans—and the world—that he deserves.

Paul Lewis

New York City

xi

*If the American Revolution was a blessing,
and not a curse, the name and character of Samuel Adams
ought to be preserved. It will bear a strict and critical
examination even by the inveterate malice of his enemies.
. . . His merits and services and sacrifices and sufferings
are beyond all calculation.*

—John Adams
Second President of the United States

THE GRAND INCENDIARY

Chapter One

In the first quarter of the eighteenth century, when all Americans had not yet been created equal by declaration, few families in the Massachusetts Bay Colony were more equal than the large, prosperous Adams clan. And no Adams was wealthier or held in higher universal esteem than Samuel the elder, a man of many parts, who had moved to Boston from his native Braintree, where the first John Adams who had come to the New World had settled several generations earlier.

Known to his intimates as "the Deacon," Adams, at the age of twenty-four, had married a handsome Bostonian, Mary Fifield, and together they became pillars of society. Adams owned a brewery, and his diligence, combined with his friendship with the city's wealthiest merchant, Thomas Hancock, enabled him to expand his horizons and operations. Hancock supplied him with the finest quality of West Indian molasses, and the Deacon distilled the best rum found anywhere in North America, quite an accomplishment in a land where the making of the liquor abounded. He bought a large property on Purchase Street, overlooking the harbor, and on it he built a comfortable house, less elegant than the Hancock mansion on Beacon Hill, perhaps, but nevertheless one of the showplaces of the city. From the observatory on the top floor Deacon Adams could watch the arrivals and departures of the schooners and brigs of the Hancock fleet, in which he acquired an interest, and as the years passed he could gaze on other properties he bought, among them private dwellings, shops and lodging houses.

If he knew that the Hancock ships engaged in smuggling, successfully avoiding the payment of taxes to the Crown, he did not speak of the matter. And if several of the waterfront lodging houses he owned were used as brothels, that was none of his business, as he was not responsible for the activities of the people to whom he rented his buildings. The Deacon was a firm pillar of the Congregational church, and Mary Adams was said to be the most devout woman in Boston, her reputation inspiring well-deserved awe. Neither the ale nor the rum made by the Adams brewery was served under the roof of the house on Purchase Street, no man dared to smoke or take a pinch of snuff there, and every day at sundown the mistress of the household conducted private worship services.

A public-spirited man, Samuel the elder was a deacon of the Old South Church and a founder of the Summer Street Church, commonly known as the New South. He, together with Hancock and a few others, was a member of a self-appointed group known as the Caucus Club, or the Caucus, which controlled local politics and nominated citizens for public office. Availing himself of the generosity of his friends, the Deacon served at various times as a justice of the peace, a member of the Boston Board of Selectmen, or alderman, and as a representative in the Massachusetts House of Assembly. He made it his business to be on good terms with the Crown-appointed governor of the colony, whoever he might be, and that official returned the compliment, so it was no idle family boast that Samuel the elder was one of the most influential men in Boston, a man in a position to do political favors for friends and associates.

The Deacon and Mary Adams had twelve children, but the infant mortality rate was shockingly high, and only three survived. The eldest of the trio, Mary, was born in 1717; her brother, Samuel the younger, came into the world on September 27, 1722; and a younger son, Joseph, arrived two years later. The Deacon was an exceptionally busy man, so the rearing of the children was left largely in the capable hands of his wife, who was described as "severely religious" by members of the family, and was an earnest disciple of the Reverend Jonathan Edwards, subsequently regarded as the strictest disciplinarian of all New England clergymen.

Religious influences were paramount in the life of young Sam Adams from his earliest childhood, and when his mother was not on hand to supervise him, his sister took charge. He was taught his alphabet by reading the Bible, he was rocked to sleep to the tune of hymns, and at the age of two he knew the Lord's Prayer. He was allowed to play in the extensive gardens behind the house, but the fruit that grew there was forbidden, which made it easy for him to understand the story of Adam and Eve in the Garden of Eden. Since he was an Adams, he was not allowed to wander off and enjoy the company of other children, but he was so lonely that he quietly disobeyed, and from early boyhood demonstrated his democratic tendencies by consorting with the sons of longshoremen and other waterfront dwellers.

Many years later he enjoyed telling stories of his childhood, but by then he had become so adept in the art of spinning a tale for its own sake that his accounts cannot necessarily be regarded as factual. It may or may not be true that the crews of merchantmen allowed him to roam through the ships at anchor in the harbor, that dock workers allowed him to inspect the merchandise from many lands that was piled in warehouses, or that he listened to political debates in the taverns frequented by workingmen. It cannot be denied, however, that in spite of the isolation to which his family tried to subject him, he gained a remarkable understanding of the thinking and aspirations of the ordinary man.

At the age of seven Sam was entered as a pupil in the Grammar School of Boston, an institution favored by Boston aristocrats for the education of their sons. Neither the rod nor religious education were spared, and the boy was forced to write such noble sentiments as "Learning is more important than riches." The emphasis was laid on mathematics, a subject in which he did poorly, rhetoric and grammar, at both of which he excelled, and the classics, which he devoured.

Relatively little is known of Sam's childhood, and posterity has been unable to authenticate the anecdotes concerning that period of his life. He was forced to maintain a discreet silence in his mother's presence, it being taken for granted that children should be seen but not heard, so he was exceptionally verbose in the company of his peers. Athletic pursuits were of little interest to him, but like most boys of the period, he learned to swim at a very early age, and in the winter he ice-skated.

As he grew older his father paid more attention to him, as befitted an elder son, and taught him deportment, a proper regard for being an Adams, and riding, at that time considered a gentleman's accomplishment by the prosperous and a necessity by everyone else. Ambitious for his son, the Deacon had a professional career in mind for him, and tried to encourage his interest in either medicine or the law. Mary Adams, to be sure, wanted him to become a clergyman, but in spite of the pressure she applied, the boy failed to respond positively to the idea. Sam showed no strong leanings toward any particular field of endeavor, and his parents demonstrated their good sense by making no decision for him, waiting instead to see how his interests developed.

In 1736, when the boy was fourteen, he was entered as a freshman at Harvard College, where all male members of the house of Adams were educated. Most of his peers were approximately his own age, and he was ranked fifth in a class of twenty-two, according to a scale based exclusively upon family social standing and wealth. His status remained unaltered during the four years he spent at Harvard.

Little is known of Sam's life as an undergraduate. He displayed remarkable sobriety and diligence, believing he should take full advantage of the opportunities being offered him, and he had only one black mark on his record, earned when he once missed morning prayers because he overslept. Like most students of the period, he concentrated on the classics, philosophy and theology, and he was fascinated by the works of John Locke, the English Father of the Enlightenment, who had died three decades earlier. The influence of Locke on young Adams, and through him on the development of the nation he would be instrumental in founding, is incalculable.

Adams took to heart Locke's political theories and moral philosophy, accepting many of the great thinker's principles without reservation. Government is a trust, and men in power who fail to act for the public good automatically forfeit that trust. The authority of the ruler is always conditional, never absolute, and the governed always retain many rights of their own. The ultimate authority lies in the people, who are sovereign. The functions of government should be separated and vested in executive, legislative and judicial branches, each of which should be independent of the others.

Young Adams's notebooks contained a number of significant quotes from Locke, most of them heavily underlined:

> It is the right of the people to withdraw their support from that government which fails to fulfill its trust. If this does not persuade government to live up to its obligation, it is the right of the people to overthrow it.

> Freedom of men under government is to have a standing rule to live by . . . a liberty to follow my own will in all things where that rule prescribes not, not to be subject to the inconstant, uncertain, unknown arbitrary will of another man.

> The function of government . . . is a right of making laws, with penalties of death, and consequently all less penalties for the regulating and preserving of property and of employing the force of the community in the execution of such laws, and in the defence of the commonwealth from foreign injury, and all this only for the public good.

The phrase "only for the public good" was doubly underlined in the notebook. Young Adams also wrote exclamation points in the margin next to a quotation to the effect that the lawmakers should be elected by all people, under universal franchise. And where Locke indicated that the executive was usually a monarch who inherited his position, the student scribbled in the margin, *"Why hereditary?"*

Out of the welter of Locke's sometimes inconsistent approach to morality, Adams also found a sentence he particularly liked:

> Moral good and evil is only the conformity or disagreement of our voluntary actions to some law, whereby good or evil is drawn on us, from the will and power of the law-maker.

Locke's ideas were already creating a new political atmosphere in England, where such men as future Prime Minister William Pitt the elder were influenced by them. Loyalty to the Crown prevented even the most dedicated of political thinkers from carrying the precepts of Locke to their logical conclusion, as would be done in America and subsequently in France. More moderate in the application of Locke's theories, English politician-philosophers were satisfied with a less drastic approach, and were changing the atmosphere rather than discarding institutions. The Age of Reason made an appearance gradually, and not even its most devoted practitioners thought in terms of revolution, Locke's penultimate extreme.

Nothing practical grew out of Locke's philosophy in Great Britain's North American colonies. Foreign affairs and commerce were controlled by the Crown and Parliament, exercising their wills through the governors of each colony, most of whom were appointed by the monarch. Local affairs were conducted by legislatures, many of which were given a free hand in passing laws that did not conflict with royal policies, but all of which were subject to gubernatorial veto.

No one thought of protesting against the system because the colonies were undergoing such rapid physical and economic expansion that there was no time to question principles and methods of government. Immigrants by the thousands from England and Scotland, and smaller numbers from Ireland, were arriving on every ship, and there was an ever-growing demand for the timber, furs, agricultural products, minerals and other raw materials of the New World.

But the seeds of future trouble were already being sown, although few men on either side of the Atlantic realized it. Until the middle of the eighteenth century, England and her colonies lived comfortably in accordance with the system that had developed naturally. The colonists sent nature's bounty to the Old World, receiving manufactured goods in return, and everyone prospered.

The rapid growth of the American population, most noticeable in such cities as Boston, Philadelphia and New York Town, was gradually creating demands for local manufacture which Parliament was quick to recognize. Attempting to preserve the profitable status quo, the House of Commons promulgated laws that were ignored in the colonies: no manufactures were permitted in the colonies, and even such simple items as iron cooking pots had to be imported from England. Tiny foundries were springing into existence everywhere, people were buying locally made pots and pans, and the legislatures looked the other way. Royal governors, in the main dependent on colonial aides for law enforcement, were either kept in ignorance or chose not to interpret the law too strictly.

So it is no wonder that young Sam Adams did not take the injunctions and advice of John Locke literally. As a student he was interested in pure theory for its own sake, and the thought of taking part in an armed insurrection did not occur to him. Colonial life in the late 1730s was serene; his own family was one of the wealthiest in Massachusetts Bay, and he had no cause for complaint. He was no agitator in his youth, nor were his friends, among them James Otis, the future lawyer who would be the first of the Massachusetts Bay leaders to advocate a break with the mother country.

There can be no doubt that the influence of Locke on the young student was profound, however, and in the early spring of 1740, a few months before he was granted a Bachelor of Arts degree by Harvard, he proposed that the members of the graduating class debate the subject of "Liberty." He was declared the winner of the contest by a jury of faculty members and peers, and it is unfortunate that no record of his remarks was preserved.

According to family tradition, Sam Adams had decided, by the time he won his degree from Harvard, that he wanted to make his career in politics. His great-grandson, William V. Wells, writes to that effect in his exhaustive biography of his illustrious ancestor, published in 1865, but offers no details of verification. Wells so busily defends Adams's reputation that it is not possible to accept all of his claims at face value.

One thing is certain: in the summer of 1740, only a few weeks after Sam Adams left Harvard, he saw and felt the results of Parliament's cavalier treatment of the American colonies. Hard currency was scarce in the New World, so colonial legislatures conveniently printed their own, unsupported paper money, which was generally accepted locally and in intercolonial transactions. It was also used extensively in commercial transactions with the mother country, but because of wild fluctuations, English merchants sometimes suffered severe losses. For their protection Parliament passed a bill in 1740 that restricted the use of this paper money, in effect devaluing it.

Samuel Adams the elder was doing most of his business with this paper money, and the new law caught him before he could dispose of his holdings. As a consequence he lost a large sum, perhaps one-third of his entire fortune. He condemned what he regarded as Parliamentary interference, and his son, aware of his parents' distress as well as the diminution of his own inheritance, was equally bitter.

The question of his own future was as yet undecided, and as he was regarded as too young to make his way in the world, he agreed when his parents urged him to return to Harvard and study for a higher degree. He spent three more years there, and in 1743, at the age of twenty-one, he was awarded a Master of Arts degree. The subject of his master's thesis, written in Latin, is significant: "Whether It Be Lawful to Resist the Supreme Magistrate, if the Commonwealth Cannot Be Otherwise Preserved."

His position was a strong affirmative, but in 1743 this was not considered particularly daring. The young man's argument was surely academic, and he had no known intention of taking an active stand against either Parliament or the Crown. The conservative faculty was unperturbed, and the governor, who attended the commencement exercises, showed no alarm. A student was privileged to choose any subject he wished for a thesis, and it occurred to no one, including young Adams himself, that he was already laying the groundwork for his future activities as the great American rebel of his era. No copy of the thesis has been preserved in the files of Harvard College or elsewhere, so the substance of his arguments is not known.

By this time the young man was showing definite signs of wanting a career in politics, and since it was universally accepted that only lawyers were suited for high public office, his father urged him to obtain a law degree. He began to study for the bar, but quickly discovered that he had no real inclination toward the law. His mother intervened and is credited with the responsibility for urging her son to become a man of business.

Young Adams abandoned law and obligingly took a position in a countinghouse, the eighteenth-century equivalent of a bank. His employer was Thomas Cushing, who not only owned the largest and most successful countinghouse in Boston, and hence in all the colonies, but was a close family friend. In spite of these connections the relationship was unhappy; young Adams was diligent and hard-working, but money as such meant little to him, commerce bored him and he vastly preferred to discuss and debate the issues of the day with his contemporaries. His second cousin, John Adams, wrote in 1772 that he "became steadfast and immovable" in the advocacy of colonial rights in the early 1740s.

He had no talents as a merchant, Cushing decided, saying that although he was active in both mind and body, he found politics too engrossing. Young Adams left the countinghouse by mutual consent, and borrowing one thousand pounds from his father, went into business for himself The nature of the venture is not known, but the results caused the family great embarrassment. Adams took a partner, to whom he obligingly gave half of the company's stock; the partner was totally inefficient, and ran through the firm's assets in less than six months. Adams, who had paid scant attention to his friend's activities, was astonished to find that he was in debt.

The company was dissolved. His weary father paid off the debts and, perhaps as a last resort, took Sam the younger into the brewery. The Deacon had so many business activities that "the malt business," as the brewery-distillery was known in the family, occupied relatively little of his time. So there was an opportunity for an aggressive young man to expand a prosperous enterprise; but the twenty-two year old was consistently demonstrating that he had no interest in making money.

He was content to play the role of a very junior partner, to do what he was told and to take no initiatives of his own as a brewer. He spent his days in his office, supervising an operation that virtually ran itself, and devoted his evenings to political discussions with his friends. The Deacon, who was very active in local politics himself at this time, did not protest. On the contrary, he welcomed his articulate son as an ally in furthering the so-called popular cause of obtaining a greater degree of self-government, free of Parliament's "interference."

The elder Adams was a member of the Massachusetts Bay General Assembly, and was so active that, in 1746, he was vetoed by the governor when his name was placed in nomination for a place on the Council, a consultative body with more prestige than power. The rebuff was bad enough in itself, but it was also complicated by a number of other factors. The colonies had joined England in a new fight with France, a conflagration known in the New World as King George's War, and under the leadership of Governor William Shirley of Massachusetts Bay a great victory had been achieved the previous year. The supposedly impregnable French fortress of Louisburg on Cape Breton Island, off the Canadian mainland, had fallen to a joint force of Royal Navy warships and an army of Massachusetts-led frontiersmen from seven colonies.

Shirley was by far the most efficient of the Crown representatives in the colonies, perhaps the best governor in the history of Massachusetts Bay, and, until the insult to the Deacon, had been supported by Samuel Adams the elder and his son. It must be presumed that his success in banding together the men of a number of colonies under one flag, the first time this had ever been achieved, was not lost on the younger Adams.

But the blow to his father could not be countenanced, and the young man declared private war on Governor Shirley. There was a vacancy in the Assembly caused by the elevation of Andrew Oliver to the Council in the place the elder Adams had wanted, and a special town meeting was held on June 4, 1746, to fill the post. There were no political parties as such; officeholders were roughly divided into two groups—those who supported the Crown and those who sought greater selfrule. Only one name was placed in nomination, that of the younger Adams, and he was elected by acclamation.

The Deacon was the acknowledged leader of the forces intent upon embarrassing Governor Shirley, and his son immediately joined in the cause. Together they opposed, successfully, a bill that would have granted the royal viceroy an increase in salary. They formed a committee to investigate Shirley's war expenditures, and they even opposed the governor's sensible proposal that Massachusetts form a joint commission with New Hampshire to settle a running dispute concerning the precise location of the boundary that separated the two colonies.

The harassed Shirley took note of the Adamses' activities in his annual report to the king, written and dispatched in January 1747. The elder, he said, was a gentleman of ability who was disgruntled because of his failure to win appointment to the Council, a post that had been denied him because his views were too liberal. His son, Shirley said, was the more dangerous of the pair because of "the indefatigable zeal" he displayed in seeking his goals.

The day was yet far distant when Samuel Adams the younger would be the exclusive subject of special reports to the king, but the career of a political genius was truly launched.

Chapter Two

From the beginning of his political career, Sam Adams never allowed himself to forget the fundamental concept he had learned from reading John Locke: sovereign power was vested exclusively in the people. Therefore full public support was needed to assure the success of any campaign, and this could best be achieved by educating and informing the people. On this keystone Sam Adams built his entire career, and ultimately persuaded his fellow Americans to seek a total separation from Great Britain.

A number of informal political associations were in existence in Boston in the fourth and fifth decades of the eighteenth century, most of them primarily social. The most important of these was the Caucus Club, and only insiders knew the truth of the rumors that the canny Deacon Adams sold beer and rum to his wealthy colleagues at special prices for their dinners, meetings and picnics. A lack of seniority and influence kept Samuel Adams the younger from membership in the Caucus, so he and several others of his age formed a club of their own late in 1747.

It had no name, but it was unique because it had a specific goal:

it would publish a weekly newspaper to be known as the *Public Advertiser*, and printed circulars distributed as early as late October 1747 promised that the members, all of them "elected representatives of the people," would contribute articles and essays on important issues of the day. The editor, who would also become the *Advertiser*'s chief editorial writer, did not allow his own name to appear in the prepublication literature that solicited subscriptions. It was typical of Sam Adams to remain in the background and operate semianonymously.

Not enough is known about him at this stage of his life to determine whether he was shy, but in the presence of his blustering, deep-voiced father he was always inclined to be somewhat withdrawn. The real reason for his anonymity, however, was his belief that an editor functioned more effectively if the public did not become too much aware of him and his doings.

None of the articles were signed, so their authorship is unknown, but within a short time the "anonymous" editor was also writing the bulk of the newspaper. The first issue appeared in early January 1748, and according to the printer, Isaiah Thomas, Sam Adams was contributing three-quarters of the published material by the following month, his colleagues devoting their principal efforts to obtaining greater circulation. All of them, Thomas declared several years later in his *History of Printing*, were "Whigs who advocated the rights of the people against those measures of government which were supposed to infringe upon the privileges of the Province secured by charter."

On the masthead of the four-page paper was a cartoon representation of Britannia, shackled and choked by a rope tied to France; with her one free hand Britannia held a pair of scissors she was using to cut the rope. The first issue offered space to readers who wanted to express their own views, and subsequent issues repeated the invitation. Taken at face value, the response indicated that a great many Bostonians availed themselves of the opportunity, but as Sam Adams's distinctive style developed, a different picture emerged. Beginning at the age of twenty-six he printed "letters to the editor" that heartily concurred with the opinions he expressed in his articles and essays—as well they should have, since he wrote all of them himself. It was a practice he maintained for the next quarter of a century, until the impending outbreak of the War of Independence caused the British authorities to suspend publication of the *Advertiser*.

The paper printed virtually no news, either domestic or foreign, and its columns were devoted almost exclusively to the goal of arousing public opinion in favor of granting increased rights to the people of Massachusetts Bay by taking various privileges from the Crown. The long-range success of the venture was extraordinary, and the continuous publication of the *Advertiser* from 1748 to 1775 was a tribute to Sam Adams's stubborn pursuit of his aim as well as to his skill.

The paper paid for itself, but made almost no profit, principally because editor-publisher Adams and his colleagues, who became known as the Whipping-Post Club, sought as broad a circulation base as possible and refused to charge more than the original price, a half-penny per issue. Even in later years, when Sam Adams's financial mismanagement brought him to the verge of bankruptcy, he refused all pleas to increase the price of the *Advertiser*.

One of the more noteworthy of his first essays was called "Loyalty and Sedition," and even in this initial stage of his career Adams demonstrated his instinctive talents as a master propagandist. He presented his themes in simple, direct terms, reducing even the most complicated of issues to fundamentals. He presented his arguments in strong language, using extreme images and freely sprinkling his prose with exaggerated adverbs and adjectives that would sway his readers. There were few grays in the written world of Sam Adams; his convictions were presented as unalterable truths, and to oppose them he set up straw men he then demolished. One hundred years later, when the French novelist George Sand was acting as the minister of propaganda for the provisional French Republic established after the downfall of King Louis Philippe, she freely acknowledged the use of Adams as her model, calling him "the most persuasive user of the written word for political purposes in all history."

Several excerpts from "Loyalty and Sedition" not only indicate the thinking of the young writer, but illuminate his approach:

> . . . we oftentimes perceive such significations assumed by those who find the wrong use of words conducive to the increase of power or gain, that it is difficult to tell whether loyalty is really commendable or sedition blameworthy. True loyalty in the sense just now explained is the beauty and perfection of a well-constituted state. It cannot indeed subsist in any arbitrary government, because it is founded in the love and possession of liberty. It includes in it a thorough knowledge of our Constitution, its conveniences and defects as well as its real advantages; a becoming jealousy of our immunities, and a steadfast resolution to maintain them. It delights in the quiet and thankful enjoyment of a good administration, and it is the scourge of the griping oppressor and haughty invader of our liberties.
>
> But sedition is founded on the depraved and inordinate passions of the mind; it is a weak, feverish, sickly thing, a boisterous and unnatural vigor, which cannot support itself long, and oftentimes destroys the unhappy patient. It proceeds from gross mistake or great wickedness, from lust of power or gain, in the first promoters of it, and from untamable obstinacy and a vitiated palate that cannot relish the happiness of a free state in the creatures of their designs.
>
> It is a very great mistake to imagine that the object of loyalty is the authority and interest of one individual man, however dignified by the applause or enriched by the success of popular actions. This has led millions into such a degree of dependence and submission, that they have at length found themselves to homage the instruments of their ruin at the very time they were at work to effect it. The true object of loyalty is a good legal constitution, which, as it condemns every instance of oppression and lawless power, derives a certain remedy to the sufferer by allowing him to remonstrate his grievances, and pointing out methods of relief when the gentle arts of persuasion have lost their efficacy.
>
> Whoever, therefore, insinuates notions of government contrary to the constitution, or in any degree winks at any mea-

sures to suppress or even weaken it, is not a loyal man. Whoever acquaints us that we have no right to examine into the conduct of those who, though they derive their power from us to serve the common interests, make use of it to impoverish and ruin us, is in a degree a rebel—to the undoubted rights and liberties of the people.

He that despises his neighbor's happiness because he wears a worsted cap or leathern apron, he that struts immeasurably above the lower size of people, and pretends to adjust the rights of men by the distinctions of fortune, is not over loyal. He that aggravates beyond measure the well-meant failings of a warm zeal for liberty, he that leaves no stone unturned to defend and propagate the schemes of illegal power, cannot be esteemed a loyal man. Indeed, the reverse of these words may possibly find authorities in some parts of the world where language and sense are deluged in the torrent of arbitrary power.

This essay contained the blueprints for Sam Adams's future conduct. His concepts of popular liberty, the prerogatives of "remonstrating grievances" and the carefully worded attack on the principle of the divine right of kings showed the great agitator of the pre-Revolution already hard at work. Certainly it was no accident, either, that from the very first he made an open bid for the support of the artisans and working people. The common man was Sam Adams's constituency.

It may be for this very reason that he was either ignored or underrated by the colonies' few intellectuals as well as by Crown authorities. Governor Shirley knew the young author of purple prose, regarded him as a nuisance and forgot him; the conservative clergymen and attorneys who sympathized with the Crown dismissed him as a misguided thinker totally lacking in influence. What all of them failed to take into account was the cumulative effect of Sam Adams's teachings. For year after weary year he pounded away at one theme, the liberty of the people, and although it is impossible to measure his influence over the period of any single year, he persuaded uncounted tens of thousands over the period of twenty-five years to accept his opinions. Still not satisfied, he continued to write on the same theme for another fifteen years. As he said in the second issue of the *Advertiser:*

> There is no one thing which mankind are more passionately fond of, which they fight with more zeal for, which they possess with more anxious jealousy and fear of losing, than liberty. . . . There is, there certainly is such a thing as liberty, which distinguishes man from the beasts, and a society of wise and reasonable creatures from the brutal herd, where the strongest horns are the strongest laws. And though the notions of men were ten times more confused and unsettled, and their opinions more various about this matter than they are, there yet remains an internal and essential distinction between this same liberty and slavery. . . .

Adams accurately regarded himself as a disciple of Locke, but he did not pretend to himself or others that he, too, was a philosopher. He contributed no original thoughts to the principles Locke had espoused, nor did he examine the philosophy of Locke either critically or in depth. He saw himself for what he was, a popularizer of Locke's views, an enunciator of a simplified version of Locke's thinking.

What makes Adams astonishing is that he grasped the essence of a growing popular mood long before anyone else was aware of it, recognizing an opportunity on behalf of the American people that was unique in all human history, the chance to transform abstract concepts—in which he himself believed—into practical, political realities. His activities more than a quarter of a century prior to the outbreak of the War of Independence of which he was the first sponsor can be explained only in terms of his genius.

Although reasonably ambitious politically, he had no overwhelming desire to hold high public office. Indeed, he sought office only because he wanted new podiums from which he could reiterate his views. His love of liberty—unyielding, intractable and constant—was the single most important force in his long life. He was so completely convinced that Locke was right and that a society unlike any other on earth, one based on the philosopher's reason, could be established in the New World that he was willing to make any personal sacrifice for it.

As early as the appearance of the first issues of the *Advertiser,* many of his contemporaries, including Harvard classmates and other gentlemen of substance, began to avoid him. They regarded him as a missionary for a strange faith, someone who lacked balance and stability and therefore was less than respectable.

Adams himself was indifferent to the opinions his peers held of him. When he deemed it necessary or desirable, at sessions of the Assembly or his own wedding, he could appear in solid-colored broadcloth, as grave and distinguished as any successful lawyer or merchant prince. Most of the time, however, his vision so obsessed him that his appearance meant nothing to him. His suits were rumpled, his boots lacked polish and printer's ink smudged his cuffs, soiled his stock and stained his fingers.

At an early stage of his career he was recognized by fellow Bostonians as a radical, and even such future great Patriots as his lawyer cousin, John Adams, were shocked by his insistence that revolution to establish a truly free government subservient to the will of a free people was inevitable. Regardless of what dock workers, artisans or other ill-paid rabble thought of him and the utopia he espoused, his social and financial peers shrank from him. A man who stood for the principle of insurrection against the Crown, even though he was not yet actively advocating such an upheaval, was either a lunatic or a dangerous traitor, and in either event was a man to be avoided.

All thinking Bostonians and all men of substance wanted less Crown interference in their daily lives, of course, but they, like so many Englishmen in positions of power, assumed that good-will and the exercise of restraint on both sides of the Atlantic would smooth the abrasions that were beginning to mar England's relations with her American colonies.

Sam Adams's intransigence—some called it bigoted intolerance—forced him to seek the like-minded as his friends. He grew close to James Otis, a member of the Harvard class of 1743, who was already making a name for himself as a brilliant lawyer. Otis was known to suffer occasional mental aberrations, to be sure, so the gentry were inclined to give him a wide berth, too. Another of Adams's friends was the younger John Hancock, the nephew, adopted son and principal heir of the wealthiest man in Massachusetts Bay. Young Hancock, in spite of his great wealth, made members of the establishment uneasy: no one blamed him because he inherited his uncle's penchant for smuggling, but he took the unique position that it was his inalienable right to pay no taxes to the Crown on goods he brought to Boston in his own ships. Only such dreamers as Adams and Otis listened to him with sympathy, agreed with him and encouraged him to defy the royal governors.

In the early years of Sam Adams's career, it must be stressed, few people paid much attention to his political activities. The Assembly was not an important forum, and the *Advertiser* had virtually no influence, selling only a handful of copies to idealists totally lacking in influence. Those who knew the young man best were afraid he was impractical, a bumbler who had so far shown no promise in the art of earning a living that was expected of an Adams.

In March 1748, the young man's problems were complicated by the sudden death of his father at the age of fifty-nine. Under the terms of the Deacon's will, his two sons and his son-in-law, James Allen of Boston, were named the executors, and the bulk of the estate was left to the widow. The elder son, who now became the nominal head of the family, was excused from repayment of his debt to his father's estate of the one thousand pounds he had lost in his foolish business venture, and was specifically charged with taking command at the brewery-distillery.

Sam Adams made a gallant attempt, aided by his mother's urging, to walk in the steps prescribed for him. He moved into his father's office and tried, without discernible success, to expand the operation. Fortunately for the estate, Joseph Adams and James Allen took charge of the late Deacon's various real estate holdings and ventures. Certain tasks could be performed only by the head of the family, however, and one of them was acting as his mother's escort to worship services. All members of the

Adams clan attended the New South Church, whose rector, the Reverend Samuel Checkley, had baptized Sam the younger on the day of his birth.

The Reverend Checkley and his devout wife had a daughter of twenty-four named Elizabeth, whose modesty and shyness may have been caused by the fact that she was descended from five generations of God-fearing clergymen, every one of whom habitually delivered Sabbath sermons of three to five hours' duration. The girl was both pious and plain; suitors had been intimidated by her father, from whose nostrils, it was said, smoke had been seen to curl, and it appeared that she might suffer the fate of a spinster. But Mary Adams and the girl's mother, Elizabeth Rolfe Checkley, were old and dear friends, and the two ladies saw eye to eye in certain matters.

Sam Adams may have been the only young gentleman in Boston who was somewhat surprised when, on October 17, 1749, he found himself marrying Elizabeth Checkley, the bride's father performing the ceremony in his house. Bride and groom were distantly related, as Sam's grandfather had married a Checkley.

The marriage was successful, in part because Adams blithely went his own way, delving into politics and paying no more attention to business than was necessary. The couple enjoyed a high social standing, but their finances suffered a steady decline, and the mild-mannered Elizabeth could neither curb her husband's enthusiasms nor persuade him to devote more time to the brewery.

During this period Adams was also plagued by some troubles he had inherited from his father. The Deacon had been a member of the board of directors of an organization known as a Land Bank, one of many such institutions in the colonies. It had been created for the purpose of putting paper money into circulation, and when forced out of existence by an act of Parliament, the directors found themselves financially responsible for the bank's considerable liabilities.

Adams had joined the bank's board, too, a few years prior to his father's death, and now he was saddled with paying off a crushing debt. His payments were slow and erratic, making it necessary for the Crown to bring a succession of lawsuits against him, and he found himself in and out of court until 1758. This steady drain on his resources was a major cause of his bitterness toward England, and it has even been argued that he would not have sought American independence had his attitude toward the mother country not been so frequently exacerbated by the lawsuits he lost with such regularity.

He and Elizabeth Checkley had five children in eight years, but only two survived infancy and grew to adulthood. The elder, Samuel, became a physician, served as a surgeon in the Continental Army and died a bachelor. The other, Hannah, married Captain Thomas Wells of the Continental line and lived a long life.

In the summer of 1757 Elizabeth suffered from a fever that her doctors could neither diagnose nor cure, and after an illness that lasted three weeks, she died on July 25. Her heartbroken husband was saddled with the care of two small children he was ill-equipped to rear alone. He was a loving father, but inattentiveness to detail made living conditions under the Adams roof haphazard. The master of the house frequently stopped in at a tavern for conversations with fellow members of the Caucus Club, to which he had been elected after his father's death, and these discussions were so intense that he often forgot to come home for dinner. Certainly the children would have run wild had it not been for the steadying influence of old Mary Adams, who took her grandchildren to church, supervised their meals and saw that they did not go out to their play yard as "half-naked savages," a description that amused her increasingly absentminded son.

Never had Adams needed to concentrate harder on his business affairs, and never had he found the brewery more boring. Even his mother was willing to admit that he had no aptitude for a life of commerce, and it appeared that he was destined to live and die in mediocrity.

Chapter Three

Few of the more prominent citizens of Massachusetts Bay took their politics seriously or became deeply involved in political matters in the fourth and fifth decades of the eighteenth century. The Crown continued to hold the reins of power, and the local matters in which elected or appointed officials had authority were too minor to concern them. The public was equally indifferent, no more than a handful attending town meetings or bothering to vote, so a small group, principally members of the Caucus Club, held most offices.

Sam Adams continued to regard politics as something more than an avocation, and in 1753 he was elected one of the town assessors of Boston, a post of little significance or power and even less prestige. Three years later, in 1756, his friends rewarded his diligence, however, and he won election at a town meeting to one of the few important posts open to colonials, that of Boston tax collector. He could go no higher, other than to win appointment to the Council, an empty honor.

As tax collector he was regarded as a member of the governor's administration, but in spite of this association he openly defied the Crown in an incident that occurred in 1758, perhaps the most significant public event in his life up until that time. He was so badly in arrears in his Land Bank restitution payments that the sheriff was ordered to confiscate his property and offer it for sale at a public auction.

According to custom, a notice to that effect was published on August 4 in the Boston *News-Letter*, stating that the auction would take place the following day at the Exchange Tavern, and listing the house and gardens on Purchase Street, the brewery, a wharf, several private dwellings and apartments as places that would be put on the block. In the following morning's issue, however, Adams published an open letter to the sheriff, charging that the proceeding was "illegal and unwarrantable." Not only would he bring a personal countersuit that would place the sheriff's estate in jeopardy, he declared, but he was "determined to prosecute to the law any person whomsoever who shall trespass" on his property.

This unprecedented act created no stir whatsoever, and if the Crown representatives in Boston realized that one of George II's loyal subjects was thumbing his nose at the majesty and authority of the monarch, they elected not to recognize the fact. The only person who took any notice of the challenge was the sheriff, Stephen Greenleaf, who had no desire to become personally embroiled in a countersuit. Apparently he received no support or other help from the governor or anyone else in higher authority, and he announced that the auction was being postponed until September 22. Twenty-four hours before the scheduled event it was postponed again, until the twenty-ninth, and this time Greenleaf appeared to mean business, for his advertisement stated that the auction would take place between twelve and one o'clock.

Adams paid no attention to these notices, and it is not known whether he privately repeated his threats to the sheriff. For whatever reason, the auction was forgotten, and the various properties remained in Adams's possession. The incident can be regarded as more than the success of an individual in defying the Crown: Sam Adams claimed his refusal to bow to authority as his legal right, an argument that became the core of his position when he stirred up intercolonial insurrection a decade and a half later.

In the meantime he enjoyed a notable lack of success as the Boston tax collector, and was so lax that Thomas Hutchinson, later the governor of Massachusetts Bay, charged him with malfeasance. The charge was false, but Hutchinson cannot be blamed for thinking as he did. By 1763 Adams's account was several thousand pounds in arrears, and when he left office in 1765 the debt amounted to more than eight thousand pounds.

In the next two years he reduced the total by one-half, but thereafter it became necessary to sue him repeatedly for the remainder. One of these suits was brought, in one of history's stranger sidelights, by his good friend and fellow Patriot, James Otis. In 1769 exasperated officialdom relieved him of further responsibility in the matter and directed the new tax collector to obtain the sum.

Contrary to Hutchinson's assertions, Sam Adams had not embezzled a single penny. The worst that can be said is that he was guilty of gross negligence and incompetence. He was incapable of handling any sum of money, large or small, and he fell into arrears because he was so kind-hearted that he could not force himself to bring legal action against fellow citizens who were delinquent in the payment of their taxes. Presumably he won the gratitude of these gentlemen, but he caused himself considerable embarrassment.

His position as tax collector managed to take up so much of his time and effort, however, that he further neglected the brewery, and his father's once prosperous business declined steadily. By Sam Adams's fortieth birthday in 1762, he had no financial standing, had accomplished nothing of note in any field and, judged by any standards, was a failure in life.

On the rare occasions when he took care to dress well he was a reasonably handsome man of medium height and build, with only a slight paunch. In the years ahead he would become heavier, thanks in part to the bread baked by his second wife. His brown hair was receding, but he rarely bothered to wear a wig, even though such headpieces were universally regarded as a necessity for anyone who wanted to be considered a gentleman. His blue eyes were keen, and he had not yet started to use the spectacles that always sat on the bridge of his nose in later life.

He had already formed the habit of spending time in the waterfront taverns frequented by sailors, dock workers, prostitutes and, presumably, the small Boston class of criminals and roughnecks. He did not neglect his friends in the Caucus Club, and dined frequently with them in the better taverns. By the late 1760s this group was composed of men whose names would become familiar to every American schoolboy. The most articulate and verbose was the meteoric James Otis, a lean, fiery man who became the spokesman for those who grew to oppose the Crown and was considered by many to be the leader. Perhaps the most cogent speaker was Josiah Quincy, subsequently regarded as the greatest orator of the day; another was the mild-mannered Dr. Joseph Warren, later a major general of Massachusetts militia and a hero of the Battle of Bunker Hill. One of the least conspicuous members of the group was young John Hancock, who had inherited his uncle's mercantile and shipping empire and was proving equally adroit as a smuggler and tax evader.

These men were Sam Adams's peers, and he enjoyed his relations with them, but he was equally at home in the waterfront bars and eateries. Some of his early biographers, his great-grandson included, tried to excuse his penchant for seeking low company by claiming he deliberately went to the waterfront to learn and test the temper of people generally regarded as the brawling scum of Boston. This was undoubtedly true, but Adams was a waterfront habitué for the rest of his life, which indicates he found pleasure in such company.

As a mature man in his forties he had developed into a highly complicated character. Still a Puritan, as he would be for the rest of his days, he never shed the influence of his mother. He was modest, almost unassuming, and was never known to raise his voice. He attended church services regularly, without fail, and in spite of his poverty always managed to contribute as much or more than he could afford. He was circumspect in his personal life and was never known to be unfaithful to either of his wives, but was himself the first to admit, cheerfully, that he enjoyed and appreciated the company of a pretty woman.

It has been said that he was a virtual teetotaller and it has also been claimed that he frequently drank to excess, but in all probability neither charge is true. Coffee disagreed with him and he gave up tea after one of the more spectacular events in his nation's early history, an incident he himself organized. Some of his more devout fellow churchmen refused to touch either liquor or tobacco in any form, but Adams was no fanatic and apparently felt it was no sin to sip a mug or two of flip, a mixture of rum and sack that was lethal if consumed in quantity, or to take an occasional pinch of snuff.

It seems unlikely that he spent long periods in either the better inns or lower-class taverns in total abstinence, particularly in the years immediately prior to the outbreak of the American Revolution, when he all but abandoned his business interests and made his day-long headquarters in a harbor tavern owned by John Hancock. Neither then nor during the long war years did anyone ever see him intoxicated, although hearsay reports to that effect cropped up in his later years.

John Adams, thirteen years his cousin's junior and his protégé at the beginning of his own public career in 1765, was always partial to kinsmen, but it was unusual for him to stress Sam Adams's sobriety as forcefully as he did in his published *Works*, first printed in 1819. Without demeaning himself to enter into a controversy on the subject, he seemed to be replying to unfair criticism of the relative and friend with whom he was closely associated for more than a quarter of a century during and after the long struggle for freedom.

It may be accidental that Sam Adams's second marriage coincides with his rise to prominence and achievement of greatness, but the praise heaped on his new wife by many contemporaries may be an indication that she was to some degree responsible for his growth and rise in public esteem. His bride was the fifth daughter of Francis Wells, an English merchant who migrated to Boston with his family in 1723, and the bride was twenty-four years of age when the marriage took place on December 6, 1764.

Her husband was forty-two, a dismal failure in virtually everything he had ever attempted.

The second Elizabeth Adams was known as one of the loveliest young ladies in Massachusetts Bay, and was so high-minded that she won the lifelong approval of Cousin John's acerbic, sharp-eyed wife, Abigail, who habitually saw the flaws in everyone she encountered. Elizabeth had a lively disposition and a needed sense of humor, but was in no wise frivolous, and no dissipation was ever seen or countenanced under her roof. She was far better educated than most women of the period, having been taught by tutors until the age of twenty-one. In addition to everything else she was an excellent, budget-minded housekeeper, and was endowed with a talent for stretching money. In brief, she was a perfect companion for a man with whom she could discuss political problems and whose meager income she could utilize to the last penny.

The Adams family continued to live in the Purchase Street house until 1774, when it was partially destroyed by British troops during the military occupation of Boston. Elizabeth bore no children, but treated her stepson and stepdaughter as though they were her own, and they reciprocated her love. Perhaps she was less of a paragon that she has been represented, but there can be little doubt that she needed all of her qualities of mind and body in the years immediately following her marriage and, to a somewhat lesser extent, for many more years thereafter.

She married a quiet, unassuming man of little or no consequence, and soon afterward saw him transformed into a blazing political comet, an organizer and propagandist, a man who recklessly squandered his time and health on a seemingly lost cause, a hero to his fellow Americans and villain to the British, a leader whose traits were recognized and applauded by others in the forefront of the struggle for liberty. For a time her husband was a refugee from British justice, and for the better part of a decade she was separated from him for long periods, never knowing when she would see him again, and in the meantime forced to live on a pittance.

Neither Elizabeth nor anyone else in Boston could have been

intellectually or emotionally prepared for the political hurricanes that swept through Massachusetts Bay and the other colonies with increasing intensity in 1764 and the years that followed. Thanks to the farsighted, conciliatory policies of Governor Shirley, perhaps the best of the royal governors, the bonds that tied Massachusetts to the mother country were firm on both sides.

A Sam Adams might grumble because of the laws that worked in his disfavor in such matters as his continuing Land Bank problems, but even he was not thinking in terms of revolution. He might write essays for the *Advertiser* on the sovereignty of the people, but he was engaging in an intellectual exercise, and the thought of actively organizing opposition to Crown policies and Parliament's laws had not occurred to him. Even his defiance when the sheriff threatened to confiscate his real estate holdings was no more than an isolated, personal act dictated by necessity, although it did indicate the temper of the man who would soon assume leadership in what he came to regard as a sacred cause.

It cannot be stressed too strongly that the Sam Adams of 1764 was no political activist, no advocate of violent revolution. Like all members of his clan, including his young cousin John, who would come to Boston from Braintree the following year to practice law, he was a God-fearing, law-abiding man, something of a dreamer who enjoyed writing abstract articles and essays about an ideal state. It might be exaggeration to say he was a nonentity, but even in Boston he was not considered a real leader. Few people living elsewhere in Massachusetts had ever heard of him, and he was literally unknown in other colonies. He had never traveled beyond the boundaries of Massachusetts Bay, as far as is known, and he never displayed the slightest desire to see other places.

His worst vice was a craving for raw oysters, fish chowder and poultry stuffed with a rich dressing of sage, chopped nuts and sausage. Clothes meant as little to him as did other worldly belongings, and he was indifferent to the arts. As far as is known he never attended a theatrical performance or concert, and his home contained no paintings or tapestries, a situation that Elizabeth tried to remedy within the strict limitations of her budget.

Even his library was modest, and contained virtually no contemporary works, his sole interests being philosophy and politics.

His outlook until this time was completely provincial, and there is no known evidence indicating an interest in the affairs of other colonies. He read only Boston newspapers, and appears to have been indifferent to life in Pennsylvania, Virginia and New York, Massachusetts' rivals for colonial leadership. A compleat city man, he rarely went to the country, never hunted or fished, and walked to his office and the various taverns he frequented. There were several horses in the stable behind the house, but they were used almost exclusively by Elizabeth and the children, as he had abandoned his daily canters through the countryside.

Boston, with a population of thirty to forty thousand, may have been the largest and most prosperous city in the New World, but it was essentially a provincial town, and Sam Adams was one of the most provincial and least successful of her sons. He had played no part in the business boom that had made others wealthy; he had achieved nothing of note in any other field, and had disgraced himself as an official in the one responsible post he had held.

But he was better prepared for the future than anyone suspected. The time soon would be ripe for a practical application of John Locke's theories, and no American was better acquainted with the works of Locke or admired them more. Equally important, Sam Adams appears to have understood what every successful revolutionary leader has always known: that it is not necessary to win broad public support for a political or social upheaval, and that only a hard core of enthusiastic and hardworking followers is needed for the task. Nothing in his known reading or his experience could have given him this knowledge, which seems to have been instinctive. Perhaps the biggest surprise of all is that a man who had done nothing of consequence for the first forty-two years of his life should have blossomed, almost overnight, as a genius.

Chapter Four

Until the early 1760s few cracks could be found in the cement that had bound England and her North American colonies together for a century and a half. Frictions had been few, the relationship had been enormously beneficial to the mother country, and the ever-growing and expanding colonies had been steadfast in their loyalty to the Crown. Now, however, a number of new factors were at work.

Parliament had gradually assumed the ascendancy over the Crown since the Revolution of 1688, and by the middle of the eighteenth century, the power of the legislative branch was supreme in Britain. But that situation changed when George III came to the throne in 1760, determined to regain the authority lost by his ancestors. He achieved his ends by political means, gaining control of the ministry and, through it, of the Commons by playing the game of the politicians and beating them at it. A man of high principles and even higher honor, he was handicapped by other traits: he was shortsighted, insanely stubborn and lacked almost all qualities of statesmanship, including tact.

King George sought what he called "the glory of Britain," and his practical aims were identical with those of the landed aristocracy and mercantile interests who, in effect, ruled the country. They viewed the colonies as sources of raw material and little else, and as early as 1733 such laws as the so-called Molasses Act tried to preserve this desired status quo. But the colonies remained quiet and contented because most such laws were regarded as foolish and were conveniently ignored. For example, it was said that not one colony obeyed a ruling to the effect that woolen clothing and hats made in one colony could not be sold in another.

Britain had traditionally refrained from interfering in the so-called home rule of the colonies, permitting them self-government in their internal affairs. During the various wars with France the Commons had been tempted to raise troops and impose special taxes by direct legislation, but had wisely refrained. Such revenue-raising laws as the Molasses Act and various customs tax acts were avoided with great skill by colonials who became experts in the art. The Hancock fortune was only one of many that had been built by smuggling, and most customs officials in the colonies were local citizens who sympathized with their compatriots, looked the other way when it was convenient and subsequently were rewarded for their lack of effort, often by being given directorships in companies they had assisted. Royal governors and their English aides knew what was happening, but so much wealth poured into England that they chose to do nothing that would interrupt the flow of gold into the coffers of English merchants.

By the 1760s a vast if invisible gulf was beginning to separate England her colonies. Men in the mother country continued to regard their outposts of empire as civilizations that existed only for the benefit of England herself. But the North Americans held a far different view, and thought of their provinces as semi-independent states or commonwealths; they themselves were independent subjects of the Crown, which formed their only real link to the mother country. Long accustomed to self-government, they made their own tax laws and raised their own revenues.

The French and Indian War, which was still being fought

when George III ascended the throne, was at least partly responsible for the crisis that came to the surface in 1763 and grew more
intense with each passing year. The cost of the war had been
tremendous, and England had been shocked and angered when
her colonists, many of whom felt a bond of kinship with the
French settlers in Canada, had allowed the mother country to
assume the major burdens of the war. Britain had been forced to
send an army and a navy to the New World, and the British
taxpayer was suffering.

A new prime minister, George Grenville, who totally failed to
understand the American mentality, assumed the task of realign-
ing the relationships with the colonies in order to relieve the
taxpayer at home of an unjust burden, and he was supported
without reservation by King George. Amazed to discover the
extent of smuggling, Grenville was personally responsible for
the new Sugar Act of 1764, which not only reduced the tax on
molasses in the hope that smuggling would cease, but simultaneously imposed customs duties on a wide variety of other products
Americans imported, among them silk, coffee, wine, salt and
ironware.

In 1765 Parliament passed a billeting act which required those
colonies in which Crown troops were stationed to provide hous-
ing and food for the soldiers. Various trade regulatons that long
had been ignored or neglected were tightened, and new, honest
officials were appointed to make certain the law was obeyed. Still
determined to force the colonies to pay for their cost to the
Crown, Grenville proposed a new concept in taxation: since the
colonies objected so vociferously to any direct form of taxation,
he asked the Parliament to pass a bill establishing an indirect tax
that would bring in vast revenues. It was called the stamp tax,
and no business agreement in the colonies, no contract and no
legal document would be regarded as binding until and unless
the new type of Crown stamp was purchased and affixed to the
paper.

The American whom England regarded as the leading citizen
of the New World was called to testify before a committee of the
House of Commons on the proposed measure. Benjamin Frank-

lin of Philadelphia, in effect the lobbyist in London for Pennsylvania, was blunt in his advice. His fellow Americans, he said, would ignore the new tax on molasses and would smuggle in the other goods on which duties had been imposed. But they would not object to the new Sugar Act itself. On the other hand, they drew a sharp distinction between customs duties and internal taxation, and their reaction to the Stamp Act would be violent. When told by a member of the committee that troops would be sent to America, if necessary, to compel the colonists to obey the Stamp and Quartering acts, Franklin replied, "Then, sir, you will not stem a revolution but will create one."

His advice was ignored, and in February, 1765, Parliament passed the Stamp Act without serious debate. In order to cushion the blow and permit the colonists to become accustomed to the idea of new taxation, the act was not scheduled to become effective until November.

In general the Americans accepted the Sugar Act of 1764 quietly, although the merchants of the principal cities protested. Most people saw nothing new in the measure, and, as Franklin had predicted, were prepared not only to continue smuggling molasses but to smuggle in the other products that had been added to the tax list as well. The uproar over the Stamp Act did not break out until several months later.

But Sam Adams was not one who remained docile after the passage of the Sugar Act. Governor Francis Bernard, a somewhat stiff-necked and tactless executive, was determined to enforce the new law, and the Boston merchants, utilizing the services of the brilliant James Otis, were determined to find either a loophole in the law or some means of obstructing its enforcement. Sam Adams was no lawyer, and although he could discuss philosophy with his peers, it was a hallmark of his rapidly emerging genius that he sought, from the beginning of his opposition to the Sugar Act and later measures, to simplify complicated issues for the general public.

In this connection it is of the utmost significance to understand that the American Revolution at no time was a spontaneous uprising of an indignant, united people. It was the handiwork of a vocal minority whose propaganda campaign endeavored to clarify issues by reducing them to basics. And no man was more persistent, more clever in the creation and maintenance of this long-term campaign than Sam Adams. People were not interested in abstract issues, he felt, and he moved in his own way to arouse support for opposition to the Sugar Act.

The self-styled radicals in the Massachusetts Assembly launched an attack less simple than it appeared on the surface. Their aim was the adoption of a measure that would condemn all taxation of the colonies by Parliament, and specifically would single out the Sugar Act as unacceptable. Then, it was decided at a meeting of the Caucus Club, an attempt would be made to obtain similar resolutions from other colonies and present them together to Prime Minister Grenville and Parliament.

The members of the informal Caucus Club, all of whom sympathized with their colleague, John Hancock, and with his fellow merchants, were unwilling to permit the Crown to encroach on their prerogatives, no matter what Parliament directed. A series of meetings was held in an atmosphere of emergency, with Sam Adams presiding. He realized—and James Otis stressed—that no resolution passed by the Assembly would be effective as long as Chief Justice Thomas Hutchinson remained in office. Hutchinson, a man of complete integrity, was devoted to the Crown, and had the power to compel Massachusetts to obey an act of Parliament, no matter what the Assembly did. Therefore they made it their ultimate goal to force Hutchinson from his office.

A list of instructions was prepared for the direction and guidance of Boston's respresentative in the Assembly, and ostensibly was issued by the town of Boston. In actuality the "instructions" had no legal basis whatever, and were not issued by the Boston electorate. They were the work of one man, Sam Adams, and constitute the first known practical political document prepared by him.

Hutchinson was not mentioned by name, but the instructions made his identity clear. In addition to his post as chief justice, to which he had been appointed by Governor Bernard, he was also lieutenant governor by virtue of a Crown appointment, and automatically held a seat on the Council. Adams directed the Boston representatives to vote for a measure prohibiting any member of the Council from holding more than one appointment from the Crown or governor, and to declare vacant all seats occupied by any man who held more than one such position. They were also instructed to withhold funds for the payment of the salary of any judge in the colony who held any position in Massachusetts Bay other than his place on the bench.

The directive also exhorted the representatives to make every effort to improve the colony's commerce "for the benefit of all the people." They were also advised to protect the economy from "all unreasonable impositions" on it, and to make clear to London their urgent desire for the repeal of the Sugar Act. In order to make this plea more effective they were instructed to coordinate such moves with similar efforts in other colonies.

While there was nothing startling in the directives, as such, it was obvious to Adams that he had to base them on principle, real or assumed, if he wanted to avoid the charge that he and his cohorts were acting out of selfish, partisan motives. Remembering that most citizens of Massachusetts were not required to pay the new taxes, and consequently were indifferent to them, and that an attack on a man of Hutchinson's stature had to be couched in lofty terms, he acted accordingly. His task was complicated by the fact that no real principle was involved; other men in high places had held more than one office at a time, and the taxes imposed under the Sugar Act were no more than a realignment and expansion of taxes imposed under the thirty-year-old Molasses Act.

He solved his problem in a manner that would become typical of Sam Adams's approach, and it made complete sense to his readers, provided they did not probe and analyze too carefully. First he paid lip service to form, urging the representatives to make it clear that they were loyal subjects of the king and to acknowledge Massachusetts' "dependence upon and subordination to Great Britain," further stressing the "ready submission" of the colony's merchants "to all just and necessary regulations of trade."

Every member of the Assembly, he said, was required to uphold "the invaluable rights and privileges of the province . . . as well as those rights which are derived to us by the Royal Charter, as those which being prior to and independent on it, we hold essentially as free born subjects of Great Britain." He took care to assume that his readers understood these rights, which he did not spell out, but he cleverly served his own end by adding, "for if our trade may be taxed, why not our lands, their produce, and in short everything we possess or make use of?"

Now, having established a base that would make every citizen of Massachusetts uneasy, he proceeded to enlarge on the theme: "This we apprehend annihilates our charter rights to govern and tax ourselves. It strikes at our British privileges, which, as we have never forfeited them, we hold in common with our fellow subjects who are natives of Britain."

At last he came to the heart of his argument, and for the first time presented a line that had some small degree of legal substance. "If taxes are laid upon us in any shape without our having a legal representation where they are laid," he demanded, "are we not reduced from the character of free subjects to the miserable state of tributary slaves?" Here was the origin of what would become the rallying cry of the American Revolution, that the colonies would not tolerate taxation without representation.

He was on shaky ground, of course, and must have known it. From the standpoint of strict legal interpretation, his argument was specious, no law ever having been passed by Parliament that granted the colonies the right to tax themselves. This privilege was the outgrowth of custom only, and there was no valid legal reason that Parliament could not impose on the colonies any taxes it pleased.

But his stand immediately proved popular. The Boston town meeting adopted his instructions, and James Otis presented the arguments to the Assembly with flair and verve. Adams deliberately kept himself in the background, and after the representatives adopted the directive by an overwhelming vote, he flooded the legislatures of other colonies with copies, taking care to send additional, printed versions to individual leaders in Pennsylvania, New York, Virginia, New Jersey and Connecticut.

Their enthusiastic replies were encouraging, and Adams immediately opened an informal correspondence with them, urging them to follow the example of Massachusetts. As the self-appointed spokesman for opponents of the Sugar Act, he succeeded in arousing men throughout America to the "dangers" of Parliament's act. Eventually he became chairman of a committee of four, authorized by the Assembly under a special act submitted by Otis, that was formed for the purpose of obtaining the formal concurrence of the other colonial legislatures.

Governor Bernard, a far more able and farsighted man than the people of Massachusetts realized, followed these developments with great interest. He regarded the opposition to the Sugar Act as unimportant in itself, and the attack on Hutchinson left him undisturbed, even though it was temporarily inconvenient to have the salary of the chief justice suspended. What alarmed him, however, was the formation of the committee authorized to contact the other colonies. This, he said, was a "foundation for connecting the demagogues of the several governments in America to join together in opposition to all orders from Great Britain which don't square with their notions of the rights of the people." Afraid he might be going too far in his belief that serious disaffection could result, he added, "Perhaps I may be too suspicious. A little time will show whether I am or not."

What neither he nor anyone else on either side of the Atlantic relaized was that an obscure Boston brewer who had dabbled in local politics on the side had suddenly found himself. For years Adams had written in philosophical generalities, filling the columns of the *Advertiser* with lofty, abstract observations that had been read only by a tiny handful of friends who already agreed with him. Now, by applying the principles expounded by John Locke to specific, large problems that affected all Americans everywhere, he found himself dealing with a vast, sympathetic audience in thirteen colonies, as well as in Canada, newly incorporated into the empire after being formally ceded by France under the terms of the peace treaty that ended the French and Indian War in 1763.

The overnight change in Sam Adams was dramatic and almost inexplicable. The bumbling failure became a self-assured man with a mission, endowed with almost superhuman energy, who devoted himself with compulsive, single-minded zeal to the task of arousing the American people to unsuspected dangers. The reaction to his instructions in Massachusetts Bay and the other colonies taught him something that he was quick to grasp, something that few other men of his era realized: it was a simple matter for a man who dealt with broad issues on a popular level to create and arouse the emotions of the public.

Governor Bernard had been more accurate than he knew when he expressed his fear of demagogues. Sam Adams's success made him a quiet demagogue, a man content to use his pen and his organizational talents to create overwhelming public responses. A new career beckoned, and the forty-two-year-old failure was ready for it. His success in forming the opposition to the Sugar Act and giving voice to its proponents coincided with his second marriage, and his personal happiness, as well as the knowledge that his children were at last in competent hands, left him free to devote all of his time and furious attention to what would become a struggle to the death against a great giant.

Whether Adams recognized the odds against him, whether he was even aware of the fact that he was a puny David challenging the Goliath that was the greatest power on earth, is not known. But it is unlikely that, at the end of 1764, he could look that far into the future. What neither he nor anyone else could realize was that the acts Parliament would pass in the next year would spur him to even greater efforts, formalize his opposition to the Crown and give him the great cause he sought. The ill-starred relationship of Great Britain and her North American colonies developed with the inevitability of a Greek tragedy, and the errors made by King George III and his ministers gave Sam Adams the firewood to throw into the flames that illuminated his crusade.

Chapter Five

The passage of the Stamp Act and the Quartering Act by Parliament early in 1765 created an unprecedented uproar in the colonies, but the reaction was not spontaneous. In the center of the whirlwind, directing its movements and fanning it to ever greater furies, was the unpretentious figure of Sam Adams.

No man seemed a less likely candidate for the role Adams played with such distinction. Certainly he was aware of his past failures, and making light of them, tried to portray them as strengths, telling his cousin John he "never looked forward in his life, never planned, laid a scheme, or formed a design of laying up anything for himself or others after him."

According to Ralph Volney Harlow, who wrote a psychological study of Adams a half-century ago, this son of a hard-driving, successful father and a mother who filled him with a sense of guilt may have suffered from an inferiority complex. If so, perhaps he worked with compulsive fervor in an attempt to overcome his feelings. The evidence at hand is only circumstantial, but it has been definitely established that at the age of forty-two, and for the rest of his life, Sam Adams suffered from some sort of nervous or emotional disorder.

According to Wells, his great-grandson, the affliction first came to light in 1765. Wells said he suffered from "a constitutional tremulousness of voice and hand, peculiar to his family, which sometimes continued for several weeks together, and then disappeared for as long a time." His handwriting, sometimes so crabbed and shaky that it was almost illegible, substantiates Wells's statement.

There can be little doubt, either, that Adams's behavior became obsessive after he enjoyed his first success in 1764. Politics became his whole life, and nothing else mattered to him. He loved his wife and children, but took them for granted, and only a rare woman would have tolerated his neglect. He no longer cared what he ate—even raw oysters failed to tempt his palate— and his attire became so slovenly that Elizabeth Adams had to supervise changes in his suits, shirts and underclothes. He acquired a reputation for forgetting his hat and greatcoat when leaving a meeting, even in midwinter, and he frequently walked out of the house without a penny in his pockets. He abandoned his few avocations, and was known to leave the dinner table in ill-disguised disgust if the conversation veered away from politics. He forgot the names of nonpolitical friends, yet could recall, verbatim, a letter written to him years earlier on a political subject.

Oddly enough, Adams himself was one of the few who recognized as successful his venture into politics on a large scale in 1764. Judged by surface standards, he had failed again. The merchants of Boston and other cities disagreed with his radical tactics and preferred to write privately to members of Parliament and businessmen in England, urging the repeal of the Sugar Act because it would result in a loss of sales. Thomas Hutchinson was not the villain Adams painted him, and moderates rallied to him, managing to reverse the Assembly's action and restoring his salary. In fact, James Otis believed he had gone too far, and for more than six months rejoined the moderates himself.

But Sam Adams knew he had aroused the emotions of men in all thirteen colonies, and was unperturbed when opposition to the Sugar Act virtually vanished early in 1765. He believed he would have another chance, and it came even sooner than he expected. In April, 1765, news that Parliament had passed the Stamp and Quartering acts reached the colonies, and the fat was in the fire.

The Stamp Act was made to order for Sam Adams's purposes because it struck hardest at the most prosperous, best educated and most articulate men in the colonies, the lawyers, the merchants and the publishers and printers. Adams and the other Boston radicals held meetings and tried to organize opposition to the Stamp Act, heaping public ridicule on Andrew Oliver for accepting appointment to the office of stamp distributor, but the conservatives held a comfortable majority in the Assembly as well as in the Council, and it appeared for a time that the radicals' efforts would be thwarted.

But Adams was rigid in his opposition to the new law, as was an obscure Virginia legislator, Patrick Henry. The two men acted more or less simultaneously, each without knowledge of the other. On May 24 Henry delivered a blazing address in the Virginia House of Burgesses that was a call to arms to all Americans and created a sensation when it was reprinted throughout the colonies.

Meanwhile Adams went to work in his own way. His first step was to form an alliance with the printers-publishers of the Boston *Gazette*, Gill and Edes, who opposed the measure because they would be required to purchase a stamp for every copy of their newspaper that they sold. They joined forces with Adams and with Otis, who came back to the radicals and the Caucus Club in June, and a number of unsigned articles and editorials, written in Adams's style, began to appear in the newspaper's columns. The *Gazette*, with a weekly circulation of more than two thousand, was the largest and most influential periodical in New England, and was read by colonial leaders elsewhere, so it served as an admirable forum for Adams's views. Like Patrick

Henry, he pounded at the theme that the Stamp Act was outrageous and illegal because it taxed the colonies without their consent.

These editorials proved insufficient to arouse the general public, however, so Adams readjusted his sights. He had discovered that he could arouse the feelings of the dock workers, merchant seamen and other lower-class friends whom he saw in the waterfront taverns, and it occurred to him that, if they were organized, they could exert a powerful influence. Working with great care and cunning, he proceeded to band them together in what was at this time an informal group. Not until later would he dignify the organization by naming it the Sons of Liberty.

A "spontaneous" demonstration would awaken all Boston to the perils of the Stamp Act, he decided, and he chose August 14, the birthday of the Prince of Wales, for the occasion. On that morning, residents of Boston crossing the Common on their way to work saw effigies of Oliver and Lord Bute, King George's lieutenant in the House of Lords, hanging from large elm trees. The governor wisely elected not to create an unnecessary incident, and although the windows of his office faced the Common, he developed an acute if temporary myopia. The effigies swayed in the breeze all day, and that night a large, noisy crowd of future Sons of Liberty took charge. The discipline exerted by its leaders was remarkable, and at no time did a mob spirit prevail. If Sam Adams was present in person he hovered on the outside fringe of the crowd, directing its activities, but since he later wrote at length about the supposed spontaneity of the gathering, it must be presumed that he kept completely out of sight.

This was the first time he had gathered a group of willing disciples for the purpose of creating future propaganda, but he had found his true calling at last, and there were no untoward disorders. Casual passersby were treated with every courtesy, and those who declined polite invitations to take part in the demonstration were permitted to go their own way.

The crowd, later estimated by Hutchinson to number about one hundred and fifty men, but described in the *Gazette* and single-sheet circulars by the optimistic Adams as "an indignant band of thousands," marched to the Common through the streets of Boston. They chanted, "Liberty, property and no stamps!"— a slogan Adams said was impromptu but that, through no accident, had appeared the previous week in an essay he had published in the *Gazette*.

The effigies were hauled down and burned, and, as Lord Bute was beyond the reach of the demonstrators, the crowd marched to a building owned by Oliver, reputedly the future office of the stamp distributor, and used axes to chop the interior to kindling. Then, to emphasize the point Sam Adams was trying to make, the windows on the ground floor of Oliver's house were broken. With a good night's work done, the crowd dispersed. It may or may not be true that the faithful who found their way to certain waterfront taverns, notably one located in a building that Samuel Adams the elder had purchased forty years earlier, were treated to free ale and cider by a generous and grateful host who chose to remain anonymous.

Early the next morning Andrew Oliver proved himself sensitive to hints and resigned his office as stamp distributor. This fact was announced triumphantly in a special issue of the *Gazette*, which also contained a glowing account of the previous night's festivities. Governor Bernard, who was not amused, said in his report to the Colonial Office in London that he suspected that the story of the spontaneous uprising had been written before the event had taken place. The governor had good reason to feel uneasy, and expressed feelings that were shared by many Bostonians of substance: "All kinds of ill humours were set on float. Every thing that for years past had been the cause of any popular discontent was revived; and private resentments against persons in office worked themselves in and endeavored to execute themselves under the mask of the public cause."

Sam Adams had reason to be pleased with the results of the evening's gathering, and immediately sent off letters to leaders of public sentiment in other colonies, with whom he was now corresponding regularly, telling them what had happened. The longest and most detailed of these communications went to Patrick Henry, and in it Adams wondered—with remarkable innocence—whether a similar spirit had as yet manifested itself in Virginia.

But the new master of Massachusetts rebels quickly discovered that once a mob has been unleashed, it is no easy matter to bring emotions under control. On the night of August 26 a group of approximately three hundred men gathered at the junction of Newberry, Orange and Essex streets, and there, beneath the spreading branches of what Sam Adams soon would call the Liberty Tree, in an open space he named Liberty Hall, made plans for another evening's entertainment. John Adams is the authority for the statement that the leaders had met a short time earlier in the counting room of the Chase and Speakman distill-ery in Hanover Square. He did not indicate whether they sam-pled the establishment's fine rum, but he must have known that Cousin Sam was its proprietor.

John Hancock has been unjustly blamed for some of that night's activities, although he had no advance knowledge of what would happen and disapproved of the violence that ensued. Un-doubtedly the finger of suspicion pointed at him because he, along with every other shipowner and importer in Massachusetts Bay, benefited from the destruction of virtually all official records of overseas commercial transactions.

The office of the registrar of the Admiralty Court was the first target of the mob, which burned every paper in the building. Then the office of the customs comptroller was attacked, and by that time the mob lost all self-control. The three hundred, accom-panied by an even larger throng of curious bystanders, marched to the private dwelling of Chief Justice Hutchinson, which was universally regarded as the finest house in the colony and which John Hancock had called the one home in Boston superior to his own Beacon Hill mansion.

The interior was totally wrecked, and the mob stole plate, silver and bric-a-brac worth a fortune. Hutchinson's library of more than ten thousand books, perhaps the most extensive in New England, was used to feed a bonfire in the side yard, and the destruction was so thorough that even fruit trees behind the house were chopped down. Hutchinson, his wife and children barely escaped with their lives, and had to take refuge in the harbor fort used as a garrison for the governor's honor guard of British troops.

All of Boston's responsible citizens, including the radical leaders, were shocked by the mob's action, and Sam Adams wrote a strong editorial in the *Gazette* condemning the riots. He and James Otis were among a group of prominent citizens who offered a statement of formal apology and regret to Hutchinson, and both took part in a campaign to collect twenty-five hundred pounds as a repayment, at least in part, of the chief justice's losses.

Several contemporary sources and a larger number of later historians have suspected that Sam Adams played a part in the planning of the events of August 26, short of the personal attack on Hutchinson, but there has never been any evidence to support this view. His anger appears to have been as great as that of anyone else, and had he or any other member of the Caucus Club been responsible, as the authorities knew they had been for the earlier demonstration, they would have been arrested and tried. As it was, however, no arrests were made and no charges were filed against any individual. On this unhappy occasion, at least, the mob Sam Adams had been instrumental in forming became faceless.

A short time later the Sons of Liberty was formally organized as a semisecret organization, but it was no secret that Sam Adams gave the group its name. A shoemaker named Mackintosh, a member of the Sons, took credit for the leadership of both riots; it may have been true that he was the physical leader, but he was an illiterate who could not have planned the first demonstration.

New tensions could be felt in the streets of Boston, and Governor Bernard wanted to form a special military battalion of volunteers to protect Crown officials from further attacks. But Sam Adams and James Otis learned of the project and paid calls on members of the Council, who refused to grant the governor the necessary approval. Bernard tried again and again to persuade the Assembly to investigate the riots, but was thwarted by an almost satanically clever Sam Adams.

Called to the governor's mansion and threatened with legal action unless he withdrew his opposition to an investigation, Adams promised his full cooperation—and provided it in his own way. He and Otis had gained virtually complete control of the radicals in the Assembly, and through their manipulations a committee of investigation was formed without delay. The group consisted of their followers, in the main, and although it went through the motions of conducting its inquiry, it actually did nothing.

Governor Bernard knew when he had been beaten, and admitted as much: "The people know that at present they may choose whether they would be taxed or not, and in such a deliberation it is easy to say what their choice will be. . . . Surely it is not known at Whitehall how weak and impotent the authority of American Governors is in regard to popular tumults. For my part, I am entirely at the mercy of the mob, and the power and authority of Government is really at an end." He exaggerated, but coming events cast long shadows.

In the early autumn of 1765 Sam Adams officially became the leader of the Massachusetts radicals. A prominent member of the group, Oxenbridge Thacher, was forced to resign his seat in the Assembly because of consumption, and Adams was elected by a special Boston town meeting to replace him. By this time Sam Adams was sufficiently well known to be regarded as a co-leader of the group with James Otis, but it happened that Otis, increasingly erratic and showing signs of the insanity that would totally incapacitate him four years later, was attending a meeting of the Stamp Act Congress in New York. It was typical of Adams that, after being instrumental in organizing the intercolonial meeting, he did not attend it himself as a delegate.

The Massachusetts Assembly met on September 3, and the radicals lost no time in electing as their leader "S. Adams, Esq., a Boston merchant and church-goer of distinction," as the *Gazette* called him. He had no immediate opportunity to display his talents in the House of Representatives, however, because Governor Bernard, unwilling to give him a chance to create new mischief, prorogued the Assembly on September 4.

Lack of a formal forum was no obstacle to the inventive Adams, and he utilized the technique that had stood him in such good stead the previous year. He wrote a letter of instructions to Boston's representatives in the Assembly, and the town meeting dutifully ratified the document, notwithstanding the fact that everyone knew he was the author of the paper and therefore had written a directive to himself. The *Gazette* printed the instructions in full, which enabled other Massachusetts towns to issue identical instructions; the first to do so was Braintree, still the official residence of John Adams.

The paper, a typical Sam Adams product, read:

At a time when the British American subjects are everywhere loudly complaining of arbitrary and unconstitutional innovations, the town of Boston cannot any longer remain silent without just imputation of inexcusable neglect. By the royal charter granted to our ancestors, the power of making laws for our internal government, and of levying taxes, is vested in the General Assembly; and by the charter, the inhabitants of this Province are entitled to all the rights and privileges of natural free-born subjects of Great Britain. The most essential rights of British subjects are those of being represented in the same body which exercises the power of levying taxes upon them, and of having their property tried by juries. These are the very pillars of the British Constitution, founded on the common rights of mankind. It is certain that we were in no sense represented in the Parliament of Great Britain where this act of taxation was made, and it is also certain that this law admits of our properties being tried in controversies arising from internal concerns by courts of admiralty without a jury. It follows that at once it annihilates the most valuable privileges of our charter, deprives us of the most essential rights of Britons, and greatly weakens the best security of our lives, liberties, and estates, which hereafter may be at the disposal of judges who may be strangers to us, and perhaps malicious, mercenary, corrupt, and offensive. Moreover, this act, if carried into execution, would become a further grievance to us, as it will afford a precedent for the Parliament to tax us at all future time, and in all such ways and measures as they shall judge meet, without our consent. We therefore think it our indispensable duty, in justice to ourselves and posterity, as it is our undoubted privilege, in the most open and unreserved, but decent and respectful terms, to declare our greatest dissatisfaction with this law. And we think it incumbent upon you by no means to join any public measures for countenancing and assisting in the excution of the same; but to use your best endeavors in the General Assembly to have the inherent, inalienable rights of the people of this Province asserted and vindicated, and left upon the public records, that posterity may never have reason to charge the present times with the guilt of giving them away.

This masterpiece of propaganda was printed in full by the Boston *News-Letter* as well as the *Gazette*, an unprecedented act in the history of New England journalism, and was adopted without change by thirty-seven smaller Massachusetts towns. Adams thoughtfully sent copies to the radical leaders and newspapers of other colonies, where it also became a model. John Adams later said that the letter of instruction was adopted verbatim by more than six hundred cities and towns from New Hampshire to Georgia. Increasingly adept in his new profession, Sam Adams thoughtfully mailed copies to prominent leaders of the Whig opposition in England, among them William Pitt the elder, now the Earl of Chatham, Edmund Burke and a young member of Parliament just coming into prominence, Charles James Fox. It was not surprising that his arguments fell on sympathetic ears, and that these men supported his stand.

Adams's activities overwhelmed Governor Bernard, and the rattled Englishman made two serious errors in his attempt to stem the tide of public sentiment swinging in favor of opposition to the Stamp Act. Hoping the politicians would talk out their grievances, he permitted the Assembly to convene, and in an address that opened the session he compounded this first mistake by charging that the radicals took the position that the law of Parliament should not be enforced.

This was not only a misstatement of fact but a political blunder, and Sam Adams lost no time taking full advantage of the slip. He made a full reply in a long, sarcastic speech, then made sure his remarks would be widely circulated by printing them at his own expense. His opening paragraph set the tone for the address, which required three and one-half hours to deliver:

> Your Excellency tells us that the Province seems to be upon the brink of a precipice! A sight of its danger is then necessary for its preservation. To despair of the Commonwealth is a certain presage of its fall. Your Excellency may be assured that the representatives of the people are awake to a sense of its danger, and their utmost prudence will not be wanting to prevent its ruin.

The real importance of this speech, almost obscured by Adams's rhetoric, was in the doctrine he advanced here for the first time. He suggested that the people of Massachusetts Bay refrain from resorting to violence, and instead follow a passive policy of nonresistance which would make the Stamp Act inoperable. This doctrine, although not clearly enunciated, was the forerunner of a far more important weapon, the boycott of British goods, to which he would resort a few years later.

In an effort to make certain that the other Massachusetts towns would join Boston in her campaign, Adams sent personal messengers, under the banner of the Caucus Club, to every community in the colony. Their efforts were so successful that Lieutenant Governor Hutchinson called them "super incendiaries," and a weary Governor Bernard declared that "a considerable part of the Province has taken their complexion from this town, more than was ever known before."

Adams gave the Crown representatives no respite, losing no opportunity to attack them. In October 1765 the stamps intended for use under the terms of the act he despised reached Boston by Royal Navy warship, and as Governor Bernard was afraid they would be burned if they were stored in the town, he placed them in Castle William in the harbor for safekeeping. Still apprehensive, he issued a decree authorizing the raising of a special military company to guard the stamps. Adams promptly pounced on him.

The Assembly, he said, had not ratified the raising of such a company, and it was a matter of supreme indifference to him that the legislature had never previously exercised such a right. In a resolution condemming Bernard's move, he thundered that an executive who raised one company of troops on his own whim would have a precedent for creating ten companies, perhaps as many as one hundred, and would be in a position to deprive the people of their "remaining liberties."

Growing still bolder, Adams presented another resolution in the Assembly, this one demanding that no citizen of Massachusetts Bay consent to accept the position of stamp distributor. Although he was the leader of the new radical majority, some of the more timid members hesitated. The debate became so incendiary that Governor Bernard again prorogued the session.

This had no practical effect, however, because Adams, Otis and their cohorts were ready for their trump move. November 1 arrived, and on that date no business or legal document would be valid unless one of the new Crown stamps was affixed to it. No stamps were sold in the entire colony, however, for the simple reason that all business requiring the use of stamps was suspended. Commercial houses closed their doors, the law courts were empty, and even John Adams, who approved of the strategy, could not help bemoaning the situation. "Debtors grow insolent; creditors grow angry," he said. "This long interval of indolence and idleness will make a large chasm in my affairs, if it should not reduce me to distress."

Other colonies followed the example of Massachusetts Bay, but only in Virginia, where the enthusiastic Patrick Henry took charge, was the success as complete. In these two colonies, and to a somewhat lesser extent elsewhere, all business, commercial and legal activities came to a complete halt, a situation that grew increasingly grim over the period of a month and a half.

It was obvious to thinking men, Sam Adams among them, that the Crown could better afford to play a waiting game than could colonists, who would be forced into bankruptcy. The Caucus

Club held a series of emergency meetings, and John Hancock is credited with devising a new plan that represented a shift in tactics. Every American merchant would write without delay to the British firms with which he did business, stating that he would purchase no more goods from that source and would cancel all current orders unless the Stamp Act was revoked.

This scheme met with an immediate, favorable response, and on December 9, 236 Massachusetts Bay merchants sent identical letters, the draft of which had been composed by Sam Adams, to merchants in England. No coercion was used in this instance, and the unanimity of the business community was remarkable. In the letter Adams forcefully reminded British commercial interests of the benefits of colonial trade, and lost no opportunity to expound on his favorite theme, the "natural rights of Englishmen, including those who lived in the colonies."

The success of this campaign in Massachusetts inspired Adams to expand the scheme, and he wrote to all of the leaders of other colonies, including copies of his own letter and urging that the same tactics be applied elsewhere. According to Benjamin Franklin, more than two thousand such communications flooded the offices of British merchants and bankers in the opening months of 1766.

But Sam Adams knew that more immediate steps were required if business was to be revived. Members of the Caucus Club, often accompanied by brawny Sons of Liberty, paid visits to the customs officials, urging them, in the name of patriotism, to grant clearance—without stamps—to the cargoes of merchant ships that clogged Boston's harbor. At the same time a petition was sent to Governor Bernard, "respectfully" requesting him to reopen the courts and allow the dispensation of justice—again without the use of stamps.

The customs officers were the first to buckle under the extreme pressure, and they were soon followed by the judges, bailiffs and other officials of the lower courts. Cargo poured into Boston, the courts resumed functioning, and so many men were involved in breaking the law that, as Sam Adams smugly observed, it would be impossible to punish "the entire population of the town."

Only the Superior Court remained closed; but by March 1766, Chief Justice Hutchinson could no longer resist the pressures created by the backlog of cases that mounted higher with each passing day. He and the governor capitulated, and the business life of Boston was restored to normal. Sam Adams, a scant two years earlier a nonentity, had won a victory that strengthened his control of the Boston town meeting, the legislature and the smaller towns that were now more willing than ever to follow his lead. No one could argue with Governor Bernard, who bitterly remarked that Adams had become the single most powerful man in the colony.

Chapter
Six

In 1766 George III and his ministers were forced to swallow and then digest the most unpalatable of political truths: Parliament might be the supreme legislative force in the British Empire, but the North American colonies could not be persuaded or coerced to obey a law enacted by Parliament and signed by the monarch. Although no one was willing to admit the obvious, a drastic change had taken place in England's relations with her colonies, and the old state of affairs could not be restored. The monarch and members of the group known as "the King's party" had no intention of surrendering their prerogatives permanently, to be sure, and made private plans to bide their time and wait for a more opportune moment to assert their authority.

In the meantime, however, immediate face-saving was necessary. Since it was inconceivable that King George himself would back down in public, thereby weakening the structure and tarnishing the image of the Crown as an institution, a scapegoat had to be found. Grenville was the natural candidate, so he and his Cabinet resigned. The first order of business was to mend relations with the colonies, to restore order there and to placate English merchants who had suffered severe losses and were demanding the immediate repeal of the Stamp Act.

Pitt and Lord Camden supported the American position that taxation without representation was illegal, which embarrassed the ministry, and an outspoken member of Parliament, Colonel Isaac Barré, delivered an impassioned speech in the Commons, hailing the victory of the colonists in terms far more outspoken than those heard anywhere on the other side of the Atlantic.

Late in March a new and somewhat complicated formula was devised: the hated Stamp Act was repealed, but at the same time Parliament asserted its supremacy in unequivocal terms. A Declaratory Act was passed by an overwhelming majority, and stated in part that Parliament possessed and retained the authority to "bind the colonies and the people of America, subjects of the Crown of Great Britain, in all cases whatsoever." An amused Pitt offered an amendment to the effect that a single exception should be made: money should not be taken out of the colonists' pockets without their consent. Parliament did not share his sense of humor, and the amendment was rejected.

The Sugar Act was modified at the same time. The tax on molasses was reduced from threepence per gallon to a penny, and the tax on other goods was to be collected at the time merchandise was exported from Britain to the colonies and added to the price of the items before the goods were received in America. In this way, it was reasoned, the colonists would not even realize they were being taxed.

The news reached America in April, and nowhere was there greater rejoicing over the repeal of the Stamp Act than in Boston, where the stature of Sam Adams was enhanced immeasurably. He and his friends were not in the least impressed by the Declaratory Act, believing Parliament had passed it as a mere face-saving device. And, as expected in London, the changes in the Sugar Act were virtually unnoticed. The Quartering Act was still operative, but few troops had been sent to the New World, so no real issue was raised except in New York Town. A brigade of fifteen hundred men was sent there, and the residents promptly resisted, refused to provide quarters for the troops and ignored all provisions of the act.

Lord Rockingham became prime minister, including in his Cabinet men sympathetic to America such as Camden and Lord Shelburne, so it was considered unlikely by most men on both sides of the Atlantic that another effort would be made to force the Americans to pay taxes they regarded as unfair. But the basic issue had not yet been resolved, and two Americans, Benjamin Franklin and James Otis, were candid in their statements that further, even more serious troubles would arise unless questions of basic principles were settled.

Sam Adams recognized the problem, too, but elected to remain silent for a time. Instead he devoted himself to the settlement of the final issue for which he had campaigned, the discharge of Thomas Hutchinson from the Governor's Council. Hutchinson was particularly disliked in Massachusetts because, unlike other Crown officials, he was a native of the colony, and Adams again displaying his genius for simplifying issues, attacked the chief justice on the grounds that he was disloyal to his fellow Americans. Inasmuch as all Americans were subjects of the Crown this argument was legally invalid, but it was nevertheless effective, and Hutchinson was now compelled to resign from the Council. Adams's victory was complete.

A study of Sam Adams's position in the fight against the Stamp Act reveals certain fundamentals that only a few scholars, down to the present day, have realized. His arguments, if carried to their logical conclusion, demanded a complete separation of the North American colonies from the mother country. No one realized this more than Adams himself, as his correspondence in 1765 and 1766 clearly indicates.

In a letter to a friend in England, identified only as "G. W.," he wrote at length about what he called the natural rights of all Englishmen and those rights as they applied particularly to Americans. The first settlers in the New World, he declared, had come to the colonies as free men, with total, unlimited authority to establish an independent state, had they chosen to do so. But they had not exercised that privilege, and instead had "voluntarily" entered into a "compact" with the British Crown. Consequently they remained British subjects, and their "natural rights" were reaffirmed in the charters that established each of the colonies.

Now, however, *the Stamp Act had vacated the charter.* In other words, the government of Great Britain had deliberately broken its contract with the American people, and this left Americans free to act accordingly. He stopped short of stating that this automatically made Americans an independent people, but he hinted strongly that he took this position.

From the beginning of his dispute with the Crown, Sam Adams realized that his position would be stronger if cloaked in legality, and it did not matter to him that his argument was historically inaccurate and legally specious. The colonists had not moved from England to territory claimed either by another power or by no power. They had crossed the Atlantic as British subjects, and had voluntarily settled in lands claimed by the Crown. The colonial charters had not been contracts, nor had they been so regarded by either the Crown or the colonists. On the contrary, they had been grants which had given the immigrants to the New World permission to settle on Crown property, to develop it for mutual benefit and to retain their standing as British subjects because they were acting on behalf of the Crown.

Adams's position is further clarified by the stand he took on representation in Parliament. Unlike Otis, who actively wanted and aggressively campaigned for the right of the colonies to send representatives to the House of Commons, Sam Adams was opposed to the idea, making his position unmistakable in his speeches in the Assembly, in essays he wrote for the *Gazette* and in his letters to friends in England. As realistic in his approach to politics as he was inept in business, he was aware that on issues such as taxation a small delegation from the colonies would be consistently overwhelmed and outvoted by a mammoth English majority. So, even if Americans sat in the Commons, they would be unable to prevent the colonies from being subjected to special, discriminatory taxes; moreover, they would lose all right to protest and would have no legal grounds whatever for disobedience.

This placed Adams in a paradoxical position: he argued on the one hand that the colonies had the right to disobey acts of Parliament because they had no representation there, but stated in the very next breath that such representation was undesirable. Adams recognized the equivocal nature of his stand; his correspondence shows his attempts to resolve the contradiction with an ingenious display of reason. In a letter to Dennys Deberdt, the Massachusetts Bay agent in London, he declared:

> The several subordinate powers of legislation in America seem very properly to have been constituted upon their (the colonists) being considered as free subjects of England, and the impossibility of their being represented in Parliament, for which reason these powers ought to be held sacred. The American powers of government are rather to be considered as matters of justice than favor,—without them, they cannot enjoy that freedom which, having never forfeited, no power on earth has any right to deprive them of.

In a subsequent statement in the Assembly, he hammered at the same theme, saying in part: 'So long as we shall have our charter privileges continued, we must think ourselves inexcusable if we should suffer ourselves to be intimidated in the free exercise of them. This exercise of our rights can never, with any color of reason, be adjudged an abuse of our liberty."

Liberty was the magic word in all of his addresses, correspondence and writing for publication, and he took care not to define it too closely. Astonishingly shrewd in his judgment of public reaction to the times, he believed that the American people were not yet ready to think in terms of the establishment of an independent nation. First the groundwork had to be laid, and as issues arose he would be able to move toward the goal he had already chosen.

The method he selected to handle the Sons of Liberty is instructive. Having obtained almost absolute control of the Caucus Club, he and his friends, among them Thomas Cushing and John

Hancock, themselves became members of the Sons. No longer operating from the outside, they made the semisecret organization the activist arm of the Caucus Club. Thereafter, the Sons invariably supported the position of the Caucus Club in any political controversy.

Adams also revealed a degree of farsighted patience that was new to him. Thanks to his initial suggestion in his correspondence with the radical leaders of other colonies, chapters of the Sons of Liberty had been established in New York Town, Philadelphia, New Haven, Providence, Hartford and other towns. The idea of combining and forming a national organization occurred to many of them, and they deluged the original founder with requests that he take the lead.

While he did nothing to discourage them from taking action on their own, Adams nevertheless made no attempt to band the various Sons of Liberty groups together. A common purpose had been evident in the fight for the repeal of the Stamp Act, but that goal had been accomplished, and there was no cement to hold a national organization together. The successful campaign to drive Thomas Hutchinson from the Massachusetts Council had proved that the Sons of Liberty could be effective if they concentrated on local matters, and until a new issue arose that required concerted action, Adams felt, it would be wiser to act separately.

He was afraid that a national group would collapse because it would have nothing to do, and once chapters were disbanded it would be exceptionally difficult to organize them again. Nowhere did he better demonstrate his ability to sacrifice short-term goals for the sake of achieving long-term gains. But he took care to offend no one. The replies to the various requests, although written in his style, were polite communications that never bore his own signature.

If other chapters of the Sons of Liberty wanted to join hands, Boston wished them well, but her members were occupied with affairs in their own town, and the replies hinted that others might do well to follow her example. Careful not to push any other town's nose out of joint, Adams also maintained his correspondence with individual radical leaders elsewhere. Otis had met some of these men at the abortive Stamp Act Congress, but Adams himself was not yet acquainted with any of them, and the failure of that congress in no way discouraged him. The next time a major issue arose, he confided to young John Hancock, who was rapidly assuming the position of his first lieutenant, the experience they had gained in the crisis of 1765 would better enable them to work in concert again.

Mending his fences for the sake of the future, Adams made it his business to write regularly even to those leaders in other colonies from whom he received no replies. He gave them news of events in Boston, passed along gossip from other places that he had gleaned and sent them copies of the *Gazette* containing essays and articles he had written. These successful efforts to keep his lines of communication open ultimately led to the formation of the enormously effective and far more formal Committees of Correspondence, the semiofficial groups that exchanged ideas and news, and out of which grew the First Continental Congress.

The comparative reign of quiet in 1766 made it possible for Adams to consolidate his position in Massachusetts, where, in the elections of that year, the radicals not only gained control of the Assembly and of most town meetings, but were able to exert considerable influence on appointments to the Council. James Otis was the orator, the man whom the general public applauded, but behind him stood Sam Adams, the man to whom the Caucus Club in Boston and the leaders of small towns came for guidance, help and direction.

Governor Bernard and Chief Justice Hutchinson recognized him as the most potent force in the radical movement and kept close watch on his activities. Adams obliged by keeping them busy, losing no opporunity to fire a new salvo on behalf of the principles he had already elucidated. He was the only colonial leader of prominence who recognized the dangers inherent in the Declaratory Act that asserted Parliament's ultimate authority, and he not only condemned the measure at length in the *Gazette*, but was responsible for the passage of resolutions in the Assembly attacking it.

Posterity has tended to treat Sam Adams and his colleagues of this period as cardboard figures, in part because so few details of their private lives are known, so the observations of John Adams are illuminating. On December 23, 1766, he visited the Caucus Club to dine with his cousin and the other leaders, and recorded the following in his *Diary* afterwards:

The behavior of these gentlemen is very familiar and friendly to each other, and very polite and complaisant to strangers. Gray has a very tender mind, is extremely timid. He says when he meets a man of the other side, he talks against him; when he meets a man of our side, he opposes him; so that he fears he shall be thought against everybody, and so everybody will be against him. But he hopes to prepare the way for his escape at next May from an employment that neither his abilities nor circumstances nor turn of mind are fit for.

Cushing is steady and constant and busy in the interest of liberty and the opposition, is famed for secrecy and his talent at procuring intelligence.

Adams is zealous, ardent, and keen in the cause, is always for softness and delicacy and prudence where they will do, but is staunch and stiff and rigid and inflexible in the cause.

Otis is fiery and feverous; his imagination flames, his passions blaze; he is liable to great inequalities of temper; sometimes in despondency, sometimes in a rage. The rashness and imprudencies into which his excess of zeal have formerly transported him have made him enemies, whose malicious watch over him occasion more caution and more cunning and more inexplicable passages in his conduct than formerly; and, perhaps, views at the Chair, or Board, or possibly more expanded views beyond the Atlantic, may mingle now with his patriotism.

The Il Penseroso, however, is discernible on the faces of all four.

Adams, I believe, has the most thorough understanding of liberty and her resources in the temper and character of the people, though not in the law and Constitution; as well as the most habitual, radical love of it of any of them, as well as the most correct, genteel, and artful pen. He is a man of refined policy, steadfast integrity, exquisite humanity, genteel erudition, obliging, engaging manners, real as well as professed piety, and a universal good character, unless it should be admitted that he is too attentive to the public, and not enough so to himself and his family.

This last observation probably was not made during the visit to the Caucus Club, but may have been noted when he dined several evenings earlier at the house on Purchase Street. On that occasion Cousin Sam had arrived home late, to the obvious distress of Cousin Elizabeth, who had tried in vain to hide her feelings. Then, after gulping his meal, Sam had hurried off to another meeting, notwithstanding the presence at his table of his young relative.

Other men were relaxing in 1766, delighted that the Stamp Act tempest had ended and happy to live normal lives again. But Sam Adams knew that other storms would gather, and he was putting his political house in order so that he would be ready for any gale.

Chapter
Seven

The illness of the Earl of Chatham in 1767 caused almost immediate repercussions in Great Britain's relations with her North American colonies. Not only was Pitt no longer able to control a Parliament that resented the attitude the Americans had displayed during the Stamp Act crisis, but the Rockingham ministry became unstable and was forced to resign. Chatham accepted the office of lord privy seal in a new ministry, but lacked the physical strength to play an active role in the affairs of state.

The Duke of Grafton, a Tory, became the new prime minister, but the real power in his Cabinet was the leader in the Commons, Charles Townshend, who had been one of the authors of the Stamp Act. Townshend shared the views of King George and of a majority in Parliament that the American colonies were not contributing their share to the maintenance of the empire, nor were they even paying their own way. The new chancellor of the exchequer also felt it was imperative that the Americans be made to realize they owed more than lip service to the Crown if they were to enjoy the benefits of being British subjects.

He immediately went to work to promote a complex series of

bills in the Commons that became known as the Townshend system. Having learned nothing from Grenville's mistakes, failing to understand the American mentality and shrugging off the influence in the New World of such radicals as Sam Adams, Townshend deliberately waved a very red flag under the nose of the American bull.

One measure was even more drastic than it appeared. The New York legislature had refused to appropriate funds under the terms of the Quartering Act, so Parliament suspended that assembly, forbidding it to convene again unless and until it agreed to provide money as required by the act. This measure further asserted that the New York legislature's very existence was predicated upon the original charter grant given by the Crown, hence its suspension made it evident that Parliament stood supreme, its acts invalidating any action taken by a lesser lawmaking body.

With the rights of Americans to legislate and appropriate funds denied, it was now clear that no colonial rights were inviolable.

Townshend again tightened the noose around American smugglers. One new law established a Board of Customs Commissioners, which would sit in Boston; it was specifically authorized to issue writs of assistance, or general search warrants, to ferret out smuggled goods.

Townshend believed he had found a way to raise revenues in America without creating new colonial opposition. Bills were passed that exacted duties on a variety of goods, including glass, paper, paint and tea. These taxes would be paid at the American ports of entry by the importers, hence the consumer would pay no tax.

In order to soften the blow still more, Townshend's bills made it clear that all revenues raised in America would be spent in America; specifically, the funds would be used to pay the salaries of Crown officials in the colonies. What he failed to understand, tragically, was that the colonial legislatures were zealous in guarding the power of the purse strings. They were pleased to pay the salaries of Crown officers because it gave them a strong measure of control over these officials, who, if paid by the Crown, would not be responsible to the American constituents whose activities they administered.

Townshend also let it be known that the items taxed were only the beginning. As the system developed, other English products would be added to the list, and he blithely, if foolishly, promised the British people that a very large revenue would be raised under his system.

The Townshend system resulted in a form of spontaneous combustion everywhere in the colonies. Southern planters immediately organized a boycott. The New York Assembly held a rump session in defiance of Parliament's order of suspension. And John Dickinson, the mild Pennsylvania Quaker, declared in a fury, "If Great Britain can order us to come to her for necessaries we want, and can order us to pay what taxes she pleases before we take them away, or when we land them here, we are as abject slaves as France and Poland can show in wooden shoes and with uncombed hair."

Sam Adams had been relatively somnolent during the spring and early summer of 1767, prior to the arrival of news of Parliament's passage of the Townshend Acts. He had continued to consolidate his hold over the Massachusetts legislature and to concern himself with the routine minutiae of the colony's affairs, but nothing had happened to arouse his imagination or ire. He is not known to have written one newspaper essay, editorial or article during that time; his correspondence fell off; and for the first time since his remarriage he was able to devote a reasonable amount of time and attention to his family. He spent more time in the brewery, although it was now too late for him to prevent it from sinking deeper into a financial swamp, and on Saturday afternoons, if at no other time, he resumed his horseback rides in the country with his children.

Governor Bernard's correspondence during this time reveals that the chief executive of Massachusetts Bay was delighted by the situation. The radicals had come to power in the colony because they had galvanized the opposition to acts promoted by Grenville, and now that serenity had been restored, Adams and his friends had been robbed of any reason for political being. If peaceful, harmonious relations between the mother country and her North American colonies were maintained, "Sam'l Adams and his breed will vanish into limbo," Bernard predicted.

Charles Townshend lacked Bernard's foresight and understanding; the acts bearing his name began to pass Parliament at the end of June 1767, and continued to move through the legislative mill for the next month. When news of the measures was received in Boston, Sam Adams reacted instantly, and the following morning a special issue of the *Gazette* appeared on the streets. Written in a style recognized by everyone familiar with the Stamp Act controversy, the *Gazette* editorial expressed astonishment and scorn as well as anger:

> Have these men forgot the year 1765, when the old *new english* spirit was roused? Let them not deceive themselves. The colonies are still united, as they are embarked in the same bottom; and I dare say, rather than submit to slavery, they would still risk their ALL.
> *Governors* INDEPENDENT!!!
> What a sound is *this!* It is discord in the ear of a Briton. *A power without a check!* What a solecism in a free government!

The piece was signed *"Brittanus Americanus,"* a new name in colonial letters. No one doubted the identity of the author, but Sam Adams had moved a giant step closer to advocating open insurrection, and had to maintain a slender fiction of identity. By saying that the colonists were willing to risk their all he was hinting broadly that they were willing and eager to revolt rather than submit to the Townshend Acts, and he well knew that an irate Governor Bernard could order his arrest for treason. What he failed to realize was that Bernard, a loyal subject of the Crown who would, in time, be knighted for his services in Massachusetts, was as shocked and dismayed by the news as was everyone else in the colony.

Old hands now in the fine arts of political combat, Sam Adams and his Caucus Club associates were confident of victory as they prepared for battle. Adams immediately drafted a new plan far more drastic than anything tried in the previous struggle: he proposed a complete boycott of all British goods, saying that the people would eat, drink, wear and "use no instruments or tools or other devices" made in Great Britain. The agreement to enter into this boycott would be universal, and would extend to people of every class and occupation in the entire colony.

The Caucus Club quickly approved of the plan, which was endorsed without argument or discussion by the Sons of Liberty, and the boycott was announced in the *Gazette* and *News-Letter* on July 23, 1767. The Boston town meeting endorsed the scheme within a week. As the legislature already had been summoned for a regular session scheduled to begin on August 4, it was assumed that Governor Bernard would intervene. But he wisely took no action, afraid he would make the situation still worse, and in a brief address marking the opening of the Assembly, he urged a preservation of the calm that had prevailed for months. Majority leader Adams paid no attention to the advice, and on August 6, a scant day and a half after the Assembly began its new deliberations, an act calling for a total boycott of British goods was passed.

Sam Adams's virtuoso demonstration of power and speed inspired awe throughout the colonies. Less than two weeks had passed since receipt of the first news of the passage of the Townshend Acts, and a boycott was already under way in Massachusetts! It did not matter that the acts would not become operative until November; the colonists were displaying their muscle, and thousands were already refusing to buy anything that was British made.

John Hancock was so wealthy he could tolerate a heavy financial loss, but not many of his fellow merchants could fall back on large fortunes. The majority faced ruin, and the newspaper that was their mouthpiece, the Boston *Post*, expressed the first discordant note by coming out in opposition to the boycott. It approached the problem in philosophical rather than patriotic terms, and argued that a compulsory boycott would, in and of itself, destroy the liberties Americans were trying to preserve.

Sam Adams replied in his own way at a session of the Boston town meeting held on October 28. The members, after a remarkably brief debate, voted in favor of a resolution urging the people of Boston to "take all prudent and legal measures to encourage the produce and manufactures of this province." This resolution ignored the fact that manufacturing in the colonies was forbidden.

A companion resolution pretended to be unaware of the informal embargo on British goods that was already in effect, and demanded that an "official" boycott be instituted on December 31, 1767.

Sam Adams had no intention of resting on his laurels. He realized that a long time might pass before the Assembly was called into session again to endorse the resolutions, and he knew that similar situations might exist in other colonies, where royal governors well might prorogue the legislatures. So he decided to circumvent them, and spent an entire night and day at the printing plant of his good friend and fellow Caucus Club member, Benjamin Edes, co-publisher of the *Gazette*. Two thousand copies of the twin resolutions were printed, along with a brief, open letter from the town meeting, urging other communities to follow Boston's example.

These communications were sent at once to every city, town and village in Massachusetts, and special messengers carried them to literally every city and town in British North America. Only in Canada were they ignored. Elsewhere selectmen, boards of aldermen and other authorities quickly accepted the "Boston Idea," as the boycott was at first known. Before the year ended, hundreds of communities had pledged to engage in a total boycott of British goods by the end of the year.

Adams accompanied these moves with a furious propaganda barrage, keeping his messengers busy riding up and down the Atlantic seaboard with letters, editorials, essays and proclamations. He thought of every contingency, and even included already prepared resolutions that could be used by a city or town whose officials felt they could not write an appropriate document of their own. Special expressions of sympathy and support were sent to the cities and towns of New York, whose Assembly had been forbidden to meet.

Not content with flooding America with propaganda, the tireless and indefatigable Adams turned his attention to friends and foes in Great Britain. Seeking sympathy and support wherever he could find it, he flooded the mother country with memorials, addresses and resolutions, almost all of them prepared in the name of the Massachusetts Assembly. Letters went off to Chatham, Rockingham, Camden and Shelburne, and he opened a personal correspondence with a number of these men, as well, hammering at his theme of justice, which could only be served by granting the colonies representation in Parliament. Since he did not actually believe such representation was practical or would serve America's ends, he was in reality conducting an extraordinary exercise in propaganda on the highest level, and although his arguments won the New World no converts in either the Commons or the Lords, he did keep America in the consciousness of men already disposed toward the cause of Britain's sons across the Atlantic.

Perhaps his boldest and shrewdest moves were made in his communications to those he regarded as his enemies. He wrote a long, eloquent petition to King George, respectfully worded yet presenting his position in forceful terms. Similar addresses were sent to the Lords of the Treasury, collectively and individually. He also prepared strong drafts of a circular letter to be approved by the legislatures of other colonies, urging them to follow the lead of Massachusetts in calling the attention of Parliament as a whole to the "plight of the colonies."

Nothing better illustrates his adroit mixture of flattery and pressure than a letter he sent to a leader of the Commons, Henry Seymour Conway, who had already indicated that he thought the claims of the colonies were just:

It is the glory of the British Prince, and the happiness of all his subjects, that their Constitution hath its foundation in the immutable laws of nature; and as the supreme legislative as well as the supreme executive derives its authority from that

Constitution, it should seem that no laws can be made or executed that are repugnant to any essential law in nature. Hence a British subject is happily distinguished from the subjects of many other states, in a just and well-grounded opinion of his own safety, which is the perfection of political liberty.

Recognizing that Lord Rockingham had already demonstrated his friendship for America, Adams nevertheless knew the statesman to be a man who believed in the supremacy of Parliament over all subsidiary legislative bodies. In order to make certain Rockingham's support did not waver, the increasingly masterful propagandist altered his tactics accordingly, and became soothing. The address he sent in the name of the Massachusetts Assembly dealt specifically with the issue, and was as specifically reassuring:

My Lord, the superintending power of that high court (Parliament's) over all His Majesty's subjects in the Empire, and in all cases which can consist with the fundamental rules of the Constitution, was never questioned in this Province, nor, as the House conceive, in any other. But, in all free states, the Constitution is fixed; it is from thence that the supreme legislative as well as the supreme executive derives its authority. Neither, then, can break through the fundamental rules of the Constitution, without destroying their own foundation.

In his address to Lord Camden, the lord chancellor, who was a devoted champion of the principles of liberty, Adams again readjusted his sights, sharpened his pen and wrote a communication he believed would appeal to such a man:

This House can speak only for the people of one Province. But no Assembly on this continent, it is presumed, can long be silent under an apprehension that, without the aid of some powerful advocate, the liberties of America soon will be no more.
If it is an essential, unalterable right in nature, ingrafted into the British Constitution as a fundamental law, and ever

held sacred and irrevocable by the subjects within the realm, that what is a man's own is absolutely his own, and that no man hath a right to take it from him without his consent, may not the subjects of this Province, with a decent firmness which has always distinguished the happy subjects of Britain, plead and maintain this natural constitutional right?

The position that taxation and representation are inseparable is founded on the immutable laws of nature. But the Americans had no representation in Parliament when they were taxed. Are they not, then, unfortunate in these instances, in having that separated which God and nature had joined? Such are the local circumstances of the colonies at the distance of a thousand leagues from the metropolis, and separated by a wide ocean, as will forever render a just and equal representation in the supreme legislative utterly impracticable.

Adams used the same arguments in his address to the great Earl of Chatham. Once again he tailored the communication to its recipient, and keeping in mind that Chatham's illness had forced his partial withdrawal from active politics, the Massachusetts agitator played on a personal note of sympathy in order to exert pressure:

Nothing would have prevailed upon the House to have given Your Lordship this trouble but the necessity of a powerful advocate when their liberty is in danger. Such they have more than once found you to be; and as they humbly hope they have never forfeited your patronage, they entreat that your great interest in the national councils may still be employed in their behalf, that they may be restored to the standing of free subjects.

Sam Adams's instinctive understanding that the most effective propaganda lay in constant repetition of a single theme, simply stated, is seen throughout his correspondence. Nowhere did he tailor his approach more stringently than in his appeal to the Lords of the Treasury. His approach was crisp, devoid of frills, and it is unlikely that he had any real hope that he would influence men whose attitude indicated their minds were already made up. At the same time, however, he knew that the release of copies of the address to British businessmen—as well as to merchants in America—could create complications for the men who were responsible for the policy of taxing the colonies. This communication declared in part:

By act of Parliament, your Lordships are sensible that the Colonies are restrained from importing commodities, the growth or manufacture of Europe, saving a few articles, except from Great Britain. By this policy, the demand of British manufactures from the Colonies is greatly increased; and the manufacturers have the advantage of their own price. Hence it appears, that what is gained by the subjects in Britain is a loss to those in America . . . . If the colonists were allowed to purchase such commodities at foreign markets, they might have them at cheaper rates . . . or the British manufacturers might be necessitated to reduce their price. This regulation . . . the house is not at this time complaining of, but they beg your Lordships' consideration, whether, in addition to these burdens, it is not grievous to their constituents to be obliged to pay duties on British manufactures here; especially considering that, as consumers of these manufactures, they pay a great proportion of the duties and taxes laid upon them in Britain . . . .

It is humbly submitted whether His Majesty's Commons in Britain have not, by these acts, granted the property of their fellow subjects in America, without their consent in Parliament. Your Lordships will allow that it is an unalterable rule in equity, that a man shall have the free use and disposal of his property. This original principle, to the lasting honor of our British ancestors, was in early time ingrafted into the British Constitution, and is the greatest security as well as the brightest ornament of a British subject . . . . All British subjects are alike free.

The blessings of the British Constitution will forever keep the subjects in this Province united to the mother state, as long as the sentiments of liberty are preserved; but what liberty can remain to them, when their property, the fruit of their toil and industry and the prop of all their future hopes in life, may be taken from them at the discretion of others? They have never been backward in affording their aid to His Majesty, to the extent of their ability . . . . From the days of their ancestors no subjects have given more signal proofs of zeal for the service and honor of their sovereign, and affection for the parent country. . . .

The House entreat Your Lordships' patience . . . while they just mention the danger they apprehend to their liberties, if the Crown, in addition to its uncontroverted right of appointing a governor, should also appoint him a stipend at the expense of the people, and without their consent. . . .

It is humbly hoped that Your Lordships will conceive a favorable opinion of the people of the Province, and that you will patronize their liberties, so far as, in your great wisdom and candor, you shall judge to be right.

Sam Adams bared his teeth for the first time, though his grimace was polite, and the significance of his words could not have been lost on those who read the long address. After protesting the loyalty of Massachusetts, he made it clear that the colony intended to remain united with the mother country *as long as the sentiments of liberty were preserved.* In the next breath he protested that they were being denied. He left his threat hanging in the air, but the implication was clear. If the rights he described as fundamental under the British Constitution—one of his favorite phrases in his constantly repeated attempt to cloak his activites in an aura of legality—were denied to the colonists, it was their *right* to seek recourse by any means at their command. He did not spell out his hints, but men who were already growing fearful of a possible revolt in America were allowed to form their own conclusions.

Having encased in a well-tailored glove the fist he had shaken at the Lords of the Treasury, he took an even more subtle approach in his memorial to George III. His tone was humble, his protestations of undying loyalty were strong, and he took pains to recall the loyalty of the Crown's subjects in America from the days of the earliest settlers. After stating that "the crown was settled in Your Majesty's illustrious family," and that "the inhabitants of this Province shared in the common blessing," he abruptly changed to a tone of bluntness:

> They [the colonists] then were indulged with another charter in which their Majesties were pleased, for themselves, their heirs, and successors, to grant and confirm to them as ample estate in the lands or territories as was granted by the former charter, together with others the most essential rights and liberties contained therein; the principal of which is that which Your Majesty's subjects within the realm have held a most sacred right, of being taxed only by representatives of their own free election.

No one had ever issued such a direct challenge to the monarch, and it is not surprising that Sam Adams gained no popularity at Whitehall. It is improbable that he thought for one moment that his words would soften or change King George's attitude. He was, in actuality, writing the appeal for the benefit of his fellow colonists, and a thrill of excitement traveled up and down the length of the Atlantic seaboard.

The few men who knew the identity of the author of the Massachusetts Assembly's resolution regarded Sam Adams as a courageous hero, and he undoubtedly gained a measure of satisfaction from that recognition. What was far more important to him, however, was the fact that Americans everywhere knew they could thumb their noses at the Crown. The appeal of the Assembly to the king might well be regarded as the first shot fired in the American War of Independence.

Chapter Eight

Anecdotes illuminate the lives of most great men, but they are strangely lacking in the story of Sam Adams, in part because he so sublimated himself to his cause that he became one with it. Equally important is that, in the furious years prior to the outbreak of the revolution he fomented, he had virtually no private life, devoting all of his time to the formation of public opinion. But he was no wide-eyed innocent; more than four decades of failure had conditioned him and given him a cynical outlook that made him better able to cope with the situation he was creating.

Late one night in the opening months of 1768, when he was at work in his study putting the finishing touches on the Assembly's petition to the Crown, his daughter Hannah came into the room and looked over his shoulder. Impressed by the document, she said it would undoubtedly be touched by the royal hand.

Her father glanced at her over the rim of the spectacles he now needed for close work, grinned and said, "My dear, it is more likely this splendid piece of paper will be spurned by the royal foot." Obviously he knew how his efforts would be received at

Whitehall; but even at this stage, seven years before the war erupted, he was thinking only of his American audience. The British government would not change, no matter how many of America's friends might rise to her defense in Parliament, and it is difficult to resist the speculation that Adams would have been disappointed if the King and his ministers had granted all of the colonies' demands. This he more or less admitted in a letter to the Massachusetts lobbyist in London, Dennys Deberdt, written on January 30, 1768:

> You will observe that the House still insist upon that inesti-mable right of nature and the Constitution, of being taxed only by representatives of their own free election; which they think is infringed by the late acts for establishing a revenue in America. *It is by no means to be understood that they desire a representation in Parliament,* because, by reason of local circum-stances, it is impracticable that they should be equally and fairly represented. *There is nothing, therefore, the Colonies would more dread.*
>
> The few gentlemen in the House who did not give their votes declared this as a reason,—that they feared if the House should insist they could not be legally taxed, because they were not represented in Parliament, it would be construed as if they would be content to be represented. And I hope you will, as you have opportunity, make it known to the Ministry, that the people here, as they always have done, will cheerfully afford their utmost aid for the honor and service of their sover-eign, and the interest of the mother state, to which they are inviolably attached. All they desire is to be placed on the standing in which they were originally put, and to have, as free subjects, the honor and privilege of voluntarily contribut-ing to the service of His Majesty at all times, when His Majesty shall be graciously pleased to order his requisitions to be laid upon their own representatives.

Having interpreted colonial history to suit his own purposes, Adams was now proceeding along careful lines toward a fixed goal. First he claimed that an injustice was being perpetrated, although he did not want that injustice rectified; then he insisted that the colonies would remain loyal to Great Britain provided certain concessions were made. At the same time, he was enough of a realist to know that British national honor and the exigencies of British politics would make it impossible for any government in London to grant the colonies' demands.

At no time, either in private correspondence or in those documents intended for public consumption, did he even hint that independence was his ultimate aim. On the contrary, he took care to protest his own loyalty to the Crown as well as that of his fellow colonists. Having discovered a formula that was unassailable, that handcuffed his opponents in Britain and gagged the genuine loyalists at home, he utilized it to the hilt. His calm was as deadly as his good cheer was feigned.

Governor Bernard was one of the few who recognized his game, and in a letter to the Colonial Office, written early in February 1768, he singled out Sam Adams as "the most dangerous man in Massachusetts, a man dedicated to the perpetration of mischief." A scant week later Adams broadened his scope so much that soon every official of consequence in London knew his identity.

After preparing the draft of a petition to both Houses of Parliament, which the Massachusetts Assembly obligingly passed after almost no discussion, he sent a strong circular letter to the legislatures of the other colonies, urging them to add their signatures to it. Radicals like Patrick Henry of Virginia were delighted to join him, and the legislatures of the other twelve colonies obliged. Sam Adams did not reveal himself as the author of either the circular letter or the petition itself, but most of his contemporaries knew he had written them. One exception was Cousin John, whose *Works*, published in 1819, indicated his belief that James Otis had been the author and Cousin Sam the editor. But the style was that of Sam Adams, not Otis, and the sentiments expressed were identical to those which Adams had written on numerous other occasions.

The circular letter created sensations on both sides of the Atlantic. Governor Bernard was so alarmed he sent a messenger to

London by a special ship asking that a Royal Navy fleet and a minimum of five regiments of troops be dispatched at once to preserve order and prevent the outbreak of an insurrection. Members of the Tory party in both Houses of Parliament magnified the handwriting on the wall, became convinced that a full-scale revolution was imminent and demanded that the Americans be punished for their temerity.

The initial reaction in America was one of astonishment that a mere circular letter could cause so much consternation in high places. The fact that Governor Bernard and his London colleagues reacted so strongly taught Sam Adams and his colleagues in other colonies a lesson they quickly learned: in union there was strength, and what one colony could do alone, if necessary, thirteen colonies acting together could accomplish more effectively.

The circular letter and the response to it in official circles were responsible for the formation of the Committees of Correspondence in the late spring and early summer of 1768. Sam Adams suggested the idea; the name itself originated informally due to lack of an official designation anywhere. No organization worked harder for intercolonial unity or achieved more than the Committees of Correspondence, which have rightly been called the prerevolutionary lifeline.

The immediate descendants of Sam Adams exaggerated, however, when they wrote that he alone was responsible for the creation and success of the committees. He provided the original spark, to be sure, and as the author of the majority of letters written in Massachusetts, he was one of the key figures in the development of the committees. But it must not be forgotten that men in other colonies worked equally hard and were equally devoted to the cause; as many as fifty or sixty, in all, may have been involved.

Sam Adams's friends needed no urging to leap into the growing controversy with him. On February 29, 1768, the Boston *Gazette* printed a letter, signed "A True Patriot" and presumed to have been written by Otis, that was the most direct attack on Bernard yet. He was called an enemy of Massachusetts and was assailed for his "cruelty to a loyal people" and his "obstinate perseverance in the path of malice."

More and more radicals adopted Otis's terminology and called themselves Patriots, a word Sam Adams happily and quickly adopted. The abolition of the new taxes was still the immediate goal of these men, but the beleaguered Bernard was correct when he wrote London that "the spirit of insurrection so inflames Adams and Otis they would no longer be satisfied with the repeal of every tax now laid upon the colonies." Nothing less than a complete break with the mother country and the creation of a separate nation would cause them to cease their activities, he declared.

The dream that Sam Adams had perceived dimly was taking shape, and it was shared by compatriots in every colony. Contrary to the traditional teachings of American history, however, there was no widespread, overwhelming clamor for independence. The dreamers were a tiny minority, and they were viewed as extremists by most Americans. It may be that a majority wanted the taxes repealed, but certainly they neither yearned for independence nor demanded it.

Sam Adams, ultrasensitive to public opinion, did not push too hard. In 1768, in fact, he expressed himself with far greater caution and conservatism than did the increasingly reckless Otis, who would lose his sanity the following year. Adams was no less eager for independence, but he realized that a groundswell of public opinion was necessary in order to achieve it. He was willing to wait, to advance one small but firm step at a time toward his goal.

Most colonists, he knew, were supremely indifferent to the idea of independence, and the reaction of the small towns of Massachusetts to the new taxes proved it. Their representatives took no initiative in the Assembly, and the fight against the taxes was conducted principally by the Adams-led Boston faction, who cajoled and bullied their colleagues into joining them.

Of all Adams's activities in opposition to the Townshend Acts, the most important and far-reaching were his attempts to persuade—and, if necessary, force—merchants through the colonies to sign nonimportation agreements. He had his work cut out for him. The financial depression that had afflicted the colonies in the wake of the French and Indian War had ended, and business was booming. There had never been so much money available in America, Governor Bernard wrote, and his estimate was accurate. American merchants were earning more than ever before, many of them living and working on generous loans extended to them by firms in London with which they traded. It was no easy matter to persuade such men to sacrifice substantial earnings for the sake of hazily defined principles.

In March 1768, at a meeting of the Merchants' Club of Boston, a resolution demanding that no Boston businessman import any goods for a period of twelve months was submitted by John Hancock. The principles expressed in the document, as well as its style, made it the handiwork of Sam Adams, although James Otis may have contributed to its preparation, too. To the astonishment of Governor Bernard and others unfamiliar with what was happening behind the scenes, the members of the Merchants' Club adopted the measure by a heavy majority.

On this occasion Sam Adams elected to remain completely out of view. Hancock, of course, worked openly for the adoption of the resolution, and was supported by the leaders of the organization, Captain Daniel Malcomb, perhaps the most efficient of the Boston smugglers, and the wealthy John Rowe. What Governor Bernard failed to realize was that Adams had been courting such key men as Malcomb and Rowe for weeks, inculcating them with his views and persuading them to adopt his ideas.

It was obvious that a nonimportation agreement would be effective only if adopted by all of the colonies, and the Massachusetts Committee of Correspondence went to work. In other words, Sam Adams sent scores of letters to colleagues elsewhere, and Patrick Henry quickly obtained the approval of Virginia merchants, whose example was followed by businessmen in the Carolinas. Connecticut was directly influenced by Massachusetts, and New York, whose merchants were enjoying unprecedented prosperity in the fastest-growing city in America, also voted in favor of the scheme.

Then Philadelphia balked; her conservative merchants refused to forgo their profits for Sam Adams's high-sounding phrases. In other communities the threats of mob violence by Sons of Liberty undoubtedly had influenced hesitant or reluctant merchants, who had no desire to see their warehouses burned and their shops ransacked. But the businessmen of Philadelphia refused to be intimidated, and their stand caused the total collapse of the scheme, which had to be abandoned elsewhere. Sam Adams was forced to concede defeat; but he regarded it as temporary—merchants, like other Americans, had to be educated, and the time would come when effective nonimportation agreements would be useful weapons.

The failure of the nonimportation scheme destroyed the core of the resistance to the Townshend Acts, and although Adams continued to thunder in the pages of the *Gazette* and elsewhere, his weapons had no sting. The opposition to the new taxes would have died away had not the British government made its worst blunder to date. London took the warnings of Governor Bernard, supported by letters from Chief Justice Hutchinson, so seriously that it was decided to send a reinforced brigade of troops to Boston to preserve order and compel compliance with acts of Parliament.

The news of this forthcoming move reached Boston in early summer, and was a gift of pure manna that Sam Adams would have been the last to overlook. Boston, the *Gazette* screamed, soon would become an occupied city, and the liberties of the people, their precious constitutional heritage as free-born British subjects, would be taken from them.

Rhetoric was not enough, as Adams well knew, and he moved swiftly before the troops actually arrived. He concluded that Boston, still the leading city in the colonies, with the largest volume of trade, would have to act alone. If she provided a concrete example, other communities might well follow suit, especially if prodded by the Massachusetts Committee of Correspondence—and if representatives of the Sons of Liberty paid persuasive calls on leaders of the organization elsewhere.

It was essential that the unanimous support of Boston businessmen be obtained, and Sam Adams left nothing to chance. Hancock, Rowe, Malcomb and others made it plain to their colleagues that they would be regarded as social pariahs if they failed to join the movement. One courageous merchant, John Mein, refused to yield, but after fires broke out in his warehouses on three successive nights, a small merchantman that flew his flag was sunk and the windows in his house were broken early one morning, he wavered, then changed his mind.

James Otis openly called on merchants and made his own position in the matter clear, but Sam Adams preferred to remain in the shadows. The Caucus Club became his headquarters, and he was infrequently seen in his office at the brewery. Merchants who supported his position visited him throughout the day, as did the "mechanics"—or artisans—who were the nominal heads of the Sons of Liberty. As far as is known, Adams did not hold one personal conversation with the nonpolitical merchants, nor did he sign his own name to any of the innumerable letters of persuasion these gentlemen received.

But he did his work so well that, when the Merchants' Club held another meeting in August 1768, all sixty-eight of the businessmen who attended voted in favor of a total boycott of British goods, beginning on January 1, 1769, and not one voice was raised in dissent during the brief "debate" before the vote was taken.

Adams's activities in the summer of 1768 were among the least admirable of his life. He acted in the name of liberty, but his conduct was a mockery of the word. He used intimidation freely, resorting to violence through brawny lieutenants when necessary, and literally forced the merchants of Boston to disobey the law, regardless of their own wishes, loyalty to the Crown or desire to earn a living as they saw fit. The continuation of these activities over a period of years eventually compelled a number of respectable merchants to leave Boston and migrate either to Halifax, where a large number of refugees settled, or to London. The imminent arrival of British troops hardened Sam Adams's resolve and stepped up his timetable; he was merciless, giving no quarter to those who opposed his ends, and at the same time expecting none.

But his nature was contradictory. He used and manipulated the mob for his own ends, in the manner used by dictators for thousands of years, yet he was no tyrant and sought no power for himself. He was a man increasingly obsessed by a dream, and wanted only to establish an independent nation governed according to democratic principles. He yearned for no powers as a ruler, avoided the limelight and was courteous, friendly and pleasant in all of his personal dealings. If he realized he was utilizing authoritarian methods as vicious as those he condemned, he did not admit it. Like so many idealists, he was convinced that the principles in which he believed were for the good of all the people, and he was determined to realize them, even if he had to stamp on the toes of those who either actively opposed him or inadvertently stood in his path.

It is as impossible to question his sincerity as it is to deny his devotion to the cause he originated and espoused with such fervor. But in his demand for the rights, as he conceived them, of British subjects in the colonies, he ignored and trampled on the rights of law-abiding Americans who were either indifferent to the desires of the radicals or who remained loyal to the Crown. Nothing in Adams's private correspondence, much less his actions, indicates that he was even aware of what he was doing in "the sacred name of liberty"; the best that can be said for him in this regard, and it is a feeble excuse, is that it did not occur him that he might be harming men who wanted only to live their lives in their own way under the guarantees of freedom provided them by the British Constitution. Like all crusaders, he was a zealot, and by 1768 he had become a true crusader, a man who lived and worked only for the establishment of a nation based on the philosophy of John Locke. The bumbling tax collector, the brewer who could not make business ends meet, the patrician who had no desire to play a leading role in the social, educational or philanthropic life of his community, had found himself at last. The odds against him were formidable, but they acted as a spur, and he intended to let nothing stand in his path.

Chapter
Nine

The members of the new Board of Tax Commission-
ers assigned by the chancellor of the exchequer to supervise the
administration of the Townshend Acts arrived in Boston late in
1767, set up offices for themselves and rented homes. Most of the
radical leaders had more pressing matters on their minds at the
time and paid scant attention to them, but Sam Adams was never
too busy to ignore what he regarded as legitimate objects of
attack. He began with a series of assaults in the *Gazette* on the
personal characters of the new commissioners, saying that men
of stature found it necessary to shun them and observing that
they were "useless" as well as "very expensive." Warming to his
theme, he wrote that the commissioners were "extremely dis-
gustfull to the people," and he predicted that Bostonians would
not tolerate their presence for more than a very limited time.

To Governor Bernard and Chief Justice Hutchinson, who
were all too familiar with Adams's methods of operation, the
threat had an ominous ring. They predicted in letters to the
Colonial Office that there might be an outbreak of physical violence against the commissioners at any time, and they were sur-

prised when nothing happened during the first months of 1768.

Then Sam Adams found or made the time to devote greater attention to the board, who would not have been popular under the best of circumstances, and on the evening of March 4 a large crowd gathered in front of the adjoining homes of two commissioners named Williams and Paxton. For an hour the mob shouted slogans, but resorted to no violence and dispersed quietly. Governor Bernard breathed easier, but Sam Adams was just beginning a new campaign.

Two weeks later, on the night of March 18, effigies of Williams and Paxton were hanged from the Liberty Tree, and then a mob estimated at more than eight hundred strong marched to the houses of the luckless commissioners. But Adams's lieutenants were able to exert firm discipline, and there was no rioting; the crowd again broke up without resorting to physical abuse. John Rowe and other wealthy, respectable radicals publicly voiced their relief that no untoward incident had disrupted the peace.

But Sam Adams was biding his time, allowing pressures to build, and everyone in Boston knew it. Tension remained high through the spring, partly because of a depression in the shipbuilding trade, one of the city's leading industries. Boston wages were so high that ship owners were placing orders in smaller towns, so large numbers of carpenters and other Sons of Liberty were out of work, their mood increasingly ugly.

Adams cannily waited for an occasion that could be dramatized in terms sufficiently simple for the entire public to comprehend, and early in June he had his opportunity. A brig that belonged to John Hancock's merchant fleet, a ship fortuitously called the *Liberty*, reached Boston carrying an expensive cargo of wine. Her captain, following the owner's specific instructions, filled out a customs declaration that indicated only a small fraction of the cargo's real worth.

That night a holiday atmosphere prevailed at the Hancock wharf. Bonfires were lighted on shore, and dock workers, aided by scores of volunteers, unloaded the ship with great show, making it obvious to everyone in the crowd that gathered to watch the fun that the wine was worth far more than the customs declaration stated. Adams, Hancock and the other members of the Caucus Club subsequently tried to play innocent, insisting that the unloading had been a spontaneous celebration, but the incident was too well organized, and neither Governor Bernard nor posterity accepted their flimsy claim.

It was apparent to the Crown representatives that a deliberate attempt was being made to defy the authority of the tax commissioners. This could not be tolerated, so the commissioners retaliated, in their own way and in their own good time. They waited a few days until Bostonians seemed to be forgetting the matter; then the *Liberty* was seized and towed by the collectors' boat to the far side of the harbor, where a seventy-four-gun Royal Navy ship of the line, H.M.S. *Romney*, rode at anchor.

It has never been determined, down to the present day, whether the events that followed were completely planned or were partly spontaneous. A town meeting was held behind closed doors, and according to a later deposition by the tax commissioners—who did not cite their sources of information—Sam Adams made a rabble-rousing speech. In it, they alleged, he declared that, should the people be called upon to defend their sacred honor, he "hoped and believed that they would one and all resist, even unto blood." Another deposition, submitted by an innkeeper named Richard Sylvester, who claimed he was present, asserted that Adams said: "If you are men, behave like men! Let us take up arms immediately—and be free—and seize all the King's officers! We will not be alone! Thirty thousand men from the country will join us!"

In all probability this allegation is an exaggeration of the truth. Certainly Sam Adams knew that the smaller towns of Massachusetts remained indifferent to the issue and that it would be impossible to raise even a fraction of a force of thirty thousand. It is also unlikely that he advocated taking such a bold stand at that time: the seizure of Crown officials would have been a premature gesture that public sentiment would not have supported.

The action taken by the mob that formed "spontaneously" more nearly fitted the circumstances. Scores of men dragged the customs boat onto shore, poured pitch over it and burned it.

Then the windows of the commissioners' homes were stoned, and two members of the board were caught as they tried to escape through doors at the rear. Their clothes were torn, the sword of one was broken and both were subjected to verbal abuse.

Promptly deciding that discretion was by far the better part of valor, the commissioners fled to the safety of the *Romney*, and thereafter established themselves at Fort William, a vantage point from which it would be impossible for them to carry out their duties. Sam Adams and his cohorts had succeeded in driving them out of Boston, and had won their greatest victory to date.

Realizing that London would be forced to react, the town meeting sent its own version of the affair to its agent in England; this highly colored account also appeared in the *Gazette*, with its author Sam Adams modestly hiding behind a pseudonym, "Determinatus," that fooled no one. His article was a masterpiece of bland propaganda that twisted facts and ignored the truth. There had been no riot, he said; on the contrary, the patriotic ardor of the people had been "stirred" because, "without reason assigned or apparent," the property of a distinguished Bostonian had been seized "under a pretense of law, at an unseasonable time, with the aid of a military power." The commissioners had remained in Boston for an additional seventy-two hours, during which time no one had molested them, and then, determined to place guilt on the people of the city, they "took it into their heads to go down to the castle." Since that time, he added, "the town has been in perfect peace."

He made no mention of Hancock's illegal declaration or the equally illegal landing of the cargo, nor did he indicate that the commissioners had acted, as required under the law, in response to that challenge. He also chose to ignore the stoning of the commissioners' windows and the acts of violence perpetrated against them. "That man," Governor Bernard said when he read the account in the *Gazette*, "is the devil incarnate!"

The errors perpetrated by Crown officials in London who failed to understand the mentality of Americans were legion in the years prior to the outbreak of the Revolution, and the announcement that a brigade of troops was being sent to Boston could not have been more ill-timed. The news arrived when the excitement over the *Liberty* affair was at its peak, late in June 1768.

Governor Bernard, the one man who truly understood Americans, had not asked for troops, had not wanted them and was certain that their dispatch to Massachusetts could only create increased turmoil. There can be no question that the ministry in London played into the hands of Sam Adams, James Otis, John Hancock and the other Caucus Club radicals, who had enjoyed the support of only a small, vocal minority until that time.

The news of the brigade's impending arrival was made to order for Sam Adams, winning him the support of elements of the population that heretofore had considered him a troublemaker and had given him wide berth. Most Boston merchants were conservative, law-abiding gentlemen who paid lip service to the Crown, even while they engaged in smuggling. Now, however, it was obvious to them that the troops were being sent to uphold the authority of the tax commissioners, and they could envision their businesses being ruined by the strict imposition of taxes under the Townshend Acts. The dispatch of troops guaranteed that the merchants of Boston would band together and sign a binding nonimportation agreement.

Even more important, other members of the city's large and influential middle class, as well as the prosperous farmers of Massachusetts, were alarmed. Troops over whom they, as voters, exercised no controls truly constituted a threat to their liberties as free-born British subjects, precisely as Adams asserted. Heretofore reluctant to accept his claims, they were now forced to admit he was right.

Not content with the folly it was creating, the ministry in London compounded an already complex problem by sending firm instructions to Governor Bernard in July 1768 directing him to order the Massachusetts Assembly to rescind its circular letter condemning the Townshend Acts and to request the support of other colonial legislatures. Bernard must have shuddered when he read his instructions, but he had no choice, although he knew he would be demanding the impossible and giving the radicals yet another golden opportunity to win converts to their growing cause.

The Assembly received the order from the governor, duly noting that the body would be dissolved if it failed to obey, and for nine days the issue was "debated," although the outcome was never in doubt. Those nine days were among the busiest in Sam Adams's life. He not only wrote for the *Gazette*, but the conservative *Post* requested and received articles from him, too. He sent long letters to other colonies and he directed the flow of rhetorical invective in the Assembly, for the first time enjoying the support of virtually every man in Massachusetts.

The Assembly refused to rescind the circular letter; a vote of 92 to 17 indicated clearly where the members stood. Its resolution, written by Sam Adams, was a masterpiece of relative brevity:

> We cannot but express our deep concern, that a measure of the late House, in all respects so innocent, in most so virtuous and laudable, and, as we conceive, so truly patriotic, should have been represented to administration in the odious light of a party and factious measure, and that pushed through by reverting in a thin house to, and reconsidering, what in a full Assembly had been rejected. It was and is a matter of notoriety that more than eighty members were present at the consideration of the vote against application to the other Colonies.
>
> The Circular Letters have been sent, and many of them have been answered; those answers are now in the public papers; the public, the world, must and will judge of the proposals, purposes, and answers. We could as well rescind those letters as the resolves; and both would be equally fruitless if, by rescinding, as the word properly imports, is meant a repeal and nullifying the resolution referred to.
>
> You have also thought fit to inform us that you cannot think yourself at liberty, in case of the dissolution of this, to call another Assembly without the express order of His Majesty for that purpose; and, at the same time, Your Excellency has been pleased to assure us that you have communicated the whole of Lord Hillsborough's letter and your instructions, so

far as relates to the requistion. In all this, however, we cannot find that Your Excellency is more than directed to dissolve the present Assembly in case of a non-compliance on the part of the House. If the votes of the House are to be controlled by a minister, we have left us but a vain semblance of liberty.

This communication held hints to Bernard of the next steps the Assembly planned to take, and the governor undoubtedly saw what was coming; but he could do nothing to prevent the inevitable. Acting in accordance with his own instructions from London, he prorogued the Assembly, ordering it to dissolve without conducting any further business.

But Sam Adams, who was enjoying the greatest success of his life, had no intention of complying without making additional moves. At his instigation and that of Otis, the Assembly voted, by a count of 99 to 3, to establish a special committee for the purpose of requesting the Colonial Office to recall Governor Bernard. The chairman of that committee, who was specifically authorized to write the letter demanding the governor's recall, was, of course, Sam Adams.

The letter was already prepared, and in order to insure its "legality" it was dispatched before the Assembly followed the governor's order and solemnly voted to adjourn. It is significant, in the light of what followed, that the members specifically did not vote themselves out of existence.

Sam Adams did not reveal his hand prematurely, however, and first concentrated on whipping up enthusiasm for the celebration of "our glorious American holiday," the third anniversary of the outbreak of opposition to the Stamp Tax. The date was August 14, a Saturday, so the festivities were held the following day in order to draw a bigger crowd. The Union Jack and other flags were draped on the branches of the Liberty Tree, and fourteen cannon were fired. A large crowd paraded through the town, then gathered for a band concert; everyong sang the "American Song of Liberty," to the tune of "God Save the King," the new lyrics being provided for the occasion by none other than Sam Adams. Free beer and quantities of stronger spirits were on hand, courtesy of the Adams brewery and distillery, which could scarcely stand the expense, and a number of toasts were drunk, among them one to "the memorable 14th of August, 1765." Others were offered to "the glorious Ninety-two" (the Assembly members who had refused to rescind the circular letter), the Magna Charta and the Bill of Rights.

All of the voluble members of the Caucus Club were on hand, but no speeches were made, perhaps because the occasion spoke for itself. The ceremony ended with the firing of ninety-two shots by the cannon, and those who had carriages or horses repaired to the Greyhound Tavern in Roxbury, where a "frugal but elegant" repast was served, and forty-five more toasts were consumed. It is presumed that some of the more abstemious celebrants, Sam Adams among them, managed to return to their homes without assistance.

Thereafter Adams turned to more serious matters. According to family tradition it was roughly at this time that he decided that British policy toward the colonies was unalterable and that he consequently made up his mind to seek the permanent separation of America from the mother state. No correspondence or other data has survived to indicate that the summer of 1768 was the turning point in the life of the forty-six-year-old Adams, but by now his actions certainly indicate that he was burning his British bridges behind him at a furious rate. He issued his initial call to arms, the first to appear in any American publication, in an editorial signed "Determinatus" in the *Gazette* of August 8:

> When the people are oppressed, when their rights are infringed, when their property is invaded, when taskmasters are set over them, when unconstitutional acts are executed by a naval force before their eyes, and they are daily threatened with military troops, when their Legislative is dissolved! and what government is left is as secret as a *Divan*, when placemen and their underlings swarm about them, and pensioners begin to make an insolent appearance,—in such circumstances the people will be discontented; and they are not to be blamed; their minds will be irritated as long as they have any sense of

honor, liberty, and virtue. In such circumstances, while they have the spirit of freemen, they will *boldly assert their freedom*! They are to be justified in so doing. I know very well that to murmur, or even whisper a complaint, some men call a riotous spirit; but they are in the right of it to complain, and *complain aloud*, and they *will* complain till they are either redressed or become poor, deluded, miserable, ductile dupes, fitted to be made the slaves of arbitrary power.

Having prepared the groundwork, Adams struck on September 5, when he wrote another piece in the *Gazette*, this time signing himself "Clericus Americanus." Although the Assembly had been prorogued, he wrote, the people of Massachusetts were determined to govern themselves, and he called for the establishment of a new General Convention, or legislature, to be elected by the people and to serve the functions of the dissolved Assembly, regardless of whether it was recognized by the governor, the ministry in London or the Crown itself.

This was the supreme act of defiance for which he had been preparing the people for several months, and in a final paragraph "Clericus Americanus" left no doubt that, if necessary, he recommended open, armed rebellion:

If an army should be sent to reduce us to slavery, we will put our lives in our hands, and cry to the Judge of all the earth, who will do right, saying: Behold, how they come to cast us out of thy possession, which thou hast given us to inherit. Help us, O Lord, our God, for we rest on Thee, and in thy name we go against this multitude!

Not even the most pessimistic members of Governor Bernard's administration had allowed themselves to think the colonist would go this far. Several aides recommended that, pending the arrival of troops, Royal Marines from the *Romney* and other warships in the harbor be used to prevent a rump legislature from meeting. But the governor knew there would be rioting he could not control if he tried to clamp down, so he wisely did nothing. No law or decree prevented private citizens from gathering together for purposes of holding a meeting, and in his eyes the members of the General Convention of 1768 were the most private of citizens. No matter what they said or did, he had no intention of recognizing the group as an official Assembly.

From the outset it was the intention of Adams, Otis, Cushing, Warren, Hancock and the other members of the Caucus Club to cloak the Convention in as much legality as they could muster. Letters of invitation—written by Adams—were sent to every town in the colony, and word was disseminated quietly to the effect that each community would be given the same number of seats it had held in the last Assembly. The Boston town meeting assigned the same delegates—Adams, Otis, Hancock and Cushing. In a number of towns the citizens were given no choice in the selection of their representatives, and the Sons of Liberty chose the delegates.

The representatives met in Boston on September 22, with delegates from ninety-six towns and eight districts on hand, the same number that had sat in the last legal Assembly. The chairman was Thomas Cushing, the last Speaker of the House. The group remained in session for a week, and Sam Adams was even busier than usual, writing a set of resolutions, two petitions to the governor and a letter of instructions to Massachusetts' London agent.

The mere fact that the gathering took place was an act of defiance of the Crown, and Adams and his associates took great care not to add insult to injury. The resolution offered no resistance to the troops, who actually reached Boston the day prior to the Convention's adjournment, and the assemblage made it clear that it did not regard itself as an authoritative governmental body. The petitions stressed the urgent need for a meeting of the Assembly, and specifically requested the governor to call for new elections. So great care was taken to preserve the pacific mood of the congress.

But feelings were running so high that wild rumors flooded Boston, and Governor Bernard believed most of them. According to one account, the Convention had sent out secret instructions to every town meeting in the colony, asking that citizens provide themselves with muskets and ammunition to resist the troops. Another story claimed that, at the instigation of the Convention, residents of Boston were gathering huge quantities of kindling and planned to set the city on fire rather than "surrender" it to the troops under the command of General Thomas Gage. Bernard not only accepted these fabrications, but was inclined to believe that an attempt might be made on the night prior to the landing of the regiments to seize Fort William.

Never before had Sam Adams played such a devious, complicated game. The meeting of the rump legislature was an act of rebellion, but its declarations were so mild that no one in authority could be offended by them. At the same time, the wild rumors—which Adams well may have instigated, although it still cannot be proved—kept Boston in a ferment of excitement. Thanks to Adams and his colleagues, and to the blunders of the London ministry, what had been an attempt by a handful of radicals to stir up opposition to certain Crown acts had now spread, and an aroused, unified colony was on the brink of revolution.

Chapter Ten

Sam Adams's subtlety may have been his greatest asset, and he altered his approach to fit every new circumstance. Governor Bernard and his aides were afraid the arriving regiments would be greeted with stones and riots that would have resulted in inevitable bloodshed; but Adams had no intention of sparking an insurrection until the people of Massachusetts and the other colonies were prepared to support a rebellion and accept the sacrifices required in time of war. The tactics he chose to greet the British troops were totally unanticipated and remarkably effective.

Not one Bostonian was on hand to witness the debarkation of the brilliantly uniformed regiments. The docks were deserted, the windows of homes in the waterfront area were shuttered, and no one was to be seen on the decks of small merchantmen and fishing boats that rode at anchor in the harbor. In the days and months that followed, people looked through Redcoats on the street, not seeing them; even the highest-ranking generals and colonels received no dinner invitations from local aristocrats, and soldiers who tried to make purchases in local stores were politely informed that the shop no longer carried the merchandise requested.

The boycott of the regiments was as total as it was cruel; the diaries and letters of various officers who were members of the new garrison indicate they were surprised by the treatment they received and did not know how to respond to it. Sam Adams was indifferent to their reaction, and did not care that both officers and enlisted men quickly came to resent the snubs. His campaign had two purposes, and both were being fulfilled. First, he was fostering the unity of the people; by portraying the Redcoats as enemies, as troops of occupation in an alien city, he was creating a wider gulf between the Crown and the king's New World subjects. Almost equally important, he was keeping tensions at a high pitch, making Boston's residents and visitors from other colonies uncomfortable and reminding them that they were being deprived of their fundamental liberties. It was irrelevant that the troops did nothing to interfere with the freedom of press or speech, the right of assemblage or any of the other rights that Britons held dear. The very presence of the regiments was enough to create more bad blood.

Yet the Crown authorities had no legitimate cause for complaint. No man displayed overt hostility to the troops even though it was almost inevitable that someday there would be a fight of some kind. Sam Adams was conducting what may have been the first modern campaign in psychological warfare, and neither Governor Bernard nor General Gage could cope with it. When the quartermaster could buy no supplies for the regiments in the Boston markets, he sent teams into the countryside, only to be informed by taciturn but polite farmers that they had suffered recent crop shortages and had no foodstuffs to sell. It did not matter that the quartermaster and his superiors knew the Americans were lying. The troops had two choices, both unpleasant: they could seize the supplies they needed, paying what they deemed appropriate, and knowing they would arouse still greater enmity, or they could ask that provisions be brought from England by the Royal Navy. They chose the latter course, and Sam Adams won yet another victory.

It is impossible to overemphasize the astonishing change in Boston's attitude toward the mother country that was manifested during the turbulent months of 1768. Until that year the vast majority of the city's residents were law-abiding men and women who were loyal to the Crown. Now, thanks to the manipulations of Sam Adams and his friends, combined with the shortsighted policies pursued in Whitehall, a deep rift had been created, and the gulf became steadily wider. Adams's arguments were making sense to conservative men, and even the town's patricians resented the presence of the regiments so much they refused to extend the hospitality of their homes to the officers.

Adams enjoyed his greatest popularity with the artisans and other workingmen of Boston, and the discipline he exerted through the Sons of Liberty was firm. Fights were avoided in taverns throughout the city by utilizing a simple method: when a Redcoat walked into a bar, the other customers immediately departed. Even the trollops of the town vanished when soldiers went in search of girls.

No better example of the shift in Boston's spirit can be found than in the attitude of the Massachusetts Bay Council, which had always been subservient to the will of the colony's chief executive. In 1768 the Council became so independent and so contrary that it criticized every move the governor made, and by October the situation became intolerable. The beleaguered Bernard disbanded the Council, one of the colony's oldest and most respected political institutions, and replaced it with a committee of three of his Crown-appointed aides.

Sam Adams sharpened his quill again, and charged that the people were being denied one of the last vestiges of popular government. The accusation was true, of course, and no one knew it better than Bernard, who had his back to the wall. Weary after struggling so long and convinced that he could not win the fight, the governor privately petitioned London for relief, writing that he wanted to retire as soon as a suitable replacement could be chosen.

Adams learned of the request, probably picking up the news from one of the governor's house servants, as many members of the staff quietly kept him informed of developments there, and he reacted with a cunning that had become typical of him. Rather than release the news and claim a victory, he chose another tactic, and deliberately stepped up the campaign demanding Bernard's recall. Certain that the governor would return to England within the fairly near future, he knew he then would be in a position to claim that the people had won yet another victory. Even though deprived of their legislature and Council, they were potent enough to force the resignation of a chief executive they regarded as a "tyrant."

Late in October a new crisis threatened, and Adams demonstrated his flexibility. The troops of the two British regiments, the fourteenth and nineteenth, had been sleeping in tents on the Common, but the weather was turning colder and General Gage applied to the town meeting for winter quarters. Under the terms of the Quartering Act, individual citizens could have been required to take soldiers into their homes, but the Crown authorities were reluctant to provoke the townspeople. Sam Adams, on the other hand, did not want to give the regiments the excuse to use force until he found an issue with a very broad popular appeal. Afraid he would be defeated in court if he tried to take a legal stand against the Quartering Act, he privately suggested to the selectmen that they offer Faneuil Hall to the army. This was done, Gage accepted and the regiments moved into their winter quarters.

Adams had no intention of losing this opportunity to create new propaganda. Letters of protest were sent to the *Gazette* by indignant citizens whose style of writing was suspiciously similar to that of the man who appeared to spend the better part of each day with his pen in hand, and other newspapers received similar communications. Then Adams sent off a letter to Dennys Deberdt, Massachusetts' agent in London, calling the quartering of the troops in the meeting place of the Sons of Liberty "a new and intolerable grievance." The people of Boston were protesting, he declared, and were more determined than ever not to buy any item of British manufacture.

This communication was read on the floor of the House of

Commons by a member of Parliament friendly to the American cause, the London newspapers printed excerpts, and Governor Bernard was said to smile wearily when clippings sent across the Atlantic reached his desk. General Gage was reported to have cursed, and perhaps he began to understand the cleverness of the man who was his self-appointed adversary.

But Adams was just beginning his fight. A long essay appeared in the *Gazette* under the signature of one "Principiis Obsta" which warned that military rule was imminent in Massachusetts and that tyranny always resulted when civilian rule was supplanted. Soon thereafter he wrote another essay for the *Post*, signing it "Cedant Arma Togae"; this was a more learned piece, befitting the *Post*'s erudite readership, and consisted of a complicated—if specious—legal argument to the effect that there was no precedent under British law for the quartering of British troops in Boston.

The harried General Gage soon faced another problem. Most of the troops in his regiments were very young men who hated the treatment they were receiving from the colonials. Themselves the products of England's lower classes, which long had looked to the New World as a land of opportunity, they began to desert, and by the end of 1768 more than one hundred Redcoats had vanished. Local citizens were questioned, but were uniformly blank; not one of the missing men had been seen, and not one citizen knew their whereabouts. A sum of ten pounds was offered as a reward for information leading to the return of any deserter, but the money went unclaimed. The reward was increased to a staggering fifty pounds, as much as many dock workers earned in a year, but no one came forward.

The army stepped up its own search, and ultimately ten deserters were captured. They were sentenced to be whipped in the Common at noon on a Sunday, when townspeople habitually went for a stroll in the open, and an essay signed "Humanitarian" appeared in the *Gazette*, condemning the cruelty of beatings and insisting that if any of the deserters died, their blood would stain Bernard and Gage.

One of the deserters had married a Massachusetts farmgirl

during his absence from the army, and his distraught wife appealed to Sam Adams to intervene on her husband's behalf. No citizen of Massachusetts was eligible for a colder reception at either the governor's mansion or the brigade's headquarters, but Adams nevertheless went to Gage, presumably because he believed he could make propaganda capital out of a refusal.

To the astonishment of Adams and his friends, General Gage granted clemency to the soldier, canceled his punishment and granted him his discharge from the army. Adams guessed the reason for this extraordinary act, as his daughter later revealed: he believed an attempt would be made to persuade him to abandon his opposition to the Crown. He received overtures from Gage within a month, but he rejected them so brusquely that the general, who soon left Boston for a sojourn in New York, thereafter regarded him as a personal enemy.

By the early months of 1769, Sam Adams's neglect of the business he had inherited from his father resulted in the closing of the brewery. No longer able to make ends meet, he lacked the capital for badly needed improvements, and what remained of a loyal market continued to shrink. He could not meet his payroll, but showed no visible signs of regret as he closed the place for the last time. He received several offers for the property, which was valuable, but refused to sell, saying he had nothing else to leave his wife and children.

His only known source of income, scarcely more than a token, was the infinitesimal salary he was paid as clerk of the Assembly, and not even as thrifty a manager as Elizabeth Adams could have fed and clothed the family on that sum. The source of Sam Adams's income in 1769 and the years that followed is something of a mystery, and little is known other than that he and his family lived on very little. It has been assumed, but never proved, that John Hancock paid him the equivalent of a consultant's fee for a number of years, and that the rental of the Adams wharf also brought in a fairly substantial sum.

If others were worried about him, however, Adams himself remained supremely indifferent to the problems of earning a living. Thanks to the unremitting efforts of his faithful wife, there was enough food on the table and everyone in the family was neatly dressed. He asked for nothing more, but his absent-mindedness must have tried the patience of a wife who had to make certain he wore matching shoes and a waistcoat that buttoned before he left the house each day.

As the crisis he was precipitating became increasingly grave, he saw even less of his family. Elizabeth joined him for an early breakfast before he hurried off for a long day of meetings; he rarely dined at home, and he spent his evenings in his study, closeting himself there until the early hours of the morning as he poured out an endless stream of essays, articles, letters and addresses. His devotion to his crusade had become a mania, and nothing else mattered to him. He and Elizabeth had no social life, and only when he attended church on Sunday mornings did he put his campaign out of his mind for a short time. He kept up the gruelling pace for years, and did not relax it until American independence was assured. Cousin John did not exaggerate when he wrote that Cousin Sam's devotion and energy made the Revolution possible.

Few of his contemporaries realized how much he did. Late in 1768 he began to write a series of essays for the *Post* under the signature of "Candidus," and simultaneously prepared another series for the *Gazette*, in whose columns he now called himself "Vindex." A month or two later he also became a regular contributor to the *News-Letter*, and in the next few years used as many as a score of pseudonyms there.

The public may not have realized that so much propaganda was the product of one man's pen, but Governor Bernard and Lieutenant Governor Hutchinson knew it, and early in 1769 it was rumored that Adams, Otis and one or two others soon would be placed under arrest and taken to England, where they would be tried for treason. The Crown authorities thought of taking such action, but Bernard wisely refrained, as did Hutchinson, who succeeded him. It was best to ignore the men who called themselves Patriots, they reasoned, and not make martyrs around whom the public could rally.

No attempt was made to limit Adams's activities in any way, and in the spring of 1769, when Francis Bernard received word that he was being permitted to return to England after spending a decade as governor of Massachusetts Bay, he allowed the Assembly to resume its meetings. Sam Adams promptly caused him to regret his lenient policy by involving him in a personal dispute: the legislature refused to pay the governor his salary, even though he would keep his title for the better part of a year thereafter, claiming he could not earn it unless he remained at his desk in Boston.

At about the same time that Bernard returned to England, where he was made a baronet as a reward for his faithful service to the Crown, James Otis engaged in a violent fistfight with a British official in Boston. Adams, never one to miss any opportunity, tried to make it appear in all three of the newspapers for which he was writing that Otis had been attacked because he was a Patriot. It soon became apparent that the brilliant attorney had lost his sanity, however, so the press charges were dropped.

The disappearance of Otis from the active political arena made Sam Adams the sole leader of the radicals, and thereafter he alone remained in command of the informal coalition until the actual outbreak of the Revolution. Hancock, an able administrator but lacking in agility, gradually became his first lieutenant, and Cousin John, rapidly moving into the front ranks of Massachusetts attorneys, became increasingly active in the radical cause.

No incident, real or feigned, was ignored by the press. The Sons of Liberty held rallies, paraded through the streets and met at dinners. Hundreds of Boston housewives signed round-robin pledges, swearing they would buy no British merchandise. Lieutenant Governor Hutchinson, who would assume the title of governor the following year, was subjected to a social boycott, as were others who remained loyal to the Crown. And Sam Adams was the puppet master: nothing was done by his colleagues without his knowledge and approval.

King George personally paid him a backhanded compliment in

the late spring of 1769, in his Speech from the Throne. Not deigning to mention Adams by name, he nevertheless acknowledged his influence by attacking "the radical agitator and his small band of followers who attempt in vain to stir sedition in the breasts of our loyal American subjects." The *Gazette*, the *Post* and the *News-Letter* gleefully reprinted appropriate excerpts from His Majesty's address, then went on to "prove"—without offering any details as verification—that the demand for liberty was becoming irresistible everywhere in the colony.

To an extent, at least, they were right. The Assembly, completely dominated by the radicals, was demonstrating no dependence on the mother country. And the courts were becoming more American-oriented, too, with the judges relying more on New World precedents than on British common law in making their decisions. What had started as an attempt to cause the downfall of the Townshend Acts was turning into the creation of a new political system in Massachusetts.

By the early months of 1769, the nonimportation agreements had been signed by every merchant in Boston. A few who had refused to join in the boycott had quietly left town, and Sam Adams could claim complete success in his campaign. Not all of the credit was his, however. The presence of British regiments in Boston caused such continuing resentment that men whose loyalty to the Crown previously had been unquestioned now called themselves Whigs or Whig-Patriots.

But the Colonial Office remained blind to what was happening in the most rambunctious of the American provinces, and in the summer of 1769 two additional regiments arrived from Halifax. Since there was literally nothing for these troops to do, Hutchinson prevailed upon General Gage to transfer one unit to New York Town and send another back to Halifax. He realized, if his superiors in London did not, that the mere sight of Redcoats in the streets of Boston gave weight to Sam Adams's arguments.

Respectable citizens were joining the radicals in ever-growing numbers, Hutchinson wrote to the Colonial Office in the autumn of 1769. Adams had gained so much power that his friends were inspecting the manifests of ships that landed in Boston and were confiscating cargo from Great Britain. Adams and his Caucus Club cronies were guilty of "democratical despotism," he declared, quoting General Gage, and he gloomily predicted that a serious incident was certain to explode in such a tense atmosphere.

Chapter
Eleven

Sam Adams conducted an incessant campaign against the maintenance of the British regiments in Boston, and a resolution passed by the town meeting late in the autumn of 1769 clearly expressed his views. The stationing of royal troops in the city was a "gross infringement of Constitutional rights," and it was essential to the peace of the community that they be withdrawn. This was the opening salvo in a vigorous new crusade, and Adams, emboldened by the success of the nonimportation agreements, hammered without pause at his new target, insisting that the troops be withdrawn to Fort William without delay.

The authorities became so apprehensive that Andrew Oliver, who succeeded Hutchinson as Lieutenant Governor, publicly charged that Adams and his friends intended to find some means to drive the regiments out of town if they were not withdrawn peacefully. Adams replied at once in the columns of the *Gazette*, hotly denying the allegation, but developments in the early months of 1770 seemed to indicate that Oliver was right.

Members of the artisan class, always Adams's strongest and most loyal supporters, began to go out of their way to pick quarrels with the troops. On one occasion, in late January, a platoon was subjected to a barrage of snowballs by a crowd of men, but the young officer in command did not permit his men to halt. Gage's deputy, Colonel Dalrymple, sent a letter to his superior in New York, reporting the incident in full. Aware of the radicals' aims, he said:

> These people appear to be determined to embroil things entirely, to effect which they will leave nothing undone to render the situation of the troops embarrassing, and indeed insupportable. The men are rendered desperate by continued injustice.

The discipline of the troops, all of them professionals, was superb, but sergeants reported to their superiors that they could not keep the men under control much longer if the abuse continued. And even the younger officers were heard to mutter that the day would soon come when it would be necessary to teach the colonials a lesson.

The situation was made to order for Sam Adams, and he chose his setting with care, selecting the North End of Boston, where a battalion headquarters of the Twenty-ninth Regiment had been established near a cluster of small rope-making factories. The rope-makers, of course, were ardent Sons of Liberty and Sam Adams's followers. On March 2, 1770, a heavy barrage of snowballs filled with stones knocked off the high helmets of several soldiers, who tried to ignore the matter. The incident was repeated on the third and again on the fourth, with larger numbers of rope-makers taking part each time. These young men began to brandish clubs and homemade spears, shouted insults at the troops and cursed them. The *Gazette* duly noted the occasions, calling them "skirmishes," and treating them as battles between bloodthirsty troops and peace-loving townspeople.

The affair on March 4 was far more serious than the incidents that had taken place on the three previous days. Unable to tease the troops into retaliating, the rope-makers made a concerted rush on the infantrymen's line, and two soldiers were battered by clubs, one suffering a broken arm and the other sustaining injuries to his face.

That night Governor Hutchinson presided at a meeting of Crown officials, and it was the estimate of most who attended that the rope-makers, having drawn blood, now would desist. Colonel Dalrymple made it plain, however, that the patience of his men was limited and that they would be forced to protect themselves if again subjected to physical assault.

The taunting of the Redcoats was resumed on March 5 in the presence of a large crowd of bystanders, and again the rope-makers ran toward the infantry line. What happened in the next few moments has been the subject of endless debate for more than two hundred years.

According to one version, the troops fired a volley over the heads of the crowd, and the mob dispersed.

According to a second story, the soldiers fired into the crowd, killing four civilians. This is the generally accepted version, and was contained in Governor Hutchinson's official report of the tragedy to the Colonial Office. It was also noted in the diary of John Rowe, perhaps the most responsible of the radicals.

The third account was that disseminated by Sam Adams, who so completely aroused the ire of his fellow Bostonians that a truly spontaneous uprising of virtually the entire city was averted by the narrowest of margins. Men of every class appeared in the streets, many armed, and it seemed unlikely that a major catastrophe could be averted.

A special edition of the *Gazette* was published, and although it cited no precise figures, it indicated that a great many citizens had been either killed or severely wounded. Sam Adams gave the ugly incident the name that posterity has called it, a heavy black headline proclaiming:

BOSTON MASSACRE!

Fortunately a snowstorm drove people to their homes that night, but the following morning a mammoth crowd went to Faneuil Hall and overflowed into the streets. The session that ensued was called a special town meeting, and a committee of fifteen was elected to call on Governor Hutchinson to demand that both the twenty-ninth and fourteenth regiments be withdrawn to Fort William without delay. Sam Adams emerged from the shadows and was named the chairman of the committee.

The crowd followed its spokesmen to the governor's mansion, where Hutchinson appeared on a balcony and tried to address the throng. But he was jeered so loudly that no one could hear him, and he went inside again. Then the members of the committee were admitted to the building, and Sam Adams had his first face-to-face confrontation with his old enemy.

Precisely what happened at the dramatic meeting is unknown; Adams and Hutchinson told vastly different stories. But some solid facts do emerge from the confusion of conflicting claims. Adams presented the demands of the "town meeting," and emphasized the point that he could not guarantee the keeping of the peace if the troops remained in the city. This was no exaggerated claim, and Governor Hutchinson well knew it. Some of the younger radicals had been demanding since early morning that the people of Massachusetts arm themselves, take the law into their own hands and drive the two regiments into the sea. At the moment the troops were being held in their barracks, but they would not remain supine if attacked. It was obvious that they would be supported by the guns of the eight Royal Navy ships in the harbor, and it was no comfort to either side to know that these vessels had already stripped for action.

The situation was so ugly that Sam Adams was as frightened as Governor Hutchinson. He had not intended to carry his defiance of the regiments to such lengths, but affairs were out of hand now, and the insurrection at which he had hinted for so long was on the verge of breaking out momentarily. He and Hutchinson shared the desire to preserve peace and prevent serious bloodshed, and they were forced to work together toward that end.

They finally agreed that the regiments would be withdrawn to Fort William that same day. In return the people would keep the peace, and no assaults would be made on the troops as they departed, for Hutchinson made it clear that they would retaliate if attacked.

Adams and the other committee members returned to Faneuil Hall, where the crowd was so enormous that the chairman had to speak from the front steps of the building. He informed the people of the terms of the agreement, then asked for "volunteers" to police the fragile peace. The Sons of Liberty provided an escort, and the troops marched to the waterfront in a grim silence; but there were no further incidents.

When quiet was restored it was apparent that Adams had won his greatest victory to date. Thanks to the Boston "Massacre," the impossible had been accomplished and the troops had departed from the city. There was an unexpected bonus when the customs commissioners, afraid to remain in Boston without troop protection, also withdrew to the castle and stayed there for the next nine months.

Hoping to cement his victory, Adams demanded that the soldiers who had fired the shots and the officer commanding the company be placed on trial. The principal counsel for the defense, appointed by the justices of the Superior Court, was none other than John Adams. In spite of his strong radical leanings, he conducted himself so commendably that men of every political persuasion, from Governor Hutchinson to Cousin Sam, publicly praised him. Not only did he make his own reputation by defending his clients with great zeal and skill, but he succeeded beyond the expectations of even the most optimistic Tories and won the exoneration of the officer and soldiers. And he was so scrupulously fair that Cousin Sam and the other members of the Caucus Club did not condemn him.

Boston might have been happy to forget the "massacre," but Sam Adams gave the people no chance to put the unfortunate affair out of mind, and articles under a number of pseudonyms appeared in the newspapers, keeping the tragedy alive. Adams lost no opportunity to utilize the incident elsewhere, too, and letters to Committee of Correspondence members in other colonies caused increased restlessness up and down the seaboard.

The Boston radicals seized their chance to move one step closer to armed rebellion, and the Sons of Liberty encouraged young men to conduct military drills for the sake of self-defense. Wooden muskets were used, to be sure, in order to demonstrate that no one was thinking of an actual revolution against the Crown, and Sam Adams blandly remarked that "our young men seem of late very ambitious of making themselves masters of the art military."

Had Massachusetts been allowed to regain its composure, the "massacre" well might have receded into the background, but Lord Hillsborough, the head of the Colonial Office, had a genius for rubbing Americans the wrong way. Scarcely had the furor over the troops died down than Hutchinson received new orders from London. Since Boston was a hotbed of sedition and dissension, he was informed, the Assembly would not be permitted to sit there, but would hold its sessions across the Charles River in Cambridge. Hutchinson issued his instructions accordingly, although he knew a fresh storm would break over his head.

Sam Adams enjoyed no dispute more thoroughly than a fight over political abstractions, and he plunged joyously into the new controversy. The Assembly met at Harvard College, but refused to transact any business other than to elect Dr. Warren as Speaker and vote Clerk Sam Adams the sum of ninety pounds for his services.

New elections were held in May; the radicals remained in firm control of Boston, and the town meeting issued its customary instructions, with Adams writing that the executive had no right to dictate to the legislative branch of the colonial government. The legislature, he stressed repeatedly, derived its authority exclusively from the people. And he moved a distinct step closer to the coming Revolution when he declared:

Nor do we concede that even His Majesty in Council has any Constitutional authority to decide such questions, or any other controversy whatever that arises in this Province, except only such matters as are reserved in the Charter. It seems a great absurdity that, when a dispute arises between the Governor and the House, the Governor should appeal to His Majesty in Council to decide it.

The implications of this new policy line were made clear by a newspaper that had just begun publication a few months earlier, the *Massachusetts Spy*. Adams himself did not start to write for the *Spy* until later in the year, but he had an exceptionally able alter ego in a newcomer to politics, Josiah Quincy, whose writing was as fiery and controversial as that of the master.

The new Assembly met in July, convening in the chapel of Harvard College, and after the election of Thomas Cushing as Speaker and Samuel Adams as Clerk, it refused to transact any other business. Not until they were permitted to return to Boston, the Adams-inspired members declared, would they attend to any business. Hutchinson was tempted to prorogue the session, but forced himself to refrain, realizing he would serve no useful purpose and would merely play into the hands of Adams.

By allowing the House to remain in session, however inactive, he gave Adams the chance to keep the new controversy alive. The verbose propagandist wrote a letter of more than ten thousand words to Hutchinson, and the legislature awakened from its lethargy long enough to endorse it without the change of a comma. In this remarkable document Sam Adams reviewed the entire subject of the rights of the colonies in general and their legislatures in particular, citing John Locke when he found it convenient, and at other times quoting "authorities" he did not name. Those experts, a close study of his words indicated, were none other than Adams himself, writing under various pseudonyms in the public prints.

Again he denied the authority of the Crown over the Assembly, and this time he went even farther, saying, "We contend that the people and their representatives have a right to withstand the abusive exercise of a legal and Constitutional prerogative of the Crown."

He was not content to deal with abstract matters, to be sure, and utilized the propaganda value of the communication to the utmost. Unleashing one of his more memorable harangues, he declared:

That the Province has enemies, who are continually defaming it and their Charter, is certain; that there are persons who are endeavoring to intimidate the Province from asserting and vindicating their just rights and liberties, by insinuations of danger to the Constitution, is also indisputable. But no instance happened, even in the execrable reign of the worst of the Stuart race, of a forfeiture of a charter, because any one branch of a legislative, or even because the whole government under that charter, refused to do business at a particular time under grievous circumstances of ignominy, disgrace, and insult; and when their charter had explicitly given to that government the sole power of judging of the proper season and occasion of doing business.

We are obliged, at this time, to struggle with all the powers with which the Constitution has furnished us, in defence of our rights, to prevent the most valuable of our liberties from being wrested from us by the subtle machinations and daring encroachments of wicked ministers.

We have seen of late innumerable encroachments on our Charter: Courts of Admiralty extended from the high seas, where by the compact in the Charter they are confined, to numberless important causes upon land; multitudes of civil officers, the appointment of all which is by charter confined to the Governor and Council, sent here from abroad by the Ministry; a revenue not granted by us, but taken from us; armies stationed here without our consent; and the streets of our metropolis *crimsoned* with the blood of our fellow-subjects. These and other grievances and cruelties, too many to be here enumerated, and too melancholy to be much longer borne by this injured people, we have seen brought upon us by the devices of ministers of state. . . .

Are these things consistent with the freedom of the House? or could the General Court's tamely submitting to such usage be thought to promote His Majesty's service? Should these struggles of the House prove unfortunate and ineffectual, this Province will submit, with pious resignation, to the will of

Providence; but it will be a kind of suicide, of which we have the utmost horror, thus to be made the instruments of our own servitude.

Hutchinson, who was an honest, conscientious man and an able administrator, lacked the ability to stand apart emotionally from such arguments, a quality that had served Francis Bernard well. The new governor was himself a colonial, and shared the love of his fellow Americans for political debate. Instead of ignoring the letter from the Assembly, he made the mistake of replying to it, thus adding fuel to the flames and giving Adams the opportunity, which he utilized, to write yet again. The most effective aid to propaganda, Sam Adams knew, was repetition, and the harried governor grew so weary of the controversy that he prorogued the Assembly until September. Adams immediately attacked him as a tyrant who wanted to rule Massachusetts alone, and Hutchinson wrote to Sir Francis Bernard that he couldn't help but wish that he, too, could retire.

But the worst mischief Sam Adams could devise was yet to come.

Chapter Twelve

The death of Charles Townshend and the attempts of a vocal Whig minority in Parliament to improve Great Britain's relations with her North American colonies might have ended the growing rupture had the new ministry appointed by the Crown been more broad-minded. But Lord North, the new prime minister, was subservient to the wishes of King George, and although an amiable and honorable man personally, he thought of the colonists as wayward children who required strict discipline.

One of the first moves made by the new administration in the early spring of 1770, even before news of the Boston "Massacre" reached England, appeared on the surface to be favorable to the colonies. The Townshend Acts were repealed. The salaries of the customs officials cost more than the revenues the taxes brought in, and it was obvious that the policy was a total failure, thanks to the nonimportation agreements sparked by Sam Adams. At the personal insistence of King George, who declared that a principle was at stake and had to be upheld, a tax of threepence per pound, a minimal sum, was still levied on tea imported by the colonies.

Most colonists rejoiced when the news of the repeal reached the New World, the nonimportation agreements were forgotten and merchants happily did business as usual. But Sam Adams was as stubborn as his monarch, and editorials in the *Gazette*, *Post*, *News-Letter* and *Massachusetts Spy* immediately demanded a total boycott of tea. Going farther than ever before, Adams insisted that anyone who bought a single pound of tea was a traitor to the cause of liberty.

Copies of the editorials were sent to other colonies, where campaigns against the importation of tea were also initiated. But everywhere—even in Boston—most men had grown weary of the long struggle. Large quantities of Dutch tea were smuggled into the colonies from the Netherlands West Indies, and everyone who served tea made it clear that he never bought the British product. All the same, the boycott was far from general, and John Adams wondered, in his *Diary*, whether the tea he had been served at John Hancock's dinner table really had been imported from Holland.

The repeal of the Townshend Acts caused Sam Adams to make his first serious mistake, created problems for him unlike any he had ever before faced and almost cost him the permanent leadership of the radicals. The change in the British stance in no way changed his own outlook, and he was in favor of keeping up the nonimportation agreements, arguing that the boycott should be relaxed only after all British troops were withdrawn from all the colonies.

Only Josiah Quincy and a few other of the other younger men agreed with Adams. Such merchants as Hancock and Rowe, who had suffered severe financial reverses, were anxious to repair their fortunes, and saw no reason why they should maintain the nonimportation agreements when their colleagues in other colonies were once again earning handsome profits. Adams was angered and disgusted by the attempted desertion of his old comrades, and rallied his forces. But those who flocked to his banner, among them Cousin John, Quincy, Joseph Warren and Thomas

Cushing, were neither merchants nor bankers. The first real split loomed in the ranks of the radicals.

Had Sam Adams been content to relax and permit Massachusetts to follow the lead of other colonies, all would have been well. But he was outraged by the revolt, demanded obedience to the principles he had so long been advocating and insisted that the Merchants' Club be polled on the issue. The poll was taken in midsummer 1770, and the Adams faction suffered a crushing defeat—the merchants voted 68 to 5 to end the boycott.

Stunned by the reversal, Adams tried to recoup when the Assembly met again in September. The question of nonimportation was more important to him than that of doing no business while the legislature sat in Cambridge, so he ignored the latter issue and tried to push through a bill that would have required individual citizens to pledge that they would buy no British-made goods. Again he failed to read the temper of the times: the people of Massachusetts were tired of the long struggle; they saw no reason to make new sacrifices and refused to follow his lead. So little enthusiasm for the bill was generated that Adams knew he faced certain defeat, and he withdrew the measure before it came to a vote.

This blunder cost him the total command of the Assembly he had so long maintained. The members, enjoying their new freedom, went on to consider other measures, conducting business as usual, and paid no attention to his renewed pleas that the Assembly should remain inactive until the governor permitted sessions to be held in Boston.

Adams failed to read other signs of the times, too. The *Post* and *News-Letter* published more noncontroversial pieces and asked him for fewer essays and articles. The *Gazette*, which continued to print his work under any pseudonym he cared to use, suffered its first substantial loss in circulation, dropping from about twenty-two hundred copies per issue to approximately seventeen hundred. And the *Massachusetts Spy*, by far the most revolutionary of all the newspapers in the colony, almost went into bankruptcy in the final months of 1770 and early part of 1771.

Adams tightened his belt. He wrote in the *Gazette* that the nonimportation agreements had been doomed to fail from the outset because merchants were too soft for the struggle against America's "implacable enemies." Those foes, he declared, understood only one language, that of force, and he concluded, "Let us then ever forget that there has been such a futile combination, and awaken our attention to our first grand object." That object was the achievment of liberty, which he did not define, and he stopped just short of using another word, *independence.*

Only a few stalwarts of the radical old guard and some of the younger men heeded his fulminations. The pendulum had swung in the opposite direction; conservatism had come into its own again, and men were no longer ashamed of proclaiming their loyalty to the Crown. Only a crusader was able to get excited about a token tax on tea.

The change in sentiment was so marked that a majority of men who shared Governor Hutchinson's moderate views were elected to the Council in the autumn of 1770, and for the first time since 1766, harmony between that body and the chief executive was restored. And late in October, the Assembly, still meeting in Cambridge, decided by a vote of 59 to 29 to resume full business.

The Sam Adams of this period was a somewhat pathetic figure. He had enjoyed six years of unending success, but now, in his forty-ninth year, he found himself unable to bend with the winds of public sentiment. His own feelings had hardened rather than changed, and no matter how sincere Great Britain might be in wanting to find an accommodation with her colonies, he continued to regard her as the "implacable enemy." Why were others proving so fickle? He could not understand it. Caring nothing about money himself, he found it incomprehensible that men like Hancock and Rowe were eager to recoup their financial losses. Indifferent to the joys of relaxed living, he was angered and saddened when others failed to share his desire to maintain pressure on the mother country.

In his bewilderment he seemed incapable of comprehending that a crusader needed active issues illuminating an active cause if he hoped to build and keep a following. Few were able to hate in the abstract, and he felt betrayed: he had devoted his substance, personal and professional, to a cause that appeared to be vanishing before his eyes.

His correspondence with other colonies indicated a similar lethargy elsewhere. One of the few who agreed with him was Patrick Henry of Virginia, and it was small consolation that other young Virginians, among them such unknowns as Thomas Jefferson and James Madison, felt the same way. Most Americans, Adams believed, were being lulled by a cunning foe.

Some of his friends were in favor of going into hibernation until the atmosphere again changed. Business was flourishing everywhere in the colonies; farm products, lumber and other raw materials were commanding exceptionally high prices, and prosperity was general. And taxes were so low it was difficult, if not impossible, to campaign against them. The tax on molasses was only a penny per gallon, so ship owners no longer bothered to smuggle it into the country. As for tea, the East India Company —which had a monopoly on its sale throughout the British Empire—was making a major effort to enlarge its American market. So the colonists could buy it at the attractive price of three shillings per pound, precisely half of what the British housewife paid. The threepence per pound tax was so negligible that most people did not care if they paid it. The good women of Boston who had supported the nonimportation agreements so enthusiastically knew a bargain when they saw one, shrugged off the advice Adams gave them in the *Gazette* and stocked their larders with British tea.

It is axiomatic that politicans quarrel when their fortunes decline—success is the only glue that binds them together; so it was inevitable that wide fissures should appear in the ranks of the Massachusetts radicals. The process was hastened by the total withdrawal from politics of John Adams, who decided to look after his own affairs as a lawyer during a time when the political crosscurrents were too tricky to be safely negotiated. He resigned his seat in the Assembly, ostensibly to make a place for James Otis, who was enjoying a temporary recovery in his long struggle with insanity. The defection of the younger Adams, whose acute sixth sense kept him out of politics throughout 1771 and 1772, robbed Cousin Sam of an ever-reliable supporter and lieutenant.

The growing rift with John Hancock was far more serious. Ultrasensitive and quick to take offense, inclined toward pomposity and convinced of his own importance, Hancock had never been easy to handle. As early as the spring of 1770, he threatened to resign from the Assembly and leave politics because some of Sam Adams's friends had made "insulting" remarks about him, and only a letter from the radical leader had persuaded him to remain in the fold. This communication demonstrates the blending of flattery and firmness necessary to hold him in line:

Boston, May 11, 1770.

Dear Sir,—

Your resolution yesterday to resign your seat gave me great uneasiness. I could not think you had sufficient ground to deprive the town of one whom I had a right to say is a most valuable member, since you had within three of the unanimous suffrages of your fellow-citizens, and one of the negative votes was your own.

You say you have been spoken ill of. What then? Can you think that while you are a good man, that *all* will speak well of you? If you knew the person who has defamed you, nothing is more likely than that you would justly value youself upon *that* man's censure as being the highest applause. Those who were fond of continuing Mr. Otis in that seat were, I dare say to a man, among your warmest friends. Will you then add to their disappointment by a resignation, merely because one contemptible person, who perhaps was hired for the purpose, has *blessed* you with his reviling? Need I add more than to entreat it as a favor, that you would alter your design.

I am, with strict truth,
Your affectionate friend and brother,
Sam. Adams

Hancock kept his seat, but his relations with his mentor continued to decline over the next year, and the process was hastened by the return of James Otis to the political arena. Accustomed to the limelight and to the deference of men who had regarded him as their leader, Otis resented the rise of Adams to a place of preeminence. Aware of Hancock's susceptibility to flattery, Otis heard of the slight coolness between the pair and made immediate efforts to widen the breach.

Excitement over the Townshend Acts having subsided, John Hancock began to think in terms of his own long-range future. He owned the largest fleet of merchant ships in New England and the greatest number of warehouses in Massachusetts, and his money was invested in a score of enterprises. His home was the finest in Boston, a magnificent mansion that straddled the crest of Beacon Hill, and men of every political persuasion were his guests. He had been a leader of the radicals for several years, but his wealth and power made him acceptable to the Tories, too.

So, with Thomas Hutchinson now formally installed as governor, Hancock wondered why another American might not hold that appointment at some future date. Sam Adams was horrified, and the mere thought that Hancock might "sell out to the enemy" outraged him. Conscious of the younger man's sensitivity, however, he made certain that Hancock learned nothing of his views. Otis, on the other hand, actively encouraged Hancock's ambitions.

Matters came to a head in the summer of 1771, when conservatives in the Assembly introduced a routine bill offering congratulations to Thomas Hutchinson on his formal appointment as governor. Adams decided to make the measure a test of radical loyalty, and passed the word to his followers to vote against the bill. He selected a flimsy issue for his fight, perhaps because no controversies of real substance could be found, and from the beginning found it difficult to round up votes, even though the radicals commanded a four or five to one majority in the legislature.

The breach in the radical leadership came into the open after Adams made an address opposing the passage of the bill. He was followed on the floor by Otis, who made a speech praising Hutchinson, and then Hancock made a similar address. The bill was defeated by a single vote, the narrowest of margins, and it was apparent to everyone interested in politics that Sam Adams's power had eroded. His opposition to an American-born governor was regarded as ungracious, and even men who had no love for Hutchinson resented him for it.

Hancock pressed his own suit by having friends propose him for a seat on the Council. The legislature nominated him for one of the places under its jurisdiction, and Adams carefully voted for his former lieutenant, as did others who were influenced by him.

Governor Hutchinson was inclined to accept Hancock, having been informed in so many words that the wealthy merchant was breaking completely with Sam Adams. But John Hancock was too honest a man to make a public disavowal of the radical position he had previously advocated, so Hutchinson was obliged to veto the appointment. The disappointed Hancock withdrew from politics, announcing his intention to devote his future efforts exclusively to his business enterprises.

Many members of the Assembly who had willingly followed Sam Adams's lead now fell away from him, and even in the Boston town meeting, the source of his strength; he found it difficult to command a majority. There was full employment in Boston, the shipyards were booming, and men who were working had little time for Sons of Liberty celebrations. Adams tried to hold ceremonies of various kinds at the Liberty Tree, but the crowds were small, and when he invited the citizens to a discussion of "the powers of the Governor," fewer than one hundred persons showed up at Faneuil Hall.

For all practical purposes Sam Adams now stood alone. He had lost his business because of his devotion to politics, and his family would have gone hungry had he not continued to rent the Adams wharf to outside interests for a large fee. He had no friends except his political associates, and his personal future was as bleak as his political prospects.

But his attitude, both private and public, was remarkable. He had recovered his good humor after suffering his first disappointments, and was able to view his situation with an emotional and philosophical detachment he had never before displayed. Nothing had altered his conviction that Great Britain would make further attempts to curb the liberties of the colonies, and he was still convinced the day would come when Americans would have to make a complete break with the mother country.

Consequently he would hold to his own course, and in time the defectors would recognize the error of their ways and return to fight again under his banner. He made no concessions to anyone, and was prepared to fight alone, if necessary.

Governor Hutchinson, as sensitive as anyone else to the change in the temper of Massachusetts, thought the time was ripe to strengthen the cause of those loyal to the Crown, and he either wrote or inspired a number of political essays that the *Post* and *Gazette* obligingly published. Sam Adams immediately accepted the challenge, and replied at great length in his own essays, which he wrote under the name of "Candidus." Issues that other men regarded as dead were very much alive in his own mind, and he wrote with a fervor as great as any he had displayed during the battles for repeal of the Stamp Act and Townshend Acts.

His consistency was also revealed in his correspondence with Benjamin Franklin, who, already representing a number of colonies in London, became the agent of Massachusetts as well when Dennys Deberdt died in 1771. There was no hint of retreat in the long letters he sent to Dr. Franklin, whom he admired and whose genius he recognized. He made his basic thinking clear late in 1771, when he declared:

> If Great Britain, instead of treating us as their fellow-subjects, shall aim at making us their vassals and slaves, the consequences will be that, although our merchants have receded from their non-importation agreement, yet the body of the people will vigorously endeavor to become independent of the mother country for their supplies, and sooner than she may be aware of it, may manufacture for themselves. The Colonies, like healthy young sons, may have hitherto been cheerfully building up the parent state; and how far Great Britain will be affected, if they should be rendered even barely useless to her, is an object which we conceive is at this very juncture worth the attention of a British Parliament.

Adams's refusal to back down in the slightest degree from the position he had taken through the long crisis was annoying to those who had grown weary of bickering over the rights of man. But he paid no attention to their criticism, and the subject remained paramount in his own mind, as he indicated in a letter to a London banker, Stephen Sayre, one of his many correspondents:

> The people here are indeed very tenacious of their rights, and I hope in God they will ever firmly maintain them. Every attempt to enforce the plan of despotism will certainly irritate them. While they have a sense of freedom, they will oppose the efforts of tyranny; and although the mother country may at present boast of superiority over them, she may perhaps find the want of that superiority when, by repeated provocations, she shall have totally lost their affections. All good men surely wish for a candid harmony between the two countries. Great Britain can lose nothing which she ought to retain by restoring the Americans to their former state, and they, I am satisfied, will no further contend. While the struggle continues, manufactures will still increase in America, in spite of all efforts to prevent it; and how far Great Britain will be injured by it ought certainly to be considered on your side of the Atlantic.

It was during this same drab period that Sam Adams opened what became a voluminous correspondence with a young lawyer, Arthur Lee, who was a member of one of Virginia's most prominent and patrician families. Lee, even more kindred in spirit than Patrick Henry, agreed heartily with Adams's suggestion that attempts should be made during this time of quiet to strengthen the ties between the colonies. The Committees of Correspondence, now increasingly inactive and in disarray, were unofficial bodies, so even the expressions of opinion they fostered were only the ideas of individual, private citizens who sought the same goals. It occurred to Adams that these groups would be greatly strengthened if the legislature of each colony appointed a number of its members to serve on a committee that would keep in touch with the committeemen in sister colonies. In this way a truly intercolonial organization would be formed, and in the event of an emergency would be in a position to coordinate legislative and other efforts.

Arthur Lee was in favor of the plan, but neither the Massachusetts Assembly nor the Virginia House of Burgesses showed any active interest in it. No disputes of consequence were ruffling relations with Great Britain, and legislators in both colonies shrugged off attempts to persuade them to prepare for future trouble.

These efforts won Adams the public condemnation of Governor Hutchinson, who took him to task in an address opening the Assembly in the autumn of 1771. Men of goodwill, he declared, were making efforts to mend the ties that "forever" bound the mother country and the colonies, but they were opposed by a small, vocal minority led by a "director and principal incendiary." There was no need for him to name that individual.

Sam Adams willingly accepted the designation. Convinced that the day would come when America would be forced to terminate her relationship with Great Britain and become an independent nation, he was spoiling for a fight, and since no opponent would meet him in or out of the ring, he was reduced to shadow-boxing.

Chapter Thirteen

"Candidus" so exhausted himself writing long essays for the *Gazette* and *Post* that he was succeeded by "Valerius Poplicola," and as there was little else to occupy Sam Adams's energies in the closing months of 1771, his political tracts became even longer. In most of these works he dealt with abstractions because there were so few matters of immediate substance to occupy his attention. He quarreled with the governor over the payment of public officials' salaries, but the public yawned through the dispute.

In December 1771, the arrival of twelve Royal Navy warships created a mild stir when it was learned that the commodore in command had been instructed to make Boston his home port. Adams immediately charged that Britain was trying to intimidate Massachusetts, but few people took the charge seriously. Long experience had taught the city that shopkeepers and tavern owners benefited from the presence of a Navy fleet, the ship repair yards did a brisk business, and as Navy discipline was strict, sailors were on their good behavior when they came ashore.

The two regiments of troops were still cooped up at Fort William, and the ministry in London contemplated taking possession of the island and paying the colony for it. Adams promptly thundered that the land belonged to the people of the colony and could not be purchased without their active consent. Other matters were occupying the attention of Lord North and his Cabinet, so nothing came of the plan; public lethargy was so great that Adams made no attempt to claim a victory.

He was writing under such a variety of names now that few of his contemporaries knew many of his identities, and it has never been possible, down to the present day, to learn all of them. His descendant, William V. Wells, listed a number of them in his *Life of Samuel Adams:*

Determinatus
Principiis Obsta
T. Z.
A Layman
A. B.
Cedant Arma Togae
E. A.
A Bostonian
A Tory
Populus
An Impartialist
Alfred
Candidus
Vindex
A Chatterer
An Elector in 1771
An Elector in 1772
An Elector in 1773
An American
A.
Valerius Poplicola
A Son of Liberty
Shippen

Z.
Observation
Sincerus
A Religious Politician

John Adams, who was deeply impressed by Cousin Sam's literary output, was bewildered by the sheer volume of that work over the period of more than a half century. In his *Diary* he asked rhetorically, "But where are his writings? Who can collect them? and if collected, who will ever read them?" Cousin John estimated that his kinsman used fifty to one hundred pseudonyms during his long life as an author for various periodicals. When Sam Adams was an old man, he one day confessed to a visitor that he himself had forgotten most of them. But it did not matter, he said, because "they served their purpose."

That goal was still far distant in the opening months of 1772, when not many agreed with Adams's estimate that the colonies were enjoying a lull before the storm. During that period his quarrel with John Hancock deepened, and some believed that the radical cause was destroying itself. Hancock's retirement from politics was brief, and in the spring of 1772 he ran for a seat in the Assembly, declaring that he was compelled to vindicate his good name. It seems that Sam Adams, in one of his *Gazette* essays, had urged Bostonians to live frugally, claiming that the more they spent, the more money they put in British pockets. Hancock, who lived regally, was convinced he had been deliberately insulted.

Adams welcomed the return of his former protégé to politics, regardless of his motives. In fact, many years passed before most of Adams's colleagues realized how hard he worked to elect a radical slate throughout Massachusetts in 1772. The loss of his overwhelming majority in the past two years had convinced him of the need to build a new, loyal following. But with the radical leadership fragmented, he was satisfied with the election of anyone who called himself radical, Whig or Patriot.

For many years he had done virtually no traveling and had rarely ventured farther from Boston than Cambridge, but in the late winter and early spring of 1772, he visited more than fifty Massachusetts towns. He preached radical unity everywhere, and his efforts were rewarded by a sweep in which the radicals won 80 per cent of the seats.

Most of these men actually were moderates, however, a fact he learned when John Hancock, no longer regarded as an extremist, was elected Speaker. Overnight Hancock proved himself master of the legislature, winning heavy support for a petition to Governor Hutchinson requesting the return of the Assembly to Boston. This was precisely what the governor wanted, and the Assembly could not or would not heed the argument of Sam Adams, who insisted that the submission of a petition meant the abandonment of the principle that the legislative branch of the government was the equal of the executive.

One man agreed with him: Governor Hutchinson promptly granted the petition. The Assembly returned to its own quarters in Boston, and Adams momentarily lost his calm, writing an angry newspaper piece in which he charged Hancock with a betrayal of principles. But his good sense quickly reasserted itself, and the article did not appear in print; in fact, its existence was not discovered until his death, when it was found among his papers.

Certainly Sam Adams suspected that the Crown was pursuing a deliberate policy of wooing Hancock. The new Speaker was invited to dine at the governor's mansion, and the always generous and courtly Hancock returned the invitation soon thereafter. On the surface only the amenities were being observed, but Adams confided his fears to the Massachusetts agent in London, and the astute Benjamin Franklin replied that he had heard rumors in Whitehall to the effect that a serious attempt was being made to win Hancock's friendship for the king's cause.

But Adams refused to say or do anything that would further alienate his former friend. They were both still members of the Caucus Club, where they met regularly, and the strain could be seen only on Hancock's side. Adams was always amiable, and went out of his way to defend the younger man to outsiders. Arthur Lee, then in London, wrote a worried letter to Adams, saying that a mutual acquaintance named Wilkes had told him Hancock had deserted the cause. Adams's reply was firm:

> Mr. Wilkes was certainly misinformed when he was told that Mr. H. had deserted the cause of liberty. Great pains had been taken to have it thought to be so, and, by a scurby trick of lying, the adversaries effected a coolness between that gentleman and some others who were zealous in that cause; but it was of short continuance, for their falsehood was soon detected. Lord Hillsborough, as I suppose, was soon informed of the imaginary conquest, for I have it upon such grounds as I rely upon, that he wrote to the Governor that he had it in command from the *highest authority* to enjoin him to promote Mr. H. upon every occasion. Accordingly, though he had before been frowned upon, and often negatived both by Bernard and Hutchinson, the latter, who can smile sweetly even upon the man he hates, when he is instructed or it is his duty to do so, fawned and flattered one of the heads of the faction, and at length approved of him, when he was again chosen by an unanimous vote a councillor last May. To palliate this inconsistent conduct, it was previously given out that Mr. H. had deserted the faction, and become, as they term each other, a friend to government. But he had spirit enough to refuse a seat at the Board, and to continue a member of the House, where he has, in every instance, joined with the friends of the Constitution in opposition to the measures of a corrupt administration; and, in particular, no one has discoursed with more firmness against the independency of the Governor and the judges than he.

That communication was a masterpiece concocted by a genius in the art of the writing and dissemination of propaganda. Fact, fancy and innuendo were freely mixed, and even the strong hint that King George himself was involved in the conservative wooing of Hancock was included in the story. Sam Adams well realized that Arthur Lee was a Patriot, but decided that it was best, even when dealing with a good friend, to pretend that the radical leadership in Massachusetts was united. If everyone's face was saved and no harsh observations were made to leave a residue of bitterness behind, it would be far easier to join hands again and face a common foe when the time was ripe. Certainly John Adams did not exaggerate when he wrote that Cousin Sam was too broadminded and generous a man to carry a grudge, and that he put the cause he held sacred ahead of every personal consideration.

The Boston conservatives were well aware of the split between Adams and Hancock, of course, and in the town meeting elections of late May 1772, they made a supreme effort to deny their most dangerous adversary the core of his power. If Adams lost his seat as a representative in the Assembly, he would be retired to private life and the radicals would lose their most effective leadership.

Discreet and conservative in what little private life he allowed himself, Sam Adams knew that an attitude of reserve and dignity was necessary if he wanted to preserve his political career and prevent himself from being inundated by the Hancock moderates. When he was told at Caucus Club meetings that the conservatives had made him their primary target and were campaigning hard against him, he merely shrugged. When articles attacking him appeared in the newspapers, he did not deign to answer them either under his own signature or under pseudonyms. The assaults continued, and in the last week before the election, he finally wrote brief letters to the press under his own name, saying he had considered the source of the attacks, found them unworthy of his notice and therefore had nothing to say.

Thomas Cushing, Joseph Warren and Josiah Quincy all urged him to speak in his own defense, or, at the very least, to permit one of them to campaign for him, but Adams refused. Boston knew him and the principles of liberty for which he stood, and he intended to abide by the will of the people. The people spoke, and he defeated his conservative opponent by a crushing two and one-half to one margin. Those who had believed he was no longer a force in Massachusetts politics were forced to reconsider.

This demonstration of strength was not lost on John Hancock, and in the autumn of 1772 he ended his feud with his mentor. The reconciliation was quiet—Hancock casually extended a supper invitation and Adams calmly accepted it. The news that they stood together again spread quickly, and Governor Hutchinson regarded it as sufficiently important to devote an entire report to the subject when he next wrote to the Colonial Office.

The friendship became so close that Hancock engaged Boston's leading artist, John Singleton Copley, to paint two full-length portraits, one of himself and one of Adams. These were displayed in the Hancock drawing room for the better part of half a century, excluding the years of the British occupation of Boston, and thereafter were removed to Faneuil Hall.

The reunited radicals directed their gunfire at an old and familiar target, the governor, and having no issue except his salary, which he was now accepting from the Crown rather than from public funds, they concentrated on that. A bill written by Adams and passed by the Assembly in July 1772 indicates that he had not lost his talent for transforming even mundane state business into crises of major importance:

> Resolved: That the Governor's having and receiving his support independent of the grants and acts of the General Assembly is a dangerous innovation, which renders him a Governor not dependent on the people as the Charter has prescribed, and consequently, not in that respect such a Governor as the people consented to at the granting thereof. It destroys that mutual check and dependence which each branch of the Legislative ought to have upon the others and the balance of power which is essential to all free governments. And this House do most solemnly protest, that the innovation is an important change in the Constitution, and exposes the Province to a despotic administration of government.

An examination of the resolution illustrates the way in which Sam Adams created propaganda. First, his claim that the "Charter prescribed" the method of the payment of the governor's salary was nonsense. Four or five different charters were granted to various groups that first settled Massachusetts, and none even mentioned the payment of the governor's salary, merely stipulating that he would be appointed by the Crown. Payment by the legislature was a custom, not a charter-prescribed law. The new method of payment did not destroy the balance of the legislative and executive branches of the government, but by denying the Assembly the power of the purse strings over the governor's personal income, it did deprive the legislature of its hold over him. Adams's claim that the "innovation" was an "important change in the Constitution" was unadulterated gibberish, and every lawyer in the Assembly well knew it. Parliament voted the king an annual stipend, to be sure, but there was no inviolable precedent in the unwritten English Constitution stipulating that a colonial governor had to receive his income from the legislature of the province he governed.

But it did not matter if the Crown authorities and those who opposed them knew Adams's arguments were specious. They had the *appearance* of validity, and therefore were convincing to laymen who knew no better and accepted them at face value. Other great propagandists had used a similar approach, not the least of them Julius Caesar and Charlemagne, but as far as is known, Sam Adams copied no one. On the contrary, he seems to have developed the technique himself, instinctively understanding what was required.

There can be little question that his efforts kept the radical cause alive at a time when the colonists' grievances against Great Britain were minor and few. Those who continued to follow him and the newcomers who joined him—among them Paul Revere, a prosperous silversmith and businessman—formed the hard core of the movement that would develop swiftly in 1773 and thereafter. The softer, passive elements had fallen away, and the survivors formed a solid phalanx behind Sam Adams in the grim struggle for American independence that would soon begin.

In the autumn of 1772 Sam Adams made one of his more notable contributions to the nation he was instrumental in founding. At that time he was concentrating most of his propaganda fire on the efforts of the Crown to pay the salaries of the justices of the Massachusetts Superior Court out of funds provided by the Colonial Office rather than permit them to be paid by the Assembly. In the fight against this further diminution of the legislature's power, Adams saw an opportunity to further one of his favorite projects.

The Boston town meeting held a special session on November 2, 1772, and Samuel Adams delivered a brief but pungent address:

> It is proper for this Town to take what the Tories apprehend to be leading steps. We have long had it thrown in our faces, that the country in general is under no fears of slavery, but are well pleased with the measures of Administration, that the Independency of the Governor and Judges is a mighty harmless and even desirable maneuver. In order to ascertain the true sense of the people of the Province, I do submit, herewith, a resolution to the effect that a special committee of twenty-one persons be appointed to open a communication with every town in the Province. Thus will the people be enabled to prosecute to effect the methods for the redress of grievances.

The town meeting voted the first official Committee of Correspondence into existence, and Adams could now pursue, officially, what he and volunteers elsewhere had been doing privately for several years. Other colonies, he hoped and believed, would follow the Massachusetts example—and they did. In Virginia, Henry, Jefferson and Richard Henry Lee sponsored a bill in the Burgesses for the appointment of a Committee of Correspondence that would work with similar, official groups elsewhere, and within six months the legislatures of the other eleven colonies also appointed official committees. Thus a dream long dear to Sam Adams was realized, and its importance cannot be emphasized too strongly. The skeleton of a formal intercolonial organization was created, simplifying and strengthening coordinated activities, and the First Continental Congress was a direct outgrowth of this organization.

Sam Adams became chairman of the Massachusetts committee, and went to work without delay. By the end of the month he and his colleagues produced a remarkable document, in the form of a report, that became the first of the celebrated state papers of the American Revolution. Subdivided into three separate reports, it considered the rights of the Americans as men, as Christians and as subjects of the Crown. Adams was the sole author of the first section, and had a hand in the preparation of the other two.

Every newspaper of substance in New England printed the report in full, as did the major newspapers in other colonies. Benjamin Franklin, who was still in England, published it there, and it made a deep impression on everyone concerned with what was now generally recognized as "the American problem." For a time Franklin was assumed to be the principal author, and Adams, displaying his usual modesty, made no attempt to assert his own claims.

Although he was not an original thinker, he adapted and applied the philosophy of John Locke to the American experience that had developed over the period of a century and a half, and his section of the report, which he called "Natural Rights of Colonists as Men," became the intellectual base on which Americans built thereafter. Jefferson's debt to Adams in the preparation of the Declaration of Independence less than four years later is obvious. The report said:

> Among the natural rights of the Colonists are these: *First*, a right to life; *Secondly*, to liberty; *Thirdly*, to property; together with the right to support and defend them in the best manner they can. These are evident branches of, rather than deductions from the duty of self-preservation, commonly called the first law of nature.
> All men have a right to remain in a state of nature as long as they please; and in case of intolerable oppression, civil or

religious, to leave the society they belong to, and enter into another.

When men enter into society, it is by voluntary consent; and they have a right to demand and insist upon the performance of such conditions and previous limitations as form an equitable *original compact*.

Every natural right not expressly given up, or from the nature of a social compact, necessarily ceded, remains.

All positive and civil laws should conform as far as possible, to the law of natural reason and equity.

As neither reason requires nor religion permits the contrary, every man living in or out of a state of civil society has a right peaceably and quietly to worship God according to the dictates of his conscience.

"Just and true liberty, equal and impartial liberty," in matters spiritual and temporal, is a thing that all men are clearly entitled to by the eternal and immutable laws of God and nature, as well as by the law of nations and all well-grounded municipal laws, which must have their foundation in the former.

In regard to religion, mutual toleration in the different professions thereof is what all good and candid minds in all ages have ever practised and both by precept and example, inculcated in mankind. And it is now generally agreed among Christians that this spirit of toleration, in the fullest extent consistent with the being of civil society, is the chief characteristical mark of the true Church. Insomuch that Mr. Locke has asserted and proved, beyond the possibility of contradiction on any solid ground, that such toleration ought to be extended to all whose doctrines are not subversive of society. The only sects which he thinks ought to be, and which by all wise laws are excluded from such toleration, are those who teach doctrines subversive of the civil government under which they live. The Roman Catholics or Papists are excluded by reason of such doctrines as these, that princes excommunicated may be deposed, and those that they call heretics may be destroyed without mercy; besides their recognizing the Pope in so absolute a manner, in subversion of government, by introducing, as far as possible into the states under whose protection they enjoy life, liberty, and property, that solecism in politics, *imperium in imperio* (a government within a government), leading directly to the worst anarchy and confusion, civil discord, war, and bloodshed.

The natural liberty of man, by entering into society, is abridged or restrained, so far only as is necessary for the great end of society, the great good of the whole.

In the state of nature every man is, under God, judge and sole judge of his own rights and of the injuries done him. By entering into society he agrees to an arbiter or indifferent judge between him and his neighbors; but he no more renounces his original right than by taking a cause out of the ordinary course of law, and leaving the decision to referees or indifferent arbitrators. In the last case, he must pay the referee for time and trouble. He should also be willing to pay his just quota for the support of government, the law, and the constitution; the end of which is to furnish indifferent and impartial judges in all cases that may happen, whether civil, ecclesiastical, marine, or military.

The *natural* liberty of man is to be free from any superior power on earth, and not to be under the will or legislative authority of man, but only to have the law of nature for his rule.

In the state of nature men may, as the patriarchs did, employ hired servants for the defence of their lives, liberty, and property; and they should pay them reasonable wages. Government was instituted for the purposes of the common defence, and those who hold the reins of government have an equitable, natural right to an honorable support from the same principle that "the laborer is worthy of his hire." But then the same community which they serve ought to be the assessors of their pay. Governors have no right to seek and take what they please; by this, instead of being content with the station assigned them, that of honorable servants of the society, they would soon become absolute masters, despots, and tyrants. Hence, as a private man has a right to say what wages he will give in his private affairs, so has a community to determine what *they* will give and grant of their substance for the administration of public affairs. And, in both cases, more are ready to offer their service at the proposed and stipulated price than are able and willing to perform their duty.

In short, it is the greatest absurdity to suppose it in the power of one, or any number of men, at the entering into society, to renounce their essential natural rights, or the means of preserving those rights; when the grand end of civil government, from the very nature of its institution, is for the support, protection, and defence of those very rights; the principal of which, as is before observed, are Life, Liberty and Property. If men, through fear, fraud, or mistake, should in terms renounce or give up any natural right, the eternal law of reason and the grand end of society would absolutely vacate such renunciation. The right to freedom being the gift of Almighty God, it is not in the power of man to alienate this gift and voluntarily become a slave.

The principles Sam Adams espoused in "The Natural Rights of the Colonists as Men" became "the guide of a people in its march to freedom," according to Wells, and for once he did not exaggerate. The consequences of the document's publication were widespread and immediate. Accepted almost without exception or discussion by the radicals of the younger generation in other colonies, the "Natural Rights" profoundly influenced British opinion, too. Until that time Great Britain demonstrated a reasonable desire to find a balanced accommodation with its New World offspring, but Adams slammed the door so hard that many moderates in and out of Parliament began to assume that the issues separating the antagonists could be settled only by the use of force.

It did not matter that the grounds on which Adams based his demands for colonial self-rule were filled with errors. The crusader may have been sincere, and possibly convinced himself that the charters guaranteed the colonists the rights of self-government, but that had become a matter of secondary importance, too. The atmosphere was becoming so emotional that the "reason" to which Adams paid lip service was receding more and more into the background. His propaganda campaign was so successful that men everywhere not only believed in freedom, but felt that history, precedent and right were on their side.

Many years later, shortly after Thomas Jefferson took office as the third president of the United States in 1801, he wrote to his "ever respected and venerable friend," who lay dying:

> Your principles have been tested in the crucible of time, and have come out pure. You have proved that it was monarchy, not merely British monarchy, you opposed. A government by representatives, elected by the people at short periods, was our object, and our maxim at that time was, "Where annual election ends, tyranny begins."

The publication of the "Natural Rights" almost overnight made Sam Adams famous throughout the colonies, winning him the grudging respect of the fence-straddlers who were in the majority as well as the enthusiastic support of the radicals who were coming to political power in every colony, due at least in part to his efforts of so many years. It has been said that, after Franklin, he became the best-known man in America. Certainly the British were more aware of him, too, and his friends and foes alike called him by the name Governor Hutchinson had given him, "the Grand Incendiary."

Adams responded by increasing his already crushing workload, and gave additional substance to the philosophical concepts he was teaching the American people by stressing the importance of representative government. "The representative body of a people are the proper judges of all other powers, and officers in the state," he declared, writing under one of his pseudonyms. "They are the foundation of all government, and the original of all authority in a nation." Here he carried his thesis to its logical conclusion, asserting that the legislature of Massachusetts had authority greater than that of the Crown.

His concepts were taking specific shape, and he justified them in the *Massachusetts Spy* under yet another pen name, saying:

> Virtuous houses of commons are the great bulwark of liberty; and the only way to keep them virtuous, is to choose them annually. They are the foundation of the great building, of which the other powers are but the top stories, and to them

all officers in the state should be accountable; they must be the watchful guardians of the rights, liberties, and interests of the people, never suffer the authority to be infringed in the least, for they are the greatest power and are the highest court in a nation, being chosen by the people, who are the original of all power and authority among men. If the houses of commons suffer their authority to be infringed, and are controlled by other powers, the foundation of civil liberty will be sapped, and the heavenly flower will soon wither and die.

Still exerting pressure with undiminished bluntness, he insisted that no house of commons had the right to tax a people it did not represent. In fact, he said wryly, the houses of commons in America had as much right to tax Great Britain as a house of commons in Britain had the right to tax America.

Finally, in a *Gazette* essay in December 1772, Adams declared *"This people has no connection with Great Britain,"* thus carrying his proposals to their logical and inevitable conclusion for the first time. Thereafter, under his own name and a bewildering variety of pseudonyms, he began to demand complete independence for the colonies. At last he "unmasked himself," as a deeply perturbed Hutchinson wrote in a report to the Colonial Office. By this time, however, his unremitting efforts finally had changed the emotional climate of America sufficiently so that only the true conservative element was alarmed. Moderates, as well as the vocal radicals, were quick to agree that it made sense for the colonies to sever all ties with the mother country.

In January 1773, writing as "An American," he issued a direct challenge to the Crown itself, saying, "If Your Majesty should become forgetful of the rights of your subjects, Your Majesty can have no dependence on their loyalty, unless you pay a sacred regard to all their liberties, for it is an established maxim with the Americans that nothing binds them to the Prince, but the Prince's fidelity to them . . . that their liberties are to be secured at any rate, if it be even at the expense of his ruin."

Governor Hutchinson was sorely tempted to place the Grand Incendiary under arrest for treason, but he refrained, afraid a trial in Massachusetts would create still more dissidents and that the removal of Adams to England for trial would make him a martyr. The day would soon come when Hutchinson would admit that his failure to act against Sam Adams early in 1773 was the greatest mistake of his life.

Chapter Fourteen

A product of the Age of Reason and a leading propo-
nent of the principles of the Enlightenment, Sam Adams believed his own preaching that man was logical, and this led him
to make an assumption that was his gravest error. Reason convinced him that the British colonies in North America should be
free and independent, and should form their own nation; he had
been successful in persuading large numbers of his fellow countrymen to share his views, and thus all that remained to accomplish his goal was to use similar persuasion in Britain. He was a
civilized, peace-loving man, and until the eve of the American
Revolution he probably did not take seriously the possibility that
Britain would use force of arms to subdue rebellion and force the
colonies to remain within the fold of empire.

Reason alone could and would persuade Crown and Parliament to grant the American colonies their independence because
it would be in the best interests of all concerned. His attitude was
naive in the extreme, but it must be remembered that Adams was
an exceptionally unsophisticated man. He wrote and spoke in
large terms, but his horizons were narrow, basically bounded by

the limits of Boston, or, when stretched, extending to the boundaries of Massachusetts Bay. He had spent his entire half-century of life in Boston, rarely going farther than Cambridge, and aside from a single tour of the colony that had taken him no farther than Worcester, he had never traveled. Other Boston aristocrats knew London, and a few had gone to Paris, Spain and the Low Countries; but Adams had never visited even Rhode Island or New Hampshire, Massachusetts' nearest neighbors.

Apparently he felt no need to travel, and if he was curious about Philadelphia and New York, the second and third cities of the British New World, he contained his curiosity. His correspondence with Arthur Lee and Patrick Henry, who felt as he did, assured him that Americans everywhere shared his sentiments, which, as a disciple of the Enlightenment, he considered right and natural. So he took it for granted that Britons were cut from the same mold, and needed only to have their eyes opened in order to share his vision of justice, order and right.

In December 1771 he had published an open letter to King George in the *Gazette*, but it had been ignored. Now, with the applause for "Natural Rights" still ringing in his ears, he decided that the time had come to make an appeal to the people of England, Scotland, Wales and Ireland. So he wrote them an open letter that was reprinted throughout the colonies, due to the efficiency of the new Committees of Correspondence, and the alert Franklin saw to it that the document received an airing in the British Isles as well. Two key paragraphs of the letter, which was first published in January 1773, illustrate his ingenuous faith in human nature, which was so at odds with his cynical approach to the creation and dissemination of propaganda:

> If the Americans are disunited from her, and allied with another nation, it will be such a diminution of Britain's wealth and power, as must be fatal to her. The Americans well know their weight and importance in the political scale: that their alliance, and the privilege of a fair trade with them, will be courted by all the powers in Europe; and will turn the balance in favor of any nation that enjoys it. Their situation is such,

their natural advantages so great, and so immense will be their sources of wealth and power, that instead of being subject to any foreign power (as some have vainly imagined) they may soon become the arbiters among nations, and set bounds to kingdoms—be the patrons of universal liberty, and the guardians of the rights of mankind.

The most eligible course for the Americans, and that which they will probably take, is, to form a government of their own, similar to that of the United Provinces of Holland, and offer a free trade to all nations in Europe. This plan will naturally and effectually secure the Americans from the invasion of foreign enemies, for it will be the interest of the European powers to prevent any one nation from acquiring more interest in America than the rest. . . . this . . . policy . . . will secure the Americans, if they should immediately dissolve their union with Great Britain. And if she still pursues false maxims and arbitrary measures, they will undoubtedly soon do it. They have all the advantages for independence, and every temptation to improve them that ever a people had. By dependence on Great Britain, and submission to her laws, the Americans sacrifice about six millions sterling annually.

Adams's vision of the future was almost astonishingly accurate, as this document proves, but his reason failed to convince Britons that America should be granted its independence. Franklin told him as much, but Adams continued to insist that his letter be published, and he was surprised and angry when some of his English correspondents wrote him that British resolve to put the colonies in their place was increasing.

This reaction inspired his own increased irrationality, and his appeals to his compatriots became more emotional and violent. He appeared to lose his composure completely under such pseudonyms as "Vindex," declaring in the *Gazette* of February 1773: "Merciful God! Inspire thy people with wisdom and fortitude, and direct them to gracious ends. In this extreme distress, when the plan of slavery seems nearly complete, O save our country from impending ruin—let not the iron hand of tyranny ravish our laws and seize the badge of freedom, nor avowed corruption and the murderous rage of lawless power be ever seen on the sacred seat of Justice!"

His charges were false and unsubstantiated, inasmuch as no attempt was being made to subject the American people to the shackles of tyranny, and the regime of the stern Hutchinson was notably free of corruption. But as reason had failed, Adams put his propaganda campaign into high gear, and his fanatical diatribe contravened the very principles for which he stood. He resembled the Crusaders of the Dark Ages, who were willing to destroy the Jerusalem they were so intent on saving. Independence had become his sole goal, and such students as Harlow have stated flatly that no reconciliation with Britain, regardless of the terms, would have been acceptable to him.

Like all zealots, Adams gradually came to believe his own propaganda, and in January 1773, he closed a letter to Arthur Lee with a wild outburst: "The Tribute, the Tribute is the indignity which I hope in God will never be patiently borne by a people who, of all the people on the Earth, deserve most to be free."

The ranks of the radicals were growing, to be sure, and Adams was winning many converts, particularly among the younger business and professional men. Bankers and merchants were quick to see the increased profits they could enjoy in an independent nation, and many lawyers, doctors and teachers were intoxicated by Sam Adams's dreams. But the truth of the matter was that Britain and her colonies were enjoying unprecedented mutual prosperity. An increasing band of America's friends in Parliament, among them the brilliant young Charles James Fox, were seeking an equitable solution of the problem. Middle-aged moderates like Dr. Franklin and Colonel George Washington, the prosperous Virginia planter, hoped that extremes could be avoided. Men of goodwill on both shores of the Atlantic were working toward an understanding that would tighten the bonds of empire and make both the mother country and her colonies still stronger and wealthier. Certainly Franklin, in his letters from London, believed that goal within reach.

Sam Adams refused to believe it because he would be satisfied with nothing less than independence. George III was a tyrant, his ministers were cunning rogues and American liberties were in critical danger of being destroyed. His increasingly violent demands for action alarmed the British, who assumed he spoke for the majority of the American people, and although he confidently assumed such a pose, it was far from the truth. It is startling to discover that the Boston town meeting of November 2, 1772, was attended by fewer than three hundred persons, or only 18 per cent of the eligible voters. Most of those present were radicals—their opponents did not bother to attend the session—and thus an overwhelming majority voted in favor of the establishment of the Committees of Correspondence.

But Sam Adams was not unopposed in his efforts; Governor Hutchinson was a worthy opponent, and in an address opening a session of the Assembly in January 1773, he presented telling arguments to counter the logic of the "Rights of the Colonies." The assumption made by the authors of that document as to the unlimited powers of the legislature was false, he said. Historically and legally the various charters establishing self-government in Massachusetts conferred on the legislature the right to make laws that were *consistent* with British laws. Consequently the laws of England were binding on her colonies. Furthermore, he insisted, the colonies were either subject to imperial control or were independent; they could not be both. And finally, in a powerful plea for reason, he declared that in the event Parliament abused its power in making laws for the colonies, it was the duty of the colonists, as reasonable, honorable men, to seek redress through legal means available to all British subjects rather than to claim that Parliament had no such rights in the first place.

Many of the towns that had not yet ratified the agreement setting up the Committees of Correspondence found it difficult to counter the logic of the governor's position, and hesitated for months before Sam Adams and his radicals exerted extreme pressure urging them to fall into line. In the main, however, Adams held his fire—because he was not yet ready to strike.

His caution is best seen in advice he gave a group of Rhode Islanders who came to him for help after a truly spontaneous crisis erupted in Providence late in 1772. The commander of a

Royal Navy warship, the H.M.S. *Gaspee*, had been meticulous in hunting down smugglers, and a group of furious radicals had set the ship on fire and destroyed it. This was an open, outright act of armed insurrection, and if Britain retaliated in kind, the colonies were not yet ready to band together in revolt. It was necessary to buy time, Sam Adams believed, and writing to various Rhode Island radical leaders in January and February 1773, he urgently counseled circumspection:

> I think it justly may be considered that, since the Constitution is already destined to suffer unavoidable dissolution, an open and manly determination of the Assembly not to consent to its ruin would show to the world and posterity that the people were virtuous, though unfortunate, and sustained the shock with dignity.
>
> You will allow me to observe that this is a matter in which the whole American continent is deeply concerned, and a submission of the Colony of Rhode Island to this enormous claim of power would be made a precedent for all the rest. They ought, indeed, to consider deeply their interest in the struggle of a single Colony, and their duty to afford her all practicable aid. This last is a consideration which I shall not fail to mention to my particular friends when our Assembly shall sit the next week.
>
> Should it be the determination of a weak administration to push this measure to the utmost at all events, and the Commissioners call in the aid of troops for that purpose, it would be impossible for me to say what might be the consequences— perhaps a most violent political earthquake through the whole British Empire, if not its total destruction.
>
> I have long feared this unhappy contest between Great Britain and America would end in rivers of blood; should that be the case, America, I think, may wash her hands in innocence; yet it is the highest prudence to prevent, if possible, so dreadful a calamity. Some such provocation as is now offered to Rhode Island will, in all probability, be the occasion of it. Let us, therefore, consider whether, in the present case, the shock that is coming upon you may not be evaded, which is a distinct part of the question proposed. . . . I beg first to propose for

your consideration, whether a Circular Letter from your Assembly, on the occasion, to those of the other Colonies, might not tend to the advantage of the general cause and of Rhode Island in particular. I would think it would induce each of them at least to enjoin their agents in Great Britain to represent the severity of your case in the strongest terms.

The Rhode Islanders followed Adams's advice, and their Committee of Correspondence sent a mild letter to the committees in the other colonies, asking only for legislative support. Adams, in so many words, suggested evasion, so Rhode Island sidestepped, thus avoiding a direct confrontation that would have made it necessary for Britain to send troops and ships to Providence. After admitting the "inevitability" of war and piously cleansing America's hands of responsibility, the Grand Incendiary urged that no large fires be lighted for the moment.

By the early months of 1773, Sam Adams had so much become the recognized leader of the independence movement that there was a change in his personal habits. Radical leaders from other colonies who came to Massachusetts for conferences were his house guests, and Boston radicals sought him out more frequently at home. So he spent less time in taverns, and his study became the literal center of the conspiracy against the Crown. But it was an open conspiracy: none of his visitors tried to conceal his presence or identity, even though it was known that Governor Hutchinson kept a list of all those who came to the house.

The influx of visitors placed an increased burden on the uncomplaining Elizabeth, whose slender means were strained by the need to provide food and drink for them. It was fortunate that, through no efforts of her impractical husband, their income was slightly increased. The Assembly now paid Adams one hundred pounds per year as clerk, a raise of ten pounds, and the general prosperity Boston was enjoying enabled him to charge a higher fee for the rental of the Adams wharves. Thanks in large part to the suggestion of Arthur Lee, who was familiar with Adams's precarious financial situation, newspapers and periodicals that reprinted his essays and articles throughout the colonies sent him sums of one or two pounds for the privilege. It has been assumed that these voluntary contributions increased his income by an additional one hundred pounds or more each year, but no precise figures have ever been found. Adams was so preoccupied with the struggle with Britain that he paid little or no attention to such mundane matters as the income he earned, and Elizabeth was far too busy making ends meet to keep a ledger. Somehow guests were entertained and fed, the family was clothed and the master of the house could go about his business without worry. It was not surprising that Cousin John, once again active in politics, whose lure he could not resist, noted in his *Diary* that Elizabeth Adams was "the best and most frugal housewife in all of Boston, and was second to none in her devotion to her husband."

The diversions of the Adams household were few in these trying times. Grace was always said by the master himself when he dined at home, and no matter how pressing his business, some member of the family always read aloud from the Bible after dinner. But the portrait of Adams as a blue-nosed Puritan painted by some of his contemporaries was somewhat exaggerated. According to his son and daughter he greatly enjoyed the company of young people, and when he could spare an evening he loved to play word games with them.

In the warm weather he occasionally could be persuaded to sail down the bay in one of John Hancock's merchant ships, outings on which the radical leaders combined business and pleasure. A sedentary life was making Adams plump, in spite of his indifference to food, so he resumed a habit of his younger days and took brisk horseback rides into the country when the weather permitted.

One of his diversions was never mentioned by his relatives. He continued to frequent the waterfront taverns, where he sat with dock workers, merchant sailors and the trollops of Boston, enjoying the company of the city's lowest class. These visits cannot be described purely as relaxation, however. Adams was continuing to mend his political fences, and it was no accident that the artisans of Boston remained his strongest supporters. Whether he drank, used snuff or smoked an occasional pipe in the taverns is unknown; he may have abstained, but if he did not, his friends protected him by surrounding him with a wall of discreet silence.

His son, who was graduated from Harvard in 1770, undertook the study of medicine as an apprentice to Dr. Joseph Warren, and in 1773 received his degree as a Doctor of Medicine. He opened his own private practice, but later gave it up to join the Continental Army as a surgeon.

Sam Adams remained close to his sister Polly, now Mrs. James Allen, and she often visited the Adams house in Boston, accompanied by her three children. Adams's wife and daughter returned these visits each summer, but the head of the family permitted himself no holidays. The needs of the cause were too urgent, he claimed, but the truth of the matter was that his own obsessions permitted him no respite.

In all probability Adams was faithful to his wife. No scandal concerning him was ever mentioned by the British, who would have been delighted to blacken his name. Unlike Hancock and several of his other close associates, he never acquired a reputation as a ladies' man.

Sam Adams demonstrated his love of liberty in his personal life when he and his wife were presented with a black slave girl as a gift in 1765. He immediately granted the young woman, Surry, her freedom, and she remained with the family as their cook for a half-century. She became Adams's strongest supporter, and visitors were warned not to quarrel with him at the dinner table, even on impersonal political subjects, because an indignant Surry might rush out of the kitchen and empty a cooking pot over the head of one who dared to disagree with the head of the household.

As the war approached Adams made more and more enemies, and he was frequently urged to permit the longshoremen and artisans of the town to provide him with an informal bodyguard; but he always laughed and said he needed none. He was right: his constant companion as he went about the city was a huge, fiercely loyal Newfoundland dog named Queue. It could not have been accidental that the animal hated the sight of a Redcoat uniform and had to be restrained whenever he saw a British soldier. On several occasions a Redcoat slashed at the beast with a sword or musketbutt in self-protection, but Adams liked to boast that Queue bore a charmed life and could never be killed by a Briton. The dog lived to a very old age, and his master was grief-stricken when he died.

Until the early 1770s Sam Adams enjoyed remarkably good health, but at approximately the time the crisis with Great Britain entered its final, convulsive stage, he began to be troubled by arthritis. His son declared that he got too little exercise, and insisted that he spend an hour each day working in his garden. Adams obeyed—but he held political meetings there, with his colleagues following him as he dug out weeds, pruned and clipped. Occasionally an associate helped him, and it was a standing joke in Boston that any radical leader who had a scratch on his hand had acquired it in Adams's rose garden.

Early in 1773 John Adams made a significant entry in his *Diary* that indicated Cousin Sam was not as indifferent to personal appearances as he liked to have it appear. The entry read:

> Spent this evening with Mr. Samuel Adams at his house. Had much conversation about the state of affairs,—Cushing, Phillips, Hancock, Hawley, Gerry, Hutchinson, Sewall, Quincy &c. Adams was more cool, genteel and agreeable than common; concealed and restrained his passions, &c. He affects to despise riches, and not dread poverty; but no man is more ambitious of entertaining his friends handsomely, or of making a decent and elegant appearance than he. He has lately new covered and glazed his house, and painted it very neatly, and has new papered, painted and furnished his rooms; so that you visit at a very genteel house, and are very politely received and entertained.
>
> Mr. Adams corresponds with Hawley, Gerry and others. He corresponds in England and in several of the other Provinces. His time is all employed in the public service.

This account, written by a distinguished relative of impeccable virtue, is at odds with all other stories of the life Sam Adams led, but it is impossible to imagine Cousin John being less than totally truthful. It appears possible that Sam Adams deliberately created an impression of indifference to anything but the cause because the image helped the propaganda he was creating. He missed no opportunity to advance his great crusade, as he proved to the entire civilized world later in 1773.

He was far more complicated a character than most of his contemporaries realized, and this deception, which Cousin John indicated was deliberate, suited his purposes. If his campaign for American independence was going to succeed, it was necessary to create the impression that the desire of the American people for freedom was spontaneous and self-generating, which meant that the man who provided the principal dynamic energy for the movement had to remain faceless. But 1773 was an extraordinary year in the developing deterioration of the relationship between Britain and her colonies, and Adams found that the events he inspired thrust him permanently into the limelight.

Chapter Fifteen

Parliament had consistently refused to force a show-down with its North American dependencies, as Prime Minister Lord North proved himself more malleable than his later attitude indicated. King George was irritated by the attacks made on him by the vocal minority of American radicals, but his advisers assured him the group was harmless and persuaded him to turn the other cheek, a difficult feat at best for the proud, stubborn head of the House of Hanover. So, until 1773, an uneasy balance was maintained, and fundamental issues were ignored, enabling the decentralized empire to remain intact.

But Great Britain was subjected to the pressures of govern-mental centralization evident on the Continent, and an economic crisis of the first magnitude made it necessary for her to contem-plate a major shift in her relations with her colonies. There was a risk involved, to be sure, but the ministry and Parliament misread the American temperament and considered the possibil-ity of causing an explosion to be slight.

The crisis was caused by a grave decline in the affairs of the East India Company, a private organization that, because of its power and wealth, had achieved a quasi-official standing. It ruled the subcontinent of India and was the largest single mercantile company on earth, so its success or failure in any given year played a large role in the determination of the British economy.

For decades the East India Company had enjoyed a unique, privileged status and had been allowed to attend its own affairs without molestation. But the liberal Whigs—the same men who had repeatedly demonstrated their sympathy for the American colonists—had become convinced that the abuses perpetrated by the company were endangering the whole British system of government, and in 1773 they mustered enough strength in Parliament to pass the Regulating Act, which clamped controls on the company's operations.

These handcuffs made it far more difficult for the company to function, and the problem was severely aggravated by the fact that the officers of the organization found themselves with a huge surplus of China tea on their hands. Unless they could find a market for the product, it appeared they might be forced into bankruptcy, which could ruin the economy of Great Britain herself.

Until 1773 the company's methods of distribution had been cumbersome and old-fashioned, which had permitted large profits to be drained away by others. It had sold its products at public auctions in London, and thereafter middlemen had distributed the wares, earning the larger share of profits. Now, in the hope of getting rid of the vast quantities of tea and restoring its financial credibility, the company offered a deal to Parliament. It would accept the Regulating Act with good grace, but in return it asked for a monopoly on trade in the North American colonies, where it proposed to sell tea direct to the retailer through its own agents.

This solution sounded reasonable to Parliament. Approximately 97 per cent of all tea consumed in America had come from the company, the rest being purchased from Holland, so there would be no change in the basic situation. The elimination of the middleman would not only enable the company to earn much larger profits, but would make it possible to sell tea to the American consumer at a far lower price, which, Parliament reasoned, should make the prospect appealing to the colonists.

But the American merchant, like his British counterpart, was frozen out of the new operation. A large number of prosperous Americans, John Hancock among them, had kept their own agents in London, and had themselves purchased company tea at auction. Now they would be excluded, and the profits they had earned would go directly into the coffers of the East India Company.

The American agents in London worked frantically to prevent the granting of the monopoly to the company, but the package proposal was so attractive that they were ignored. Benjamin Franklin and a few other Americans of stature in Britain warned that the plan was dangerous, that their fellow countrymen would feel they were being exploited, even though the cost of tea would be reduced dramatically. Americans would resist, they warned, and as virtually the entire population drank tea, the opposition would be even greater than it had been under the Stamp Act and the Townshend Acts.

But Franklin and his colleagues could not stem the tide. There was a residue of resentment in Parliament against Americans for their past resistance to the supreme authority of the empire, and the scheme was so eminently sensible, solved so many problems, that even men normally friendly to the colonies believed the predictions of gloom to be exaggerated. The scheme would be beneficial to virtually everyone, a handful of British and American merchants excepted; Americans would pay much less for their tea, and the public outcry, if any was raised, soon would die away.

Sam Adams must have been aware of the ominous situation, for John Hancock, who corresponded frantically with his agent in London, is sure to have kept him informed. But he made no mention of it in his correspondence or newspaper articles, and if he braced himself for what lay ahead, he must have smiled in private. The gathering storm was perfect for his purposes.

In the meantime he kept busy, enjoying himself thoroughly as he debated with Governor Hutchinson on the abstract question of Parliament's supremacy over colonial legislatures. Only by keeping the issue alive could he hope to gain his ultimate ends.

On March 5, 1773, he supervised the celebration of the anniversary of the Boston "Massacre," saw to it that the Sons of Liberty filled Faneuil Hall for the occasion and then thoughtfully had copies of the address delivered by Dr. Benjamin Church printed in large numbers. These were sent to Committees of Correspondence in other colonies and to America's friends in Britain.

He also stepped up the pace of his personal correspondence with John Dickinson of Pennsylvania, whose *Farmer's Letters*, written in much the same spirit as Adams's articles and essays, had been keeping the spirit of rebellion alive in Pennsylvania, Maryland and New Jersey. They discussed the idea of calling a congress consisting of the members of the several Committees of Correspondence, but agreed that the time was not yet ripe. A major issue was needed that would unite the colonies, and a premature meeting might dissolve in squabbling prompted by individual or regional interests.

At about this same time Adams began to develop an even more important correspondence with Richard Henry Lee of Virginia, a kindred spirit whose ideas on independence and its achievement were identical to his own. Arthur Lee's brother was assuming a position in the South similar to that held by Adams in New England, and was providing the spark that kept the "torch of liberty" lighted. The pair were frank and cheerful conspirators, and their letters freely discussed ways and means to spread the "urge for freedom," as they called it. In one of his first letters, written on April 10, 1773, Adams said, in part:

> I had often thought it a misfortune, rather than a fault, in the friends of American independence and freedom, not taking care to open every channel of communication. The Colonies are all embarked on the same bottom. The liberties of all are alike invaded by the same haughty power. The conspirators against their common rights have indeed exerted their brutal force, or applied their insidious acts differently in the several colonies, as they thought it would best serve their

purpose of oppression and tyranny. How necessary, therefore, that *all* should be early acquainted with the particular circumstances of *each*, in order that the wisdom and strength of the *whole* may be employed upon every occasion. We have heard of bloodshed and even civil war in our sister Colony of North Carolina, and how strange it is that the best account we have of that tragical scene should be brought to us from England.

This Province, and this town especially, have suffered a great share of ministerial wrath and insolence. But God be thanked, there is, I trust, a spirit prevailing which will not submit to slavery. The compliance of New York in making annual provision for a military force designed to carry acts of tyranny into execution, the timidity of some, and the silence of others, are discouraging. But the active vigilance, the manly generosity, and the steady perseverance of Virginia and South Carolina give us reason to hope that the fire of true liberty and patriotism will at length spread itself through the continent. The consequences would be the acquisition of all we wish for. The friends of liberty in this town lately made a successful attempt to obtain an explicit sentiment of a great number of towns of this Province, and the number is daily increasing. The very attempt was alarming to our adversaries, and the happy effects of it mortifying to them. I would propose it for your consideration, whether the establishment of Committees of Correspondence among the *several* towns, in *every* Colony, would tend to promote that general union upon which the security of the whole depends. The reception of the truly patriotic resolves of the House of Burgesses of Virginia gladdens the hearts of all who are friends to liberty.

Our Committee of Correspondence had a special meeting on the occasion, and determined to circulate immediately printed copies of them in every town in the Province, in order to make them as extensively useful as possible. I am desired by them to assure you of their veneration for your most ancient Colony and their unfeigned esteem for the gentlemen of your Committee. This, indeed, is a poor return. I hope you will have the hearty concurrence of every Assembly on the continent. It is a measure which will be attended with great and good consequences. Our Assembly is dissolved, and writs will soon be issued, according to the Charter, for a new Assembly to be holden the last Wednesday in May next. I think I can almost assure you there will be a return of such members as will heartily co-operate with you in your spirited measures. The enormous stride in erecting what may be called a court of inquisition in America is sufficient to excite indignation in every heart capable of feeling.

I am expecting an authentic copy of that commission, which I shall send to you by the first opportunity after I have received it. The letter from the new Secretary of State to the Governor of Rhode Island, which possibly you saw in the newspapers, may be depended upon as genuine. I received it from a gentleman of the Council of that Colony, who took it from the original. I wish the Assembly of that Province had acted with more firmness than they have done; but, as the court of inquiry is adjourned, they may possibly have another trial. I have a thousand things to say to you, but am prevented by want of time, having had but an hour's notice of the sailing of this vessel. I cannot conclude, however, without assuring you that a letter from you, as often as your leisure admits, would lay me under great obligations.

The groundwork was being laid with firmness and dispatch by the Grand Incendiary. He and three radical colleagues, Cushing, Hancock and Phillips, were elected as Boston's representatives to the new Assembly by an almost unanimous vote of the town meeting on May 6. The new "instructions" which Adams wrote for himself and duly publicized thoughtfully provided for full cooperation with "our noble, patriotic sister Colony of Virginia." Thereafter the legislatures of the two colonies, led in Massachusetts by Adams and his cohorts and in Virginia by Richard Henry Lee, Jefferson and Henry, worked closely together in all matters, setting an example for the other colonies and exerting a tremendous influence on their neighbors.

Governor Hutchinson viewed these developments with growing alarm, and wrote to London that he expected an outbreak of armed hostilities whenever the American radicals felt the time was ripe. Only the firm exercise of British strength, or conversely, the use of great restraint, he believed, would prevent a serious insurrection.

Copies of letters from Hutchinson, Lieutenant Governor Oliver and other Crown officials fell into the hands of America's friends in England, and were given to Benjamin Franklin, who was asked that they not be made public. He forwarded them to Sam Adams, who had the gallery cleared, and then, in his perennial capacity as clerk, read carefully selected excerpts to the Assembly "proving" that the Crown officials were engaging in a nefarious scheme to deprive the people of their liberty.

The Assembly responded with appropriate indignation, and Adams promptly wrote a resolution condemning Hutchinson and Oliver, which he followed with a strongly worded petition to the Crown, demanding their dismissal as well as a promise that neither would ever again hold appointive office in Massachusetts or any other colony.

It is difficult to determine whether Adams seriously expected the request to be heeded, but he succeeded in widening the breach between the executive and legislative branches. This further heated the atmosphere prior to the crisis that soon would break, and may have carried a greater long-range effect than Adams had dared to hope, for Hutchinson was recalled in the winter of 1773–1774. He was an able official, although not as wise and far seeing as Sir Francis Bernard had been, and he governed Massachusetts under circumstances that would have tried the mettle of any man. His worst offense, in the eyes of Sam Adams and his colleagues, was that of being loyal to the king in the first place. They expected nothing else from a governor who was an Englishman, but Hutchinson was a "traitor" because, as a native-born American, he continued to support the Crown, and they had gone so far in influencing public opinion that many of their fellow colonists shared their view.

By the summer of 1773 the radicals had forged a remarkable degree of union. Not one town had been able to withstand internal and external pressure to form its own Committee of Correspondence, in actuality an insurrectionist executive body, and every community represented in the Assembly now had its own committee. The Lee brothers and Henry were enjoying a similar success in Virginia, and Sam Adams confidently looked forward to "an Union among the Colonies . . . an *Assembly of States.*" Great Britain, he predicted with a confidence that was not misplaced, would need strong, very competent ministers to deal with such a body.

Rumors were heard everywhere in the colonies during the summer of 1773 that a congress would be held in the near future, and moderates shared the view of the radicals that such a meeting was inevitable unless the differences between the mother country and her offspring were settled in the near future on a mutually amicable basis.

As yet there was no single issue on which the colonies could unite, but the spirit of unrest deepened. The ubiquitous Sam Adams continued to contribute substantially to the cause, his essays in the *Gazette,* the *Massachusetts Spy* and other journals indicating that a reign of tyranny and oppression was already under way. His correspondence increased even more, to the point that it appears to have been almost impossible for any one man to have written so much.

Yet he continued to stay in the background whenever possible, knowing that at this stage of development he could operate more effectively in anonymity. Governor Hutchinson heard the rumors that an intercolonial congress would convene in the near future, but even he failed to realize what a large role Sam Adams was playing behind the scenes. In a report to the Colonial Office written in July 1773, the Massachusetts governor declared that he had heard that the Speaker of the Rhode Island Assembly was the force behind the proposed congress. It is obvious from this that he had no idea that the Rhode Islanders acting as stalking horses were responding to constant suggestions from the Grand Incendiary, who wanted to make it appear that some colony other than Massachusetts occasionally took the lead.

Adams's private correspondence in the spring and summer of 1773 fails to indicate clearly whether he envisioned complete home rule within the ranks of the British Empire for the American colonies, or whether he wanted a totally independent state. It is probable that he himself did not know, believing it would depend on the response of Britain to the American demands, which were being asserted more loudly with each passing month. His letters to strangers indicated his abhorrence of war, and he frequently repeated the pious hope that bloodshed could be averted. But in his correspondence with men to whom he could speak more freely, he made it plain that he knew Britain could not accept such a direct challenge to her authority and would be compelled to respond with force. "How many regiments will be thought necessary," he asked Arthur Lee in an outburst of shrewd rhetoric, "to penetrate the heart of a populous country and subdue a sensible, enlightened, and brave people to the ignominious terms of slavery?"

No one knew better than Sam Adams that people would not revolt or take a stand together in defiance of authority for the sake of an abstract principle. Words such as *liberty* and *freedom* were rallying cries, but he needed specific incidents. The sinking of the *Gaspee*, an accident in which a merchantman was attacked by a Royal Navy warship, late in 1772 had been perfect, but he had not been ready for a crisis at that time, and consequently had kept the lid tightly screwed on the emotions of his fellow countrymen.

Now, a half-year later, he was better prepared. Every town in Massachusetts had its Committee of Correspondence representatives, so the network of insurrection was formed and ready for action. Virginia was similarly prepared, and Rhode Island, Connecticut, Delaware, Pennsylvania and South Carolina were not far behind. Of the more populous colonies, only New York was lagging, in part because of the presence there of General Gage, whose regiments were an intimidating influence.

Making the most of the material at hand, Adams tried to persuade the Massachusetts Assembly to impeach Governor Hutchinson on the basis of the correspondence sent from England. But, even though the legislature was usually subservient to his will, the members balked. The evidence was too flimsy for the lawyers, and not even the most ardent Patriots among them could find a shred of authority in the various charters granted the colony for the removal from office by the people's representatives of a Crown-appointed viceroy.

Sam Adams was eager to test his new strength, knowing the public would grow weary of his propaganda unless he could produce specific results. Parliament obligingly filled the vacuum, and in May 1773, the Tea Act was passed and became law.

Chapter Sixteen

Economic determinist historians led by the late Charles A. Beard have argued that the merchants who were deprived of income by the Tea Act sparked American opposition to it, but their approach is somewhat oversimplified. Such merchants as John Hancock were in the vanguard of the opposition, but the initial impetus was provided by practical politicians like Sam Adams, who had been searching for precisely such an issue.

On the surface the Tea Act did little to threaten American liberties. It continued the tax of threepence per pound to which the colonists had objected mildly, but when the news of the act's passage crossed the Atlantic, the housewives of America reacted as Parliament had believed they would. They were delighted that the retail price of tea had been cut almost in half.

According to an early nineteenth-century historical myth that survives even today in the schoolbooks of America, King George and his ministers intended to use the new Tea Act as a means of testing American sentiment in order to determine whether new, additional taxes should be imposed on the colonies. Those who accepted this view simply adopted Sam Adams's propaganda line without subjecting it to a critical scrutiny.

There was no reason for the king or Lord North to test the waters of America, for the colonists had been paying the new tax without serious complaint for three years. While it was undoubtedly true that for each pound of tea on which a tax was paid, at least three additional pounds were smuggled into the colonies, the major merchants were paying a considerable tax on the tea they imported regularly. The records of the tax commissioners in Boston indicate that many hundreds of thousands of pounds of tea moved through that one port. In September 1773, prior to the imposition of the new act, John Hancock quietly paid the tax on the importation of 110,000 pounds of tea.

Had the new law been passed a few years earlier, it would have attracted little or no attention anywhere in the colonies, and even such radicals as Sam Adams would have had feeble grounds on which to protest. By 1773 the radicals had done their work so well, however, that even this mild law, which benefited the people of America as a whole, could be attacked as an instrument intended to deprive the colonists of their precious liberty. Tension had been kept at a high pitch for so long that propaganda, properly presented, could create precisely the crisis Sam Adams, Richard Henry Lee and others sought. Through appropriate manipulation of the issue, they could compel Britain to surrender to the radicals or go to war in order to enforce the authority of Parliament and the Crown.

Sam Adams realized he could not forever maintain a crisis atmosphere without producing results. For years he had been crying that American freedom was being destroyed by tyrants, but he had been able to manufacture only a few relatively minor incidents to prove his contention. And he had carefully sidestepped when the *Gaspee* had been burned. Certainly the opportunity offered him now was an act of Heaven rather than of Parliament, and he responded accordingly. It was no accident that opposition to the new act first crystallized in Boston.

In June 1773, Adams received a letter from Arthur Lee that convinced him the time was precisely right for a major show of opposition to the Crown. Historians have been unable to determine whether he received this letter before or after he heard about the passage of the Tea Act, but their quarrels are irrelevant. He must have heard the two unrelated items at approximately the same time, and what is important is that he related them in his own mind. Lee wrote, in part: "The prospect of a general war in Europe strengthens daily; and it is hardly probable that another year will pass away before that event. You cannot, therefore, be too speedy in preparing to reap full advantage of this opportunity. . . ."

Lee must have been indulging in wishful thinking, interpreting political developments in Europe so they fitted his own desires. The facts disputed his contention: France had not yet recovered from her defeat a decade earlier, and no other Continental power was ready to challenge Great Britain, the strongest nation on earth.

But Sam Adams happily accepted his friend's prediction because it so perfectly fitted his own aims. A Britain threatened with a major European war would need peace within her own household, and therefore would be inclined to yield to the demands of her colonies. The time for mere rhetoric had passed, and although he maintained a steady propaganda barrage in the press, writing under a variety of pseudonyms as usual, he was preparing for real action, devoting the entire summer of 1773 to that end.

Historians have long argued whether Sam Adams or Benjamin Franklin first made the specific proposal for the holding of a full-scale intercolonial congress, but it appears they conceived of the idea at approximately the same time. Their aims were far from identical, however: Franklin wanted to find some mutual accommodation with Great Britain, if possible, while Adams was thinking only in terms of determining common grounds on which to unite in opposition to Britain.

Even the friends who shared his desire for independence were afraid he might be going too far, and Arthur Lee, then in London, wrote him a pointed letter in the summer of 1773:

You have with great propriety mentioned, in your answer to the Governor's first speech, that the drawing a line being an arduous undertaking and of general concernment, you would not attempt it without a general Congress. Of the justice of this I am clear, but doubtful of its policy. I cannot help thinking that the leading men in each Assembly, communicating with one another, would form a plan more wise and well-considered than could be expected from a public body. And there would be no danger of effectual opposition to it in the different Assemblies, when the time came in which they could demand a ratification of it from this country, with assurance of success.

My great objection to a public Congress is, that it will arouse this country, and perhaps incense her to some hostile measure. The only contention in which we are unequal to her is that of arms. It is not wise policy, therefore, to provoke this issue of the dispute, if our purpose can be accomplished without it. For with all her ill usage, Britain is still our mother country.

But Adams continued to press for a congress, meanwhile preparing the Massachusetts Committee of Correspondence for an emergency. In September 1773, he made his intentions plain in an essay he wrote for the *Gazette* under the pseudonym of "A." This diatribe so alarmed Governor Hutchinson that he sent a copy of it to the Colonial Office, finding it necessary to remark only that the minister to whom Adams referred was Lord Dartmouth, the head of that department. The essay read, in part:

If we will now petition in such a style as his Lordship will call decent and temperate, that is, so as administration shall be able to avail themselves in Parliament in saying that we have, to use their own words, virtually given up our claim, we shall then have everything else we want, and his Lordship will endeavor that the acknowledged right of Parliament shall never be exercised, except a case of absolute necessity should happen. But who is to be the judge when this case of necessity happens? I fear if these revenue acts should be repealed on this principle, it would very soon be deemed necessary, by other acts, to give and grant to the King the property of the Colonists again, and enable him to apply it to the purpose of establishing a tyranny over them. His Lordship, I dare say, will not in this case think it safe to pledge himself to the Colonies.

If ever another petition should be sent from America, relating to the common rights, it is presumed it will employ the joint wisdom of whole, in a Congress, or in some other way, conformable to the plan of union proposed by Virginia, and adopted by the Assembly of this and such other Colonies whose Assemblies have had opportunity of meeting since. It certainly would be inconsistent with that plan of union for this or any other Colony to come into a new system of American policy without consulting the whole.

But why should administration expect any further petitions? Our sentiments and resolutions are sufficiently known to them already. We have spoken without reservation. We scorn to say anything that looks like duplicity or cunning. Our petitions have always been expressed in terms decent and temperate, as well as explicit. If they expect we shall alter our tone with a view of having it thought we have altered our sentiments, when in reality we have not, this is a low artifice which Americans will always despise, and therefore it is highly probable they will find themselves mistaken. Solomon tells us there is a time to speak and a time to be silent; and perhaps it requires as much wisdom to determine the time as what to speak. Speak ye every man the truth to his neighbor, however inconsistent it may be with the maxims of cunning politicians, is a rule which ought to be, and ever will be, regarded by an honest community as well as by every honest individual whenever he speaks at all. It is certainly not a time now for Britain and the Colonies to prevaricate with each other. The matter in controversy is of too serious and important a nature to be trifled with. It will be folly for Britain, and with half an eye she may have discerned it already, to attempt to settle this controversy by mere power and brute force. If, perchance, it should be admitted that at present she is powerful, would it not for all this be wiser for her to consider how long she is likely to remain so. America is daily increasing in numbers and consequently in strength; and the balance of power may be shifted before the most sagacious are aware of it. . . .

It was plain that Adams was spoiling for a fight. A few days later on September 27, 1773, again writing in the *Gazette*, this time as "Observation," he shrugged off the advice of those who believed the time inappropriate for the holding of an intercolonial meeting:

> The very important dispute between Britain and America has, for a long time, employed the pens of statesmen in both countries, but no plan of union is yet agreed upon between them; the dispute still continues, and everything floats in uncertainty. As I have long contemplated the subject with fixed intention, I beg leave to offer a proposal to my countrymen, viz. that a CONGRESS OF AMERICAN STATES be assembled as soon as possible; draw up a Bill of Rights, and publish it to the world; choose an ambassador to reside at the British Court to act for the united Colonies; appoint where the Congress shall annually meet, and how it may be summoned upon any extraordinary occasion, what further steps are to be taken, &c.
>
> The expense of an annual Congress would be very trifling, and the advantages would undoubtedly be great; in this way the wisdom of the continent might, upon all important occasions, be collected and operate for the interest of the whole people. Nor may anyone imagine this plan, if carried into execution, will injure Great Britain; for it will be the most likely way to bring the two countries to a right understanding, and to settle matters in dispute advantageously for both. So sensible are the people of America that they are in possession of a fine country and other superior advantages,—their rapid increase and growing importance—it cannot ever be thought they will give up their claim to equal liberty with any other people on earth; but rather, as they find their power perpetually increasing, look for greater perfection in just liberty and government than other nations or even Britain ever enjoyed. . . .
>
> No people that ever trod the stage of the world have had so glorious a prospect as now rises before the Americans. There is nothing good or great but their wisdom may acquire, and to what heights they will arrive in the progress of time no man

can conceive. That Great Britain should continue to *insult* and *alienate* the growing millions who inhabit this country, on whom she greatly depends, and on whose alliance in future time her existence as a nation may be suspended, is perhaps as glaring an instance of human folly as ever disgraced politicians or put common sense to the blush.

Copies of this appeal, which combined a proposal for the holding of an intercolonial congress with chauvinism and a prophecy of things to come, were sent to every town in Massachusetts, to the Committees of Correspondence in other colonies and to newspapers throughout America. Sam Adams was preparing with great care for the tempest he intended to create, and he overlooked no angle. Writing under the aegis of the Boston town meeting, he sent out a circular letter advocating a "Confederacy of the whole continent," and copies of this document also were widely disseminated. Other Massachusetts town committees were urged not to abandon their rights, no matter what pressures were applied against them, and Adams wrote at length to Joseph Hawley, the radical leader in the Massachusetts interior, telling him to prepare for the storm. On October 21 he sent another circular letter to the other colonies' Committees of Correspondence, directly suggesting that a congress be convened as soon as arrangements could be made.

Not the least extraordinary aspect of the campaign for American independence in the period prior to the actual outbreak of the war was the brazen attitude of the men who inspired, instigated and conducted the movement. Throughout history revolutionists have been conspirators who have functioned in the dark, concealing their activities from the authorities they have wanted to supplant, but Sam Adams and his colleagues made no attempt to act, write or speak with discretion. They had grown so strong and were so confident of their local political power that they openly thumbed their noses at Crown officials, advertised their aims in the press, held their meetings in public places and exchanged long letters with careless abandon.

Certainly the attitude displayed by the Colonial Office and its representatives made a mockery of the claim that the colonies were being subjected to oppression and tyranny. The long British tradition of personal freedoms was still being scrupulously observed, and no attempts were being made to initiate censorship, restrict the right to hold meetings for any purpose or clamp down on individuals. It had long been rumored that the principal agitators, Sam Adams in particular, might be placed under arrest and taken to England for trial; indeed, the ministry had contemplated such a move, but had refrained from taking it.

This reluctance was prompted, in part, by the Cabinet's desire to avoid violating the personal freedom that—as Adams was so fond of saying—was sacred to British subjects. Lord North and his associates were also motivated by sound political considerations; they knew the arrest of Adams and his colleagues would arouse sympathetic support for the rebels on the part of men who previously had not responded to their propaganda. But above all, the deep-rooted belief of British officials that the would-be insurrectionists were merely bluffing was responsible for the lack of a positive response.

It was inconceivable to the ministry and Parliament that men who were members of the class that most nearly formed an aristocracy in America were serious in their proclamations, that they meant it when they said they were willing to go to war for their independence. Richard Henry Lee and Arthur Lee were members of one of Virginia's most aristocratic families. Sam and John Adams bore one of the most respected surnames in Massachusetts. John Hancock was New England's wealthiest merchant, and Dr. Joseph Warren was a physician of great stature. Gentlemen, the ministry reasoned, might indulge in rhetoric, but would not actually raise the banner of revolt.

One man who knew better was Governor Hutchinson of Massachusetts, who was distressed because the Colonial Office failed to heed his repeated warnings. Unable to stem the rebel tide, outmaneuvered at every turn by Sam Adams, he knew his days in office were numbered and he began to think of his own future. Hutchinson was the first to read the handwriting scrawled in such large letters on the walls of Boston, and even before he was inundated by the storm over the Tea Act, he wrote several letters to the Colonial Office suggesting his appointment to various posts he considered suitable for a former colonial viceroy. In spite of his forebodings, he did not escape in time.

Chapter Seventeen

East India Company agents reached their posts in the three principal American cities—Boston, Philadelphia and New York Town—on or about October 1, 1773, and word was received soon thereafter that the merchant ships laden with tea would sail from England around the middle of the month, arriving in the New World in mid-November or soon thereafter. The radicals prepared to act, and on October 13, Arthur Lee wrote to Sam Adams from London:

> The introduction of the tea ought, I think, to be opposed. . . . The confidence with which the least appearance of safety inspires cowards should make us cautious in permitting Administration to succeed in any of their measures. The commodity may, under this maneuver, come cheaper to the consumer, the merchants' commission &c. being avoided; but whatever touches our liberties should, under every temptation, be shunned. Besides, when once they have fixed the trade upon us, they will find ways enough to enhance the price. But I rest in your wisdom.

Pennsylvania was the first to act; on October 18 its legislature passed a resolution condemning the Tea Act and urgently requesting the East India Company agents to resign. A few days later a "committee" of Philadelphians called on the frightened commissioners, who decided that the air of the New World was bad for their health. Submitting their resignations on the spot, they immediately engaged passage for the return voyage to London.

No action was taken in New York where the presence of General Gage and two regiments of Redcoat regulars was an inhibiting factor. Citizens might glare at the agents in the streets, but no one threatened them or raised a hand against them. Radicals elsewhere sympathized with their New York colleagues, but knew they could do nothing.

The spotlight was on Boston, where Sam Adams made his careful plans and followed the Philadelphia example. On the night of November 1, unknown persons tacked notices on the doors of the houses rented by the agents, requesting them to appear thirty-six hours later at the Liberty Tree and publicly resign their commissions. The dramatic scene was scheduled to take place at noon, and at 11:00 A.M. the church bells of the city began to ring, summoning citizens to the event. The town crier spent the morning announcing the meeting as he made his way around the community, and neatly printed notices, posted everywhere, read:

TO THE FREEMEN OF THIS
AND THE NEIGHBORING TOWNS

Gentlemen,—You are desired to meet at the Liberty Tree this day at twelve o'clock at noon, then and there to hear the persons to whom the tea shipped by the East India Company is consigned to make a public resignation of their offices as consignees upon oath; and also swear that they will reship any teas that may be consigned to them by the said Company, by the first sailing vessel to London.

O.C., Sec'y.

Boston, November 3, 1773

SHOW ME THE MAN THAT DARE TAKE THIS DOWN!

Sam Adams, duly accompanied by the other Boston representatives in the legislature, the selectmen and the town clerk, made their appearance at the Liberty Tree together, arriving shortly before noon and receiving the wild applause of a crowd estimated at approximately one thousand persons. Neither on that occasion nor at any other time was "O. C., Sec'y" identified, nor was it explained of what organization he was the secretary.

The East India Company agents were conspicuous by their absence, so the vigilantes, substituting their own terror for order, marched to Clark's warehouse, where the commissioners had established their office. Several leaders, Sam Adams among them, went inside and presented the agents with a resignation already written for their convenience, and they were urged to sign it without delay. But the commissioners were more courageous than their colleagues in Philadelphia and they refused, possibly because of the presence of several British warships in the harbor and the proximity of troops at Fort William.

The mob almost escaped from control when the word was passed that the agents refused to sign, but the leaders wanted no bloodshed. At the urging of Adams, Hancock, Phillips and several others, the crowd dispersed.

A town meeting was held on November 5 to consider the situation and take appropriate action. As the citizens gathered they were given printed handbills called "Tradesman's Protest," and Sam Adams, who was acting as chairman of the meeting, ordered the document read. This was accomplished to an accompaniment of jeers, for the handbill advocated the admission of tea to Boston. Its authors were requested to identify themselves, which they did, and the citizens availed themselves of their franchise by voting unanimously in favor of the exclusion of the tea. Sam Adams was named chairman of a committee which was directed to inform the East India Company agents of the vote.

Governor Hutchinson had not been idle through these developments. Knowing his own authority was being challenged, he sought to clarify the issue by securing the immediate appointment of his own two sons as additional agents for the East India

Company. The committee found it difficult to read them the resolutions passed by the town meeting, since both were in residence at the governor's country estate in Milton, where a Redcoat honor guard refused to admit the committee members. After great difficulty the five agents were finally found and the resolutions were read to them. All persisted in their refusal to resign, and the *Gazette* took the lead in calling them "insolent."

No details whatsoever regarding the secret meetings held by the radical leaders during the next few days have ever been unearthed, and the precise identity of those who participated in these talks has never been learned. It has been assumed that the sessions were held in the offices above the printing plant of the *Gazette*, but this has never been proved. Sam Adams has been credited by posterity—including Wells, his great-grandson— with being the leader and moving spirit of these conclaves. And in his own day Adams never denied the allegation.

In any event, it was decided at these meetings that the landing of East India Company tea would be opposed by force. This signaled the inauguration of a new policy, and everyone concerned undoubtedly knew that its potential consequences were grave. The colonists were forcing a direct confrontation with Great Britain, which would not be able to condone or ignore acts of violence and would be forced, for its own honor and authority, to retaliate in kind. In order to protect the identity of those who would participate in the operation, it was decided that they would wear Indian warpaint and would be identified only as "Mohawk braves."

In some mysterious manner similar preparations were made soon after in Philadelphia and New York Town, where bands of Mohawks sworn to secrecy also were enlisted. It has been assumed that these arrangements were made after the receipt of letters or messages, presumably written by Adams, which were then destroyed.

No one knew the consequences of impending events better than Sam Adams, who sent Arthur Lee copies of the *Gazette* and wrote him on November 8:

I have but just time to enclose you a newspaper, by which you will see that Lord Shelburne was not mistaken when he said that "things begin to wear a very serious aspect in this part of the world." I wish that Lord Dartmouth would believe that the people here begin to think that they have borne oppression long enough, and that, if he has a plan of reconciliation, he would produce it without delay; but his Lordship must know that it must be such as will satisfy Americans. One cannot foresee events; but from all the observations I am able to make, my next letter will not be upon a trifling subject.

Additional attempts were made to persuade the East India Company agents to resign, but, prompted by Governor Hutchinson, they replied that it was "not in their power" to comply. A schooner reached Boston on November 17, and an official of the East India Company who was on board confirmed the fact that the tea ships were on the high seas and might be expected to arrive in the near future.

A final town meeting was held on the eighteenth. The citizens of nearby towns were invited to attend, so the session was not confined to Boston voters, and an attempt to maintain the fiction of legality was observed by calling it a meeting of "the Body." No action was taken at this session, which was designed exclusively as a show of strength, but a report was read to the effect that the replies received from the company's agents were "not satisfactory." Those attending the meeting were informed that hereafter the crisis would be managed by the Committee of Correspondence, an official unit of the Assembly.

In view of what was to come, it is somewhat surprising that Sam Adams, the chairman of the Committee of Correspondence, should have allowed himself to be so closely identified with future events. But he was playing a game as bold as it was careful: on the surface he was observing legalities, hence it would be far easier for him to disclaim any participation in an act of violence.

The tension continued to grow, and rumors to the effect that the cargo would be destroyed were heard everywhere. The company's agents picked up the stories and proposed a compromise solution that would prevent the destruction of property: they asked that the tea be moved to warehouses, where it would be placed under the guard of sentries appointed by the Committee of Correspondence. There it would remain until they received further orders from London regarding its disposition.

This plan was probably devised by Governor Hutchinson, and was a clever scheme that might have defused the time bomb the radicals had planted. If the tea were stored in warehouses for an indefinite period, the town's passions would cool.

But Sam Adams did not intend to allow the crisis he had engineered to be dissipated. Replying on behalf of the committee, he rejected the offer, saying that if the tea were landed, the tax of threepence per pound would have to be paid. Under no circumstances, he said, would the people of Boston "pay tribute." By this declaration he served notice on the governor that he was still in command of events to come.

Several of the East India Company's agents reached the hasty conclusion that winter had come early to Boston, and one evening they had themselves transferred to the warmth of Fort William by a Royal Navy launch.

Adams made certain that no one in Massachusetts would forget the crisis. On November 20 the Committee of Correspondence held a meeting in the Selectmen's Chamber at Faneuil Hall, with the committee members from the principal outlying towns in attendance. For the convenience of the participants, Adams had already prepared a circular letter to be sent to the committees of every town in the colony, and the document was adopted without change. It read:

> . . . if we are prevailed upon implicitly to acknowledge a right to tax us, by receiving and consuming teas loaded with a tax imposed by the British Parliament, we may be assured that, in a very short time, taxes of a like or more grievous nature will be laid on every article exported from Great Britain, which our necessity may require, or our shameful luxury may betray us into the use of; and when once they have found the way to rob us, their avarice will never be satisfied until our own

manufactures, and even our land, purchased and cultivated by our hard laboring ancestors, are taxed to support the vices and extravagance of wretches whose vileness ought to banish them from the society of men. We think therefore, gentlemen, that we are in duty bound to use our most strenuous endeavors to ward off the impending evil, and we are sure that, upon a fair and cool inquiry into the nature and tendency of this ministerial plan, you will think this tea now coming to us more to be dreaded than plague or pestilence; for these can only destroy our mortal bodies, but we never knew a country enslaved without the destruction of their virtue, the loss of which every good man must esteem infinitely greater than the loss of life. And we earnestly request that, after having considered this important matter, you would impress upon the minds of your friends, neighbors, and fellow-townsmen the necessity of exerting themselves in a most zealous and determined manner, to save the present and future generations from temporal, and we think we may with seriousness say, eternal destruction.

Now, brethren, we are reduced to this dilemma, either to sit down quiet under this and every other burden that our enemies shall see fit to lay upon us as good-natured slaves, or rise and resist this and every other plan laid for our destruction, as becomes wise freemen. In this extremity we earnestly request your advice, and that you would give us the earliest intelligence of the sense your several towns have of the present gloomy situation of our affairs.

In the hour of impending crisis the nature of Sam Adams's appeal to his fellow colonials for support had changed. No longer bothering to base his stand on legality, real or presumed, his call for help was exclusively emotional. His foes were vile, extravagant wretches who indulged in unnamed vices and who intended, by means of a cunning introduction of East India Company tea into Massachusetts, to reduce the people to a state of impotent slavery. His request that the citizens of others towns "rise and resist" was an open demand for insurrection that he did not bother to conceal, and he made it plain that he expected members of the Committees of Correspondence throughout the colony to utilize whatever means they found necessary to win the support of their fellow citizens. The former Boston brewer was abandoning his self-assumed role of propagandist and was becoming an eighteenth-century David who was challenging the might and majesty of the age's most powerful Goliath.

An unsigned essay published in the *Massachusetts Spy* on November 26 made it clear to the world that the radicals did not intend to permit the landing of the tea, regardless of the consequences. The style of the piece indicated that it had been produced by the pen of Sam Adams.

On Sunday, November 28, a light drizzle fell in the morning, but the air cleared by noon. Boston observed the Puritan Sabbath with its usual unyielding rigidity, but it so happened that men experienced in such matters stood sentry duty on the third floor of the highest building on the waterfront, a warehouse owned by John Hancock. At three in the afternoon they saw a merchantman of five hundred tons, the *Dartmouth*, enter the harbor and drop anchor.

Members of the committee were notified at once, and they paid a call on a local citizen named Rotch, the owner of the vessel, obtaining from him a promise that he would not try to dock before Tuesday. Then the committee held a brief meeting at the home of its chairman, and Adams was authorized to invite the committees of Dorchester, Brookline, Roxbury, Cambridge and Charlestown to a mass meeting the following morning. Messengers were dispatched without delay, and the chairman repaired to the printing plant of the *Gazette*. Soon after midnight placards were tacked up all over Boston. They read:

FRIENDS! BRETHREN! COUNTRYMEN!

That worst of plagues, the detested TEA, shipped for this port by the East India Company, is now arrived in this harbor. The hour of destruction or manly opposition to the machinations of tyranny stares you in the face. Every friend to his country, to himself, and posterity is now called upon to meet at Faneuil

Hall at nine o'clock in the morning THIS DAY (at which time the bells will ring), to make a united and successful resistance to this last, worst, and most destructive measure of Administration.

Soon after sunrise, men in the outlying towns left their homes by the hundreds and clogged the roads to Boston. In the city the Sons of Liberty went from door to door, informing the citizenry that their presence was urgently requested at the meeting—and that no absences would be tolerated. Shortly after eight, bells began to ring in every church.

The crowd was said to be the largest that had ever gathered in Boston's history. Dr. Warren, acting as temporary chairman, accepted a motion that a permanent chairman be elected and heard the name of John Hancock placed in nomination. As no other names were submitted for the honor, Hancock was elected by acclamation. He promptly recognized Sam Adams, who placed a resolution on the floor:

> As the town have determined at a late meeting, legally assembled, that they will, to the utmost of their power, prevent the landing of the tea, the question be now put,—Whether this body are absolutely determined that the tea now arrived shall be returned to the place from whence it came at all events.

By this time the turnout was so great that the overflow spilled into the street, and hundreds clamored so loudly for admission that those inside Faneuil Hall could not hear the speakers. So the meeting was adjourned to the Old South Church, the largest assemblage in its history squeezing into every available inch of space. As nearly as can be judged from contemporary accounts, at least five thousand persons were in attendance. Sam Adams repeated his resolution, and added a new question at the end in order to make the matter completely clear to everyone:

> Is it the firm resolution of this body that the tea shall not only be sent back, but that no duty shall be paid thereon?

To the surprise of no one, the affirmative vote was unanimous. The meeting was adjourned until three o'clock in the afternoon, when thousands again assembled. Francis Rotch, the owner of the *Dartmouth*, whose actual sympathies lay with the radicals, was present, and for the sake of the record entered a protest, saying that if anything untoward happened to his ship he would be forced to sue for restitution. Every attorney present recognized the wisdom of this legal maneuver. Rotch was notified, in return, that he would land the *Dartmouth's* cargo at his peril, and he was requested to convey a similar warning to the master of the ship, Captain Hall.

Adams and his colleagues knew that passions had been so thoroughly aroused that an attempt might be made to damage the ship or injure her crew, so a watch of twenty-five men was established for the night under the command of Captain Edward Proctor, a militia veteran of the French and Indian War.

Meanwhile Governor Hutchinson summoned the justices of the peace to a meeting and instructed them to arrest any man who incited a riot or attacked property, private or public. The radicals professed to be insulted.

The watch was changed on the morning of November 30, and a short time later the East India Company agents offered to place the tea in a warehouse, without payment of the customs duty, until they received new instructions from London regarding its disposal. The offer was refused without explanation.

Yet another mass meeting was held that afternoon, and various odds and ends were given the semblance of legality by unanimous votes:

The owners and masters of all ships were warned that they would land tea anywhere in Massachusetts at their peril.

Armed patrols would be maintained to watch over the *Dartmouth* until the present issue was resolved, and men who wanted to volunteer for such duty were requested to leave their names at the *Gazette* office.

Any man who cooperated with the Crown authorities and made an effort of any kind to land tea would be regarded by "all decent people" as "an enemy to his country."

The landing of tea would be prevented by force, and those present swore they would abide by this decision "at the risk of their lives and property."

Messengers were sent to Philadelphia and New York Town to inform the Committees of Correspondence in those cities of the sense of the meeting, and special couriers also carried the word to every seaport in Massachusetts in order to make certain that no tea would be landed elsewhere in the colony.

During the first week in December, three more merchantmen laden with tea reached Boston. Their masters were directed to anchor near the *Dartmouth* so that the guard keeping watch over one ship could perform the same function for all. The Sons of Liberty posted placards around the city announcing their determination to resist any attempts made by the governor to land the tea, and sentries were posted around the *Gazette* office to prevent the seizure of its presses.

One of the oldest organizations in Massachusetts was a paramilitary group known as the Cadets, which traditionally served as an honor guard for the governor on ceremonial occasions. Martial fervor ran so high that there was talk to the effect that the Cadets would be mobilized to "defend the people." But the head of the company, "Captain" John Hancock, was too sensible, well knowing that if an armed military group formally joined in the resistance, its officers would be arrested, subjected to court-martial and hanged. No major power, even one as lenient as Great Britain, would be able to tolerate such an act, so Hancock declined to call the Cadets to arms.

Governor Hutchinson wrote to his predecessor, Sir Francis Bernard, admitting he was helpless. For all practical purposes, he declared, his place had been usurped by Sam Adams, with the Committee of Correspondence acting as an insurrectionist Council. Apparently neither the governor nor his aides thought of summoning the troops on Fort William, perhaps because their numbers had been drastically reduced and what had been two full regiments were now three weak half-battalions. Certainly Hutchinson knew, too, that the reappearance of Redcoats in the streets of Boston at this time would spark a full-scale revolt. Therefore it would be unwise to call in troops until he could muster regulars in sufficient force to cope with any situation that might develop.

Sam Adams overlooked no angle in his campaign to raise public support. The *Gazette*, which printed daily issues throughout the emergency, published promises of support from various towns throughout Massachusetts, and copies of the newspaper were sent to towns that had not yet replied. The Committee of Correspondence wrote urgent letters to the committees in other colonies, and particularly requested New Hampshire, Rhode Island, Connecticut, New York and Pennsylvania to take similar action, thus making the "tea blockade" complete in almost every major American port.

Rotch was requested to appear before the Massachusetts committee, and was asked why he had not yet sent the *Dartmouth* back to England. The question was rhetorical, and was asked only for the sake of the record, as Adams and his colleagues well knew the reasons: Governor Hutchinson had accepted the colonists' challenge, and refused to permit any ship to put to sea from Boston without a permit bearing his personal signature. Two Royal Navy sloops-of-war were stationed at the entrance to the harbor to enforce his will, and the guns of Fort William had been loaded, with expert artillerymen on duty night and day, ready to fire on any vessel that attempted to defy the gubernatorial edict.

Adams was determined to break the impasse, and on December 13 a meeting of the Committees of Correspondence of Boston and her neighboring towns was held. Sam Adams was named chairman of a subcommittee of four that was assigned to accompany Rotch to the office of the royal customs collector. This was done, and when the owner of the *Dartmouth* formally requested clearance papers so that his ship could sail, he was told with equal formality that Governor Hutchinson refused to sign any permit until cargo sent to Boston from the East India Company in London was unloaded.

The Boston Committee of Correspondence went into private

session behind closed doors, and took care to insert a notice in the *Gazette* of December 20 that "no business transacted; matter of record."

A last mass meeting was held at the Old South Church on the morning of December 16, and the thousands who attended reaffirmed their previous resolution to permit no landing of the tea. The meeting was memorable because one of the local leaders wondered aloud "how tea will mingle with saltwater," and the audience applauded at length. Only one moderate voice was heard. Quincy, who had just returned from a tour of the southern colonies on behalf of the committee and who was already suffering from the illness that would take his life, warned his friends and neighbors that the consequences would be frightful if they resorted to violence. His loyalty to the cause placed him beyond reproach, and he was applauded more for his courage than his advice.

Adams, who regarded himself as no orator and never was at his best when addressing large gatherings, made no speeches on this occasion. He sat with the other members of the committee, his face impassive, and took no direct part in the proceedings. For all practical purposes his work was already done.

The meeting was adjourned until early evening, when Rotch appeared to report that his request for clearance had been denied. Adams, who had remained silent all day, immediately rose and declared, "This meeting can do nothing more to save the country!"

As soon as he spoke a number of loud Indian war whoops were heard outside the church, and a band of forty to fifty men disguised as Indians raced down to Griffin's Wharf near the foot of Pearl Street on the errand since familiar to every American schoolchild. Sentries permitted only the "Mohawks" to go on board the merchantmen, and they went about their business with thoroughness and dispatch. Cases of tea were carried on deck from the hold of each ship, cut open and dumped overboard. The original band of Indians was augmented by others in similar disguise, and perhaps as many as one hundred and forty persons took part in the raid, which lasted for three hours. The ships themselves were left undamaged, no property other than the tea itself was destroyed and no man was injured; the Sons of Liberty were demonstrating their discipline in the ultimate hour of crisis.

Sam Adams, John Hancock and the other radical leaders did not venture near the waterfront that night, but returned to their homes, each of them making certain that witnesses of stature knew his precise whereabouts during the entire evening. On December 31 Adams wrote to Arthur Lee that 342 chests of East India Company tea were opened and dumped into the bay. Perhaps the most remarkable feature of the incident was that a full moon shone on the scene from a cloudless sky, but neither the warships at the entrance to the harbor nor the troops on Fort William intervened.

Complete secrecy was maintained regarding those who participated in the Boston Tea Party until the end of the War of Independence, at which time a number named Adams as the principal instigator of the affair.

Adams found it difficult to contain his pleasure in his letter to Arthur Lee:

> You cannot imagine the height of joy that sparkles in the eyes and animates the countenances as well as the hearts of all we meet on this occasion, excepting the disappointed, disconcerted Hutchinson and his tools. I repeat what I wrote you in my last,—if Lord Dartmouth has prepared his plan, let him produce it speedily; but his Lordship must know it must be such a plan as will not barely amuse, much less further irritate, but conciliate the affections of the inhabitants.

Philadelphia received the news of the Boston Tea Party from the Massachusetts Committee of Correspondence on December 26, and church bells pealed. The following day a mass meeting endorsed the act. In South Carolina the tea was landed and stored in cellars, where it was allowed to rot, and the Charleston agents of the East India Company resigned in a body. New York took no direct action, but the agents there were cautious, and sent the tea ships that docked in the East River back to London with full cargoes.

Great Britain was stunned by the news, and because it was obvious that the affair had been planned with great care, was forced to take action. The Boston Tea Party marked the turning point in the relations of Britain and her North American colonies, and certainly was the climax of Sam Adams's career to date.

It was obvious that neither the Crown nor Parliament could tolerate the calculated insult and that some form of punitive retaliation was required if Great Britain hoped to retain her self-respect and dignity. This was precisely what Sam Adams wanted, of course, since the Boston Tea Party had been a deliberately provocative gesture, and any action London took would add fuel to the flames of his shrill demands for "liberty." On the surface he was optimistic, but in private he wondered how far the king and the Commons would go in rebuking the colonists. America was not yet prepared for a full-scale war, and he wanted to buy more time, using the interim period to build still more pressures that would make a revolution inevitable.

He privately expected Governor Hutchinson to place him under arrest and have him taken to England for trial, and although he did not relish the prospect of being placed in a martyr's role, he was willing to make the sacrifice if it should become necessary. But none of this was reflected in a happy essay that appeared in the *Gazette* of December 31, in which, writing over the signature of "Marlborough," he wished the world his own brand of joyful new year:

> To all Nations under HEAVEN. Know ye, that the PEO-PLE of the AMERICAN WORLD, are Millions strong—countless Legions compose their united ARMY of FREE-MEN. . . . AMERICA now stands with the Scale of JUSTICE in one Hand, and the Sword of VENGEANCE in the other, and whatever Nation or People who dares to lift a hostile Hand against her, to invade her serene Regions, or sully her Liberty shall —————— —————— ——————. Let the Britons fear to do

any more so wickedly as they have done, for the HER-
CULEAN ARM of this NEW WORLD is lifted up—and Woe
be to them on whom it falls!—At the Beat of the Drum, she
can call five Hundred Thousand of her SONS to ARMS—
before whose blazing Shields none can stand. — Therefore, ye
that are Wise, make Peace with her, take Shelter under her
Wings, that ye may shine by the Reflection of her Glory.

May the NEW YEAR shine propitious on the NEW
WORLD—and VIRTUE and LIBERTY, reign here without
a Foe, until rolling Years shall measure Time no more.

Governor Hutchinson thought Adams was daring the Crown
to arrest him, but he refused to take the bait. At the same time
he made it clear in an urgent report to London, in which he
included a copy of the *Gazette* essay, that a major move had to be
made without delay to prevent the outbreak of a full-scale insurrection.

Chapter Eighteen

In promoting the Boston Tea Party, Sam Adams made one major miscalculation. He thought America's friends in England would rally to the support of the colonists, but even Chatham, Burke and Fox shared the indignation of the Tories. Parliament could not act overnight, however, and in the meantime Adams and his colleagues took steps to make their victory more secure.

The Assembly had been scheduled to meet on January 20, 1774, but Governor Hutchinson postponed the opening for a week in the vain hope that a moderate attitude would prevail. The Adams-controlled majority had its own ideas, however, and launched a new attack on all judges who accepted their salaries from the Crown. Calling themselves "the Commons of this Province," an Adams-inspired name they had no right to use, the members passed a resolution written by Adams threatening the judges with impeachment if they accepted their salaries from the Crown. This gesture was the most blatant usurpation of Crown powers that Adams had yet devised, for the Assembly had been granted no powers of impeachment under any of its charters or in any other way.

But the threat was so effective that four of the five judges promptly succumbed and agreed to accept their pay only from the Assembly itself. The fifth judge, Peter Oliver, rejected the demand of the radicals in a brilliant letter that forcibly demonstrated the legality of the position he had taken.

Sam Adams was no longer concerned with mere legalities, however, and under his guidance the Assembly approved another sonorous Adams-prepared resolution stating that Judge Oliver's conduct was perverting the cause of justice and that he was totally disqualified to hold his post. The Assembly issued an appeal to the governor to dismiss the offending judge, but Hutchinson ignored the request—precisely as Adams had known he would.

This cleared the air, and the Assembly voted to impeach the judge for "high crimes and misdemeanors." Before the members could proceed with their farce, however, Governor Hutchinson exercised a prerogative of his own and prorogued the session.

But Sam Adams and his associates had the last word. By this time they had achieved such overall control of public opinion that even the most bitter of their opponents did not dare to stand up in public against them. Jurymen called to serve in the court of Judge Oliver refused to appear, and so many took this position that it would have been necessary to make mass arrests in order to assert the authority of the judiciary. Governor Hutchinson was still unwilling to take any action that might cause major disturbances, and he felt frustrated beyond measure when he saw that, for all practical purposes, Judge Oliver was unable to function.

Adams enjoyed this victory, but he was engaging in a mere skirmish, and far more important matters occupied his time and attention. In March 1774, he revealed his hand on the occasion of the celebration of the anniversary of the Boston "Massacre." John Hancock was scheduled to be the principal speaker, and for a week prior to the event, Adams met with him daily, in effect writing the speech for him. Many years later Adams's daughter revealed that she had known of these meetings, but had been forbidden to say where they were taking place.

In this address Hancock finally came out in the open with the aims of the radicals: he urged a wildly cheering crowd to break off relations with Great Britain and establish an independent nation to be called the United States of America. Sam Adams was the first man to use the name on paper, as the notes he wrote for Hancock's speech indicate, but it is impossible to determine whether he actually was responsible for coining the name. Radicals in a number of colonies began to use it at about the same time.

In any event, Adams thoughtfully had copies of the Hancock address printed, and they were sent to Committees of Correspondence throughout Massachusetts and to the other twelve colonies. In all, more than one thousand copies were disseminated.

At more or less the same time, King George made an Address from the Throne, advising both Houses of Parliament of the state of affairs in Boston and describing the Boston Tea Party in detail. The Commons reacted swiftly, and America's friends, among them Burke and Barré, could find little to say in the defense of the colonists. Within a few days the Boston Port Bill was written and passed by an overwhelming majority in the Commons, and on March 29 it won the unanimous approval of the Lords. Under its terms the port of Boston was to be closed, at the pleasure of the king, and all trade there was to be suspended. The city would be denied all privileges of landing and discharging merchandise, or of loading and shipping any goods. The duration of the port act would depend on the future conduct of Bostonians, and would be set aside when the city paid for the tea that had been destroyed and otherwise indicated a willingness to submit to the authority of the Crown.

Not satisfied with this effort, Parliament passed another measure early in April "for better regulating the government of Massachusetts Bay." This act removed all powers from the rebellious Assembly, invested the governor with the authority to appoint and remove all Council members and judges, prohibited the calling of town meetings without the approval of the governor and granted him exclusive authority to determine what matters could be discussed at all town meetings. Juries were to be summoned by the sheriffs, who were under the governor's control, and were empowered to compel individuals to serve on juries when called.

Under a separate series of acts the administration of the Massachusetts Bay Colony was further tightened. In order to prevent riots and the subversion of justice, any man accused of murder, treason or other major crimes could be removed from the colony and placed on trial in another colony or in Great Britain itself. A special bill authorized the apprehension, at an appropriate time, of Samuel Adams, "the Chief of the Revolution," and of "his principal lieutenant," John Hancock, as well as of other persons whom the governor might consider incendiaries. At the same time these bills were rushed through Parliament, the Colonial Office forcibly retired Hutchinson and replaced him as governor with General Thomas Gage, the Commander in Chief of His Majesty's armed forces in North America, and the War Office announced that three additional regiments of troops would be sent to the New World to make certain that the will of Parliament was obeyed. For all practical purposes, civilian government in Massachusetts was suspended, and the colony was placed under military rule.

In order to strengthen the hand of General Gage, the Quartering Act of 1765 was renewed, giving the governor the authority to compel private citizens to give billets to royal troops. Yet another new act provided that Crown officials in Massachusetts could be tried in Great Britain if any charges were brought against them by colonials.

All of these measures were harsh, so it was doubly unfortunate that, at the same time, Parliament passed the Quebec Act, which was a direct outgrowth of the French and Indian War and had no intended connection with the rebellion that Sam Adams and his friends were fomenting. Under the terms of the Treaty of Paris that had ceded Canada to Great Britain, a specific promise had been given that the religious liberty and legal customs of the

French in Canada would be respected. A primary purpose of this law was that of making certain this pledge was kept.

The act also extended the boundaries of the Province of Quebec to include the area known as the Northwest Territory, a vast region that lay between the Ohio and Mississippi rivers. The fur trade in the region was lucrative, and the purpose of the measure was to discourage English settlement there, as a number of Montreal merchants were already active in that trade. The act totally disregarded the charters of Massachusetts, Virginia and Connecticut, and further aroused the resentment of these predominantly Protestant colonies by giving territory that had been promised to them to a province whose population was overwhelmingly Catholic. No premeditated slight could have more aroused the ire of the Americans.

Parliament was acting boldly, asserting its own rights and those of the Crown after years of hesitation. Some of the colonies' supporters in the Commons felt that the Americans would be forced to react and that a genuine crisis could not be averted. For that reason they advocated the passage of a simpler measure—the payment of damages to the East India Company by the perpetrators of the Boston Tea Party. From the outset this mild measure was doomed, however, for Parliament had been stung into taking more severe action. And Benjamin Franklin did not encourage the moderates, either, telling them he felt certain that Sam Adams and his colleagues would refuse to pay damages to the East India Company. So, when the harsher acts came to a vote, even America's best friends felt they had to support the dignity and authority of Great Britain.

It did not matter that Parliament and the Crown were playing into Sam Adams's hands, and that he now obtained support from Americans of every class. The property owners—the only men who held the vote—were as furious with the mother country as were the disenfranchised urban poor and the tenant farmers and hired hands of rural districts. Even before learning of the so-called Coercive Acts, Adams moved into high gear, saying in a communication to the Committees of Correspondence of the other colonies:

We have long been struggling with one grievance upon the back of another, but none seem to be so threatening to us and to all the Colonies as an attempt to render our Governor and the judges of the land independent of the people for their support. This appears to us to be the completion of the system of tyranny: for certainly that people must be slaves where another legislative claims and exercises the power of raising what moneys it pleases from them, and supporting an executive which is independent of them for their places or their continuation in office, out of the moneys thus taken from them without their consent. We cannot better convey to you the sentiments of the house of Representatives of this Province upon this subject, than by enclosing their protest and resolves thereon. The House have lately petitioned for a removal of this grievance in special; but we have certain intelligence that their petitions are displeasing to His Majesty, because the principle is therein held up repugnant to the authority claimed by Parliament to make laws binding on the subject in America in all cases whatsoever. The power assumed and exercised by the British Parliament is, in truth, the foundation of the grievance. We have petitioned against it; and if we admit that they have this right, we have no ground of complaint.

· Adams plainly set forth the core of his position, and although he did not yet know it, he was laying the groundwork for the position he would take when he learned of the passage of the Coercive or "Intolerable" Acts, as he would call them. They had no validity and Americans would not be required to obey them because they were the work of a legislative body that lacked authority to make laws governing the American people.

On March 28, 1774, a few hours before Parliament passed the Boston Port Bill, Adams outlined his views in a remarkable communication he sent to Dr. Franklin in London. An essay rather than a letter, it was nevertheless intended strictly for private consumption, and it is significant because it formed the philosophical basis on which Americans fought the War of Independence. Copies were distributed a few months later at the meeting of the First Continental Congress. Adams may have written the piece to clarify his own stand, but whatever his motives, he produced a document with which the leaders of the other twelve colonies were able to agree:

It will be vain for any to expect that the people of this country will now be contented with a partial and temporary relief, or that they will be amused by Court promises, while they see not the least relaxation of grievances. By the vigilance and activity of Committees of Correspondence among the several towns in this Province, they have been wonderfully enlightened and animated. They are united in sentiment, and their opposition to unconstitutional measures of government is become systematical. Colony communicates freely with Colony. There is a common affection among them,—the *communis sensus*; and the whole continent is now become united in sentiment and in opposition to tyranny. Their old good will and affection for the parent country is not, however, lost. If she returns to her former moderation and good humor, their affection will revive. They wish for nothing more than permanent union with her, upon the condition of equal liberty. This is all they have been contending for, and nothing short of this will, or ought to, satisfy them. When formerly the kings of England have encroached upon the liberties of their subjects, the subjects have thought it their duty to themselves and their posterity to contend with them till they were restored to the footing of the Constitution. The events of such struggles have sometimes proved fatal to crowned heads,—perhaps they have never issued but in establishment of the people's liberties.

In those times it was not thought reasonable to say that, since the King had claimed such or such a power, the people *must* yield it to him, because it would not be for the honor of His Majesty to recede from his claim. If the people of Britain must needs flatter themselves that they are collectively the sovereign of America, America will never consent that they should govern them arbitrarily, or without known and stipulated rules. But the matter is not so considered here: Britain and the Colonies are considered as distinct governments under the King. Britain has a Constitution, the envy of all foreigners, to which it has ever been the safety, as well of kings as of subjects, steadfastly to adhere. Each Colony has also a Constitution in its charter or other institution of government, all of which agree in this, that the fundamental laws of the British Constitution shall be the basis. That Constitution by no means admits of legislation without representation. Why, then, should the Parliament of Britain which, notwithstanding all its ideas of transcendent power, must forever be circumscribed within the limit of that Constitution, insist upon the right of legislation for the people of America, without their having representation there?

It cannot be justified by their own Constitution. The laws of nature and reason abhor it; yet, because she has claimed such a power, her honor truly is concerned still to assert and exercise it, and she may not recede. Will such kind of reasoning bear the test of examination? Or, rather, will it not be an eternal disgrace to any nation, which considers her honor concerned, to employ fleets and armies for the support of a claim which she cannot in reason defend, merely because she has once in anger made such a claim? It is the misfortune of Britain and the Colonies that flagitious men on both sides of the water have made it their interest to foment divisions, jealousies, and animosities between them, which perhaps will never subside until the extent of power and right on each part is more explicitly stipulated than has ever yet been thought necessary; and although such a stipulation should prove a lasting advantage on each side, yet considering that the views and designs of those men were to do infinite mischief, and to establish a tyranny upon the ruins of a free Constitution, they deserve the vengeance of the public, and until the memory of them shall be erased by time, they will most assuredly meet with the execrations of posterity.

Governor Hutchinson and his successor, General Gage, would have found it difficult to believe that Sam Adams could have been the author of such a conciliatory declaration, a paper totally lacking in the rhetorical, patriotic fervor that marked his other efforts. For Adams to have indicated in private that a reconciliation with Britain was still possible is astonishing in the light of his editorials and essays, which insisted that it had become necessary for the colonies to go their own way. In fact, he wrote to Arthur Lee a few days after sending his conciliatory declaration to Franklin and asserted that unless Britain returned to "the principles of equity," rigorous measures would be prosecuted to secure "the entire separation and independence of the colonies." And who in America more closely fitted Adams's description of a "flagitious man" who fomented divisions, jealousies and animosities?

It is difficult to believe that Adams lacked sincerity when he wrote to Benjamin Franklin, and it must be assumed that he saw himself, in private and behind his public image, as a man of common sense and moderation. Or it may be that he was even more diabolical than anyone gave him credit for being. He believed he would be placed under arrest at any time, and as a realist he could not have thought that Britain would turn the other cheek. Parliament was sure to retaliate against Boston, but if he showed himself willing to make concessions—which he was careful not to specify, naming only what he thought necessary for Britain to do—he might emerge in a better bargaining position.

There was no doubt that the radical leadership of Boston, which was expanding as such men as Paul Revere, Oliver Wendell, Richard Dana, John Rowe and Samuel Pemberton joined the cause, were willing to follow wherever Adams led. In April of 1774 his leadership was acknowledged when the *Royal American Magazine*, which was published in Boston, printed an engraving of him made by Revere and presumably taken from the Copley portrait. It was Revere who called him "the political father of us all."

Under his direction the people of Massachusetts Bay were preparing for the coming storm. The Marblehead Committee of Correspondence saw revolution and bloodshed not far away, and offered its resignation from the parent committee for the whole colony. Adams refused to accept it, and wrote a very firm reply, insisting that a time of supreme crisis was approaching and that all liberty-loving men of goodwill were required to stand together. Members of the Marblehead committee promptly withdrew their resignation.

Adams, acting through local committees, saw to it that a military company was formed in every town in Massachusetts; each elected its own officers, and regular drill schedules were established. One of the last acts voted by the Assembly before it had been prorogued had been a bill authorizing the purchase of five hundred barrels of gunpowder. Adams was chairman of the committee that purchased the powder, and his feeling of impending danger led him to move the supplies from Boston to Cambridge, where they were hidden in an old mill and placed under volunteer guard.

On May 10 the news of Parliament's passage of the Coercive Acts reached Boston, and even those who had been expecting trouble were shocked when they learned that the new laws would become effective on June 1. On that same day Samuel Adams became chairman of a group appointed to notify the other colonies of Parliament's acts, and the Committees of Correspondence of Boston's eight neighboring towns were invited to an emergency meeting on May 12 to consider the situation.

Adams wrote a letter on behalf of the Boston committee, flatly refusing to accept the punishment meted out by Britain, promising to resist to the best of the city's ability and asking all other Americans to come to her aid. "Boston," he declared, "must be regarded as suffering in the common cause."

Less than three weeks remained before the closing of the port of Boston became effective, so Adams had to work quickly. On May 13 a town meeting was held, and the new laws were called "repugnant to law, religion and common sense." By unanimous vote the other colonies were asked to refrain from engaging in all commercial intercourse with Britain and her West Indian dependencies, and to maintain the embargo until the Boston Port Act was rescinded.

The reaction of other colonies was swift and sympathetic to Boston. Paul Revere, who carried the message to New York and Pennsylvania, addressed a crowd of several hundred in Philadelphia, and brought home the suggestion offered by his hosts that a congress of delegates from all thirteen colonies meet as soon as possible to consider joint action against "the vile edicts of Parliament."

The Virginia House of Burgesses voted that the colony observe a day of mourning on June 1, and the outraged governor promptly prorogued the legislature. Richard Henry Lee, Patrick Henry, Thomas Jefferson and the other leaders of the Burgesses had not yet heard of the Philadelphia proposal that a congress be held, and on their own intiative produced the same idea. Sam Adams had done his work well, and it was beginning to bear fruit.

Chapter
Nineteen

The affable General Gage reached Boston by ship on
May 17 after a short voyage from New York Town, and was
correctly received by the inhabitants. He was escorted by the
Cadets under the command of their captain, John Hancock, and
the members of the Assembly called on him en masse. If he was
surprised when Sam Adams held out a hand to him, he gave no
indication, but he must have known that the show of civility was
only superficial. On the same day Adams sent a letter to Arthur
Lee in which he expressed confidence that the embargo on British goods would be observed throughout the colonies.

On May 26 the Assembly held its last meeting under the provisions of the royal charter, and listened to a statement from General Gage to the effect that he was moving the capital of Massachusetts Bay to Salem and that the legislature would meet there
until further notice. Thanks to the quiet maneuvering of Sam
Adams and his lieutenants, the Assembly made no reply.

General Gage was a cultured man who had been in the New
World long enough to doubt the wisdom of trying to enforce the
Boston Port Act. But the senior officers of the Royal Navy squad-

ron that had escorted him to his new command post were in favor of closing the port, and were supported by the customs officials who had been embarrassed by the Boston Tea Party. So the harbor was closed to all incoming ships at noon on June 1, and all outgoing vessels were ordered to depart no later than June 14. The church bells of the city tolled somberly, and most of the city's residents appeared in deep mourning, which they continued to wear daily.

On June 5 the Massachusetts Committee of Correspondence met to find ways to implement and enforce the nonimportation agreement, and on June 7, in response to a summons by the new governor, the Assembly convened in Salem. Sam Adams was detained by last-minute business in Boston, and a rumor swept through the legislature that he and Hancock had been placed under arrest. When he finally arrived, his fellow members greeted him with a standing ovation.

The Assembly's first order of business was the passage of a resolution, already written by Adams, condemning the Coercive Acts. General Gage refused to accept the document, and replied with a blistering counterattack of his own.

The most important matter before the Assembly, Adams believed, was the election of delegates to an intercolonial congress to be held in Philadelphia. But plans for the meeting of that body were being made in secret so that Crown authorities could not halt the deliberations before they began, and Adams acted accordingly. Tories who were in touch with the new governor were misled, and a number actually believed that the legislature planned to pass a bill offering indemnity to the East India Company.

On Thursday, June 16, the Tories in the Assembly were told that the legislature would adjourn until the following Monday, and all of them departed for their homes. But the Patriots had been told not to leave, and a total of 129 of them convened on the morning of Friday, June 17. The doors were locked, and the sergeants at arms were instructed to let no men enter or leave until the deliberations were concluded.

Secrecy having been assured, those present were asked to take an oath promising they would reveal nothing of what transpired to any outsider. After the ceremony was completed, Sam Adams arose to announce that an intercolonial congress would be held in Philadelphia on September 1, and that Massachusetts was being asked to send five representatives. The first to be elected was Adams himself, by acclamation. Other members of the group were Thomas Cushing, James Bowdoin, Robert Treat Paine and John Adams.

In spite of the attempts to maintain secrecy, the governor learned of the session and its purpose, and hastily wrote an eleven-line document dissolving the Assembly. He sent his secretary to read it from the rostrum, but Sam Adams was keeping the key to the chamber in his own pocket and, pretending to be hard of hearing, refused to open the door. So the frustrated secretary read the order on the steps of the building; it so happened that several members of the Assembly who had not reached the hall before the doors were locked were on hand and heard the reading. This, General Gage later declared, made the dissolution legal, a claim Sam Adams hotly and consistently denied. He had no interest in keeping the Assembly in session, to be sure, but he did not want to lose the opportunity to create still another legal battle with Gage.

Since it was impossible to obtain funds for the expenses of the delegates without the approval of Governor Gage, a special tax was voted, each town contributing a share in proportion to the last tax list. The rump Assembly then voted in favor of the embargo on British goods and passed a bill urging other colonies to be diligent in pursuit of the same goal. Their business completed, they adjourned, and Sam Adams unlocked the door.

The presence of John Adams on the list of delegates was the work of his cousin, who rightly regarded him as one of the foremost lawyers in New England. His involvement in politics had been slight prior to this time, but Cousin Sam had held many long, private discussions with him, and he decided to cast his lot, without reservations, with the Patriots. His election as a delegate to the First Continental Congress is rightly regarded as the beginning of his public career.

Boston was bearing its tribulations heroically, if not in silence, for contributions of food arrived daily from every community in Massachusetts Bay and all of the other colonies. By the end of June the warehouses of Hancock and a number of other merchants were bulging with corn and potatoes and rice, dried peas and wheat flour. Hundreds of barrels of pickled fish and smoked pork arrived, as did live cattle, sheep, oxen and poultry.

The facilities of the Committee of Correspondence were inundated, so a special Donations Committee was formed to dispense the food to those who needed it. Sam Adams, who seemed to have time for every function required of him, accepted the thankless task of chairman. His principal occupation was that of maintaining the steady flow of supplies, and he discharged his duties with his customary thoroughness, thereby enabling Boston to hold out indefinitely without being forced to offer compensation to the East India Company.

Adams's state of mind during this time is reflected in a letter he wrote around the beginning of July 1774:

> An empire is rising in America. Britain, by her multiplied oppressions, is accelerating that independency which she dreads. We have a post to maintain, to desert which would entail upon us the curses of posterity. The virtue of our ancestors inspires us. For my part, I have been wont to converse with Poverty, and however disagreeable a companion she may be thought to be by the affluent and luxurious, who never were acquainted with her, I can live happily with her the remainder of my days, if I can thereby contribute to the redemption of my country. Our oppressors cannot force us into submission by reducing us to a state of starvation. We can subsist independently of all the world. The real wants and necessities of man are few. Nature has bountifully supplied us with the means of subsistence; and if all others fail, we can, like our ancestors, subsist on the clams and muscles [sic] which abound on our shore.

In spite of his brave words, the Loyalists were feeling stronger, and late in June opened an attack on the Committee of Correspondence, rightly believing that the Patriots would be crippled without measure if their executive were abolished. Adams craftily adopted a generous approach to the problem, and posters announced that a special meeting would be held to discuss the subject and that all interested persons were invited.

He was elected chairman of the meeting, and very much in evidence were the dock workers and others who had lost their employment because the port had been closed. These men were inclined to be rowdy, but Adams kept them under strict control, and every courtesy was extended to the Loyalists who wanted to abolish the committee. When they had made their speeches, Adams handed the chair to Joseph Warren, descended to the floor and, in a speech his friends said was one of the most pungent he had yet delivered, he demolished the arguments of his enemies. Had the question been submitted to the voters who held the franchise, it is possible that the anticommittee forces might have made a good showing. But, by ostensibly observing the rules of democracy and giving the unemployed a vote, too, Adams easily defeated his foes, who were forced to abandon their project.

Adams realized that Boston would need help for a long time to come, and he became the moving spirit behind the formation of a new intercolonial organization in July 1774. It was called the Solemn League and Covenant, and in most places it operated under the auspices of the local Committee of Correspondence. In some localities British Army officers, acting on their own authority, made strenuous attempts to hamper the work of the league, but these efforts backfired. In New Haven a captain of Royal Artillery forbade the citizens collected on the Green to sign a pledge of support, swearing he would arrest anyone who disobeyed him. The moment he stopped speaking, more than one hundred men stood in line, and each signed the document promising to give funds to the poor of Boston.

All who joined the league also promised to purchase no goods made in England, and the popular support for Boston was so strong everywhere that many who otherwise might have continued to buy British merchandise accepted the nonimportation agreement. General Gage became alarmed, and in his capacity as commander in chief of the British Army in North America, he issued a proclamation asking all magistrates, sheriffs and other public officials to arrest and prosecute any who joined the league.

The general, who was new to politics and continued to think almost exclusively in the military terms that made him comfortable, soon realized he had bungled. Thousands throughout the colonies joined the league, many acting in sheer defiance of his authority, and it was impossible to place so many under arrest. Even worse, he gave Sam Adams fresh ammunition to use against him, and Gage, essentially a man of goodwill who had been given a task beyond his capacities, saw himself described in print as a ruthless tyrant determined to crush the American people. The Grand Incendiary, as the general learned, was never so busy as to abandon his first love, and churned out editorials and essays at his customary, furious rate.

The summer of 1774 was the critical time that would determine whether Britain and her North American colonies resolved their dispute peacefully or went to war. Parliament had issued its challenge, and the radicals—now being called Patriots everywhere—were not backing down. Sam Adams, spearheading the resistance and refusing to contemplate the payment of indemnity to the East India Company, must have known he was leading America into war.

Benjamin Franklin advocated the payment of a token sum as compensation for the tea that had been destroyed, and so did a number of prominent moderates in every colony. But the Patriots had seized the initiative; Boston was a martyred city and her plight was drawing together Americans of every political persuasion. Adams and his colleagues held firm because they might never again enjoy such an advantageous position.

What made their situation particularly favorable was the response of the small but influential American middle class. The radicals had been supported for years by the city and country poor, but they needed more than the cheers of the dispossessed. Previous attempts to place an embargo on British merchandise had been only partly successful, but the Boston merchants now had no choice and were compelled to enlist under Adams's banner. Men of substance in other colonies, reading the ominous signs, were afraid their turn would come next and therefore were more inclined to cast their lot with the Patriots.

"War fever," as such, was still almost nonexistent. Adams demanded independence in terms that grew increasingly insistent and shrill, but no sense of alarm gripped the American people yet. They felt sorry for Boston, but realized at the same time that there was a measure of justice in the punitive steps taken against the city by the Crown and Parliament.

In Boston itself the tension continued to rise, and it was exacerbated when four regiments of British regulars arrived early in July. Since the weather was pleasant, they were quartered on the Common, where their tents were a constant reminder to the people that the city was under military occupation.

Sam Adams's friends lived in constant fear that he would be placed under arrest and taken to England in a Royal Navy warship for trial, but he himself disagreed, believing that General Gage wanted to avoid the spark that would set off a general war. Massachusetts was the most populous colony in America, and Boston was the largest city. Sam Adams was more than a leader of the multitude—he had become a symbol of the colony's hopes and fears, and even the Loyalists who disliked him were forced to admire his single-minded energy and courage. John Hancock wrote that any attempt to take Adams into custody would provoke an immediate, violent reaction, that the entire colony would rise up as one man and that "four times four regiments" would not be enough to quench the fires of rebellion.

The Massachusetts Committee of Correspondence indicated some nervousness at a meeting held on the night of July 5, when it was voted unanimously that the group would continue to attend to its regular business unless prevented by "brutal force." Sam Adams himself calmly analyzed the situation in a letter he wrote a few days later to Richard Henry Lee:

Lord North had no expectation that we should be thus sustained. On the contrary, he trusted that Boston would be left to fall alone. He has therefore made no preparation for the effects of a union. From the information I have had from intelligent persons in England, I verily believe the design was to seize some persons and send them home [to England]; but the steadiness and prudence of the people, and the unexpected union of the Colonies, evidenced by liberal contributions for our support, has disconcerted them, and they are at a loss to know how to proceed further.

For the moment, it appeared, His Majesty's government preferred the velvet glove to the iron fist. According to a story told many years later by Adams's daughter, Mrs. Hannah Wells, an emissary of General Gage, one Colonel Fenton, who was the commander of one of the regiments of newly arrived troops, paid an informal call at the Adams home. After an exchange of the usual civilities, Fenton hinted broadly that a great many benefits would be showered on Adams if he gave up his opposition to the Crown. At the same time, however, the colonel warned him that persons who were adamant in their opposition could be sent to England for trial. But he concluded on an optimistic note, indicating that there could be no doubt that here was an opportunity for great personal advantage as well as the chance to reach an accommodation with the Crown.

According to Mrs. Wells's story, her father listened to Colonel Fenton in a silence that encouraged the soldier, and when he was finished speaking, replied, "Sir, I trust I have long since made my peace with the King of kings. No personal consideration shall induce me to abandon the righteous cause of my country. Tell Governor Gage it is the advice of Samuel Adams to him no longer to insult the feelings of an exasperated people."

Joseph Warren, interviewed more than a decade after the end of the Revolution, said that many attempts had been made to bribe his old friend and comrade. According to yet another account, never verified, Adams was offered a Crown pension of two thousand guineas per year for life if he would retire from politics.

Instead of succumbing to the temptations that did not interest him, Adams became chairman of yet another new group, the Massachusetts Committee of Safety. Other members were

Thomas Cushing, John Hancock, John Adams, William Phillips, Josiah Quincy and Joseph Warren. Formed originally to act as an executive charged with the responsibility of distributing the gifts received by the Donations Committee, this small body ultimately took the place of the Committee of Correspondence and directed the war efforts of Massachusetts.

In August 1774, however, Adams's thoughts were turning toward Philadelphia and the longest journey he had ever made.

Chapter
Twenty

Paul Revere and other young couriers might make the journey from Boston to Philadelphia in ten days, but the fifty-two-year-old Sam Adams, already suffering from arthritis, needed a far longer time. His personal affairs were not in good shape as he made ready for his trip: his family was impoverished, although his son, Dr. Adams, was beginning to contribute money for food and other essentials. Funds for the journey itself had been provided by means of the tax imposed on all towns in Massachusetts, but Adams had no appropriate clothes and no money to buy them.

A week before Adams was scheduled to depart, he and his family were about to sit down at the dinner table when they were interrupted by the arrival of Boston's most fashionable tailor, who was followed by a shirtmaker, a haberdasher and a shoemaker. All insisted on taking the measurements of the Grand Incendiary, but refused to say who had sent them or to explain their mission.

On the day prior to Adams's departure, he found a heavy trunk on his front stoop. It contained two complete suits of clothes, two new pairs of shoes with silver buckles, a set of gold knee buckles and another of gold sleeve buttons, a gold-headed cane, a deep red cloak and an elegant cocked hat, along with a number of minor articles of clothing. The cane and sleeve buttons, which became family heirlooms, were decorated with the device of the Liberty cap, which led members of the family to believe the gifts had come from the Sons of Liberty. But all Boston knew that Sam Adams's financial situation was precarious, so Hancock, Warren or other wealthy friends may have contributed his new wardrobe to save him from embarrassment in Philadelphia.

It is significant that everything in the trunk had been made in Boston. Many of the wealthier Bostonians had clothes made and materials dyed in England, but anyone acquainted with Adams knew he would refuse to wear anything made in England. He also would neither wear a wig nor powder his own hair, and, according to his daughter, he regarded the elaborate hairdressings of ladies as absurd. It was the custom for a woman to have her hair prepared the day before a party, then sleep in an easy chair that night so she would be ready for the following day's festivities. No woman in the Adams household dared to indulge herself in this frivolous manner.

The members of the Massachusetts delegation to the Continental Congress met at the house of Thomas Cushing on August 10, then went together to an inn called Coolidge's in Watertown, where a large company of their friends toasted them at a farewell party given in their honor. They left at 4:00 P.M., and Governor Gage took note of their departure in a report to the Colonial Office:

> The delegates, as they are called, from this Province are gone to Philadelphia to meet the rest who are to form the General Congress; and it is thought it will be determined there, whether the town of Boston is to comply with the terms of the Port Bill. It is not possible to guess what a body composed of such heterogeneous matter will determine; but the

members from hence, I am assured, will promote the most haughty and insolent resolves, for their plan has ever been, by threats and high-sounding sedition, to terrify and intimidate.

John Adams carefully noted the party's progress in his *Diary*. Silas Deane, one of the leading Patriots in Hartford, entertained them at his home, and a splendid dinner was served, complete with punch, wine and coffee. A number of members of the local Committee of Correspondence called on the visitors, and a company of gentlemen escorted them as far as Wethersfield when they took their departure. They were greeted on the approach to New Haven by some hundreds of persons, including most of the local officials. Church bells pealed as they rode into the town, and the cannon on the Green were fired in their honor. They dined with Roger Sherman, one of Connecticut's delegates to the Congress, and Sam Adams struck up a friendship that would last for many years.

Among the towns that turned out en masse to greet the gentlemen from Massachusetts were Milford, Fairfield, Norwalk, Hamford and Kingsbridge, and everyone wanted to meet Sam Adams, universally recognized as the man responsible for the creation of the Patriot cause. The party reached New York Town on the twentieth, and, fatigued by the long journey, remained there for six days, conferring with John Jay and other New York delegates to the Congress.

On August 26 they crossed to New Jersey, dined at Elizabethtown and spent the next two nights in Brunswick. On the twenty-ninth they passed the Delaware, and at Frankfort were met by a welcoming committee of prominent Philadelphians. When they reached the city, "dirty, dusty and fatigued," they were escorted to their tavern, "the most genteel one in America," and remained there for a day or two before renting lodgings in a house on Arch Street belonging to Miss Jane Port.

Sam Adams felt instant rapport with Christopher Gadsden of South Carolina, with whom he had been corresponding for eight years, and who was called "the Sam Adams of the South." He established a deep, long-lasting relationship with Richard Henry

Lee of Virginia, another of his correspondents, and respected the views of Patrick Henry, though he thought his personality a trifle too dry. Adams and Richard Henry Lee already knew they thought in similar terms, and they formed an alliance that would last through both the First and Second Continental Congresses. Another with whom Adams established friendly relations was John Dickinson, the great Pennsylvania propagandist. But, like so many others, he felt a little uncomfortable in the presence of Colonel George Washington of Virginia, whose austere, aloof manner made it difficult for anyone to get close to him.

The First Continental Congress that began its deliberations on September 1, 1774, has achieved a place of enormous significance in American history because it was the first time that representatives of twelve colonies south of the Province of Quebec (Georgia not being represented) had met under one roof. Contrary to the belief of the Loyalists, however, they were not wild-eyed radicals determined to foment revolution at any price. The majority were conservative men of substance, and many were there to protect their interests and those of colleagues at home whose fortunes and property were being jeopardized by the colonies' rapidly deteriorating relationship with Great Britain. Sam Adams, Gadsden, Lee, Henry and some others spoke of independence from the outset, but the general mood of the Congress was cautious and exploratory. Only a few of the delegates had been elected by the legislatures of the colonies, the others had been selected by extralegal "conventions"; but posterity has concluded that most shades of public opinion were fairly represented.

The spotlight was on Sam Adams from the outset. He was the leader of martyred Boston, he had corresponded with many of the Patriots from other colonies and, above all, he was recognized as the genius responsible for the Boston Tea Party. No man present was more experienced in the ways of legislatures, and he knew that important matters were decided in private conferences, not on the floor of an assembly, where a politician became a statesman and spoke for the sake of the record. The diaries and journals of First Continental Congress delegates are filled with references to the meetings of key members in lodging houses and the private dining rooms of inns and taverns. This was a game Adams could play to perfection, and he showed his muscle before the Congress opened.

He wanted the Congress to meet in Carpenters' Hall because he believed the name would appeal to the working classes of the colonies, and he rallied enough support to win acceptance of the designation. Then, acting as temporary chairman and preferring not to remain in the limelight himself, he secured the election of Charles Thomson, a Philadelphia radical, as permanent chairman. Some of the more conservative delegates indicated discomfort, and a number of southerners felt the North was trying to dominate the proceedings.

These sentiments became clear when a fight broke out over the election of a chaplain. Adams, known by all to be a prominent member of the Congregational church, obtained the floor and poured a healing balm on the chafed sensitivities of conservatives and southerners by moving that all other activity cease so that the Reverend Mr. Duché, an Episcopalian clergyman, could lead the members in prayer. Thereafter he nominated Duché for the post of permanent chaplain, and the gesture, which cost him nothing, won him a number of new friendships, among them that of Colonel Washington.

Adams and the wealthy Virginia planter had little in common, and they shared few tastes and fewer interests, but they began an association based on mutual respect that would last for the rest of their long lives. Both were realists, and both thoroughly understood the uses of power. Adams's friendship with Richard Henry Lee was personal, while that with the moderate, soft-spoken Washington was based on necessity; when the Grand Incendiary discovered that Washington was the real leader of the Virginia delegation, with the others deferring to him on questions of substance, he dealt accordingly with the man who could obtain results.

He and Washington held a number of private meetings throughout the Congress, and although no one has ever known precisely what happened at these sessions, the results speak for themselves. The delegations of Massachusetts and Virginia, the two most prominent and prestigious at the convention, almost always voted together.

The leader who became the general spokesman for the conservatives was Joseph Galloway, a Philadelphia attorney who subsequently joined the Loyalists. He was one of the principal authors of what came to be known as the Galloway Plan, which, if adopted, might have effected a reconciliation between the colonies and Great Britain. Under this plan the colonies would have formed a national assembly which would have asserted control over their joint interests, and no bill affecting the colonies would have become law without the approval of both Houses of Parliament and the new colonial council, which, in effect, would have become a third chamber of Parliament. The scheme was noteworthy because, although obviously clumsy, it might have been an important step leading to the formation of constitutional guarantees within the framework of the British Empire.

But the plan was anathema to the majority, who agreed with Sam Adams that Britain had to recognize the rights of the colonies as the colonies themselves viewed them. If possible, peaceful means would be used, but if necessary, the colonies would resort to force to gain respect for their approach. The Galloway Plan was roundly defeated.

John Adams offered an explanation of Cousin Sam's methods in his *Diary,* saying:

> We have had numberless prejudices to remove here. We have been obliged to act with great delicacy and caution. We have been obliged to keep ourselves out of sight, and to feel pulses and sound the depths; to insinuate our sentiments, designs, and desires, by means of other persons; sometimes of one Province, and sometimes of another.

But Sam Adams's discretion fooled no one. A Maryland Loyalist later wrote with great bitterness: "Adams with his crew, and the haughty sultans of the South, juggled the whole conclave of the delegates."

The Caucus Club tactics and techniques that had been so effective in the Boston town meeting and the Massachusetts Assembly worked wonders in Philadelphia, too. Sam Adams could write to his friends that the sentiments of the congressional majority precisely mirrored their own views, but he neglected to add that he was responsible for this phenomenon. The Congress was obligingly obedient to the will of a master politician.

Adams's first victory was the adoption by the Congress of the so-called Suffolk Resolves, which were drawn up by a convention in Suffolk County, Massachusetts—in other words, the Boston Patriots. The convention passed them on September 9, and Paul Revere set a new record by reaching Philadelphia with a copy one week later, on the sixteenth. On the eighteenth the Congress adopted the Resolves by an overwhelming majority, and what makes the action remarkable is that there was so little debate.

The Suffolk Resolves repeated the list of the colonies' grievances against the mother country in the exaggerated language familiar to anyone who knew the written works of Sam Adams. It was the duty of all Americans to maintain and proclaim their own rights, the document declared; the Coercive Acts were "gross infractions" of those rights, so Americans owed "no obedience" to these measures. Judges who accepted salaries from the Crown held office "unconstitutionally," and those who were involved in lawsuits were advised to settle their differences out of court. All citizens were urged to take part in regular military drills in order to prepare for the future, and a flat warning was issued to Great Britain. Americans would remain exclusively on the defensive "so long as such conduct may be vindicated by reason and the principles of self-preservation, but no longer." Thus anyone in Great Britain who could read knew that the Congress had put a chip on its collective shoulder and was daring the Crown and Parliament to knock it off.

Private agreements that the delegates reached and that never saw the light of print were equally remarkable. Adams and his Massachusetts colleagues were repeatedly assured by the members of the other eleven delegations in attendance that arms and fighting men would be forthcoming in the event Massachusetts was forced to resort to violence in the protection of "lives and liberty."

Undoubtedly Adams's greatest triumph was the formation of the Continental Association, a plan that was adopted by the Congress on October 20 by the usual lopsided majority. This document provided that after December 1, 1774, no British merchandise of any kind, with the exception of a few medicines and drugs available nowhere else, would be imported by the colonies. After September 1, 1775, all exports to Great Britain and her West Indian possessions would cease.

In order to enforce this agreement, every county, city and town in the colonies was instructed to appoint special committees whose "business it shall be attentively to observe the conduct of all persons," and to make up a blacklist of those who refused to join in the total embargo. Also, all Committees of Correspondence were urged to keep a close watch on customs entries and to take "appropriate action" against violators. It is small wonder that Joseph Galloway wrote that the conservatives were intimidated by threats of mob action, and kept increasingly quiet.

No military plans for the future were made public; Adams and his colleagues preferred to keep such matters secret. But everyone knew that the acknowledged military expert of the Congress, Colonel Washington, who had served with distinction in the French and Indian War, was holding private daily conferences behind locked doors with the members who were interested in military affairs.

The results of the Congress to date had exceeded the expectations of most delegates, but Sam Adams was not yet satisfied. Basic propaganda needs had not been filled, and the Congress had not yet issued the sort of ringing statement that the people of Massachusetts had learned to expect from their Assembly and the Boston town meeting. In his private sessions Adams stressed that it was desirable to address a direct statement to the Crown and to Parliament so that the whole world would know what was at stake. Therefore the Congress should draw up a Declaration of Rights and Grievances.

Richard Henry Lee proposed to the Congress that a committee be named to draw up such a declaration, and to the surprise of no one, Sam Adams became its chairman. The document, which contained virtually nothing that had been left unsaid previously, was similar in wording and content to the pamphlet that had been issued on the same subject by the Boston Committee of Correspondence in 1772.

The First Continental Congress ended its sessions on October 31, 1774, and Sam Adams emerged from the convention as a national symbol of opposition to the Crown. Men from all thirteen colonies recognized him as the leader of the independence movement, and he had taken no pains to conceal his aims, either in his few public addresses or many private meetings. He had "forged a network of insurrection," as Dickinson happily observed, and its links were too strong for "King George, Lord North and all their armies and navies" to sever.

By dint of constant correspondence with friends at home Adams had kept Boston and the smaller towns of Massachusetts fully informed of what the Congress was doing. As a result, occupied Boston took heart, and General Gage was having his troubles. So many men were drilling in every community in the colony that the governor, regarding Salem as indefensible, moved the capital back to Boston, at the same time sending an urgent appeal to London for more troops. A quantity of gunpowder was seized by Redcoats in Cambridge and several small artillery pieces fell into army hands in Charlestown. These acts so enraged the people of the colony that Lieutenant Governor Oliver and several other officials were forced to resign.

When General Gage learned that other colonies were following the example of Massachusetts and that men were drilling everywhere, he became still more apprehensive. Even if it had been possible for him to make conciliatory gestures, he did not know how to do it. The only language he knew was military, and he began to erect fortifications on the Neck, the only avenue that connected Boston with the rest of the colony. The city's selectmen promptly protested, but Gage paid no attention, and his troops continued to expand the fortifications.

Sam Adams continued to correspond with friends in England, too, but his reputation as an incendiary was now so great that a new note of caution crept into his letters. He still wrote boldly, but no longer signed the letters. Dr. Franklin, who was still in London, wrote that the name of Adams was regarded there as synonymous with the independence movement.

George Bancroft, the American historian, statesman and politician whose life virtually spanned the nineteenth century, wrote a story about Adams that is not necessarily accurate; Bancroft was sometimes inclined to disregard truth for the sake of emphasizing preconceived notions. In any event, according to his account, former governor Hutchinson was summoned to Whitehall for an audience. King George said he was aware that Samuel Adams was a poor man, and demanded to know the source of his influence.

Hutchinson supposedly replied, "A great pretended zeal for liberty, and a most inflexible natural temper. He was the first who asserted the independency of the Colonies upon the supreme authority of the kingdom."

Certainly Adams had come completely into the open by the time the First Continental Congress met. In a letter written on October 17, 1774, to a friend in Boston, he said:

> I have written to some of our friends to provide themselves without delay with arms and ammunition, to get well instructed in the military art, to embody themselves, and prepare a complete set of rules, that they may be ready in case they are called to defend themselves against the violent attacks of despotism. Surely the law of self-preservation will warrant it in this time of danger and doubtful expectation. One cannot be certain that a distracted minister will yield to the measures taken by Congress, though they should operate to the ruin of the national trade, until he shall have made further efforts to lay America, as he imperiously expressed it, *prostrate at his feet.*

No matter how frankly Adams spoke in his letters or in private meetings with other members of the Congress, he maintained a discreet silence on the subject of independence on the floor of the Congress itself, and his Declaration of Rights and Grievances stopped just short of recommending open insurrection. Over a period of two busy months he had formed valuable friendships with like-minded men in other colonies and the groundwork of revolution had been laid, but the public at large was not yet ready for the final step. A few additional preparations had to be made, and the ultimate blame for starting a war had to be laid at the feet of the British.

Chapter
Twenty-one

When Sam Adams and his fellow Massachusetts delegates to the First Continental Congress arrived home in late
November 1774, it quickly became apparent to them that war was
approaching and that the tide had become irreversible. The seeds
Adams had sown for so many years were bearing fruit, and the
tensions, misunderstandings and conflicts between the people of
Massachusetts Bay and the Crown authorities were becoming
unbearable. Even Adams himself appears to have been somewhat
surprised by the steady deterioration of the relationship.

This was due, at least in part, to the deliberate policies adopted
by Lord North and his ministers. While the attention of America
was riveted on the Continental Congress, the British government, regarding the state of affairs in Massachusetts as a test case,
was taking stern, rigorous steps to reassert the authority of the
Crown in the colony. North's basic failure was his inability to
realize that times had changed and that it was no longer possible
to revert to the situation that had existed prior to 1760. Until that
time the legislature of the colony had been semimoribund, no
political organizations had existed and the power of Crown au-

thorities had been taken for granted. Now a public awakened, agitated and aroused by Sam Adams was demanding its own brand of equality and would not settle for less. Organized opposition to the Patriots in Massachusetts Bay was at an end, and the people were virtually united in their support of the cause for which Adams had so long been the self-appointed spokesman.

Had Lord North known anything about the colonies and the differences between them, he might have selected a different target. Massachusetts, with a population approaching four hundred thousand, was angry, hurt, and volatile, ready to retaliate against the Coercive Acts that had been aimed exclusively at her. As Lord North would learn much later, there were still strong groups of Loyalist sympathizers in New York Town and Philadelphia, and a military governor in either of those cities might have won a measure of public support. But this was not the case in Boston, where every man was now a Patriot—in part, to be sure, because the conservatives were afraid of the Sons of Liberty and of mob action that might damage their property and injure their persons.

Town meetings were forbidden now without the express permission of the governor, but town after town continued to convene its citizens. The people believed they could openly defy the Crown because Gage had too few troops under his command to force nearly four hundred thousand people to obey the Coercive Acts. Being a sensible man, the governor knew it, and whenever he received orders from Lord Dartmouth, the colonial secretary, which he knew were impossible to obey, he replied by submitting another demand for more troops.

The inexperienced Gage was no match for Sam Adams and his pupils in the art of political jousting, and on one occasion he was made to look positively foolish. He dissolved the Assembly because it had sent delegates to the Continental Congress; then he had ordered elections for a new General Court, and had directed that it meet on October 5.

With Sam Adams guiding his disciples by letter from Philadelphia, Boston and the smaller towns ignored the governor's directive. Instead they elected members to a new, extralegal body they called the Provincial Congress, and announced that it would hold its first session on October 5, the precise date the governor had set for the meeting of the General Court.

Gage had two choices, both uncomfortable. He could use troops to prevent the meeting of the Provincial Congress, but he was afraid this might trigger the start of the war for which Britain was unprepared and undermanned. Or he could ignore the fact that the Congress meeting on October 5 was not the duly constituted Assembly, even though much of the membership undoubtedly was the same. In this event, he knew, he would become the laughingstock of Massachusetts and of other colonies. Being prudent, he followed the latter course, although it was painful to swallow his pride.

Adams, writing from Philadelphia, cautioned his colleagues at home to make certain they observed the forms authorized in the Massachusetts Bay charter. "*There is charm in the word 'constitutional,'*" he informed Dr. Warren. Then he checked with his colleagues from other colonies and wrote again, saying that Massachusetts would receive the support of her sister colonies if forced to fight in self-defense, but that no help of any kind would be forthcoming if she tried to establish an independent government. His advice was heeded, and the Provincial Congress, which met first at Salem and then transferred its deliberations to Concord, called itself the legal successor to the General Court. It was careful to observe such opening-day amenities as offering a pledge of allegiance to the Crown and sending official notification to the governor that it was in session.

Thereafter, the members did their best to upset the old order, and in less than a week they struck a major blow. All tax collectors in Massachusetts were "advised"—in other words, directed —to give no receipts to the official treasurer of the province, but to hold all funds until further notice. The following week a "receiver general" was named by the Congress, and tax collectors were told to pay all moneys to him.

Steps were taken at the same time to enforce the provisions of the Continental Association set up by the Continental Congress, and a special committee was named to supervise these efforts. It was given exceptionally broad powers, including the unprecedented right to confiscate the stock of any merchant who bought British goods or sold products or raw materials of any kind to Britain.

Many of Boston's wealthier and more prominent merchants, including some who had Patriot sympathies, believed that the Patriots were going too far, and countered the move by establishing a private association of their own. They proposed to assist each other in the event that one or more were threatened, and, adopting the language of Sam Adams, they said their purpose was the protection of life, liberty and property.

By the time Sam Adams returned to Boston in November, however, these brave pronouncements proved to be mere words. The city was still under military rule, and the people refused to support a merchant or anyone else who showed the slightest degree of loyalty to the Crown. Members of the Merchants' Association had the good sense to keep quiet, and those who had Loyalist sympathies began to liquidate their holdings and to make plans for a move to Canada or Great Britain.

By December 1774, a state of near anarchy reigned in Massachusetts. The Assembly no longer existed, its place taken by a body composed of a single house that combined the functions of the old Assembly and the Council, but this new organization was not recognized by the governor. Judges were afraid to accept their salaries from the Crown, and the towns were so lax in making payments to the Congress-appointed "receiver general" that no funds were available from the rump legislature to pay them, either. So the courts no longer functioned, and the administration of justice ground to a halt.

John Adams, who apparently had not expected this swift development, revealed his perturbation in his *Diary*:

> The difficulties we suffer, for want of law and government, are innumerable; a total stagnation of law, and of commerce almost. . . . We have no council, no house, no legislature, no executive. Not a court of justice has sat since the month of

September. Not a debt can be recovered, nor a trespass redressed, nor a criminal of any kind be brought to punishment.

Military preparations were speeded, with the Provincial Congress supervising and coordinating activities. Companies of men met daily throughout the colony for "exercise," town leaders blandly assuring the governor that no armed insurrection was intended. Company officers met to form battalions, and regiments came into being, each higher echelon electing its own officers. The Provincial Congress named a Committee of Safety for the purpose of maintaining a watch on all British troop movement so an alarm could be given in the event General Gage decided to commence military operations. And a subcommittee headed by Colonel Jeremiah Lee secretly began to purchase large quantites of ammunition and gunpowder in New York and Rhode Island. These munitions were stored in Worcester and Marblehead, out of Gage's immediate reach and guarded by Sons of Liberty volunteers who were told to use their arms, if necessary, to protect the sinews of war.

Tensions ran so high that in mid-October, while Sam Adams was still in Philadelphia, the colony reacted instantly and explosively when it was falsely rumored that British troops had launched an attack on Boston. Within a few hours, according to the *Gazette*, more than twenty thousand men were marching toward the city, all of them "completely armed." Two days later one hundred thousand men clogged the roads, reported the newspaper, and the Massachusetts militia were joined by volunteer units from New Hampshire and Rhode Island. The figures obviously were a wild exaggeration, but it was nevertheless true that men everywhere responded eagerly to a call to arms.

Only the cautious good sense of General Gage, to whom posterity has given too little credit, prevented the outbreak of open hostilities months before the war actually began. Gage was familiar enough with the temper of the colonies to know that to defeat them by force of arms would be a herculean undertaking, and his sober reports to the Colonial Office and the War Office stressed the need for fifty to one hundred thousand troops, a fleet large enough and powerful enough to seal off the Atlantic coastline and vast numbers of merchant ships that could ferry supplies of all kinds to a huge army of occupation that, because of colonial hostilities, could not be expected to live off the land.

Had Gage's advice been given greater weight, it is possible that war could have been avoided—provided that Parliament had been willing to grant the Americans total self-rule. But Lord North and a majority in both Houses of Parliament, like King George himself, simply could not accept the fact that most Americans were willing to sever all relations with the Crown and set up an independent nation. They clung to the belief that an incendiary minority continued to be responsible for all agitation in the colonies, that the Continental Congress had been composed exclusively of these Radicals and that most Americans remained loyal to Great Britain. They admitted that the situation in Boston was different, but to explain the solid opposition to the Crown there they claimed that Sam Adams had succeeded in poisoning the minds of the people.

What London completely failed to understand was that the efforts of Adams and the members of Committees of Correspondence in all thirteen colonies had been remarkably effective, thanks in part to the bungling of Lord North's ministry. The North American climate had changed drastically, and although it cannot be claimed with certainty that at this stage, before actual hostilities began, a majority of the American people wanted independence, the group in favor of such a move had increased greatly and the shrinking minority group of Loyalists was forced to remain silent. This miscalculation on the part of the British government was the last and perhaps the greatest of the blunders made in London. For all practical purposes, war was now unavoidable.

America's friends in England nevertheless renewed their efforts to find a peaceful solution of the crisis. The Earl of Chatham praised the Continental Congress's Declaration of Rights for "solidity of reason, force of sagacity, and wisdom of conclusion." And he urged the adoption of a system on the order of the

Galloway Plan as an interim measure that would keep the colonies within the British Empire while a new, permanent method of governing America was worked out by both sides. Burke, who failed to realize how advanced public opinion had become, asked for a return to the amicable relations of the period before 1763. British merchants were alarmed, and several hundred of them submitted a petition to the government requesting an immediate, drastic modification of the ministry's policies.

But the king and North were determined not to surrender to the American radicals, and an election proved they had the support of the voters, who resented the insults heaped on Britain by the colonial press. Chatham, struggling in vain, submitted a motion for the withdrawal of troops from Boston, but the measure was supported by only eighteen members. Both Houses of Parliament then went on record, huge majorities supporting Lord North and authorizing him to subdue rebellion in the New World by any means he saw fit.

Lord North himself made a belated attempt to stave off a war by putting through a bill that offered any colony exemption from taxation provided it raised a stipulated, agreed sum that would be used for support of the empire. His timing could not have been worse, and even those Americans still sympathetic to the Crown believed that the measure was an attempt to divide them.

The War Office and the Admiralty were not standing still while the political jockeying for position entered its final phase. A dozen or more regiments advertised extensively for recruits, promising many benefits to men who would join. And, as was the custom throughout Europe, negotiations were opened with the rulers of various German principalities, who hired troops to the highest bidders. The keels were laid for more than one hundred new warships, and the shipyards were working overtime. The Navy could not obtain enough new men, so press gangs roamed the streets, kidnapping the unwary and defenseless, then brutally forcing them into naval duty.

Meanwhile public opinion was crystallizing rapidly in America, and for the first time the public remained abreast of the deluge of editorials and essays that Sam Adams wrote after his return from Philadelphia. His boast, in a letter to Richard Henry Lee, that "there are no more Loyalists" in Massachusetts was not as exaggerated a claim as it appeared. In Virginia the moderates of the tideland plantation country accepted a partnership with the pioneers of the west, who were vociferous in their demands for independence, and Lee was correct when he said that Virginia and Massachusetts stood in the vanguard of those who sought a complete break with Great Britain.

The silence of the Loyalists made them appear weaker than was actually the case. Merchants in New York, Philadelphia and Charleston had no desire to terminate their union with the British Empire. The Quakers of Pennslvania and Delaware, whose creed was peace, offered no encouragement to the Patriots, and even Dickinson hesitated so long at this juncture that some of his friends wondered if he had changed sides. Tory sentiment was strong in the backwaters of the South, too, and pockets of Loyalist strength could be found in almost every colony.

But these men had no Sam Adams to unite them, to articulate their views or to present a positive program. In some instances cowed by the Sons of Liberty, in other cases simply unable to believe that the colonies would go to war for the sake of independence, they remained quiet and disorganized.

General Gage had no illusions about the future, and in one gloomy report to London after another, he declared that he had completely lost control of the interior towns and that his administration was confined to the government of Boston, which he was able to maintain only because of the presence of his British regiments. His situation was precarious, he declared, adding that he was virtually under siege in a city that regarded him and his troops as alien enemies.

Lord Dunmore, the governor of Virginia, felt equally isolated, and having no Redcoats on hand to support and protect him, was in personal, physical danger. A plan to kidnap him and his family was exposed just in time, and on one occasion he and the Virginia militia almost came to blows.

Most of the Massachusetts leadership wanted immediate independence, and Dr. Warren, in a speech delivered only a few days before Sam Adams's return from Philadelphia, urged the colony to "smash the shackles of slavery" before the new year. The *Gazette*, the *Spy* and other Patriot newspapers echoed these sentiments, and the leaders of the movement awaited the return of Sam Adams so he could take personal charge of the drive.

Adams spent a day or two assessing the situation. He read the newspaper editorials that had been written during his absence, listened to summaries of the speeches that Warren and others had made—and then astounded the men who formed the nucleus of the independence movement by telling them that they were acting prematurely. The time for independence, he said, was not yet ripe.

Chapter
Twenty-two

Many of Sam Adams's contemporaries failed to understand the seeming switch in his stance, and felt bewildered by it, as were a number of early nineteenth-century historians, who conducted a fruitless search for his supposed "hidden motives." But nothing could have been simpler than his unexpected stand in favor of moderation.

The truth of the matter was that Adams's long campaign had borne fruit too soon. Massachusetts was ready for open rebellion, it was true, but only Virginia was similarly prepared, and even there such moderates as George Washington would be reluctant to go to war unless the American people had been unduly provoked by an overt British act of hostility. Attendance at the First Continental Congress had convinced Adams, as it had Cousin John and Paine, that eleven of the colonies were not yet ready to fight. If Massachusetts struck the first blow without due and just cause, she would stand alone. It was essential, Adams had learned, that the people of the other colonies be convinced that all other avenues had been fully explored, and that the issues could be settled only by the use of force. Still the supreme realist, he knew that an isolated Massachusetts would be defeated by British troops and the Royal Navy, and forced to her knees. In that event the entire independence movement would collapse, and the waverers everywhere would proclaim their loyalty to the king. All that he had struggled to achieve would be destroyed if Massaschusetts, instead of allowing nature to take her course—which meant waiting for a British blunder—insisted upon striking the first physical blow.

The Provincial Congress reconvened late in November, and Adams hurried to Concord. There, acting in his usual manner, he held private meetings with the leaders of every delegation, impressing them with the urgency of his views. They could *hope* other colonies would come to their support if they rose up against General Gage and his regiments, but he *knew* that the others would make no move and would permit Massachusetts to fight alone. Hancock, at first astounded by the attitude of his friend and mentor, was sensible enough to change his own stand, and such faithful lieutenants as Oliver Wendell and John Pitts followed Adams's lead and added their voices to his, urging the exercise of moderation and tact.

The Royal Navy was vigorous in maintaining the quarantine of Boston, and not one merchant ship entered or left the port. Even small fishing vessels from other parts of Massachusetts were not permitted to enter the harbors, and the city chafed as her hardships increased. Adams realized that the load was increasingly difficult to bear, but, as he wrote to Arthur Lee early in January 1775, the people had no real choice, and were compelled to tolerate the unpleasantness as best they could. The present situation could not long continue, he declared, although the people were becoming increasingly discouraged because they could see no relief in sight.

Eleven regiments of British troops were now stationed in Boston, and the plan for quartering them in private homes, as provided in the Quartering Act, had proved impractical. Therefore many of them were living in the crowded facilities of the fort; but most were still stationed in the Common, and the use of strict discipline on both sides was necessary to prevent untoward incidents.

The position of the troops was not enviable. The winter was severe, and the men who were forced to sleep in tents fell ill by the hundreds. In late January Sam Adams heard that the Sixty-fifth and Royal Irish regiments had lost more than 50 per cent of their effective strength because of illness, and the story may have been true.

Neither officers nor enlisted men enjoyed any social life other than that which they provided for themselves. They were never invited to dine at private homes; even the Tories refrained from asking them to a meal because of the total ostracism to which they themselves would have been subjected. The trollops of the waterfront refused to sell their favors to the soldiers, and no young lady of the town would speak to an officer, much less permit him to call on her. The quartermasters were unable to buy any meat, fish, vegetables or dairy products on their forays into the countryside or their visits to shore towns, and literally all food consumed by the regiments had to be brought from England.

The enlisted men accepted their lot with British stoicism, having expected nothing better. But the younger officers, the captains, lieutenants and ensigns, many of them the younger sons of high-ranking aristocrats, resented the snubs, and after consuming quantities of whisky or rum to ward off the cold, were spoiling for trouble. Few people realized how hard General Gage and Sam Adams had to work in order to keep their respective forces in line.

But not even the governor had any idea of the moderating influence Adams was exerting, and in early February, after the Provincial Congress reassembled, electing John Hancock its President, Gage secretly prepared a list of Patriot leaders whom he intended to apprehend at the first sign of trouble and transport to England for trial. Espionage agents planted in the governor's office kept Adams remarkably well informed of activities there, and notified him that he held the honor of heading the list, closely followed by Hancock. The Sons of Liberty, busily forming a paramilitary organization called the Minutemen, wanted to provide him with a full-time escort, but he declined, as did Hancock, both saying it was beneath their dignity to show fear in the face of Crown intimidation.

Meanwhile the efforts that Adams and the other members of the Massachusetts delegation had made at the First Continental Congress were bearing unexpected fruit. Supplies from all of the other colonies were reaching Boston daily, carried across the Neck by convoys under the guard of militiamen. Virginia was particularly generous and donated thousands of tons of corn, meat, fish and flour to the impoverished citizens of Boston.

Early in 1775 the increasingly impatient Lord North, unable to break the city's will to resist, put a new bill through Parliament that proclaimed a state of rebellion in Massachusetts Bay and authorized General Gage to deal with it in any manner he saw fit. The London newspapers declared that Adams and Hancock soon would be hanged, and when copies reached the colonies in February, the families and friends of both men became alarmed. The two were still determined to show no fear, but finally gave in to the pleas of those around them and moved to Cambridge, where they lived in the house of Adams's father-in-law, Francis Wells.

In Cambridge, Adams stepped up the pace of his correspondence with the eldest of his brothers-in-law, Andrew E. Wells, now a resident of Savannah. Loyalist sympathies were strong in Georgia, which had sent no delegation to the First Continental Congress, but Wells and a number of other Patriots had forged a convention which had ratified the acts of the Congress. Subsequently they formed a Provincial Congress in Georgia, and some of the speeches made by Wells and several of his friends bore a remarkable resemblance to the addresses and essays prepared by Sam Adams. Wells knew he lacked his brother-in-law's powers of articulation, so he conveniently gave Adams's compositions a second airing.

Adams himself was looking beyond the day when America formed an independent nation, and at the February sessions of the Massachusetts Provincial Congress he pushed through a number of bills that encouraged the establishment of manufacturing plants. It no longer mattered to him that such factories were strictly forbidden under the terms of every charter the colony had ever been granted, and he did not care if the governor protested and Parliament roared. An independent America would need to make many products for herself, and it was essential that land and funds be made available for the creation of industries. It was not accidental that, in the years that followed, more factories were built in Massachusetts than in any other state in the newly created Union.

It was in February 1775 that Adams also turned his attention to a matter most Committees of Correspondence had been neglecting. The protection of the colonies' northern flank was important, and it had long been Adams's dream to see all of the British provinces on the continent united. He had been hampered by the lack of initiative on the part of the Canadians, who had been British subjects for less than a decade and a half. But now an organization called the Committee of Montreal had been formed in that fur-trading town, so Adams opened a vigorous correspondence with its leaders.

It soon became evident that the Canadians were in no position to join in the movement south of their border. They were a badly divided, impotent people: a majority of the inhabitants of the sparsely settled land were of French descent and Roman Catholics, and were indifferent to the struggle. The English-speaking minority, who were Protestant, sympathized with the other colonies, but they had no lesgislature, their governor was all-powerful, and it was impossible for them to generate enthusiasm for the independence movement. Adams continued to court the Canadians for many months, but he was hampered, too, by the religious prejudices of many of his colleagues, and eventually he was forced to abandon the idea of placing all British colonies in the New World under one flag.

A serious incident was barely averted on March 6, at a Faneuil Hall celebration of the anniversary of the Boston "Massacre" for which Joseph Warren was the scheduled speaker. Sam Adams was the chairman, and he knew trouble loomed when forty young British officers, all of them determined to "beat up a breeze," as he later put it in a letter, entered the hall in a body. Determined to give no one the opportunity to start a riot, he had the front benches cleared and offered them to the Redcoats. The officers occupied them, and several sat on the steps leading up to the podium. They were armed with eggs, which they obviously intended to use, and the situation was delicate.

Warren, forewarned by Adams, made a noninflammatory speech that even the Patriot newspapers called dull, and the officers had no cause to throw their eggs. They hissed, however, when plans for the following year's meeting were being formulated, and Adams halted the proceedings to ask if any of the officers wanted to speak. None accepted, and the meeting continued peacefully to its end.

Adams had judged his tormentors accurately. He reasoned that, since they were aristocrats, they would be shamed into responding in kind if he treated them as gentlemen. His adroit handling of the situation prevented certain bloodshed, and he wrote to Richard Henry Lee a few days later that if fighting had broken out, "I am persuaded . . . not a man of them would have been spared."

In March, prior to the adjournment of the Provincial Congress, Adams took additional action to provide the Americans with allies. Undiscouraged by the failure of the Canadians to join the cause, he acted at once when he learned that the British were making vigorous efforts to turn the principal Indian tribes of the western frontier against the colonists, and sent long, separate letters to each of the five nations that made up the powerful Iroquois Confederation. These communications were masterpieces of propaganda, distorting history to make their points. Addressing the Indians as "brothers," Adams pointed out at length that they and the colonists had been good neighbors for many years. The colonists and paid for all the land they now occupied, he said with a straight face, and only the wicked British had stolen the land of the Iroquois. Now the armies and navies of the British planned to use force to take away the homes and property of the colonists, and would try to steal the land, houses and hunting preserves of the Indians, too. In years past, the colonists had traded happily with the Indians, but that trade would be ended by the British, and the Iroquois would be cut off from all the products on which they now depended. This was doubly sad because the colonists knew the Indians required fire-arms for food and protection. "How can you live without powder and guns?" he asked rhetorically, then added, "We hope to supply you soon with both, of our own making."

Another of his paragraphs speaks for itself: "Brothers,—They have made a law to establish the religion of the Pope in Canada, which lies so near to you. We much fear that some of your children may be induced, instead of worshipping their only true God, to pay *his* dues to images made with their own hands."

The colonists and the Iroquois suffered the same hardships, he declared, and unless they banded together now they would fare even worse. They shared the same desire, to keep "that good land which enables us to feed our wives and children." How, if the British were not halted by joint efforts, the colonists and Iroquois alike would forfeit all they possessed.

Adams made a valiant effort, but this was one campaign he lost. The British had already beaten him to the punch, and had offered the five nations of the Iroquois more than warm words and mere promises. British agents had paid these tribes, as well as the Ottawa, the Algonkin and others, large sums of gold for their cooperation, and had armed them with new muskets, ammunition and powder. These tribes, although unreliable and erratic, served the British whenever it suited their purposes throughout the war, and caused considerable damage to the colonists' villages and farms in the Mohawk Valley and the Northwest Territory.

But Adams was successful in securing the loyalty of the Stock-bridge and other Indian tribes of western Massachusetts. He not only sent them similar letters, but also dispatched couriers to plead the American cause. These men had traded with the Indians in the past, the warriors trusted them, and the tribes swore to make the cause of Massachusetts their own. They kept their word, and the Stockbridge became so enthusiastic that more than one hundred of their braves became Minutemen. The majority were later incorporated into the Massachusetts militia, but a number became scouts for the Continental Army, the American Regulars, and served with distinction until the end of the war.

Before adjourning, the colonial Congress appointed a Committee on the State of the Province, a body whose duty it would be to approve or disapprove of any major questions that came up before the Committee of Safety, which acted as the executive arm of the extralegal Congress. The Committee of Safety, under the chairmanship of Hancock and the vice-chairmanship of Adams, was vested with supreme powers, whose exercise would then be ratified by the Committee on the State of the Province, under the chairmanship of Adams and the Vice-chairmanship of Hancock. No one doubted the identity of the men who held the reins of power.

In the latter part of March Adams occupied himself with a project so secret that nothing was committed to writing. He employed three couriers, who spent the better part of their time traveling to and from the other New England colonies, New Hampshire, Connecticut and Rhose Island. There they delivered verbal messages from Adams to leaders of the other colonies, men with whom Adams had become friendly in Philadelphia and whom he knew he could trust. These gentlemen sent him verbal messages in return.

Finally, on April 8, a meeting of the Committee on the State of the Province was held in Concord. All the members of the Provincial Congress were regarded as members of the committee, and one hundred and eight of them appeared. Spring had come late to Massachusetts and the room in which the meeting was held had no fireplace and was exceptionally cold; but guards could be placed at each of the windows, the doors could be locked and the entire building could be isolated. Therefore warmer quarters were not sought.

The first order of business was the passage of a resolution that permitted members of the committee to keep their hats on in order to ward off the cold.

Then Chairman Adams swore all present to an oath of secrecy and revealed the subject of his recent intensive negotiations. Massachusetts would join with her sister New England colonies in the formation of a single army under a unified command. Nothing would be done to activate this force until events made it necessary, but, if approved by the four Provincial Congresses, the senior commanders would meet in the immediate future to elect their generals and set up staffs. No officers below the rank of lieutenant colonel would even be told that such an army existed. As soon as arrangements could be made the commanding general of the army and his staff would meet with three delegates from each of the four colonies to determine the size of the army and resolve problems of obtaining munitions, uniforms and supplies.

The proceedings of the meeting were never written up, so the precise reaction of the committee members is not known. Presumably it was unnecessary for Adams to spell out the fact that the formation of a New England army would bring the colonies to the brink of war. Only 7 members abstained from voting, apparently shrinking from the consequences, and 101 voted in favor of the military confederation.

Less than two weeks later, events of a nature that should have been anticipated by both sides hastened the process.

Chapter
Twenty-three

A deceptive quiet in Massachusetts in the winter and early spring of 1775 lulled General Gage into a false sense of security. No untoward events of consequence had occurred, the extralegal Provincial Congress had passed no outrageous or insulting legislation and no attempts were being made to break the blockade of Boston. The governor even misinterpreted the actions taken by Sam Adams and his cohorts at the Boston "Massacre" ceremonies, mistaking disciplined discretion for a new, chastened attitude. Early in April he wrote to the Colonial Office that, although it was too early to make any definite predictions, it was possible that the spirits of the Massachusetts rebels had been broken.

There are two versions of the prelude to "the shot heard round the world." According to one, General Gage believed the time was at last ripe for him to establish garrisons in places other than Boston and, eventually, move some of his supplies from that citadel to smaller communities. The second version, universally accepted without question by virtually all residents of the thirteen American colonies, was that the governor sent out an expedition to seize and destroy secret Patriot arms caches.

Rumors to that effect were heard in Boston on April 17, and were taken so seriously by Sam Adams and his colleagues that on the eighteenth they sent special messengers to every town in the colony, summoning members of the Provincial Congress to an immediate session. Adams himself left Cambridge on the eighteenth, presumably going with Hancock to the little village of Concord.

If it is true that Gage had made up his mind to take definite action and seize the military stores, it may be equally true that he ordered the arrest of Adams and Hancock at this time. His orders were given verbally, so no one has ever known precisely what he directed.

In any event, the facts are simple and tragic. On the morning of April 19, a column of British troops commanded by a Major Pitcairn approached the little town of Lexington en route to Concord. The detachment had left Boston the previous night, but the Minutemen who comprised the informal Massachusetts militia had kept a close watch on its movements.

At an hour when most citizens of Massachusetts Bay were sitting down to breakfast, the Redcoats approached the central square in Lexington. At the far end stood the town's meeting house, and in the Green before it, in a loose military formation, was a company of colonial militia. Most were armed with long rifles rather than muskets, and many wore armbands in lieu of uniforms. It appeared to Major Pitcairn that the Americans had gathered to dispute his right to pass, so he rode forward and ordered them to disperse.

Captain John Parker, the commander of the militia unit, realized that his men were badly outnumbered and that their arms were inferior to those of the Redcoats, so he corroborated the order, directing the company to withdraw.

As Parker's men started to obey, a single shot was fired. No one has ever been able to determine, down to the present day, whether the shot came from a confused militiaman or a British soldier who misunderstood Major Pitcairn's order. That shot, nevertheless, was the beginning of the American War of Independence.

The military engagement that followed was of slight significance as such, but to those who could interpret it correctly, it had deep meaning. A brief skirmish ensued, and although the Americans stood up to their foes for a short time, they were forced to withdraw. The British detachment then marched to Concord, where another small militia unit was encountered, and after a few exchanges of shots, these Americans also retired from the field. When Pitcairn led his men back to Boston, however, the story was far different. Minutemen concealed themselves in the forests and in the high grasses of the fields, shooting at the scarlet-clad targets that stubbornly refused to break ranks. The slaughter was frightful, and the march became a complete rout. "We beat them in the fight," American humorists said, "but they beat us in the race."

The Battle of Lexington and Concord, as the minor engagement was called, proved two things. First, American militiamen with little or no military training were capable of standing up to British Regulars. Equally important, Americans could win if they ignored the formalities of battle used in Europe and concentrated instead on their own frontier tactics, which they, the Indians and the malleable French who had come to the New World had used with such great success.

General Gage refused to regard the incident seriously, and his report to London indicated that it had been only a very minor skirmish. He soon learned better, and Adams was his instructor.

One of the purposes of the Redcoats' march to Concord was the arrest of Adams and Hancock, for the governor's patience finally had been exhausted. The pair had been elected by the Provincial Congress, just prior to its adjournment, as two of Massachusetts' delegates to the Second Continental Congress, which was scheduled to begin its deliberations in Philadelphia on May 10. It had been their intention to attend the emergency session of the colonial legislature and then proceed directly to Pennsylvania.

They were the overnight guests of the Reverend Jonas Clark, a Congregational clergyman who lived in Lexington, and at his house they received word from Dr. Warren that the British would be on the march within a few hours. Eight militiamen had been standing guard duty outside Dr. Clark's house when the reliable Paul Revere arrived to deliver the message. The sergeant in charge of the detail refused to admit him, explaining that everyone in the house had retired early after requesting there be no noise in the area.

"Noise!" Revere said. "You'll have noise enough before long. The Regulars are coming out!"

The sergeant opened the door for him, Adams and Hancock were alerted, and at 1:00 A.M. the Lexington militiamen began to muster on the Green. Adams and Hancock arrived there about an hour later, by which time about 130 of the volunteer troops were on hand, and they watched the loading of two small cannon. The British had not yet appeared, so the men dispersed at about 4:00 A.M., subject to immediate recall. Adams and Hancock accompanied a number of officers to Buckman's Tavern, located about two miles from the town, for an early breakfast.

While they lingered over coffee, drums sounded the alarm, and the pair were persuaded to remain at the tavern, with a detachment of militiamen as their escort. Captain Parker brought them the news of the skirmish on the Green. The safety of the two leaders was regarded as vitally important, and they were urged to retire across open fields to the village of Woburn, out of the path of the Redcoats, who were then marching on to Concord. At first Adams demurred, but he was persuaded to behave sensibly, and again the militia provided an escort.

As they made their way through the fields Adams is reported to have remarked, "Oh! what a glorious morning is this!"

Whether he actually made the unlikely statement cannot be ascertained. Wells accepted and reported it as a fact, and in 1825 it was the subject of an address by Edward Everett, regarded as the greatest New England orator of his day. Regardless of its authenticity, the statement has been handed down to posterity as one of Sam Adams's most celebrated remarks.

No matter what he may have said, Sam Adams knew that the fight for freedom had begun. He and Hancock stayed in Woburn for two days, and during that time they issued another call for a meeting of the Provincial Congress, which convened a week later. Afraid Gage would learn their whereabouts and would again try to take them into custody, on April 21 they moved to the little village of Billerica, where they passed their time writing long, inspirational messages to be read to the Provincial Congress.

On the twenty-fourth they proceeded to Worcester, where "every man was a Patriot, and the very name of the King was an epithet." There they were to meet John Adams, Paine and Cushing, the other Massachusetts delegates to the Continental Congress. But the trio had not yet appeared, and in the absence of news of any kind from Boston, Hancock became panicky. Had the other delegates been arrested? What was the Provincial Congress doing? What were the reactions of the members and of the public at large to the stirring events in Lexington and Concord? What steps were being taken to secure the relief of Boston, which had to be wrested from the Redcoats by force of arms?

Lacking information of any kind, Hancock wrote a long letter to the Committee of Safety, his tone revealing his near-hysteria. He felt like a deserter, he said, although he knew his duty required him to proceed to Philadelphia. Adams was far calmer, and sent a quiet letter to his son, directing the young physician to burn a number of bundles of correspondence that could be used to brand himself and a number of other persons as traitors if they fell into the hands of the British.

By the twenty-seventh the pair felt they could wait for their missing colleagues no longer, and as their personal safety was considered essential to the cause, they were escorted to Hartford by a full company of militia. The Connecticut capital was completely in the hands of the Patriots, and the two delegates from Massachusetts joined the Connecticut Committee of Correspondence and Intelligence, that colony's executive body, in a secret session. At that meeting plans were made to seize Fort Ticonderoga, the strongest British citadel in New York and the key to the control of the West. Soon thereafter, the plan was carried out by Colonel Benedict Arnold of New Haven and Colonel Ethan

Allen of New Hampshire's Vermont Grants, the leader of an irregular band of militia who called themselves the Green Mountain Boys.

John Adams, Cushing and Paine, who had found it necessary to sneak out of Boston singly, caught up with their colleagues on the road to New Haven, where they were joined by the members of the Connecticut delegation to the Second Continental Congress. The two groups traveled together, and as they approached New York Town they were met by an escort of hundreds. Church bells and booming cannon greeted them in Manhattan, and New York militia guarded them around the clock.

They held private meetings with that colony's Committee of Correspondence and Committee of Safety, and after a very brief stay in the city they departed early on the morning of May 8, joined by the New York delegates to the Continental Congress. In addition to the Massachusetts delegation, the group included Roger Sherman, Silas Deane, Eliphalet Dyer, Philip Livingston, John Alsop, James Duane, William Floyd, Francis Lewis and Simon Boerum. Two hundred heavily armed militiamen escorted the delegates, whose capture by the British would have severely injured the Patriot cause, and five hundred enthusiastic New Yorkers also crossed the Hudson River to the New Jersey shore in the flotilla of boats provided for the purpose.

A troop of New Jersey horse troops and a company of heavy infantry was on hand to provide protection, and the party proceeded to Newark, where a banquet was given in honor of the visitors and many patriotic toasts were consumed. But Sam Adams was impatient to be on his way, and immediately after the meal, the group set out for Elizabethtown in a grand procession, with Adams and Hancock riding in the phaeton at the head of the line. They continued to occupy the place of honor all the way to Philadelphia.

When they reached the city the largest crowd yet assembled was on hand to greet them, and a number of men started to remove the horses' harnesses so that they could pull the carriage themselves. Adams protested, declaring that this "honor" was contrary to his democratic principles. Hancock, on the other hand, was pleased, and tried to silence his companion; but Sam Adams remained adamant, announcing that he would get out of the carriage and walk rather than permit fellow humans to "degrade themselves into beasts." This halted the effort, and the horses continued to pull the carriage to its destination.

Adams had an embarrassing personal problem to handle on his arrival in Philadelphia: he had no clothes with him except the travel-soiled suit and linen he had been wearing on his journey. He urgently needed new attire, but had no funds for the purpose. His fellow delegates from Massachusetts urged him to send the bills to the Provincial Congress, but he felt this was wrong and refused. Hancock, aware of his friend's fierce personal pride, said that he would gladly loan him the money, and at last Adams consented. Tailors, haberdashers, shoemakers and shirtmakers were summoned, and Adams was made presentable. Ultimately his colleagues did send the bill to the Provincial Congress, then meeting in Watertown, and the small sum was paid promptly; the members felt that it was the least they could do for a man who had sacrificed everything for the sake of his country's freedom.

The delegations presented their credentials on the morning of May 10, and Adams was horrified to discover that he was the leading candidate for president of the Continental Congress. Before the session opened he made it plain to his many supporters that he did not want and would not accept the honor, arguing that he preferred to work quietly in committee meetings and that holding the presidency would place him too much in the limelight. Then, in order to prevent his friends from ignoring his wishes, he nominated Peyton Randolph of Virginia, who was elected on the first ballot. This caused delegates from some of the smaller colonies to remark that the Massachusetts-Virginia axis was still in operation. Charles Thomson was elected secretary, the Reverend Mr. Duché led the delegates in prayer, and the Second Continental Congress got down to the business of organizing the affairs of a nation at war.

Benjamin Franklin later commented that at this time he had heard no talk in favor of independence, and John Adams said he would have given everything he possessed for a restoration of "the state of things before the contest began, provided we could have had a sufficient security for its continuance." Even Thomas Jefferson, the scholarly young Virginia lawyer who would be the principal author of the Declaration of Independence a year later, shrank from the idea of secession.

Sam Adams was strongly in favor of breaking all ties with Great Britain, but he found himself virtually alone. He tried to utilize his usual technique and spoke to fellow delegates one by one, but their resistance was so great that he finally realized his plan was premature. At no time did he abandon it, however, and less that a week after the Congress convened, he remarked to Richard Henry Lee that "inevitable events" would force the colonies to form an independent nation. He saw what they apparently could not or were reluctant to see, that the conflict could be settled only by the force of arms now, and that no other solutions were available.

Washington became chairman of the Committee of Military Affairs, and after approving the plan to take Fort Ticonderoga, he addressed himself to the problem of the relief of Boston. Volunteers from every colony were marching north to Cambridge, and within a few days Washington himself would go there after the Congress appointed him major general and placed him in overall command of the operation that would become the siege of Boston.

Adams and Benjamin Franklin, recently returned from London, met for the first time at the Congress after corresponding for so many years, and discovered that they liked each other in spite of the many differences in their personalities. Franklin, regarded by many as the greatest American genius of the age, an assessment confirmed by posterity, had been a journalist, too, and he was pleased to discover that Adams was far less belligerent in person than he had been in his letters. They dined together frequently, and although Franklin was irritated by Adams's refusal to eat rich foods or drink anything except watered wine, he found that the delegate from Massachusetts was an eminently sensible man and a practical politician.

The pair had no peers as propagandists, and were jointly responsible for an appeal to King George, an open letter to the Assembly of the island of Jamaica and an address to the people of Ireland. They also worked on an appeal to the people of Canada, but this document was, in the main, the handiwork of John Jay of New York, who ultimately became the first chief justice of the United States, and was the only dull, pedantic document produced by the various committees.

Adams wanted the Congress to authorize and mount an expedition to Canada, believing that men of like sentiments there would join the cause and that Canada would quickly unite with the other provinces. But a majority felt otherwise, and although Adams was supported by the other New England delegates, the idea was opposed by everyone else, and the plan was defeated. This marked one of the only times that Massachusetts and Virginia split on an issue.

President Randolph felt compelled to return to Virginia for a meeting of the Burgesses, and Richard Henry Lee immediately proposed that a delegate from Massachusetts be elected to replace him. That colony, he declared, deserved the honor above all others, and Sam Adams, the first citizen of Massachusetts, again found himself in an uncomfortable spotlight.

But General Gage inadvertently saved him from taking the post. It was known that the governor intended to offer complete amnesty to all Massachusetts rebels except Adams and Hancock, so Sam Adams, ably seconded by Cousin John, argued that Hancock was the right man for the presidency. Not only would his election show the British that the Congress meant business, but he was the wealthiest man in New England, and his elevation to the post of greatest prominence would help convince other rich men who were still wavering that they should join the cause. Hancock, who was not lacking in vanity, was delighted, particularly as it had been the Adams cousins who had nominated and seconded Washington for the post of military commander in chief. There were no other candidates, and Hancock became president, holding the post for many years and, after independence was declared, becoming the first citizen of the young nation.

The business of the Congress kept Sam Adams occupied, but nothing could lessen his worry about the safety of his family in Boston, where Gage had been reinforced by the arrival of three other general officers, William Howe, John Burgoyne and Henry Clinton. More than sixteen thousand Americans were now gathered at Cambridge, their numbers continued to grow, and a climactic showdown could not long be avoided. He prayed for the safety of his wife and children, and at the same time he confided to his friends his certainty that the war soon would spread to other colonies. Just as he had been the first to believe there would be a war, so he was convinced that others would soon share his opinion that America would be forced to declare her independence.

Chapter
Twenty-four

On June 17, 1775, the Americans under General Washington and General Gage's Redcoats fought the Battle of Breed's Hill, later called the Battle of Bunker Hill, the first major engagement of the American War of Independence. The Americans were narrowly defeated, but they proved they could stand up to the most punishing attacks that British infantry, cavalry and artillery, supported by Royal Navy gunfire, could mount. They gave such a good account of themselves that it finally dawned on General Gage that his position was untenable, and he evacuated Boston; so, although the rebels lost a battle, they won a campaign.

The significance of the battle was not lost on Sam Adams, but his pleasure was diluted by the sad news that his good friend Joseph Warren had been killed in combat. Other delegates mourned Breed's Hill as a defeat, but Adams mourned only for his friend and saw the battle in perspective. "We have tolerated the worst a powerful and vicious foe can inflict upon us," he told the Congress. "Never again will Americans be led to believe, falsely, that His Majesty's arms are invincible."

In July the Massachusetts Provincial Congress, having duly

been certified by the Continental Congress as the "official" legislature of a colony that had now formally repudiated General Gage and his administration, put its house in order. Samuel Adams was elected, in absentia, to the new post of secretary of Massachusetts, a position somewhat similar to that which he had held as clerk of the old Assembly, but on a larger scale. The position paid a salary, and his friends undoubtedly saw to his election because they knew his finances were so precarious.

In July, too, Sam Adams finally received welcome news about his family. His son had joined the Massachusetts militia as a surgeon, and would serve in that capacity throughout the war, later transferring to the Continentals. Adams's wife and daughter had vacated Boston and were now living in Cambridge with Mrs. Adams's father. But they had lost the house that had been the pride of Samuel Adams the elder, and had been able to take only a few personal belongings with them. The place was now occupied by newly arrived British officers, and the property had been confiscated by General Gage on the grounds that it belonged to a traitor.

Adams shed no tears for the loss of mere physical possessions and turned his attention to the last major task awaiting the delegates to the Continental Congress. It was the preparation of a typical Adams document, a Declaration of the Causes and Necessity of Taking up Arms. Had he prepared it alone, the paper might well have bristled, but Franklin worked on it with him, and it was cunningly devised to win the sympathies of the Whigs in Parliament and, if possible, open the door to a reconciliation with Great Britain. As much as Adams himself wanted independence, he was scrupulously fair to his fellow delegates, and the declaration represented the views of the great majority.

The full blame for all that had happened was placed on Lord North and his ministers, and the declaration stated, "We are reduced to the alternative of choosing an unconditional submission to the tyranny of irritated Ministers, or resistance by force. . . . The latter is our choice. . . . We have counted the cost of this contest, and find nothing so dreadful as voluntary slavery." The declaration assured Britain that "we mean not to dissolve that union which so long and so happily subsisted between us," and it ended with a prayer that the Ruler of the Universe would "dispose our adversaries to reconciliation on reasonable terms."

Before leaving Philadelphia Adams was distressed to learn that chaotic conditions were developing in Massachusetts, and he was alarmed by the news that many towns were discharging their schoolmasters because they believed they could no longer pay the teachers' wages. In his firm opinion the future of America rested on the education of her young, and he wrote a number of vigorous letters insisting that teachers must be retained at all costs. Education, he said, was "so well calculated to diffuse among the individuals of the community the Principles of Morality, so essentially necessary to the preservation of public Liberty."

Adams did what he could to prevent anarchy in Massachusetts, but he spent little of his time there from 1775 to 1779, and was absent again for the better part of 1781, although he was elected annually to a seat in the new House of Representatives and held the post of secretary of state throughout that time. Most of his time and energy was devoted to the affairs of the developing nation and the problems she had to overcome in her infancy.

Shortly before the adjournment of the Congress on August 1, 1775, Adams made one of his worst mistakes in judgment, and it would haunt him for the rest of his days. Until now he been a good judge of men, but he was deeply impressed by the character of a former British officer who had come to the colonies a few years earlier and had decided to cast his lot with the Americans. Thanks to Adams's influence, Charles Lee was made a major general and officially became second in command of the American armies. He was vain, ambitious and two-faced, and frittered away his considerable talent by conspiring to supplant Washington. Eventually he dealt surreptitiously with the enemy, and was prevented from doing serious, permanent damage only when he was captured by the British.

After the Congress adjourned, the Adams cousins and John Hancock spent far less time on the road than had been their custom, and emulating Paul Revere they arrived at home—which now called itself the Territory of Massachusetts Bay—on the eleventh. Adams spent a few days with his wife and daughter in Cambridge, devoting the better part of his time to conferences with General Washington and learning what was required to drive the British out of Boston. Then he hurried to Watertown, where the Provincial Congress was already in session. He arrived just in time to hear his new title changed to that of secretary of state, and to be elected, without a dissenting vote, to the chairmanship of a new Donations Committee to help Boston's suffering civilians. He served in this capacity faithfully, even after his return to Philadelphia.

He remained in Watertown until the twenty-fourth, when the legislature, now calling itself the House of Representatives, adjourned. Then, after spending a few more days with his wife and daughter and arranging for the better part of his salaries as secretary of state and as a delegate to the continental Congress to be paid to them each month, he hurried back to Philadelphia for the new session of the Congress, which began on September 13.

The Congress was forced to mark time pending word on the reactions of Great Britain to the declaration, but Sam Adams was convinced the king and Lord North would reject a policy of reconciliation, and refused to stand still. Using his time-honored technique of tackling one colleague at a time, he pushed his campaign for independence. Cousin John was one of his first converts, and the pair were regarded as inseparable, which sometimes helped but more often worked to their disadvantage. Some of the smaller colonies were afraid that Massachusetts was trying to dominate the Congress, and consequently their delegates were slow to respond. Dickinson of Pennsylvania harbored an active personal dislike for Cousin John, and campaigned against the independence movement.

Little effort was needed to convince Patrick Henry that independence was desirable, and Richard Henry Lee soon joined the group, too, as did Gadsden of South Carolina. These men formed the hard core, and worked quietly, trying to win converts but never raising the issue on the floor.

The Congress had little money of its own and no way to compel the individual colonies, soon to become states, to pay assessments. This would remain a primary problem throughout the war, much to the disgust of Sam Adams. He made it his personal crusade to obtain supplies and munitions for General Washington, and most of his efforts on the floor of the Congress were devoted to fights for the army's needs. The lack of trust civilians so often show for the military in America was already in evidence, and Adams had his hands full. Again he joined forces with Franklin, and by the end of September they were successful in passing legislation that authorized procurement of arms, munitions, uniforms and supplies for an additional army of twenty-three thousand men.

Adams was also instrumental in obtaining the passage of bills to send Continental troops to the aid of South Carolina and Georgia, where a number of wealthy planters were Loyalists, making it difficult to obtain money there. He responded even more quickly to a plea from Richard Henry Lee for aid in a situation that had developed in Virginia. Precisely as Adams had predicted, the fighting was spreading to other colonies, and Redcoat regiments had appeared in Virginia to uphold the authority of Lord Dunmore. Some of the smaller colonies felt that Virginia was populous and wealthy enough to handle the situation herself, and Sam Adams felt compelled to make one of his few major addresses in the Congress.

No verbatim quotes are available, as no precise records were kept, but Cousin John's ever reliable *Diary* and the *Journal* of Richard Henry Lee give the gist of his remarks. All Americans were in the war together, he declared, and any one colony or territory that failed to come to the aid of her sisters in a time of duress was guilty of treason. She, too, would fall because of a lack of support from the outside when her turn came. Just as it was a man's duty to help extinguish the flames when his neighbor's house caught fire, so it was the sacred duty of every colony to put the welfare of all before its own selfish considerations. The people of Boston were suffering at this very moment, living under the tyranny of enemy military occupation because they put a love of freedom for all Americans first. He himself had lost all of his property to the Crown because he had so insistently demanded liberty for all Americans, not only for his fellow Bostonians and the people of Massachusetts. The war would be won and the tyrant driven from the land only when Americans from all thirteen colonies fought side by side, as they were doing in the siege of Boston, and when they were given the undivided support of their political servants.

The debate that followed Adams's address was desultory, and the aid Virginia had requested was voted without further delay.

Adams was jealous of what would come to be called states' rights, however, and made his sentiments clear in a long letter he wrote to Elbridge Gerry, dated October 29, 1775, on the subject of the Massachusetts militia. The territory should be "cautious in putting the militia under the direction of generals of the continent, at least until such a legislative shall be established all over America as every Colony shall consent to." The Continental Army, he declared, was "very properly" under the direction of the Continental Congress. But "prudence" required that the militia of each colony "should be and remain under the sole direction of its own legislative, which is, and ought to be, the sovereign and uncontrollable power within its own limits or territory." It was the duty of the militia to fight outside the territorial limits of a colony when necessity dictated, but it should be permitted to do this only upon application to the government of the colony. The militia was the "natural strength" of a colony, and should be "employed for your own safety and strength."

This shortsighted approach would hamper Sam Adams in the years ahead, and at no time did he grasp the importance of granting supreme powers to a national government in the conduct of foreign affairs, military direction or, above all, taxation. In his mind the individual state remained the "natural" seat of all powers, and a citizen owed his first allegiance to it. It would remain for younger men with broader vision to form the concept and bring into being the national government composed of balanced branches that would administer the affairs of the United States of America.

Adams was at his best in organizing the fight for freedom, and his colleagues in the Congress were not slow to recognize this quality. As a member of a committee to improve the defenses of New York he refused to tolerate delays in the establishment of a chain of forts on the Hudson River, and pounded incessantly at his committee colleagues until they approved the projects. He became a member and eventually was elected chairman of the Military Selections Committee—there was one from each colony —that granted commissions to all army officers and approved all promotions. He was also one of a handful who fought success- fully for the establishment of a navy. Some members thought the idea insane, but he enlisted the support of Dr. Franklin and Richard Henry Lee, and Cousin John, who had become an excel- lent speaker, was the principal navy advocate in the debates that ensued on the floor of the Congress. The measure passed before the end of the year.

The cousins rented joint lodgings from a Mrs. Yard; each had his own bedchamber and they shared a large living room. They spent most of their waking hours together, making and receiving joint social calls, going for walks and dining. Cousin Sam was the "disputatious" member of the team, according to Cousin John, and when he was trapped in an argument the young lawyer could be depended upon to come to his rescue.

They were jointly responsible for the twin expeditions into Canada, led by Brigadier General Richard Montgomery and Colonel Benedict Arnold, that were authorized in the autumn of 1775. And they were among the few who were farsighted enough, at this juncture, to give their hearty approval to a plan to estab- lish a new territory being formed by the Company of Transylva- nia in what would become Kentucky and Ohio. Since the Crown had awarded this territory to Virginia under her original chart- ers, Sam Adams used his good offices in an attempt to persuade the Virginians to give up their claims to the land for the good of the entire country. But the Virginians clung to their rights, just as Massachusetts would do when her turn came, and the idea had to be abandoned.

Among those with whom Sam Adams formed friendships at this time was an immigrant from England who had become editor of the influential Pennsylvania *Gazette,* Thomas Paine. An introvert who had led a desperately unhappy personal life and who occasionally drank to excess, Paine possessed outstanding talents as a writer that Adams recognized and encouraged. He and Cousin John dined and conferred with Paine so frequently that, in January 1776, when the latter's enormously popular pamphlet *Common Sense* was published, they were assumed to be the authors.

At about this time, in the late autumn of 1775, the Adamses and John Hancock began to drift apart. They would continue to be associated in the common cause until the end of the War of Independence, but would never again be close personal friends. No single incident was responsible for the growing rift, but the differences in their life-styles could have caused the increasing chill. The Adams cousins ate simple meals at inexpensive taverns, while Hancock indulged his taste for elegant repasts at the best inns in town. He took his position as president of the Congress seriously, and sometimes put on airs, driving up to daily meetings in a coach pulled by four matching horses. Sam Adams preferred to walk, and even thought a cane ostentatious, so he was irritated by his old friend's love of ceremony.

The coolness persisted long after the war, and in 1789, when General Washington became the first president of the United States under the new Constitution, Hancock stopped speaking to the cousins. He had coveted the post himself, and held them responsible for Washington's election.

Certainly Sam Adams was close to Washington from the time of their association at the First Continental Congress. The general appreciated the talents of a man who was impatient of delays and red tape, and most of his correspondence to the Second Congress was channeled through Adams. Making sure he was a member of every committee that dealt with military affairs, Adams fought vigorously for Washington's requests. His insistence that Washington be given the arms, men and supplies necessary to win the war won him the nickname "General," and incurred the ill will of some of his colleagues.

But Adams was not a man who suffered doubts. Any cause he

espoused was the right cause, any action he took was the right action, and the presence of obstacles only spurred him to work harder to achieve his goals. What maddened his opponents was that he so frequently *was* right, as those who advocated reconciliation with Great Britain learned early in 1776.

Chapter
Twenty-five

By early 1776 even the most optimistic Tories and moderates realized that Great Britain would not accept reconciliation with her colonies. The vicious gossip that King George could read only German was untrue; but he did give the appeal from the Continental Congress short shrift, and the Battle of Bunker Hill made a far greater impression on him. The Americans were rebels, he proclaimed in a formal Address from the Throne, and he forbade all commercial intercourse with the colonies. The Whigs tried in vain to curb Parliament, but an act blockading all American ports was passed. A number of high-ranking army officers, among them Generals Howe and Burgoyne, had openly sympathized with the Americans in the past, and although they loyally carried out their assigned duties, they and many of their subordinates had little enthusiasm for the task. Within weeks the War Office would begin hiring regiments of German mercenaries, and thousands of Redcoats were piled onto transports for passage across the Atlantic.

It was at this time that Thomas Paine's *Common Sense* appeared, creating a sensation. Whether Sam Adams played any part in its composition is unknown but unlikely, as the style was distinctly Paine's, but there can be little doubt that Adams agreed whole-heartedly with the sentiments the immigrant to America expressed:

> Reconciliation . . . is a fallacious dream. . . . The blood of the slain, the weeping voice of nature cries, " 'Tis time to part." Even the distance at which the Almighty hath placed England and America is a strong and natural proof that the authority of the one over the other was never the design of Heaven. . . . Freedom hath been hunted round the globe. Asia and Africa have long expelled her. Europe regards her like a stranger, and England hath given her warning to depart. O! receive the fugitive and prepare in time an asylum for mankind.

It is difficult, two hundred years later, to imagine the impact of *Common Sense* on a people struggling to make an agonizing decision. They had been increasingly prepared for such a pamphlet over the years by the essays and editorials of Sam Adams, and the emotional appeal of *Common Sense* could not be denied. Copies were distributed by the hundreds of thousands, and it has been estimated that one came into the hands of every third family in America. Perhaps no other single influence was as strong in the final drive for independence.

The Crown's reaction effectively ended all British government in the colonies, and some set up provisional governments of a sort. Sam Adams and Richard Henry Lee urged leaders in every colony to follow the examples of Massachusetts and Virginia and set up formal legislatures, and with anarchy threatening everywhere, this was done, the opponents of such measures being swiftly disarmed.

The year of decision had arrived, and no one knew it better than Sam Adams, who saw "the chief wish of my heart" on the verge of realization. Signing himself "Sincerus," he wrote in Philadelphia an essay called "An Earnest Appeal to the People," which first appeared in the Pennsylvania *Gazette* of February 12,

1776, and subsequently was reprinted by more than a score of the more prominent American newspapers. He said, in part:

I cannot recall an idea to my mind more amazingly absurd and stupid, than the idea of Lord North's second attempt to gull the Colonies into a belief of his inclination to hold out to them terms of a safe and amiable reconciliation with Great Britain. No one is ignorant that the Americans have offered everything that can possibly be devised to bury the injurious and enslaving claim of Administration in perpetual oblivion, and leave matters on the same footing that they were before the pretence was held up. These generous proposals, however often repeated, have as yet been rejected with an insolent contempt; and yet the profound politician tells his opponents, in the British House of Commons, that he is heartily inclined to a reconciliation with the Colonies, and willing to put them in the situation they so passionately desire; that is (says he to a courtier demanding explanation), in a state of absolute dependence on the British Parliament in all cases whatsoever; for, says his Lordship, they were unquestionably thus dependent in 1763.

Had his Lordship entirely forgot the success of his former experiments, perhaps a trial of the same wretched trick over again might have appeared less ridiculous,—I may indeed say, less insulting to the lowest understanding. I would ask the most credulous votary for making up the dispute, what possible grounds they perceive to found their expectations of a permanent reconciliation upon? Has anything lately turned up which has indicated a change of disposition in the prince or his favorites? Can a majority which has been secured from one seven years to another by pure force of corruption be depended on to remain firm to a slaughtering, plundering, and desolating Court, and share the detestation of present and future ages for mere nothing? . . . I tell you, nay!

. . . It is no wonder they tell of sending a formidable fleet and army to bring over their terms of reconciliation, when they are in no one article different from the terms they first aimed to impose. Had the Ministry, or more properly, the obstinate author of all our troubles, had the remotest idea of favoring us with a government of laws which had any respect to the security of our lives and properties, he had long since granted with a good grace petitions made and repeated with the most dutiful and persevering affection, which asked for nothing more. *Sed aut Caesar aut nullus,* seems the unalterable determination of the man who soothed our already elated expectations by an inaugural declaration, that he gloried in the name of Briton, then a distinctive characteristic of the patrons of universal liberty.

If, therefore, the whole body of the governing and influential part of the governed in Great Britain be unalterably set upon exacting tribute from the Colonies; and the better to secure the collection of it, claims right to impose laws and executors of those laws, dependent only on themselves for appointment, continuance, and support, and all these extended at their sole pleasure, it may readily be determined in what condition the absolutely passive subjects of such an unnatural usurpation would quickly be. It is evident they have concluded on two things, viz. to make a bold push for our entire subjection, as their ends would be thereby more readily answered; but, that being found impracticable, we are to be tried with negotiation, in which all the craft, duplicity, and punic faith of Administration is to be expected. Pray God it may be wisely and firmly guarded against! . . .

More firmly committed than ever to the cause of independence, Adams realized that most Americans were incapable of grasping the complications of the situation, which many lawyers found it difficult to assimilate. Again demonstrating his genius as a propagandist, he simplified and personalized the issue: one man was to blame for the deterioration in Great Britain's relations with her colonies, and that villain was George III. Beginning in the winter of 1776, Adams always referred to him as "the tyrant," and so impressed this view on his compatriots that the monarch's image remains largely unchanged for Americans even today. "His speech breathes the most malevolent spirit," Adams declared, "and determines my opinion of its author as a man of a wicked heart. I have heard that he is his own minister; why, then, should we cast the odium of distressing mankind upon his minions? Guilt must lie at his door," he concluded ominously, "Divine vengeance will fall on his head."

Oddly, no one else had yet thought of this direct approach, which not only made the conflict easier for the illiterate to understand, but also appealed to a people who, once they declared their independence, would owe allegiance to no monarch and would perforce conduct an experiment in the establishment of a democratic form of government, setting up a republic whose chief executive was determined by election. Newspaper editors throughout America quickly followed Adams's lead, and thereafter the "tyrant King" was blamed for the need to fight the War of Independence.

Many members of the Continental Congress continued to resist the idea of a total separation from Britain, and Adams, never a fluent speaker, was unable to persuade his colleagues to change their minds on the subject. He promptly resorted to other means. Cushing of Massachusetts was one of the "pusillanimous waverers," and when the House of Representatives met in Watertown in March to reelect its delegates to the Continental Congress, he received no votes. Elbridge Gerry, who favored independence, was elected to take his place, and the delegation was directed to "concert, direct and order such further measures as should to them appear best calculated for the establishment of right and liberty of the American Colonies, upon a basis permanent and secure against the power and arts of the British Administration, and guarded against any future encroachments of their enemies, with power to adjourn to such times and places as should appear most conducive to the public safety and advantage." First and last a pragmatic politician, Adams did not hesitate to deal ruthlessly, even with associates of many years' standing, when they appeared to be blocking the achievement of his goals.

The opposition to independence held firm in the Congress during the first months of 1776. Adams became increasingly alarmed, and finally decided that, if a majority of colonies wanted to remain united with Britain, New England would form its own independent confederation. To be sure, he exerted a strong measure of control over the delegations from New Hampshire, Rhode Island and Connecticut. The idea was not new to him, and, in fact, he had toyed with it for a number of years, and had mentioned it in his correspondence with Benjamin Franklin, at that time the Massachusetts agent in London.

Whether Franklin got wind of the revived scheme now or whether Adams went to him with it is not clear, but they did discuss it at some length. Franklin, more patient and farseeing than his colleague from Boston, was alarmed at the suggestion that New England might break away from the other colonies. Only by standing united, he declared, could Americans achieve their ultimate aims, and if some remained British colonies while others became independent, all would flounder.

Adams could see the validity of the distinguished Pennsylvanian's argument, but he refused to promise that he would abide by it. He was convinced the time had come to strike off British "shackles," and if the timid refused to act, New England well might move on her own. Fortunately for the future of the United States, a dispute flared up in the late winter of 1776 in the Congress over the question of ownership of the Vermont Grants or Territory. Massachusetts, New Hampshire and New York each insisted that the area belonged to it, and none was willing to give up its claims. The question was not settled until 1780, when the people of Vermont decided the issue themselves by insisting upon separate statehood. Had the matter been resolved four years earlier, it is possible that the impatient Sam Adams might have put machinery in motion to establish an independent New England confederation.

Unable to proceed with his scheme, he pounded the theme of independence in dealings with the inhabitants of reluctant colonies. Pennsylvania was particularly slow to respond to the idea of independence because the influential Quakers, opposed to a plan they knew would mean all-out war, were balking. So, writing under the pen name of "Candidus," Adams wrote an "Address to the People of Pennsylvania," publishing it as a pamphlet at his own expense, a luxury he could scarcely afford. In it he effectively countered the arguments of the Quakers, but the extent to which he may have been responsible for Pennsylvania's shift toward support of independence is difficult to determine.

Events far from the scene of political jockeying in Philadelphia were of much greater importance to the formation of American opinion now. General Washington had given the command of his artillery to a mild Boston bookseller, the amiable and overweight Colonel Henry Knox, who had never fired a cannon in his life and who had learned all he knew of artillery from the books he had read. Knox, destined to become one of America's most expert generals before the War of Independence ended, succeeded in mounting his cannon on Dorchester Heights, making the British position in Boston untenable.

So General Gage was forced to deal with General Washington, and arranged a peaceful withdrawal of his troops by sea, thus sparing the city—and his army—a terrible bombardment. The Americans won their first notable victory of the war, all the more welcome because of the failure of the Canadian expedition— General Montgomery had been killed in action and Benedict Arnold, now a brigadier general, had been severely wounded. Americans moved into Boston, where they were hailed as conquering heroes, and Sam Adams joined his fellow Bostonians in saluting Washington and Knox.

The release of Boston from British occupation had a long-range effect that no one could envision in March 1776. The grateful Adams was the first to recognize the military genius of Washington, and from that time onward was the general's uncompromising champion in the Continental Congress. Through the hard years ahead, when the American armies frequently faltered and there were insistent demands in Congress for Washington's dismissal or a reduction in his authority, Adams always held firm, rallied support for Washington and insisted that he be allowed to prosecute the war in his own way.

Similarities in personality made it difficult for Adams and Washington to become close personal friends, and their association never developed beyond the stage of mutual respect. Both were austere and dignified, and shyness caused them to be somewhat remote and withdrawn in their personal dealings with each other. Adams and Washington never came to call each other by their Christian names, although they were in frequent touch with each other until the end of their lives, but this is not unusual when it is remembered that Cousin Sam and Cousin John always referred to each other as "Mr. Adams." Sam Adams saved his flamboyance for the printed word and for the ideas he conceived.

The members of the Congress were coming to know each other better as the months passed, and a number of men were beginning to emerge as leaders. John Adams and Richard Henry Lee were universally regarded as the most effective speakers, and Thomas Jefferson, who had not yet developed as an orator, was considered one of the deepest thinkers. All factions looked up to Benjamin Franklin, who rarely took sides in any dispute and, by holding aloof, often was the mediator.

The two "principal politicians," as Cousin John called them, were Sam Adams and Roger Sherman. The former rarely made speeches, but quietly accumulated power in his own way. He replaced Cushing on the Committee of Claims, and a short time later became chairman. He also won a place on the Committee on the State of the Treasury, and held his post as chairman of the Military Affairs Committee throughout the war. As independence approached, the Grand Incendiary was spending more time in his lesser known capacity as the Grand Manipulator. Sherman, doffing his hat to his friend and colleague, remarked in a letter that nothing could be accomplished by the Congress without Sam Adams's approval, and that it was almost impossible to succeed in blocking any action he wanted taken.

At the same time, however, he kept up his activities as a propagandist. The Pennsylvania Quakers held a convention in March 1776, and explained their stand in a pamphlet they titled "To the People in General"; Adams replied in a pamphlet of his own under the same title, signing it, "A Religious Politician." He chose the pseudonym with care, and wrote accordingly; the work not only reflected a respect for the Quakers' religious beliefs, but obviously was written by someone who knew his Scriptures and biblical history. It was one of his more impressive works, and his propagandistic approach, usually so blatant, was muted.

Adams had to write late at night because his labors in the Congress continued to increase. He became chairman of a new committee that was requested to recommend whether the ports of the united colonies should be opened to the free trade of the world, a question that was academic at the moment, as the Royal Navy was already beginning its blockade of American ports. But the long-range value of a congressional policy on the matter was of great importance, principally because, as Adams so heartily agreed with Benjamin Franklin, the aid of France was necessary if the Americans hoped to win an armed conflict, and any help obtained from Holland, Sweden, Spain and other nations also would be useful.

So many members were still reluctant to take the initiative in breaking any of the ties that bound the colonies to Great Britain that it was difficult to obtain a majority vote in favor of free trade. So Adams, the wily politician, had the question postponed, and although it was supposed to come to a vote early in March, he did not allow the committee's recommendation to reach the floor of the Congress until early April, by which time he and Sherman, ably assisted by Robert Morris of Pennsylvania, had managed to muster enough votes. Morris, a prominent Philadelphia banker and merchant, was one of the wealthiest men in the Congress, and was quick to understand the potential benefits of a free trade policy.

During this same period Adams and General Washington lost a major political battle. The commander in chief was irritated by the policy of enlisting troops for periods of only two to three months at a time, which made it necessary for him to recruit and train a new army for each campaign he waged. He believed that, if the issue was to be decided by the use of arms, it would be essential for him to have the services of men who enlisted for the duration of the war, and he requested the Congress to adopt a new policy in accordance with this sensible approach.

No man in the Continental Congress was more opposed to the principle of maintaining a standing army than Sam Adams, who habitually insisted that the civilian government maintain total authority over the military at all times. But he was quick to grasp the common sense of Washington's proposal, and requested the Military Affairs Committee to recommend its adoption.

His fellow members disagreed, partly because of their own fear of standing armies and partly because they hoped the conflict would soon end. Adams was one of the few who realized that no reconciliation was possible now unless the colonies surrendered all of their demands and accepted the authority of Parliament, so he submitted Washington's proposals in a minority report.

But he had failed to prepare for a congressional vote with his usual meticulous care, and even his strongest supporters, John Adams and Roger Sherman, refused to stand with him. Virtually alone, Sam Adams fought for his resolution, but only a handful of delegates voted with him, much to his chagrin and Washington's dismay. American men at arms would be forced to suffer a series of severe defeats before the wisdom of the policy advocated by Washington and Adams would be appreciated and adopted.

General Washington, gathering his forces on Long Island for an expected British assault against New York Town, wrote Adams a letter thanking him for his support, and received an immediate reply. "We needs must bide our time," Sam Adams told him, "until the wisdom of your recommendation becomes clear in the eyes of those who hope—in vain, I fear—that this conflict soon will end. I shall present it again when the time is ripe."

In a letter to his wife, who had now returned to Boston, Adams sounded the same note. The optimists who hoped the ministry and Parliament soon would accept the "very minimum" of American demands were fooling themselves. The war would be long, far more difficult than anyone imagined, and the American people would suffer agonies in their fight for cherished freedom.

Chapter
Twenty-six

It became increasingly obvious in the spring of 1776 that Great Britain intended to punish the colonies for their transgressions; there would be no reconciliation until the rebels were brought to their knees. But the Continental Congress continued to hesitate, refusing to issue a formal statement establishing the birth of a free and independent nation, and Sam Adams even had difficulty in persuading his colleagues to pass a resolution urging each colony to disarm its Tories. Unable to budge the Congress, he resorted to the methods that had brought America this far on the road to independence.

How he found the time to spew out essays and editorials in such great quantity still remains something of a mystery. Wells says that this work, if collected, would make a volume of considerable size, running some hundreds of pages, and what makes these efforts particularly impressive is that he was spending at least twelve hours of each day on the specific business of the Continental Congress. He and Cousin John continued to receive visitors and make calls during the period from March to June, so it can only be assumed that he did most of his writing late at night, when others slept.

The sometimes shrill note that had been evident in his previous writing was lacking now, perhaps because he was writing for a larger audience. Some of his articles and editorials appeared in the Boston newspapers, which were publishing again, but others first appeared in Philadelphia, New York, Charleston and other cities, their publication assured by friends in the Congress who were influential in those places. A quotation from one of these essays, written at the end of March under the name of "Candidus," reveals the new approach Adams took, a reasoned, balanced effort in which he seldom resorted to the emphases present in his earlier work:

Declare independence immediately! Issue a manifesto, containing a full view of our rights, our grievances, and the unwearied applications we have made for their redress. Apply to the state of whose readiness and power to assist us we have undoubted assurance. A neglect to improve the openings given us for that purpose may inspire those statesmen with resentment, and incite them to accept overtures from our enemies, and then we may indeed become provinces! If we can withstand the tyrant of Britain without allies, we can incontestably better withstand him with an ally that has ever commanded a very complacent behavior from him. This ally can wish for nothing more than such a share of our commerce as shall be convenient to both parties; and as that must be rather a gain than a loss to us, we must be stupid beyond conception to delay the measure.

Circumstances have strangely cooperated to open scenes no human foresight could have viewed in their full latitude. And what is there now wanting to complete the triumph of the friends of human nature, but a little fortitude, patience, and perseverance? All Europe must allow that, while America was in the greatest good humor with her old mother, a scheme was laid to keep up a large standing army in her capital towns, and to tax her at pleasure for the support of it. They see that, from time to time, the most fraudulent and violent measures have been taken to support their entirely unprecedented claim, till at last, drained of their national troops, they have applied for assistance to other nations. By the law of nations we were discharged from our allegiance, the moment the army was posted among us, or a single farthing taken from us in like manner; either of these being fundamental subversions of the Constitution. It remains then, entirely with ourselves to have ample justice done to us. We have nothing to do but to declare off, and appeal to the *droit des gens*. . . .

Family worries made this a trying time for Adams, even though the concern did not distract him from his work. His wife wrote him that the family home was uninhabitable. The young British officers who had occupied the place had cut obscene remarks into the windowpanes, burned doors for fuel, and, with apparent deliberation, made a shambles of every room and ruined the garden. As it would have cost a large sum of money to put the place in shape, the family moved to Dedham, where Mrs. Adams had relatives, and stayed there until 1778. The Purchase Street residence was in such a bad state that the tax collector, sympathetic to Adams's impoverished state, refused to charge him taxes while the house was nothing but an empty shell.

The friendship of Adams and John Hancock, which had survived since they had repaired their relations several years earlier, once again deteriorated in the spring of 1776, and the rift between the two men became apparent to their colleagues in the Congress. Some attributed it to Hancock's love of pomp and ceremony and his choice of wealthy Philadelphians and New Yorkers as dining companions, and a member of the Rhode Island delegation delivered a stern lecture to him, reminding him that he had been elected to the Congress for a purpose. But this trait in Hancock was not new.

Some early American historians claim that Adams was annoyed because Hancock failed to support the independence movement with the fervor shown by other New England delegates, and there may be a grain of truth in their appraisal. But something more appears to have happened, and Wells claims their coolness dates from the preceding September. Adams appears to have been the injured party, but refused to discuss the matter, telling anyone who questioned him that Hancock's patriotism was not an issue, and that nothing else mattered. Cousin John seems to have known the cause of the difficulty, but kept his mouth shut and his pen still; he tried to maintain cordial relations with Hancock, but as his name was Adams, too, and as he was so closely associated with his cousin, his own relations with the president of the Congress gradually became cooler.

The rift created attention throughout the colonies and in Great Britain, and in the late spring of 1776, the Tory press in England insisted that the rebel leaders were quarreling over spoils and would destroy their cause. This was wishful thinking, and had no basis in fact. But there can be no doubt that Hancock joined the conservative minority and opposed most policies that either of the Adams cousins espoused.

Some of Hancock's personal habits irritated John Adams, although Cousin Sam maintained a tight-lipped silence. Hancock was escorted everywhere by a troop of light horse, and when he traveled he incurred the wrath of innkeepers because he expected them to feed the cavalrymen without charge.

But Sam Adams had more important problems on his mind than the behavior of his one-time protégé. The war was spreading in the South, precisely as he had predicted it would, and he was responsible for the passage of a bill that raised new regiments of Continentals for the defense of Virginia and South Carolina. No one knew for certain what had happened to Gage's army, now under the command of General William Howe since Gage himself had been recalled to England. But it was rumored that the divisions had gone to Halifax and were awaiting reinforcements, both military and naval, before launching a decisive attack.

Not a delegate to the Congress could fail to see that Britain intended to wage a full-scale war. Letters from Great Britain that reached the colonies through circuitous routes stated repeatedly that large numbers of troops, including German mercenaries, were being sent to staging areas in Canada. And residents of major coastal cities could look out of their windows and see warships belonging to the mighty fleet of Admiral Lord Howe cruising offshore, ready to swoop down on any merchantmen that tried to enter or leave an American harbor.

Sam Adams increased his already frenzied work pace, and wrote what Cousin John, with whom he still shared quarters, called "hundreds" of letters. He corresponded with men in every state, as he now called each colony, urging influential citizens to persuade their delegates to the Congress to vote in favor of independence. Most of these letters have been lost to posterity, due to Adams's discretion. When Cousin John teased him for cutting piles of correspondence to shreds or throwing bundles into the fire each day, he replied, "Whatever becomes of me, my friends shall never suffer by my negligence."

This attitude reveals a personality trait in Sam Adams that was becoming more pronounced in the year that was of paramount importance to the future of America. No man realized more than he the significance of the movement he was leading, but he had no interest in making a place for himself in history. Others carefully preserved their correspondence, and many members of Congress kept copies of bills and resolutions they introduced there, but Adams did not bother. He was concerned only with the results that his political activity and his propaganda could achieve, and he did not care whether future generations remembered him.

Wells and others have called him modest, which may well be true, but they neglected another factor. Adams was the pure obsessive, driving toward his once-impossible goal with undiminished vigor and force, and only its accomplishment held meaning for him. Others might think in terms of memorials, of statues that would be erected in their honor or of cities named after them, but he wanted only results, and the sooner the better. A letter he wrote on April 3, 1776, to the Reverend Samuel Cooper, his Boston clergyman and friend, reveals his state of mind:

Is not America already independent? Why, then, not declare it? Upon whom was she ever supposed to be dependent but upon that nation whose barbarous usage of her, and that in multiplied instances and for a long time, has rendered it absurd ever to put confidence in it, and with which she is at this time in open war? Can nations at war be said to be dependent either upon the other? I ask you again, why not declare for independence? Because, say some, it will forever shut the door of reconciliation. Upon what terms will Britain be reconciled to America? If we may take the confiscating act of Parliament, or the King's proclamation for our rule to judge by, she will be reconciled upon our abjectly submitting to tyranny, and asking and receiving pardon for submitting to it. Will this redound to the safety or honor of America? Surely, no. By such a reconciliation, she would not only be in the most shameful manner acknowledging the tyranny, but most wickedly, as far as would be in her power, prevent her posterity from ever hereafter resisting it.

In April the states—some of which still called themselves colonies—edged closer to open independence. On April 6 Adams moved that British customs houses be abolished, and a large majority voted in favor of the measure. On May 10 he strongly supported a motion by John Adams which totally abolished all offices established under the Crown and urged the people of every state to replace them with officials they themselves elected.

In the spring of 1776 Sam Adams became a member of the Medical Committee of the Congress, a group charged with recruiting physicians into the Continental Army and obtaining medical supplies for them. He was also urgently working to obtain support for General Washington and Major General Philip Schuyler, commander of the northern army, in New York, both of whom were demanding muskets, ammunition and cannon.

The work done by Sam Adams in the Continental Congress has never been fully appreciated because of the dismal record of the Congress itself. This, however, was not the fault of the delegates, but of the system of government that developed in 1776 and thereafter, culminating in the adoption of the Articles of Confederation two years later. The thirteen states jealously retained most powers of government themselves, including such rights as the printing of paper money, and allowed Congress few powers of its own. So, although the Congress could pass firm resolves and sensible bills, it had no authority to enforce these measures, and a state that chose to ignore an act of Congress it disliked could do so with impunity.

Adams, a lifelong advocate of home rule, was badly torn and somewhat confused by this state of affairs. As a citizen of Massachusetts and a member of her House of Representatives every year except 1776 and 1777, he believed that she alone had the right to make laws governing her people. But as a member of the Continental Congress throughout the war, he chafed and became angry when the states vacillated, often rejecting measures passed by the Congress out of self-interest, even though obedience to the acts was necessary to the winning of the war.

A number of questions became increasingly vexing, and Sam Adams became a troubled man. Should each state have exclusive right to impose taxes on its citizens? After all, America had gone to war because it clung to this principle. If this was the case, how could the states be persuaded to pay their proper share of funds for the support of the Continental Army, the tiny but growing Navy, the courts that had to decide interstate disputes, the foreign service that conducted America's relations with foreign powers?

The painful evolution of Adams's convictions on these and other questions of states' rights versus national powers will be seen in later chapters. In 1776 he scarcely knew where he stood on such issues, and the truth of the matter is that he had not really stopped to ponder them. His goal in the spring of that year was precisely what it had been for the past eight years: he wanted independence, and he looked no farther into the future than its achievement at the earliest possible date.

Apparently it did not occur to him that there would be chaos, bewilderment and mismanagement if each of the thirteen states was sovereign and the Continental Congress functioned principally as an advisory body whose acts could be accepted, denied or sidestepped at each state's pleasure. He, more than any other American, was responsible for his nation's independence, but when it came in the summer of 1776 he was no more prepared for the establishment of a strong, efficient national government than were his colleagues in the Continental Congress or members of the various state legislatures.

Sam Adams was a practical politician whose control over the Massachusetts legislature had made him the undisputed leader of that commonwealth for many years. But he was still an idealist who accepted the philosophy of John Locke literally, and he had no experience in the administration of government on a truly national level. John Adams, Thomas Jefferson and others were far younger and even less experienced, and they, too, were forced to learn by brutal means of trial and error that prolonged the war. General Washington, the one man who had the strength and vision to create order out of national chaos in 1776, was devoting his full time and energy to the extraordinarily difficult military task he had been given. And Benjamin Franklin was more of a diplomat than an administrator, and his mind did not tend toward the creation of an intergovernmental apparatus that would be effective.

In the spring of 1776 Sam Adams was spending his few precious hours of "spare" time thinking in military terms. He wrote to General Washington, suggesting the building of a road that would extend from the mouth of the Connecticut River to Canada, and when the commander in chief heartily approved of the project, Adams rounded up enough support in the Congress to secure the passage of a bill authorizing the construction of the road. Work was started soon thereafter, but the project languished for many decades and was not completed until long after Adams's death because only the New England legislatures were willing to provide funds for the purpose; the others either demurred or, when shamed into a favorable vote, "forgot" to provide their share of the cost.

It proved to be somewhat easier for Adams to obtain the money for the construction of military hospitals in each state. His committee, after consultation with Dr. Benjamin Rush of Philadelphia and a number of other distinguished physicians and surgeons, requested funds from each state for the construction and staff salaries of such hospitals. Most states built their own, but agreed to the standards of maintenance, administration and medical capabilities that Adams's committee requested.

This task completed, Adams threw himself with renewed fury into the campaign for independence. By May it was becoming obvious that America no longer had a real choice in the matter, and Sam Adams was convinced his dream would finally come true.

Chapter
Twenty-seven

The resolution Sam Adams maneuvered through the Continental Congress on May 10, 1776, declaring that Crown government in America had come to an end and that each state should establish its own methods of operation under its own officials was a sign that the time was finally ripe for a complete break with Great Britain. In that same month Viriginia took the lead, establishing a state constitution and instructing its delegates in Congress to submit a resolution of independence. Samuel Chase of Maryland, a member of that state's delegation in the Congress and one of Sam Adams's close associates, promptly persuaded the Maryland legislature to authorize a similar declaration. No such action was required of the Massachusetts legislature, already on record in favor of independence.

On the night of June 4, Richard Henry Lee, Adams and Chase dined together and discussed strategy. The moderates in the Continental Congress were still holding back and could control enough votes to prevent the departure of America from the British Empire. On the other hand, the radicals now had gained a new momentum and were determined not to lose it. Lee proposed that Adams, the "Father of Independence," introduce the resolution, and that he and Chase second it, but Sam Adams demurred. The Massachusetts stand was already known to every delegate, and many resented what they regarded as that state's domination of the Congress. Therefore, he reasoned, the effect would be much more profound if Virginia presented the resolution and Maryland seconded it. In this way the Mid-Atlantic and southern states would be more inclined to join.

The others agreed, and on June 5 Lee introduced his resolution.

On June 8 the measure came up for consideration, and speeches in its favor were made by Lee and John Adams. Dickinson, Edward Rutledge and Robert Livingston spoke on behalf of the moderates, condemning the resolution and demanding more time.

Meanwhile Patrick Henry, writing from Williamsburg, where the Virginia Convention was working out the details of its new state government, said to John Adams, "Our session will be very long, during which I cannot count upon one coadjutor of talents equal to the task. Would to God you and your Sam Adams were here!"

But Sam Adams was badly needed in Philadelphia. The debate went into a second day, then a third, and it became apparent that all of his strength and cunning were needed. He made no speeches in favor of the Virginia resolution, leaving that task to more eloquent orators, but he went to work behind the scenes, cornering two or three moderates at a time, forcing them to accompany him into an empty committee room and then unleashing all of his powers of reason on them. Jefferson, writing of him in 1819, declared:

> . . . he was a truly great man, wise in council, fertile in resources, immovable in his purposes, and had, I think, a greater share than any other member in advising and directing our measures in the Northern war. As a speaker he could not be compared with his living colleague and namesake, whose deep conceptions, nervous style and undaunted firmness made him truly our bulwark in debate. But Mr. Samuel Adams, although

not of fluent elocution, was so rigorously logical, so clear in his views, abundant in good sense, and master always of his subject, that he commanded the most profound attention whenever he rose in an assembly by which the froth of declamation was heard with the most sovereign contempt.

No records of the day-to-day proceedings of the Continental Congress exist, but Adams appears to have played a key role in the final phase of the debate on independence, which lasted for five days. According to Elbridge Gerry, speaking on the subject many years later, Adams confined himself to personal conversations on the subject until the final day of the debate, when he finally rose and delivered an exceptionally long speech. In it he cited the many arguments in favor of independence that had been the substance of so much he had written in recent years, and several waverers promptly fell into line.

But neither side could muster a majority, and on June 10 Rutledge asked that a vote on the question be postponed for three weeks. Those in favor of independence readily agreed, and then proceeded to outwit the opposition. Sam Adams immediately presented a resolution establishing a special committee that would write a "Proclamation of Independence," and he caught the conservatives offguard, so the measure was passed without debate.

Five members were named to the committee, and four could be classified as men who favored independence. One was Jefferson, the principal author of the Declaration of Independence, who was joined by John Adams and Sherman, whose views were universally known. Dr. Franklin, a fourth member of the group, had already cast his influence and prestige in favor of independence; the only moderate among them was Robert R. Livingston, a scrupulously fair man who could see both sides of every question.

Sam Adams assumed that the declaration would be adopted, which meant that a new national government of some kind would have to be established, so he presented a resolution urging the formation of an "American Commonwealth," and after its passage joined Dickinson on the new Committee of Confederation. Neither man was an expert on the subject, and, granting that they had only three weeks in which to set up the machinery for a new American government, they did an imperfect job; the Articles of Confederation that they presented left much to be desired. The draft of the Articles was not ready on schedule, for the committee members repeatedly found new snags that slowed their task, and the document was not submitted to the Congress until July 12.

Meanwhile the Grand Incendiary, the master of the backroom caucus, whom Josiah Quincy had called "the First Politician of the World," devoted more of his time and efforts to rounding up votes for independence than attending to his own committee work. The vote was to be taken by states, and a two-thirds majority was necessary for the passage of any major measure, which meant that the approval of nine of the thirteen was necessary. Adams moved from delegation to delegation, joining those who favored independence within each group in the delicate art of arm-twisting.

He and Cousin John saw little of each other during this three-week period. The younger Adams was devoting most of his waking hours to the preparation of the great declaration. The elder Adams was spending most of his sitting at dining tables talking to the hesitant and reluctant, and his only comment, made many years later, was that during this time he ate so much unaccustomed food and drank so much coffee and green tea that he suffered from continual indigestion for the better part of a month.

Here was the great rebel at work, driving without pause now that the great goal of his lifetime was within grasp. William Tudor, the early nineteenth-century biographer of Otis, best captured the essence of Adams's character when he wrote:

He combined in a remarkable manner all the animosities and all the firmness that could qualify a man to be the assertor of the rights of the people. Had he lived in any country or any epoch where abuses of power were to be resisted, he would have been one of the reformers. He would have suffered excommunication rather than have bowed to Papal infallibility, or paid tribute to St. Peter; he would have gone to the stake rather than submit to the prelatic ordinances of Laud; he would have mounted the scaffold sooner than pay a shilling of illegal ship-money; he would have fled to a desert rather than endure the profligate tyranny of a Stuart; he was proscribed, and would sooner have been condemned as a traitor than assent to an illegal tax, if it had been only a sixpenny stamp or an insignificant duty on tea; and there appeared to be no species of corruption by which this inflexibility could have been destroyed.

The motives by which he was actuated were not a sudden ebullition of temper, nor a transient impulse of resentment, but they were deliberate, methodical, and unyielding. There was no pause, no hesitation, no despondency; every day and every hour was employed in some contribution towards the main design; if not in action, in writing; if not with the pen, in conversation; if not in talking, in meditation. The means he advised were persuasion, petition, remonstrance, resolutions, and when all failed, defiance and extermination rather than submission.

It should be remembered that Sam Adams, the human dynamo who never paused in the pursuit of his aims, was one of the two most renowned men attending the Continental Congress, sharing the honor with Franklin. It was difficult for obscure delegates from other states to stand up to this man on whose head the Crown had put a price.

Jefferson, in paying tribute to him, said he was "truly the Man of the Revolution." The man who learned politics sufficiently well himself to serve two terms as president of the United States shed light on Adams's methods, recounting that Adams was "constantly" holding caucuses "at which the generality of the measures pursued were previously determined on, and at which the parts were assigned to the different actors who afterwards

appeared in them. John Adams had very little part in these caucuses, but as one of the actors in the measures decided on in them,
he was a Colossus."

The Loyalists had their own opinions of Sam Adams, and
mounted frenzied attacks on him in June 1776. Two pamphlets
still survive, as do a handful of copies of the few newspapers the
Tories still controlled. Adams was "the Cromwell of America"
and "His Satanic Majesty," a man determined to succeed King
George and make himself the "tyrant of the New World." He
was a demagogue, a cunning, consummate knave and—as a final
blow—a "hypocrite in religion." As far as is known, Adams
totally ignored these assaults, as was befitting a man who had
victory within his grasp after a long campaign.

It is unfortunate that posterity has never been able to learn the
details of Sam Adams's machinations during the hectic month of
June 1776. But he did his work well, and when the Congress
convened on July 1, sitting as a committee of the whole, only four
states were unable or unwilling to declare themselves in favor of
independence. The New York delegation awaited instructions
from the state's legislature; South Carolina was opposed, while
Pennsylvania and Delaware were split.

Dickinson moved for an adjournment for twenty-four hours,
and the proponents of independence consulted Adams and
Franklin, who were agreeable for reasons of their own. There
was no longer any question that the Congress would vote in favor
of independence, but the two most prestigious men in the assembly well knew that negative votes would cast a pall on America's
aspirations and would lead both Great Britain, her enemy, and
France, her potential ally, to doubt that she could maintain her
independence. Consequently it was necessary to obtain a completely unanimous vote. It may be that it was on July 1, rather
than during the actual signing of the Declaration of Independence, that Dr. Franklin uttered his famous comment, "If we
don't hang together we'll assuredly hang separately."

On July 2 the arrival of Caesar Rodney, who had been absent
on personal business, assured a change in the vote of the Dela-

ware delegation. The pro-independence party made no objection when Edward Rutledge proposed another day's delay.

The New York delegates decided not to wait for instructions from their legislature. Dickinson absented himself when the Pennsylvania delegation held a caucus, and that state voted in favor of independence. South Carolina momentarily stood alone, but the pressure was too great, and her delegates changed their vote. The decision in favor of independence was unanimous, and all members of the Continental Congress, with the exception of Dickinson, signed the Declaration of Independence on July 4.

Sam Adams's great dream had been realized, but he did not rejoice. On the contrary, he was irritated, and he indicated to one of his lieutenants in the Massachusetts House of Representatives, writing on July 5 that "much . . . has been lost by delaying to take this decisive step." Had independence been declared months earlier, he believed, Canada would have become part of the United States.

In a letter to a Boston friend, however, he displayed greater tolerance, saying "our determinations have been necessarily slow." He had formerly been convinced, he stated, that if independence had been declared six months earlier, the army that had marched into Canada would have been more vigorous and the people of the Province of Quebec would have joined in the movement. Now, however, he felt less certain that would have been the result, and admitted, "Probably I was mistaken." The colonies had not been ripe for "so momentous a change. It was necessary that they should be united, and it required time and patience to remove old prejudices, to instruct the unenlightened, and to fortify the timid." In victory the Grand Incendiary could afford to play the role of the gracious statesman.

In a letter to Richard Henry Lee, who was in Virginia during the first part of July and who signed the Declaration of Independence at a later date, Adams was blunt. He was not taking independence for granted, to be sure, but he wasted no time extending mutual congratulations. He indicated deep worry about Canada, saying that the military situation there demanded the presence of a Duke of Marlborough or Prince Eugene of Savoy, but that the new United States was saddled with Major Generals Philip Schuyler and Horatio Gates. He was disturbed, too, by feuds between various generals, and "sincerely wish my apprehensions may prove to be groundless."

He entertained higher hopes for General Washington's army, declaring that the commander in chief was being bolstered by the militia of New Jersey, Maryland and Pennsylvania, which were marching north to join him. General Howe, he said, had reached New York with a force of ten thousand regulars and mercenaries, and the arrival of the main body of Lord Howe's fleet was expected at any moment. It was obvious that a major battle would take place, and though Adams expressed hopes for an American victory, a thread of doubt ran through the letter to Lee. He was neither deluding himself nor trying to fool his colleague, and he knew that a long, hard road lay ahead for the new nation before independence was assured.

His one comment on the Declaration of Independence was perfunctory. It had "given vigor to the spirits of the people," he said, and then he became bitterly realistic, again insisting that the situation in Canada would have been far different had the declaration been signed months earlier.

Adams's health seems to have suffered during the late spring and early summer of 1776, but he had allowed himself no time to minister to his physical needs. He received a letter from Dr. John Warren, urging him to take a holiday and telling him that those who loved him were concerned about his health. A day or two later he heard from his son, who prescribed a regimen for him that included "roasted meats, ample draughts of bayberry tea and no less than six to seven hours of sleep" every night.

But he refused to allow himself to rest. The Articles of Confederation were not completed until the twelfth. When they were presented to the Congress, they set off an uproar. Each state was afraid its interests were not being duly protected, and the first constitution of the new United States was torn apart by various factions. Adams plunged headlong into the new battle, and worked so hard for the adoption of the Articles that he made a number of permanent enemies.

His feud with John Hancock became deeper, too. Adams believed that the president of the Continental Congress was not working hard enough to resolve the differences between the states. Ordinarily Adams would have maintained a discreet silence in dealing with his former protégé, but he was tired now, and recklessly accused Hancock from the floor of the Congress of what he called "lassitude." Thereafter the two men barely nodded to each other when they passed.

By early August John Adams added his voice to those of the friends and relatives who were urging the fifty-four-year-old Grand Incendiary to take a respite from the labors that had occupied him without pause for the better part of a year. It was obvious that the Articles of Confederation would be debated for a long time to come, and a man who had not seen his wife and children for many months deserved a real holiday. The precise nature of Sam Adams's malady is not known, but a twentieth-century physician has described it, from the symptoms he displayed, as nervous exhaustion.

Finally heeding the advice of all who knew him well, Sam Adams left Philadelphia on August 12 for the Boston he had not seen in more than two years. He brushed aside suggestions that he might need an escort, and was accompanied only by the judge advocate general of the Continental Army, William Tudor. In a democracy, he said, no man had any cause to fear his neighbor.

Chapter
Twenty-eight

The Declaration of Independence changed the very basis of life in America, transforming a protest into a full-scale revolution. From that time forward it was impossible for Patriots and Tories to live side by side. A man either became a citizen of the new republic or, if he persisted in his loyalty to the Crown, became a traitor. Thousands of Americans were driven into exile in Canada, the West Indies or England, and their property was confiscated. Others joined Loyalist regiments that fought on the British side, or, after the fall of New York, sought refuge there behind Redcoat lines.

As Sam Adams had so long predicted, the way was now open for France to come to the aid of the new United States, but she was not ready for another direct confrontation with Britain, her ancient enemy. So several "commercial companies" were formed, and these dummy organizations "sold" arms, munitions and supplies to the Americans.

The fundamental military situation was also changed. Until now Lord North's ministry had been walking a tightrope in the hope that the strong Whig sentiments of approximately half of

Britain's people would not be offended. The Declaration of Independence enabled the British government to make a far greater effort to win a total victory, and the odds were in her favor. She had a population of about ten million, and was the strongest nation in Europe, possessing the most powerful navy and a thoroughly professional army.

The United States suffered under severe handicaps. Her total population, including the slaves of the South and various Indian tribes whose loyalty was dubious, numbered slightly less than three million. She was an agricultural nation almost totally lacking in industries, and even in New England, the most advanced section of the country, it was said that there were only three small foundries capable of manufacturing cannon.

Sam Adams declared—for public consumption—that the Declaration of Independence had been received by the people "as though it was a decree promulgated from heaven," but he knew better. Had the nation been organized for war it might have been possible to put as many as a quarter of a million fighting men into the field, and a force of this size, defending its own territory, would have been too strong for any army the British could have sent across the Atlantic. But the national government was not yet formed, and many of the states were still in the process of organizing their own rudimentary governments.

The worst handicap, in spite of Sam Adams's optimistic public expressions to the contrary, was the indisputable fact that few Americans had as yet developed any sense of a national entity. Men were citizens of Massachusetts or Pennsylvania or Virginia, and were loyal only to those states. Militiamen were determined to protect their own homes, but a farmer from North Carolina was ready to desert rather than fight to save New York, and a New Hampshire fisherman had no interest in preventing the enemy capture of Philadelphia. Years would pass before tribulation forged a national consciousness that, combined with vastly increased help from France and the contributions of liberal foreign volunteer fighting men of experience, would enable independence to become a reality.

Sam Adams was well aware of the infant nation's shortcomings, and although he was supposedly going home for a short holiday, the military situation preyed on his mind. On the evening of August 13, a scant thirty-six hours after he left Philadelphia, he sent a worried letter to Cousin John from Princeton, New Jersey:

> Before this reaches you, you will have heard of the arrival of near a hundred more of the enemy's ships. There are too many soldiers now in Philadelphia waiting for arms. Is it not of the utmost importance that they should march even without arms, especially as they may be furnished with the arms of those who may be sick at New York? Would it not be doing great service to the cause at this time if you would speak to some of the Committee of Safety of Pennsylvania relative to this matter?

On the fourteenth he reached New York, and that night he dined with General Washington and his staff. The commander in chief was well and in good spirits, and a number of his principal subordinates were summoned to a conference with the chairman of the Congress's Military Affairs Committee. All expressed their determination to defeat the enemy. Adams had no opportunity to inspect the fortifications, but was assured they were strong.

But a number of matters were not to his liking, and he discussed them at length in another letter to Cousin John. His principal concern was the brief period of a soldier's enlistment, and he rightly saw that special inducements had to be offered to veterans to persuade them to remain on active duty. It was his initial idea that, in return for three consecutive years of duty, a soldier be granted one hundred acres of land and a cash bonus of twenty dollars. He offered the idea to Cousin John for his consideration.

On August 29, Sam Adams reached Boston, immediately requesting the many friends who wanted to honor him not to celebrate his return. "This country is at war," he said, "and there is no time for pleasures." Taking his own dictum literally, he spent only a few days in Dedham with his wife and daughter, and since they wanted to be with him as much as possible, they had to return to Boston with him on September 4.

There he immediately reassumed his position as secretary of state and devoted most of his energies to the promotion of the organization of a privateer fleet. America could not yet afford to build warships of her own, so the defense of the seacoast against the powerful Royal Navy was in the hands of privateers, the owners and captains of swift sloops and other merchant ships who could run enemy blockades, capture British merchantmen and do as much damage as they could while avoiding collisions with great enemy ships-of-the-line and frigates.

Soon after Adams's arrival in Boston he learned the news of the debacle that has been known to posterity as the Battle of Long Island. Confused American regiments fled from the field, many not putting up even a token resistance, two American general officers—Stirling and Sullivan—were captured, and the rout was so complete that British trumpeters played hunting calls as the Redcoats chased American farmboys and town clerks from the field. Washington retired to Manhattan, and the complete destruction of his forces was averted only because General Howe moved so slowly that the retreating Americans slipped from his grasp and began a long march southward through New Jersey.

So decisively were the Americans defeated that Admiral Lord Howe, who had been given the powers to make peace at his discretion, sent a message to the Continental Congress offering to negotiate with the rebels. A committee consisting of Franklin, Rutledge and John Adams was appointed to meet with the admiral, and the next day Cousin John sent off a hurried note to his relative in Boston:

> Tomorrow morning Dr. Franklin, Mr. Rutledge, and your humble servant set off to see that rare curiosity, Lord Howe. Do not imagine from this that a panic has spread to Philadelphia. By no means. This is only refinement in policy. It has a deep, profound reach, no doubt. So deep that you cannot see the bottom of it, I dare say. I am sure I cannot.

Do not, however, be concerned. When you see the whole thing, as you will erelong, you will not find it very bad. I will write you the particulars as soon as I shall be at liberty to do it.

The meeting produced no results; the representatives of the Congress insisted that America would discuss terms of peace only as an independent nation, while Lord Howe refused to treat with them unless the states reverted to their former status as colonies.

Sam Adams knew none of this as he busied himself with the various affairs of Massachusetts. A new state constitution was being prepared, and he urged his followers to establish a legislature of two houses, an independent judiciary and an executive branch. He was called upon to select and approve one or more of the many plans for the improvement and refinement of Boston's land and sea defenses. He was asked to settle difficult questions of the powers of taxation to be granted the new legislature, and plans for the enlargement of the militia were submitted to him. In brief, his many friends and followers treated him as though he were the Governor and had returned home for a brief period of decision-making before departing again to deal with larger affairs.

Harried, tired and overworked, he had received no direct word from Philadelphia when the news of Lord Howe's offer and the appointment of the congressional committee to meet with the Admiral reached him. The post was unreliable, so John Adams's letter had not yet arrived, and for the first time in the struggle his composure broke.

He sat down at once and wrote a long letter to Cousin John. Nervous and on the verge of hysteria, he spoke of the honor of Congress, the resolution of the people and the resentment that would be universal if independence should be lost only a few weeks after it had been declared. It was the only time during the entire War of Independence that he is known to have completely lost his calm.

The arrival of John Adams's note within a day of the sending of his own communication reassured him, however, so he recovered swiftly and devoted himself to the dispatch of additional regiments of militia to General Washington. The legislature had to approve the departure of the troops from the state, and there was some opposition within the body to the idea, so Sam Adams made his only personal appearance before the House of Representatives in that year. He was not a member of the House in 1776, but that was a mere technicality, and he went in his capacity as Massachusetts' secretary of state.

His address must have been as pungent as it was brief, and certainly it was effective. There was no further debate, and the House immediately authorized three additional regiments to join the army of the commander in chief.

During his brief stay in Boston he also made or found the time to overhaul the system of the distribution of money and food to the poor of the city who had suffered as a result of the British occupation. It might be noted that, after his return to Philadelphia, he forwarded a substantial sum to his subordinates on what was still known as the Donations Committee, having collected pledges previously made.

Early in October, after a sojourn at home of only six weeks, Sam Adams said good-bye to his wife, daughter and friends, and hurried back to Philadelphia. Presumably he had been refreshed during the interlude of uninterrupted work that would have exhausted most other men. It is interesting to note that only after he returned did John Adams depart on a similar trip to Massachusetts. The cousins had made a private, informal agreement, and never were both absent from the seat of national government at the same time.

Plunging anew into the affairs of the Continental Congress, Sam Adams became the chairman of two new committees. One, whose operations were so secret that few of its activities have ever been learned, was charged with the preparation of "an effectual plan for suppressing the internal enemies of America and preventing a communication of intelligence to our other enemies." Thus Adams, in effect, became the head of the first counterespionage effort ever engaged in by the United States.

The second committee he headed was, more or less, a subcommittee of the Military Affairs group, and was charged with the direction of the war in the North. Adams was already familiar with that situation, and within forty-eight hours he and his committee submitted a long list of vigorous recommendations. They included the casting of new cannon at Salisbury foundry and their transportation to Fort Ticonderoga, the provisioning of five thousand men for a field expedition and of an additional five thousand to be stationed at Albany, the forwarding of medicines, the care of the sick and the punishment of delinquent physicians. Richard Henry Lee dryly remarked, "Now that Mr. Adams is once again in our midst, the Congress has awakened from its lethargy."

All through the autumn the military news was bad and continued to grow worse. General Washington was forced to retreat through New Jersey, and so many men deserted from his forces that he never knew from day to day how many effectives he could put into the field. Eventually he was forced to retreat across the Delaware River into Pennsylvania; only superb organization and superlatively conducted operations made it possible for him to salvage the bulk of his supplies. Meanwhile Sir William Howe, who had been knighted by a grateful George III after the Battle of Long Island, offered amnesty to all residents of New Jersey, and according to word that reached Philadelphia, thousands were accepting.

There was little cause for cheer in the Continental Congress. Coupled with the repeated defeats and the army defections was the apparent impossibility of obtaining recruits in substantial numbers for the Continentals, who were proving to be the military's only backbone. The public credit was virtually exhausted, and the paper money printed by the authority of Congress had no backing and was worthless. It was at this time that the expression "Not worth a Continental" came into being, and the epithet remained a part of the national language for the better part of two centuries.

People throughout the United States were becoming rapidly discouraged, and on December 9 an alarmed Congress appointed a committee to prepare an address to the citizenry at large. The co-chairmen were Sam Adams and Richard Henry Lee, and they did not tarry at their task, returning the next day with a report that was duly published within the next twenty-four hours.

How much of Adams's confidence was genuine and how much was feigned for the sake of rebuilding public confidence is difficult to determine, but there can be little doubt that the address read well. The army was being reorganized under a plan submitted by General Washington, reinforcements were being sent forward to join him and major preparations were being rushed for the defense of Philadelphia, the authors of the cheerful report declared. A frigate had been stationed on the Delaware River to prevent the passage of enemy troops to Philadelphia; all of the arms, ammunition and clothing in the nation's first capital had been placed at the disposal of General Israel Putnam, whom Washington had placed in charge of the city's defenses. Swift privateers were cruising off the shores of the Mid-Atlantic states, and already had taken a heavy toll of enemy supply vessels bringing ammunition and food to General Howe.

Had the report been true, America's military situation would have been vastly improved, to say the least. But more than 90 per cent of the address was the product of Sam Adams's vivid imagination; in a time of crisis he instinctively reverted to the propaganda approach that had proved so effective in the past.

The actual situation was worsening, and most members of the Congress were becoming panicky as the need to move the capital to Baltimore became increasingly, painfully evident. But Sam Adams had thrived on adversity for many years, and as others became gloomier and more afraid, he radiated optimism and good cheer. His letters to friends and relatives in December 1776 indicated his sincere conviction that the losses being suffered were temporary. On December 4 he felt compelled to write an "Address to the People of New England," which he sent to Dr. Warren, and in it he not only urged fellow citizens not to lose heart, but exhorted them to prepare their defenses for a campaign the following spring. Others, John Hancock among them, were beginning to wonder aloud what peace terms Great Britain might be willing to offer, but Adams refused to discuss the matter. He would fight to the end, he said, no matter what the outcome of the present campaign.

An undated note to his wife, one of the few extant, reveals his actual state of mind at this trying time:

> I am still in good health and spirits, although the enemy is within forty miles of this city. I do not regret the part I have taken in a cause so just. I must confess it chagrins me to find it so ill-supported by the people of Pennsylvania and the Jerseys. They seem to me to be determined to give it up. But I must say that my dear New England will maintain it at the expense of everything dear to them in this life. They know how to prize their liberties. Heaven bless them!

In two other letters to Mrs. Adams, written on December 9 and December 11, the latter the eve of the adjournment of the Congress to Baltimore, he remained calm, courageous and, in his appraisal of the fortitude of women, sententious. In these two communications he said, in part:

> If this city should be surrendered, I should by no means despair of our cause. It is a righteous cause, and I am fully persuaded righteous Heaven will succeed it. Congress will adjourn to Baltimore, in Maryland, about one hundred and twenty miles from this place, when necessity requires it, and not before. It is agreed to appoint a day of prayer, and a committee will bring in a resolve for that purpose this day. I wish we were a more religious people.
>
> You tell me you were greatly alarmed to hear that General Howe's army was on the march to Philadelphia. I have long known you to be possessed of much fortitude of mind. But you are a woman, and one must expect you will now and then discover timidity natural to your sex. I thank you, my dear, most cordially, for the warmth of affection which you express on this occasion, for your anxiety for my safety, and your prayers to God for my protection. The man who is conscientiously doing his duty will ever be protected by that righteous

and all-powerful Being, and when he has finished his work will receive an ample reward. I am not more convinced of anything than that it is my duty to oppose, to the utmost of my abilities, the designs of those who would enslave my country; and with God's assistance, I am resolved to oppose them till their designs are defeated, and I am called to quit the stage of life.

By this time so much propaganda had flowed from Adams's pen that, even in his letters to his wife, he could not refrain from speaking in the same vein. Some of his less serene colleagues must have been annoyed when he adopted this lofty tone with them during the most difficult days the Americans had yet known. On December 12 the Congress voted an adjournment to Baltimore, then a small town of only a few thousand people, and the journey most nearly resembled a flight. Few carriages and fewer horses were available, the military having commandeered all vehicles and mounts for the defense of Philadelphia, so the distinguished members of the Continental Congress were required to crowd into the few coaches that could be secured, with their baggage overflowing from the roofs.

Sam Adams remained as cheerful as ever, however, and according to his own account he regaled his colleagues on the journey with accounts of the reinforcements that would soon come to General Washington's help. In almost no time, he said, as the carriages slowly made their way down the roads, axle deep in mud, Sir William Howe and his "barbarous hordes in scarlet" would be thrown back to the mouth of the Hudson River. This attitude was no form of self-induced euphoria; Adams was so consistent in the maintenance of his views that it can only be assumed he sincerely believed every word he was saying. For the better part of a decade he had devoted his entire life to the cause of American liberty, and now that independence had been achieved, he was totally convinced his God would not deprive the American people of what He, with Adams's help, had seen fit to bestow on them.

In a letter to Mrs. Adams after his arrival in Baltimore he was still serene, and his judgments remained dispassionate. He was accustomed to alarms, he declared, so he had seen no need to leave Philadelphia for Baltimore so soon, but he was willing to admit that "deliberative bodies should not sit in places of confusion."

On December 20, while the Congress sat in Baltimore, Adams pushed through his plan to give one hundred acres of land and a bonus of twenty dollars in cash to every veteran who remained in the army for three consecutive years. His colleagues were convinced that this act halted the desertions and made possible Washington's Christmas night attack on the enemy across the Delaware at Trenton.

Also on December 20, acting on a recommendation from the commander in chief, Adams introduced a resolution promoting Colonel Henry Knox to the rank of brigadier general. At this time Sam Adams was so much in command of military affairs in the Congress that his bill was passed without discussion, setting a precedent in the talkative legislative body.

The business of the northern army continued to concern him, and he was chiefly worried abuut the state of defenses of Fort Ticonderoga. In a long letter to General Schuyler he urged that all available artillery be taken to the fort immediately and emplaced there, that reinforcements of no fewer than three to four thousand men be sent to Ticonderoga without delay and that adequate provisions be gathered there to withstand a long enemy siege. Had his suggestions been followed, it is possible that the fort, the key to the possession of New York and the domination of New England, would not have fallen into the hands of General John Burgoyne and his Redcoats in the campaign that ultimately led to the climatic Battle of Saratoga.

On December 27, when news of Washington's victory at Trenton dispelled the belief that the enemy was invincible, Sam Adams acted quickly and decisively to strengthen the hand of the commander in chief. A new Committee on the State of the Army was appointed, with Adams and Richard Henry Lee as its co-chairmen, which meant, for all practical purposes, that the desires of those worthy gentlemen would be realized. Within forty-eight hours they submitted a report, stating in a preamble that, although they opposed the granting of "tyrannical powers" to the military as a matter of principle, they had complete faith in George Washington's devotion to the common cause. They had "perfect reliance." they declared, in his "ability and uprightness."

Then, in the main body of the report, they recommended that Washington be invested with "full, ample and complete powers" to raise and equip a new army, establish pay standards, obtain from the states whatever militia assistance he deemed necessary, establish magazines and supply depots, appoint and displace officers, confiscate—for a fair price—any property that individuals might refuse to sell to him, arrest persons who refused to accept the Continental dollar and incarcerate those whose disaffection was "injurious to the cause of freedom."

The report was too much for the Congress to digest, and the members felt, with good cause, that they lacked the authority to vest such powers in any man. After a brief debate it was decided to circularize the report to the states, so Lee and Adams promptly wrote a long letter on the subject to the several legislatures.

That ended the most momentous year in the life of Sam Adams and the young nation he was so instrumental in founding, but he was still bursting with enthusiastic plans for the future as the United States lurched into 1777.

Chapter
Twenty-nine

      Sam Adams, who had never traveled farther from home than Philadelphia and Baltimore, may not have been the first American to think of establishing foreign alliances, but there were few who anticipated him. As early as 1775, when he left Massachusetts to attend the opening of the Second Continental Congress, the subject was very much on his mind, and thereafter it continued to prey on him. More patient men realized that little could be done until the United States became an independent nation, but he was unwilling to wait, and on July 5, 1776, he informed the Congress that it had dallied long enough. "It is high time," he said, "for us to have ambassadors at foreign courts. I fear we have already suffered too much by a delay."

      By that time a group of commissioners to France had already been elected. Jefferson and John Adams had refused the nomination, so the posts had gone to Franklin, Arthur Lee and Silas Deane, both of the former having lived in England and enjoyed extensive travel on the Continent. By the end of the year Deane was already in Paris, where he was engaging in secret negotiations with the Foreign Office and hoping to obtain substantial material assistance. During the summer Franklin and John Adams had prepared the draft of a treaty the Congress wanted to present to France, and in the meantime the first weapons, ammunition and other essential supplies were already arriving.

So much had to be accomplished in so many spheres that other foreign relations were neglected by the Congress, in spite of Sam Adams's frequent remonstrances. But the military disasters of the summer, autumn and early winter finally convinced the delegates that America could not defeat the British without help, and soon after the adjournment to Baltimore a special committee was appointed to "prepare and report a plan for obtaining foreign assistance." The matter was considered urgent, so the Congress selected as the co-chairmen the pair who could be relied on to move quickly, Sam Adams and Richard Henry Lee.

They made their preliminary report on December 28, 1776, and within a few weeks the task was completed. Adams and Lee started on the premise that their "natural allies" would be those nations that were either the traditional enemies of Britain or currently were opposed to the further expansion of the British Empire. Spain was first on the list, and a close second was the Grand Duchy of Tuscany. It was also decided to send an envoy to Prussia, and London's relations with Vienna having cooled, it was determined that the same minister-commissioner should represent the United States in Austria.

Before Franklin sailed for France he and John Adams put the finishing touches on their treaty, which the special committee recommended without reservation and which the Congress approved. Under the proposed terms the American West Indian trade would be confined to the vessels flying the flags of France and the United States; France would, in time, recapture Newfoundland and Cape Breton Island from Britain, which would be excluded from the Newfoundland Banks fishing grounds; subsequently the French Navy would capture Nova Scotia, and that territory would be divided by France and the United States. The optimism of Congress in the face of new catastrophes was totally unjustified, of course, and the hopes so glowingly outlined in the proposed treaty were never realized.

Dr. Franklin was offered the twin posts of minister to France and to Spain, but he declined, saying he had no desire to remain abroad for a protracted time and wanted to return home when his work as a commissioner was completed. So Arthur Lee, whom few in the Congress knew well, was substituted, thanks to the influence of his brother, Richard Henry, and of his good friend, Sam Adams. Another member of the prominent Lee family, William, subsequently became the American minister to Berlin and Vienna, and Ralph Izard was sent to Italy.

These appointments were overly optimistic and reflected the Americans' total lack of diplomatic experience. Arthur Lee was taken into custody at Burgos by the Spanish government and was escorted back to the French border after being told that Madrid would not accept his credentials. When Izard reached Paris en route to Italy, he was informed by the Tuscan legation there that it was pointless to continue on his journey, since the grand duke had no intention of offending Great Britain. William Lee was given the cold shoulder by the royal courts of Vienna and Berlin, and his mission, too, ended in complete failure. Only in France were the American envoys received, and even there they were not officially recognized. It was obvious that even those who hoped the Americans would succeed were convinced they would be beaten into submission.

Early in January 1777, the Congress returned to Philadelphia, General Washington's Trenton raid having convinced even the most apprehensive members that the capital was in no immediate danger of falling. So many committees were now functioning that the system had become unwieldy, and a bureaucratic tangle was hampering the effectiveness of a legislative body that, under the best of circumstances, talked a great deal but achieved little. So the entire committee system was overhauled.

Sam Adams became the chairman of the most important of them, the Board of War, and also of the subcommittee charged with supervising and directing the war in the North. He was also made chairman of the Foreign Alliances Committee, the Medical Committee and a special committee formed for the purposes of procuring cannon, which General Knox so desperately needed.

Adams also served as a member of eight minor committees, and was chairman of four.

The load would have been heavy even for a healthy man, and Adams was ill, suffering severe dysentery while still in Baltimore and not recovering his health until long after his return to Philadelphia. He concealed his ailment from his family and Massachusetts friends, however, and he rejected the advice of several physicians, including Dr. Rush, who urged him to remain in bed until he recovered. He insisted on maintaining his full schedule, even though he had to walk with the aid of a cane, and he was so weak that in late January he fainted on two occasions while the Congress was in session.

By early February he began to recover his strength, and he was cheered by the return of John Adams from Massachusetts. The cousins were again inseparable until the end of the year, when the younger Adams was sent abroad, taking up his new career as a diplomat and not returning to a seat in the Congress.

The year 1777 was the dreariest the Americans experienced in their struggle for freedom, and Sam Adams's unremitting efforts were devoted, in the main, to obtaining congressional support for General Washington. The delegates remained suspicious of any military man, and Adams had his work cut out for him, but he used the same tactics that had won the country's independence. When possible he launched frontal attacks, when necessary he assaulted flanks, but he never gave up.

As chairman of the Board of War he was active in every phase of military operations. Thanks to his swift intervention, a battalion of Continentals was sent into Maryland to put down an uprising of Loyalists in Somerset and Worcester counties. He directed the efforts of agents who were trying to establish alliances with various Indian tribes, and he maintained strict control of these activities. He and Richard Henry Lee conferred at length with the Pennsylvania Committee of Safety, with whom efforts were coordinated for the long-range defense of Philadelphia.

In addition he worked so hard on the settlement and establishment of the Articles of Confederation that he again impaired his health. Of the original committee, composed of one delegate from each state, he was the only remaining member, and hence was the only one who saw the problems in terms of a continuous development. His difficulties in trying to push through the Confederation were legion. The states quarreled about major issues and bickered about minor matters; a delay of many weeks occurred at one point in the summer of 1777 because several of the larger states were insisting that they be given several votes on matters of substance under the Articles and that the smaller states be confined to a single vote each.

Adams used his enormous influence in favor of granting each state a single vote, with its delegates deciding how to vote by means of an internal caucus. This system was adopted, and true proportional representation in the legislative branch of the United States government did not come into being until the adoption of the Constitution in 1789, when members of the House of Representatives were seated in accordance with that system.

But Adams believed that proportional representation was inevitable, and introduced a resolution proposing that a census be taken every three years and that, as the population grew and shifted, the membership of the Congress be adjusted accordingly. He stood alone in the Massachusetts delegation on this issue, and the rest of New England, the most populous section of the country, lined up against him, too. His colleagues and friends campaigned against him, and every state in the North followed the New England lead. The South, equally suspicious, joined in, and when a final vote was taken Adams was supported only by Virginia and a lone member of the Maryland delegation. His defeat was a sharp reply to the British newspapers that continued to insist that he intended to make himself the "King of America" and establish himself as a tyrant.

Adams also looked forward to the settlement of the West, and submitted a resolution proposing the admission of additional states to the Union as the vast wilderness territories were settled. But he was far ahead of his time, and twelve of the thirteen colonies strongly opposed him, all but Maryland having claims to western lands under the terms of their original charters. In spite of his defeat on this issue he took satisfaction in the knowledge that the people of the Vermont and Kentucky territories hailed him as their champion, and he wrote to a friend in Vermont that "the day is not far distant when you will be admitted to statehood." He proved to be a far better prophet than his congressional colleagues, and one of the principal reasons the Confederation eventually foundered was because of the lack of elasticity that made it necessary for a minimum of nine states to vote their approval before a new state could be admitted to the Union.

At the outset the Articles of Confederation were not seen as a series of feeble, unworkable compromises. An infant nation at war, with little experience in self-government on a national level, was incapable of producing the system that emerged a decade later under the new Constitution, which, reflecting the wisdom gleaned from events of the intervening years, rectified the original errors. The best minds of the age were devoted to the problems of establishing a national government, and the Confederation was the best that could be formed and approved by states that were jealous of all prerogatives.

The military news continued to be disheartening during 1777. Sir William Howe, eventually succeeded by Sir Henry Clinton, was still harrying Washington, and Sam Adams was one of the few who remained optimistic. It was true that the commander in chief's forces were still shrinking, but enlistments in the Continental Army had increased, and Adams, like Washington himself, placed his principal reliance on this body of regulars. The militia could not be relied on in emergencies, and Adams worked hard to encourage additional enlistments in the Continentals.

The news that "Gentleman Johnny" Burgoyne had started a march southward from Canada in May caused severe apprehensions, and Adams, charged with congressional responsibility for the war in the North, was particularly concerned. He respected the wealthy Philip Schuyler, the commander of the northern army, but believed the general was too old for a task that required youth and vigor, and due to Adams's efforts Schuyler was replaced by General Horatio Gates, a former British officer. Adams believed many qualities of leadership were lacking in Gates, too, but he appeared to be the best man available for the command. A few weeks later, when news was received that Fort Ticonderoga had fallen to Burgoyne, Adams immediately conferred with General Washington, who was then in Philadelphia. As a result of this talk, the commander in chief recommended the appointment of the most vigorous and incisive of his field generals, Benedict Arnold, as Gates's deputy, and Adams succeeded in pushing the nomination through the Congress. The task was difficult, for the volatile Arnold had offended a number of delegates by talking out of turn, but the wisdom of his appointment was demonstrated in October, when his efforts were responsible for the great American victory at Saratoga.

Prior to that triumph, however, the American cause received its most severe blow when Howe defeated Washington at the Battle of Brandywine and entered Philadelphia on September 26. Members of the Congress barely managed to escape the preceding day, and adjourned their sessions to the little inland Pennsylvania town of Lancaster. One meeting was held there, but the quarters were so cramped and the personal accommodations were so miserable that the "capital" of the United States was moved to nearby Yorktown.

The country was in despair as America suffered the worst days of the war, and even John Adams momentarily wondered whether the cause was lost. Thousands of ordinary citizens believed the end was near, and even the most frenzied efforts on the part of Patriots in Pennsylvania and her neighboring states of New Jersey, Maryland and Delaware could not prevent many from taking advantage of the British offer of amnesty and swearing their allegiance to the Crown.

Many members of the Congress had returned to their homes rather than go to Yorktown, and when deliberations began on September 30 there were only twenty members in attendance. Pennsylvania, Delaware and Georgia were unrepresented for a time, New Hampshire and Rhode Island had only one delegate each on hand, and there were just two present from New York.

Sam Adams displayed his customary calm in an hour of trial, though only he and John Hancock were excluded from the amnesty offer, and called it "the truest Congress we have ever had." The opening meeting of the truncated Congress was devoted to brief, gloomy speeches by each of the members in turn, and Sam Adams waited until everyone else had spoken before rising to his feet. His address, which appears here in full, was one of the few he ever made that was reported verbatim:

Gentlemen, your spirits appear oppressed with the weight of the public calamities. Your sadness of countenance reveals your disquietude. A patriot may grieve at the distress of his country, but he will never despair of the commonwealth.

Our affairs, it is said, are desperate! If this be our language, they are indeed. If we wear long faces, long faces will become fashionable. The eyes of the people are upon us. The tone of their feelings is regulated by ours. If we despond, public confidence is destroyed, the people will no longer yield their support to a hopeless contest, and American liberty is no more. But we are not driven to such narrow straits. Though fortune has been unpropitious, our condition is not desperate. Our burdens, though grievous, can be borne. Our losses, though great, can be retrieved. Through the darkness which shrouds our prospects the ark of safety is visible. Despondency becomes not the dignity of our cause, nor the character of those who are its supporters.

Let us awaken, then, and evince a different spirit,—a spirit that shall inspire the people with confidence in themselves and in us,—a spirit that will encourage them to persevere in this glorious struggle, until their rights and liberties shall be established on a rock. We have proclaimed to the world our determination to "die freemen rather than to live slaves." We have appealed to Heaven for the justice of our cause, and in Heaven we have placed our trust. Numerous have been the manifestations of God's providence in sustaining us. In the gloomy period of adversity, we have had "our cloud by day and pillar of fire by night." We have been reduced to distress, and the arm of Omnipotence has raised us up. Let us still rely in humble confidence on Him who is mighty to save. Good tiding will soon arrive. We shall never be abandoned by Heaven while we act worthy of its aid and protection.

Let us remember, always, that common adage, that "the darkest hour was just before the dawn of day."

This address, perhaps the best speech Sam Adams ever made, was widely reprinted in the American press, but it made little initial impression on the people, who thought the gentleman from Massachusetts was whistling in the dark. Some newspapers, owned by waverers, commented that a man who was still proscribed had literally nothing to lose by taking a firm and unyielding stand.

Then, on October 17, General Burgoyne was compelled to surrender his entire army to General Gates at Saratoga. Creasy has called this engagement one of the fifteen most decisive battles in the history of the world, and there can be no doubt that it was the turning point in the American Revolution. The grand British strategy for the destruction of the former colonies was smashed, and recruits once again began to join the Continentals. More important than anything else, France for the first time believed the Americans would win the war, and officially recognized the United States, sending the new nation men, warships and vast quantities of munitions and supplies.

Bonfires were lighted in every city and town under Patriot control as the news of the victory spread, and General Gates sent a special courier to Yorktown to inform the Congress that a military miracle had been wrought. He neglected to state, however, that the valor of General Arnold had been responsible for the triumph.

Sam Adams and Richard Henry Lee appointed themselves a committee of two to write a special proclamation of thanksgiving, a long-winded and rhetorical piece which most newspapers obligingly published. Many also reprinted Adams's speech of September 30, and someone—the finger of suspicion points at either John Adams or Lee—called him "the Prophet Samuel."

The word quickly spread, and until the end of his life Adams bore the affectionate nickname.

The Battle of Saratoga had its effect in Great Britain, too, and the long-silent Whigs came to life again. The Earl of Chatham appeared on crutches in the House of Lords to demand that the war be ended without delay, and similar speeches were made in the Commons by Burke, Fox and Barré.

Generals Gates and Schuyler, with whom Burgoyne had long discussions after Saratoga, wrote separately to Sam Adams that the defeated British commander, who had himself opposed the war as a member of the Commons in 1774, had not changed his mind and continued privately to hold the belief that Britain should grant the independence of her former colonies. The day was closer at hand than anyone believed possible, Burgoyne declared, when the Whigs would unseat Lord North and form a new ministry that the Parliament would empower to make reasonable, just peace terms with America.

Burgoyne's estimate was far too optimistic, but Sam Adams accepted it at face value, perhaps because it was what he most wanted to hear. His optimism soared to new heights, and in flurries of correspondence with the American commissioners in Paris, he repeatedly urged them to persuade the French to sign a treaty with the United States before other nations beat them to the punch.

One major, immediate task still faced the Congress, the completion of the Articles of Confederation, and that work was done by October 30. The following day President Hancock went home to Boston on leave. Sam Adams had labored without respite for thirteen months in Philadelphia, Baltimore and Yorktown, and on November 7 he and John Adams also went home on leave. Relations between the two cousins and Hancock were so strained that it did not occur to the three gentlemen from Massachusetts to go home together.

Chapter
Thirty

Last-minute snags made it necessary for Sam and John Adams to delay their departure for home until November 11. They traveled by way of Lancaster and Reading, then headed toward the Hudson River, and on the night of the eighteenth they dined at Fishkill with Dr. Samuel Adams of the Continental Army, who had not seen his father for more than two and a half years. The cousins reached Boston on December 4, and that same day, after a reunion with his wife and daughter, Sam Adams immediately resumed his duties as the Massachusetts secretary of state.

This fact makes it more obvious than ever than he had no concept of relaxation and leisure. He had no hobbies, no avocations, no interests in life outside of his work. Now fifty-five years old, he had spent thirteen years in the public service without once taking a real vacation, and apparently it did not occur to him that he might take life easy in the company of his wife and daughter. His country was still at war, fighting for her independence, so there was work to be done.

What Adams failed to realize was that, during his long absences from Massachusetts, there had been changes in the public temper. The state's fighting men were either absent from home on duty with the Continentals—many were suffering through a ghastly winter at Valley Forge with General Washington—or were on home duty with the militia. But the politicians were as active as ever, and a deep schism had manifested itself in the ranks of the Whigs. The old-line radicals, headed by Dr. Warren, remained loyal to Sam Adams and were willing to follow his lead in all things. But a younger, more personally ambitious breed had appeared, and this group drifted toward John Hancock, strongly encouraged by Hancock himself. The president of the Congress, soon to obtain for himself a militia appointment as a major general, had unlimited personal ambitions and envisioned himself as a postwar president of the Republic. It is untrue, however, that he wanted to make himself a king, a charge previously leveled at Sam Adams and one that would be used later in attacks on General Washington.

But Hancock, who lacked the common touch, was nevertheless clever enough to realize that a man who wanted a permanent niche as a national leader needed a strong power base at home. He could no longer rely on the support of Sam and John Adams, and Dr. Warren and his lieutenants would have nothing to do with a man on whom the Adams cousins had turned their backs, so Hancock felt compelled to create a following of his own. Various friends had worked on his behalf during his own absence from Massachusetts, and by the time Adams reached Boston, he found that Hancock had accumulated a strong following.

This situation might not have bothered a man totally engrossed in the war effort had it not been for ugly developments in Yorktown. During December an attempt was made by Washington's opponents in the Congress to dismiss him as commander in chief and promote Gates, who was not averse to the idea, into his place. The effort failed, and neither Sam nor John Adams knew anything about the matter until Washington was confirmed in his office. But, to the astonishment of the cousins, a rumor spread to the effect that they were responsible for the cabal.

The very idea that Sam Adams, Washington's closest associate and strongest supporter in the Continental Congress, could have had a hand in any attempt to replace the general was absurd. Adams's first act when he heard the ridiculous story was to write a letter to Washington, assuring him of his abiding affection, trust and loyalty, and the general immediately answered in kind, saying he did not believe the rumors and that his own regard for both Adamses was undiminished.

How Sam Adams came to believe that John Hancock was responsible for the vicious rumor is unknown, but believe it he did, and posterity has since ascribed the tale to Hancock, although the possibility exists that he was innocent in this matter. In any event, he did not deny that he had a hand in the incident, and some historians have leaned toward the view that he had great military ambitions of his own, and saw the appointment of Gates as temporary and believed that, in time, he himself would become commander in chief.

Be that as it may, the cool relations between Hancock and Adams had now erupted into open enmity, and Adams no longer tried to disguise his hatred for his colleague and former protégé. The rift between the two factions of the Whig party grew deeper, and in 1779 Adams strongly opposed the candidacy of Hancock for the presidency of the Massachusetts Constitutional Convention, stating bluntly that the consequences would be disastrous if "great trusts should be confided to hands incapable of managing them."

Beginning early in 1778 the puritanical Adams frequently attacked Hancock for his personal extravagances and high style of living, and after returning to the Congress he mortally and permanently offended his former friend. A motion was made to thank the president for his devotion to the cause, but Adams rallied the New England delegates and they not only voted in a solid bloc against the resolution, thereby defeating it, but went on record as holding that no president of the Congress should be thanked for the performance of his duty.

In a letter to a Boston friend after his return to the Congress, Adams wrote:

Is it true that the review of the Boston militia was closed with an expensive entertainment? If it was, and the example was followed by the country, I hope I shall be excused when I venture to pledge myself, that the militia of that state will never be put on such a footing as to become formidable to its enemies. . . . Are we arrived at such a pitch of levity and dissipation as that the idea of feasting shall extinguish every spark of public virtue, and frustrate the design of the most noble and useful institution? I hope not! Shall we not again see that sobriety of manners, that temperance, frugality, fortitude, and many other virtues which were once the glory and strength of my much loved native town? Heaven grant it speedily!

Most of Adams's attacks on Hancock were much more pointed, and his propagandist's pen held the new militia general, still the president of the Congress, up to ridicule. In a letter to John Warren he said: "Our Boston papers never fail to mark all the movements of Great Men and to give honor where honor is due. The spirited exertions of our new Major General, to be sure, ought properly to be noticed."

As will be seen, the vendetta had a number of consequences, but it occupied only a small portion of Sam Adams's time and attention. In January 1778, the Massachusetts legislature reported a new state constitution, and although Adams had played no part in the preparation of the document, he used his influence to support its passage. The stubbornly independent farmers of Berkshire County opposed passage, however, and Hancock, flexing his muscles, threw in his lot with them. So the passage of the constitution by the legislature was blocked, necessitating the holding of the convention in the following year.

In December 1777, a remarkable gentleman from Prussia arrived in Boston from Europe, bearing a letter of introduction to Sam Adams from Dr. Franklin. Baron Friedrich Wilhelm Ludolf Gerhard Augustin von Steuben was a professional soldier who believed in the American cause and had come to offer the United States his services. Adams held a number of meetings with him, dining with him on several occasions, and was deeply impressed by his sincerity. He gave von Steuben a letter to General Washington, and subsequently, after his own return to the Congress, he was instrumental in obtaining for the baron the rank of major general and the position of inspector general of the Continental Army.

Von Steuben went to the "natural fortress" of Valley Forge in the hills of Pennsylvania, where a winter of incredible hardships imbued the survivors with a new spirit and determination. Baron von Steuben, the drillmaster supreme, transformed these men into one of the most efficient, hard-bitten corps of troops on earth, and the professionalism of American men at arms was due in large part to his great efforts. He and Adams subsequently became close friends, maintaining the relationship for the rest of their lives.

General Burgoyne and his troops arrived in Boston during Adams's sojourn there to await a prisoner-of-war exchange and transfer home. "Gentleman Johnny" wanted to meet the head of the American Board of War, but Adams declined. His reasons were not personal, he emphasized, but he felt it improper for a man in his position to engage in social intercourse with such a prominent representative of the enemy.

In February 1778, John Adams sailed for France, replacing Silas Deane as a commissioner, but before he arrived there the formal treaty with France was concluded. Sam Adams received ecstatic letters from both Franklin and Arthur Lee, and the whole country rejoiced when the news was made public. The Americans would receive financial help, munitions and other supplies; volunteers were coming to serve in the Continentals and a French fleet was being dispatched to break the British blockade. The rewards of the victory at Saratoga were great, and Sam Adams, who had so long advocated an alliance with France, was convinced that the United States was certain to triumph in its military contest.

Early in May Adams again left home after his longest sojourn in Boston in years, and on the twenty-first of the month resumed his seat in the Continental Congress. On that same day he was made chairman of the new Marine Board, which was charged with the responsibility of supervising the creation of a navy, building ships and obtaining munitions and supplies, and providing the fleet with officers. He had served on previous Congressional committees dealing with the Navy, but his new assignment was similar to that which he still held on the Board of War, and he displayed his customary vigor in the discharge of his new responsibilities. Orders were given for the building of five warships in Massachusetts yards, and a number of privateers were given formal commissions, thereby creating the infant Navy almost overnight; their captains and subordinate officers accepted personal commissions and the Navy was given the same status as the Continental Army.

Something of a stir was created late in May when a group of commissioners empowered by Lord North to deal with the Americans reached New York, and Sir Henry Clinton wrote to General Washington asking that the group be allowed to travel to Yorktown. The commander in chief and Adams were unalterably opposed to the principle of conferring with the British because the Crown was still unwilling to recognize the independence of the former colonies.

As usual, Lord North and King George completely failed to understand the mood of the Americans. Two years earlier public opinion would have been overwhelmingly in favor of a conciliatory settlement that would have kept the colonies in the British Empire, but by now the nation had made too many sacrifices and the people would settle for nothing less than the establishment of their own country separate from Britain.

Adams leaped into the fray, and not only wrote the formal letter notifying the British commissioners that the Congress would not receive them or treat with them, but also prepared another of his propaganda essays. Written in the form of an open letter to Admiral Lord Howe, Sir Henry Clinton and the commissioners, it was a document of more than five thousand words, signed "An American," and it dealt at length with the American reasons for refusing to settle the conflict on any terms other than the recognition of the independence of the United States.

This treatise was published by the newspapers of eight states, and was instrumental in solidifying American opinion. The unhappy commissioners waited in New York until October, hoping for a change of mind, and then returned to London with their mission a failure. The war would go on.

But the British would continue to seek ways to end the struggle on terms that would return the colonies to the fold, and one of the most novel ideas, concocted by North himself and approved by the king, was to create an American House of Lords. In all, two hundred men would be made peers, with the highest ranks being given to Franklin, Washington, Adams and Hancock. John Adams, writing from France, informed his cousin of the scheme, and with a straight face asked if he would like to be so honored. The elder Adams was vastly amused, and replied that there was nothing he desired more than an earldom.

The arrival of the French fleet under Admiral Count d'Estaing imperiled the British in Philadelphia, and Clinton, realizing his lines were extended, withdrew from the city on June 18. This gave Washington one of his few opportunities to take the offensive, and on June 28 he attacked the enemy at Monmouth, New Jersey. The Continentals were on the verge of winning a victory as complete as the Battle of Saratoga, but General Charles Lee deliberately disobeyed Washington's orders to advance and by his dilatory tactics robbed them of the chance. Monmouth had to be regarded as a draw, but the veterans of Valley Forge gained self-confidence and knew now that they could beat the best troops Britain could field.

The Congress returned to Philadelphia on the heels of the enemy evacuation, and the city once again became the capital of the United States. On August 1, the French minister Gerard landed in Philadelphia, and Sam Adams was placed in charge of the arrangements for the presentation of his credentials, a full-dress ceremony unique in the American experience. Adams and Richard Henry Lee rode in an open carriage to the envoy's house, then escorted him to Independence Hall, where the credentials were presented to President Hancock. After the ceremony an "entertainment" was given, appropriate toasts were offered and the company sat down to a banquet. Gerard sat on the right of

Hancock, and the Frenchman was flanked on the other side by Adams; not even the fact that the two gentlemen from Massachusetts were not on speaking terms could mar the pleasure and splendor of the occasion.

In the summer of 1778, Adams played a major role in the dispatch of an expedition to effect the recapture of Newport, Rhode Island, from the British, one of the most ineffectual American efforts of the war. The entire force of ten thousand men was commanded by General John Sullivan, with the Massachusetts militia under Hancock, who took a leave from his duties in the Congress for the purpose. The American land attack was to be coordinated with an assault by sea on the part of the French fleet, but a hurricane battered the ships so severely that d'Estaing was forced to sail straight to Boston for repairs. Sullivan's troops gave a good account of themselves, and the British suffered greater casualties, but they retained possession of the Rhode Island port, the most important in New England after Boston.

Sam Adams immediately tried to blunt the criticism to which he knew Count d'Estaing would be subjected, and wrote long letters to men prominent in politics in all four of the New England states. Thanks to the vigorous assertion of his influence, which included several newspaper articles written under various pseudonyms that explained the situation in detail, New England's reaction to the unfortunate sequence of events was mild.

Adams had to develop and employ skills to which he was unaccustomed during the second half of 1778. The commissioners to Paris were quarreling, each of them jealous of what he regarded as his authority, and each of the three—Franklin, John Adams and Arthur Lee—regarded Adams as his confidant. He soothed each in turn, but he realized that frictions were unavoidable, and recommended to the Congress that one man be given the rank of minister to France, thereby ending che confusion. His idea won immediate acceptance, and Franklin, whom he nominated for the post, was appointed. John Adams, who was grateful for his relative's intervention in an embarrassing situation, returned home in the winter of 1779.

As in any war, atrocities were committed by the fighting men on both sides, and all through the summer and autumn of 1778, a rumor persisted to the effect that American prisoners of war were being badly treated. Adams, with the help of Thomas Paine, prepared a "Manifesto" issued in the name of the Congress, decrying the outrages and threatening to retaliate in kind unless the enemy desisted. The document had no effect on the British treatment of prisoners, which was actually no worse than that the Americans inflicted on their captives. But as an exercise prepared by the eighteenth century's two greatest masters of the art of propaganda, it helped to arouse, once again, the spirits of a war-weary people. The citizens of America were being "butchered," the document stated, open country was being "laid waste" and "defenseless villages" were being burned. British prisons were "slaughter-houses," and "the severest injuries have been aggravated by the grossest insults." The "Manifesto," which was unanimously approved by the Continental Congress, closed on an emotional note:

> We, therefore, the Congress of the United States of America, do solemnly declare and proclaim that if our enemies presume to execute their threats, or persist in their present career of barbarity, we will take such exemplary vengeance as shall deter others from a like conduct. We appeal to the God who searcheth the hearts of men for the rectitude of our intentions; and in His holy presence declare that, as we are not moved by any light or hasty suggestions of anger or revenge, so through every possible change of fortune we will adhere to this our determination.

For all practical purposes the war in the northern states was at an end, and in the years of the conflict that remained, the major theaters of operation were transferred to the South, with bitter campaigns waged in Virginia, the Carolinas and Georgia. In spite of the help being given by France, the American economy was anything but sound; the states competed with the Congress in printing paper money, unsupported by gold or silver, that was worth less each month.

Sam Adams had no income other than his salaries as a delegate to the Congress, a member of the Massachusetts legislature and that commonwealth's secretary of state. He was paid promptly, but his wages could not keep pace with the rate of inflation, and he refused to engage in the practice employed by so many of his colleagues, who invested in speculative land schemes. His wife and daughter continued to live simply and had no money for luxuries; he himself lived in the least expensive of Philadelphia lodgings and ate most of his meals at cheap waterfront taverns frequented principally by American and French seamen. He found it difficult, too, to clothe himself with the dignity required of a delegate to the Congress.

So he instituted a new propaganda campaign, and in a typical barrage of newspaper articles written in 1778 and 1779 under various pen names, he insisted that threadbare suits, frayed cuffs and cracked boots were "patriotic," His only requirement was that these "badges of honor" be neat and clean.

The Massachusetts legislature came to his aid by renting him, for a nominal sum, a confiscated house in Boston that had been the property of Robert Hallowell, the former Crown comptroller, who had fled to Halifax. Since his furniture had been destroyed by the British officers who had occupied his own home, the legislature obligingly sold to him, for a very small price, furniture, rugs, lamps, linens, chinaware and cooking utensils that had been confiscated from the estates of various Loyalists who had fled the country.

Some of his letters to his wife and daughter during this period have been preserved, and indicate the flavor of his relationship with them. On September 8, 1778, he wrote to "my dear daughter":

Your very dutiful and obliging letter of the 28th of August came to my hand yesterday, and brought me the afflicting news of your mother's illness. When you tell me "the doctor thinks she is on the mending hand" and "he hopes she will be cleverly in a day or two" I am apt to conclude her disorder had not much abated when you wrote. I know "she is exceedingly loath to give me the least pain," and therefore I suspect that she has dictated to you to make the best of it to me. "She begs me not to make myself very anxious for her." This is a request which it is impossible for me to comply with. I shall be very uneasy till I hear again from you. I pray God she may recover her health, and long continue a rich blessing to you and me. I am satisfied "you do all in your power for so excellent a mother." You are under great obligations to her, and I am sure you are of a grateful disposition. I hope her life will be spared, and that you will have the opportunity of presenting to her my warmest respects. I rejoice to hear that your late disorder was so gentle, and that you have got over it. I commend you, my dear, to the care and protection of the Almighty. That he may reward your filial piety is the ardent prayer of your

Very affectionate father,
S. Adams.

His letters to his wife reflect a different tone. He frequently discussed political matters with her, and in the autumn of 1778 he was upset by the continuing campaign of John Hancock's lieutenants in Boston against him. Unable to reply to the whispers of his foes, who were spreading false rumors, he rejected the attempts of mutual friends to arrange a reconciliation. In a letter to "my dear Betty," dated October 20, 1778, he said, in part:

My Boston friends tell me, with great solicitude, that I have enemies there. I thank them for their concern for me, and tell them that I knew it before. The man who acts an honest part in public life must often counteract the passions, inclinations, or humors of wicked men, and this must create him enemies. I am, therefore, not disappointed or mortified. I flatter myself that no virtuous man who knows me will, or can be, my enemy, because I think he can have no suspicion of my integrity. But they say my enemies "are plotting against me." Neither does that discompose me; for what else can I expect from such kind of men? If they mean to make me uneasy, they miss their aim, for I am happy, and it is not in *their* power to disturb my peace. They add, the design is to get me recalled from this service. I am in no pain about such an event, for I know there are many who can serve their country here with greater capacity, though none more honestly. The sooner, therefore, another is elected in my room the better. I shall the sooner retire to the sweet enjoyment of domestic life. This, you can witness, I have often wished for; and I trust that all-gracious Providence has spared your precious life through a dangerous illness to heighten the pleasures of my retirement. If my enemies are governed by malice or envy, I could not wish them a severer punishment than their own feelings. But, my dear, I thank God I have many friends. *You* know them. Remember me to them all as you have opportunity. I could say many more things to you, but I am called off.

Chapter
Thirty-one

All through the autumn of 1778 Sam Adams spoke of retirement from public life in his letters to his wife and to his cousin, John. But even his foes in Massachusetts had no real desire to see him removed from the national political scene. His prestige was so great throughout the country that he was universally regarded as the most prominent and influential of American legislators, and Hancock's supporters put up only a token opposition to his reelection as a delegate to the Continental Congress for 1779.

Most of Adams's time was spent on the Marine Board, which, like the Board of War and the Treasury, had created and built its own staff and maintained offices separate from those of the Congress. Because of French military help, his duties on the Board of War had become routine, but the need still existed for an efficient, larger and more powerful Navy.

Early in 1779 Adams was made chairman of a select committee that was given an exceptionally delicate and embarrassing assignment. The criticism of Silas Deane as a commissioner to France was persistent, and Deane was accused of being negligent as well as ineffient. The task of the special committee was to conduct an inquiry and, in effect, sit in judgment on Deane, which was ticklish for Adams because he and the accused long had been personal friends. Roger Sherman was Deane's defender, while Richard Henry Lee became his principal accuser, due to the claims of his brother, Arthur, that Deane had used public funds for private purposes. The matter became still more complicated when Thomas Paine, who was the secretary to the Committee of Foreign Affairs, entered the controversy and had to be dismissed from office when he became indiscreet and revealed secret details of the negotiations with France.

Congressional tempers flared, and the entire Virginia delegation, supported by North Carolina, implicated Dr. Franklin and demanded his recall from France. But on this issue Adams and the Lees split; Sam Adams had complete faith in the integrity of Franklin, and insisted that he continue to serve as minister to France. His will prevailed, as did his firm opinion that the charges of disloyalty and embezzlement against Deane were not proved. His friendship with the Lees was not disrupted, although his influence was paramount in winning Deane's exoneration.

In the spring of 1779 Adams suffered from fatigue, and, now fifty-seven years of age, he began to think seriously of returning to Boston and staying there. An added incentive was the Massachusetts Constitutional Convention, which was being convened in June and which he was anxious to attend.

He submitted his resignation as a delegate to the Congress, but the Massachusetts legislature would not accept it and refused to elect someone else to his seat. Under no circumstances would he miss attendance at the Convention, so he left Philadelphia late in June, reaching Boston early in July. He stayed at home for the better part of a year, and throughout that time the legislature repeatedly refused to replace him. It ultimately elected him to serve yet another term, for 1780, which proved to be his last.

Shortly after his return to Boston the British mounted a new expedition in New York and launched it against Connecticut. Adams, acting in his capacity as the chairman of the congressional Board of War and as a member of the Massachusetts War

Board, to which his friends hastily elected him, immediately coordinated New England's repulsion of the invaders. At his instigation Massachusetts raised two new regiments to aid a sister state, and he also traveled to Rhode Island and New Hampshire to obtain additional assistance from them.

The Massachusetts legislature was sitting in almost continuous session, most of its members simultaneously serving as delegates to the Constitutional Convention, so Adams's friends found a vacancy for him and promptly saw to his election as a voting member of the legislature, in which he had been serving only as secretary of state. He quickly launched a campaign to obtain flour from other parts of the country, as bread was scarce in the state, and he became chairman of the Massachusetts Marine Board, which made it possible for him to speed the shipbuilding program demanded by Sam Adams of the Congress's Marine Board.

He was one of Boston's twelve delegates to the Constitutional Convention, and had obtained the largest number of votes of any candidate. In spite of Hancock's opposition Sam Adams could still win election to any position he wanted in Massachusetts— or so it seemed. He would soon learn that his foes were more numerous and powerful than he realized.

He attended the Convention faithfully, and was an uncompromising advocate of the rights of an individual state. His attitude was remarkably similar to that displayed by Patrick Henry at the Virginia Convention; both men were unyielding in their opposition to the granting of powers to the national government of the country that both had been so instrumental in creating. Adams was so unalterably wedded to the principle of home rule that he continued to regard the state rather than the nation as the basic unit of power and administration.

The Convention actually convened on September 1, and Adams was at once elected chairman of a committee to draft a constitution; John Adams and James Bowdoin served with him. Their work appears to have been joint, and they prepared the main body of a proposed constitution together, but later in the autumn John Adams was appointed by the Congress to the post of minister and was charged with negotiating with Great Britain for a treaty of peace and commerce, as America's friends in Great Britain finally had won enough influence to force the consideration of negotiations on the basis of a free, independent United States. So the younger Adams was not present for the rewriting of the Consitutiton and the preparation of amendments.

The task of completing the Constitution was done by the spring of 1780, and Adams turned his attention to one other matter before returning for the last time to Philadelphia. He was unalterably opposed to the readmission of Loyalist refugees to any part of the United States, a stand that blurs his image as a liberal and humanitarian. He was the author of a bill forbidding their return to Massachusetts at any time, and after initial opposition he pushed it through the legislature.

Immediately prior to his departure he, together with a number of others who were philosophically inclined, applied to the legislature for the incorporation of an organization destined to become one of the most prestigious in the United States, the American Academy of Arts and Sciences. His own interests were principally in the realm of literature, and he admitted he knew little about science, but he agreed with Dr. Franklin that its encouragement was vital to the future of an independent, growing nation.

On the eve of his departure Adams was elected to membership on the Governor's Council, soon to become the Massachusetts Senate, but he declined the honor. He had not yet recovered his full physical strength and still suffered from fatigue, so he appears to have wanted no more responsibilities than he could comfortably handle. This was a new attitude, the first sign he had given that he was aware of advancing age, but no documents have ever been found that explain his refusal in detail.

A French fleet bringing troops on board transports for the capture of Newport was expected at any time, and early in July, soon after his arrival in Philadelphia, Adams wrote Cousin John, who was on the Continent:

> I wrote you several times while I was at Boston, and received your favor by the Marquis de Lafayette. Another, to

which you referred me, has not yet come to hand. This letter will be delivered to you by Mr. Searl, a member of the Congress from the State of Pennsylvania. He will be better able to inform you of the state of things than I can, who, after twelve months' absence from this city, returned but a few days ago.

The people of Massachusetts have at last agreed to the form of a civil Constitution, in nothing varying from a copy I sent you by a son of our friend General Warren. This great business was carried through with much good humor by the people, even in Berkshire, where some persons led us to expect it would meet with many obstructions. Never was a good constitution more needed than at this juncture. Among other more lasting advantages I hope that, in consequence of it, the part which that state must take in the war will be conducted with greater attention and better effect. Who is to be the first man will be determined in September, when, if our newspapers rightly inform us, the new government is to take place. The burden will fall on the shoulders of one of two gentlemen whom you know. May Heaven lead the people in the wisest choice. The first chosen Governor may probably have it in his powers to do more good or more hurt than any of his successors.

The French fleet is not yet arrived. Perhaps their long passage may turn out for the best. An earlier arrival might have found us not altogether prepared to co-operate with them to the best advantage. I now think we shall be ready to join them. One would think the exertions which Americans might make with such aid would rid us of the British barbarians. I hope this will be a vigorous and effective campaign. I left Massachusetts exceedingly active in filling up their battalions by drafts, besides raising four thousand militia in the service.

Mr. [Henry] Laurens arrived here a few days past. He will speedily embark for Holland, to prosecute a business which you are not unacquainted with.

Under their new constitutions the states were reserving most important rights to themselves and granting the Continental Congress little or no authority. So that august body, at no time powerful, was rapidly degenerating into a debating society, and its deliberations in 1780 were the dreariest in which it had yet engaged. Most of its efforts were directed toward the solution of financial and economic problems that were multiplying rapidly, but the Congress lacked the authority to impose solutions on the nation, even if it found them. Sam Adams served on his usual, many committees, but no permanent records of the proceedings were kept and his correspondence said little about new, burning issues. Therefore virtually nothing specific is known of his activities in Philadelphia during this dullest of congressional years.

By this time he had changed his mind about the dangers of a standing army, sharing the disgust of many Americans with the almost totally unreliable militia. A permanent, "well-appointed" army, he wrote, was to be preferred to the inefficient, expensive militia. During the autumn of 1780 he broke for the first time with General Washington, who proposed to the Congress that retired officers should receive half pay for life. This, Adams argued, would create a military elite that might become a threat to the democratic form of government. Displaying the same skill he had shown for so many years, he was responsible for the defeat of Washington's proposal, even though the Congress had fallen into the habit of giving the commander in chief almost anything he requested.

While Adams was in Philadelphia, Major General Benedict Arnold committed the act of treason that shocked the entire United States. The gentleman from Massachusetts was not surprised, however. In a letter to his wife dated October 3, 1780, he commented, "You know that I have had my suspicions of this traitor, and therefore it is not wonderful that I am not astonished as if some other officer had been detected of the treason." There is no explanation of this provocative comment elsewhere in the letter or in any other document, so posterity is in ignorance of Adams's reasons for suspecting that Arnold had sold out to the British. After the passage of two centuries this intriguing minor mystery appears insoluble.

In September the Massachusetts elections took place, and Adams, who had expected John Hancock to be elected governor, was nevertheless chagrined when his opponent became the first citizen of Massachusetts. He was startled, however, by his own defeat for the office of secretary of the commonwealth. It was the first time the people of his state had ever turned against him en masse, and his defeat was a sure sign that Hancock now held the real reins of power.

In the winter and spring of 1781, prior to Adams's final retirement from the Congress, he devoted most of his efforts to bolstering the Continental Army and obtaining more supplies and munitions for General Washington. The British were enjoying great military success in Virginia, the Carolinas and Georgia, and even though it was becoming increasingly clear to thinking men on both sides of the Atlantic that the war would end with the formal granting of independence to the United States by Great Britain, that had not yet occurred.

In 1781, Franklin, Jefferson, John Jay and Henry Laurens were added to the Peace Commission, but Jefferson, then governor of Virginia, declined the appointment, and Laurens, who had been taken captive by the British, was not released in time to take much part in the talks. Formal negotiations began in September 1782, and the outcome was inevitable from the start when, at Jay's insistence, the head of the British Commission, Richard Oswald, was authorized to treat with "the Thirteen United States of America."

It is significant that Dr. Franklin continued to play a major role in the affairs of his country, and would become chairman of the Constitutional Convention in 1787. But Sam Adams, sixteen years his junior, ended his principal work on behalf of his country when he retired from the Congress. Never robust, Adams literally wore himself out in the service of the United States. A year shy of his sixtieth birthday, he was, according to Harlow, the physical equivalent of a man of eighty.

His political life did not end at this point, however. As will be seen, he remained very active in a relatively minor sphere, and suddenly, the better part of a decade later, was rejuvenated, ending his career in an almost totally unexpected burst of activity and glory. So it is a mistake to say, as so many historians did for many years, that he disappeared from the mainstream of American history.

Certainly it is true, however, that he had made his principal contribution to his country by the time he retired from the Congress. Americans were completely unified on the subject of independence, and only the regiments of Loyalists fighting on the side of the British in the southern states continued to cling to the forlorn hope that the authority of the Crown would be reinstated in America. The independence of the United States was taken for granted throughout Europe, even in Spain, which, because of its own colonial empire in North America, was reluctant to grant recognition to the new nation.

The main thrust of Adams's career had lain in the creation of a new climate in America, followed by the demand and fight for independence. He was truly the Grand Incendiary, and unlike Franklin, John Adams, Jay and many others, he was unable to shift mental gears and become a peacetime statesman. His career runs curiously parallel to that of Patrick Henry, who remained active in Virginia politics but did not again rise to prominence on a national level. Of all the Founding Fathers of the Republic, he and Adams were the truest revolutionaries.

Perhaps it is a trifle unfair to the still puritanical Adams to claim, as some historians have done, that he was unable to adjust to a new and different era. He had made austerity fashionable at a time when it had been necessary for the creation and survival of a new nation, and that approach had coincided with his own convictions. So it is true that he was out of temper with the times when he objected to the more extravagant social life that spread rapidly and widely after the treaty of peace was signed in 1783.

In the political sphere, however, he did understand what was happening around him, as he proved after nearly a decade of lying semifallow. He was too feeble, as the loss of his political power in Massachusetts so amply demonstrates, to reassume active leadership. After more than six years of living alone in drab lodging houses and eating cheap food, after a decade and a half of such constant devotion to the cause he believed sacred that he had neglected his wife and family, he was in desperate physical and emotional need of the love and care that Mrs. Adams and his children could give him. He yearned for that luxury, and in every letter to his wife he spoke of the rest he hoped to enjoy at her side.

It is untrue, too, that he thought only in terms of keeping all power in the hands of the states. Wells emphasizes, based on Adams's voluminous correspondence with various friends in the period after 1781, that he was sensitive to the need to grant authority in foreign, financial and military affairs to a central government, and that he agreed with the advocates of a strong national legislature and executive in these fields.

Some of his friends in Massachusetts refused to accept his insistence that he be relieved in the Congress, and others found it impossible to believe he really wanted to go into semiretirement. In the late winter of 1781 a number of them rallied to his cause, and wrote to say they felt certain he could defeat Hancock in the September election. There would be no better man than Sam Adams as governor, they argued.

But he indicated his own frame of mind in a short, philosophical treatise he wrote to one of his strongest supporters, Caleb Davis, saying:

> You mention a certain juncture when you wish me to return. I think I can discover your motive and your own partiality for me. I do assure you I am not solicitous about anything of the kind which your letter seems to indicate. I have always desired to confine my desires in this life within moderate bounds, and it is time for me to reduce them to a narrower compass. You speak of "neglect," "ingratitude," &c. But let us entertain just sentiments. A citizen owes everything to the commonwealth; and after he has made his utmost exertions for its prosperity, has he done more than his duty? When time enfeebles his powers, and renders him unfit for further service, his country, to preserve its own vigor, will wisely call upon others; and if he decently retreats to make room for them, he will show that he has not totally lost his understanding. Besides, there is a period in life when a man should covet the exalted pleasures of reflection in retirement.

Apprehensive that his health would not permit him to spend another summer in Philadelphia, Adams wrote a formal letter of resignation from the Congress to the president of the new Massachusetts Senate, and on April 18 he left for home, arriving in Boston at the end of the month. His travels were at an end, and he never again left the state. He had not been pushed into retirement, but had deliberately chosen to lead a less active life, and was sincere in his yearning for a time of quiet contemplation. Apparently it did not occur to him that, after he enjoyed a long rest, he would feel compelled to return to the active arena.

Chapter Thirty-two

When Sam Adams returned to Boston in the spring of 1781 his family was still living in the rented house and using secondhand furniture. He had almost no funds, but friends in the legislature busied themselves on his behalf, and soon he was paid the better part of one hundred pounds still due him for his services as clerk of the Massachusetts Assembly in 1774. Now that it was becoming obvious that the war would end victoriously and that America would achieve her ends, the nation was enjoying the beginning of an economic boom. Boston, now far removed from any active theater of military operations, was the first American city in a position to enjoy the benefits of improving conditions, and many men were becoming wealthy. Adams could have availed himself of a number of business opportunities that would have given him greater security, but he still had no interest in commerce, no desire to engage in foreign trade, become a banker or open a new brewery. Politics was still his only vocation.

He was incapable of complete retirement, and in spite of the domination of Massachusetts politics by John Hancock, Adams still had an army of friends who would not allow him to slip into total obscurity. Shortly after his return a member of the new state Senate resigned, and the voters obligingly elected him to fill the vacancy. His colleagues responded equally promptly, and the day he took his seat, in late May, they made him president of the Senate. In this capacity he continued to play a role in providing men and funds for the final military operations of the war, and he had the unenviable task of trying to quiet the murmurs of the discontented who felt that Massachusetts had already done more than her share in the war effort.

His duties were not arduous, however, and for the first time in many years he had time to relax in the company of his family. In June he had the happy task of giving his daughter in marriage to the younger brother of the second Mrs. Adams. In keeping with his Puritanical beliefs he and his wife planned a modest celebration, but his many friends took advantage of an opportunity to show their affection for him, and the church was crowded. Even Governor Hancock ignored his feud with the head of the Adams clan and was on hand to kiss the bride.

After spending so many years in the Continental Congress Sam Adams could not put its affairs out of his mind, and even though his hand trembled so much now that his writing was only semilegible, he kept up a steady, heavy correspondence with his former associates. He was particularly active in obtaining financial help for South Carolina and Georgia, which had been suffering severe Loyalist raids; his efforts were not totally altruistic, as Mrs. Adams had close relatives in both states.

Soon after his return from Philadelphia he joined the Reverend Mr. Cooper and a number of other clergymen on a local committee formed "to adopt measures for the promotion of virtue and good order." In this capacity the last of the Puritans acted as the moderator of a number of town meetings, and wrote about them with grim relish to Cousin John, with whom he continued to maintain a regular correspondence.

His natural target was Hancock, whose extravagances he continued to disapprove, but contrary to his customs of the past, he refrained from writing to the newspapers under various pseudonyms. This self-control may have been the result of the efforts made by a number of prominent Bostonians to end the feud between the city's two most distinguished citizens. Adams and Hancock were persuaded to sit down at dinner together on a number of occasions, and although neither regarded the other with any great affection, they managed to reach an armistice of sorts. They stopped sniping at each other, and the people were led to believe that the Whigs were presenting a solid front again.

In his intimate correspondence with John Adams, however, the new president of the Massachusetts Senate remained highly critical of Hancock. After observing that "men of influence must form the manners of the people," he said, "*You* are well enough acquainted with the character of our first magistrate, to judge what effect his influence may have upon manners."

On October 19, 1781, after a decisive battle, General Lord Cornwallis surrendered his entire army to General Washington at Yorktown, Virginia. This was the last major military operation of the war, and although fighting continued on a small scale in Georgia and South Carolina, the end of the conflict was at last within sight. The United States rejoiced, but Sam Adams remained wary, afraid that advantages won in the field might be lost at the bargaining table.

The British were experienced negotiators, but the Americans were naive, and although Adams had complete faith in his cousin John, he was afraid that John Jay and even Dr. Franklin might be tempted to compromise in the peace negotiations. So he took it upon himself to issue a number of solemn warnings on the subject, and in his capacity as an elder statesman he wrote several long letters to the new president of the Continental Congress, Thomas McKean. In one of these communications, which set the tone for those that followed, he said:

> Are we soon to have peace? However desirable this may be, we must not wish for it on any terms but such as shall be honorable and safe to our country. Let us not disgrace ourselves by giving just occasion for it to be said hereafter, that

we finished our great contest with an inglorious accommodation.

He was particularly anxious that Americans be granted the right to use the Newfoundland fishing banks, long a pet project and one that reflected the urgent desires of Massachusetts fishermen. He pounded at this theme in his letters to McKean, mentioned the subject to John Adams and then found it desirable to write directly to Franklin and Jay on the matter, too. His correspondence increasingly indicated that the matter was urgent, and he hammered at it with an intensity that made it seem as though the people of Massachusetts were thinking of little else.

The American peace commissioners were well aware of the problem and needed no instruction from Sam Adams. In the peace treaty of 1783 they managed to obtain rights for American vessels in the Newfoundland banks, and when the issue was settled, Franklin remarked, "Now we shall be able to face Sam Adams when we return home. Had we failed to obtain these provisions he would have hounded us to our graves."

Adams went beyond partisanship in the attitude he displayed in the question of granting independent statehood to Vermont. Here he steered a cautious and somewhat devious course; his approval of the principle of independent statehood for Vermont stemmed, perhaps, from the fact that Massachusetts' claim to the territory was less solid than were those of New York and New Hampshire. Suspecting that those two states might have made a deal to carve up the area between them, Adams used his influence as president of the Senate to insure that the Massachusetts delegates in the Continental Congress would vote in favor of independence. At the same time, however, he was careful in his correspondence with Thomas Chittendon, whom the people of Vermont had elected as their governor, to address him as a private citizen. When Vermont won the dispute and was officially invited by the Congress to join the Union he was one of the first to write a letter of congratulations to Chittendon and made a point of addressing him as governor.

The Articles of Confederation had been ratified by the states after almost interminable delays and had gone into effect on March 1, 1781, prior to Adams's final departure from Philadelphia. He seems to have paid little attention to this event, however, even though he had been instrumental in the creation of the Articles. One of Adams's blind spots as a statesman is apparent here. The Massachusetts Constitution had been important to him, but he had concentrated on independence, as such, for the nation as a whole, and had been only mildly interested in the precise form of national government that was created. James Madison, Alexander Hamilton and other, younger men would devote thought and effort to the drafting of a national constitution, but Adams's views remained parochial. The United States had won her independence, and that, for the present, was enough to satisfy him.

At the meeting of the Massachusetts legislature early in 1782 both the House and the Senate unanimously elected Adams as one of the state's delegates to the Continental Congress for the year. As president of the Senate he knew what his colleagues were doing, and he protested that, at the age of sixty, he had no desire to be absent from home again. But they could not believe he would refuse what they regarded as an honor, and went through with his election. He told friends he would not serve, so the legislature was forced to send him a letter notifying him of his election, and he replied to it in unequivocal terms: "Having served in that department for more than seven years with much fatigue, and at a great distance from my family, I now beg to be relieved."

Later in 1782 a groundswell of support appeared for his candidacy for governor, a post Hancock again wanted. Adams announced he had no intention of running for the office and intended to vote for Hancock, but his friends again refused to believe he meant what he said, and placed his name in nomination. Adams asked that he be removed from contention, but his request was ignored, so he refused to engage in a campaign for the office, periodically making a statement to the press to the effect that he was not an active candidate for the office. To his relief Hancock was reelected.

Adams's supporters would not allow him to withdraw totally from public life, and the truth of the matter was that he could not afford complete retirement. His only income came from his salary as a public official, so he consented to serve another term in the state Senate, and again was elected its president, a post that paid a salary only slightly less than that which the governor received. The legislature was in session for only a few months of each year, which gave him ample time for his other interests.

His personal habits were only slightly changed, however. He continued to rise very early every morning, and after eating a frugal breakfast he retired to his study, where he spent his mornings writing to various friends in the national service. At noon he and Mrs. Adams ate a light meal, after which he recognized his advancing years by taking an hour's nap. In the afternoons he went to his office in the State House, where he held open court for his friends, and occasionally he wandered down to the waterfront taverns. He was still close to the artisans who had been his earliest political supporters, and they continued to regard him as their champion and spokesman. In spite of his formal manner they knew he understood and sympathized with them, and at no time did they transfer their loyalty to the more patrician Hancock, in whose company they felt uneasy.

Adams's associations with the artisans, sailors and more disreputable waterfront characters is one of the more obvious contradictions to be found in his nature. Ever the Puritan who disapproved of licentiousness, intoxication and sloth as much as he despised extravagance and frivolity, he nevertheless established and maintained a kinship with the uneducated poor. He knew, far better than did they themselves, that they were not responsible for their sorry situation in the world, and he never criticized them as he did men who knew better but failed to live up to his concept of their potential. Universally recognized, both in the United States and abroad, as one of the greatest of living Americans, as well as a patrician gentleman, Adams nevertheless felt at home on the waterfront. He was never seen to touch a drop of liquor, smoke a pipe or *segaro*, or take a pinch of snuff, but he never kept his distance from the harbor habitués who used liquor and tobacco.

He and Mrs. Adams ate their principal meal of the day at about five o'clock in the afternoon, and then settled down for an evening of reading. Distinguished foreigners and prominent Americans from other parts of the United States were frequent dinner guests and stayed for an evening of conversation. Adams rarely dined in public places with other men, as he had done in earlier years. His letters to his son indicate his appreciation of home cooking after so many years of eating in cheap Philadelphia taverns. And, had he gone out, Mrs. Adams would have had to dine alone, since ladies rarely accompanied their husbands to public houses.

The tremor in Adams's voice was more pronounced than it had been in earlier years and the quiver in his hands was always present; old friends who had not seen him in some time unfailingly mentioned his increasing disability in their correspondence. But his general health improved, he was less subject to fatigue, and he himself attributed his condition to what he called "the good air of the North."

The problems of peace were becoming apparent even before the formal end of the war. The public debt was staggering, returning veterans were resentful of those who were becoming wealthy, and in many places there were riots and even insurrections when citizens refused to pay the taxes imposed on them. The situation became particularly unpleasant in Hampshire County, and Governor Hancock was unwilling to send the militia there for fear of starting a revolution in miniature.

Sam Adams solved the problem, at least in that one county, when the legislature sent him to Hampshire, accompanied by two members of the Massachusetts House. During a week of conferences he patiently explained to the dissident leaders that as citizens of a free land they had obligations to both nation and state, and he was firm in his insistence that they were required to obey laws in whose making their elected representatives had participated. His prestige and logic turned the tide, and the Hampshire County rebellion collapsed.

But money remained scarce, and people continued to resent the payment of various taxes, particularly property taxes. Adams, who was no economist, developed the idea that the public treasury could survive on customs taxes alone, and he recommended their adoption on both state and national levels. He presented a bill incorporating the heart of the notion in the Massachusetts Senate, and he wrote to various members of the Continental Congress, urging them to follow his example for the entire nation. For a time he showed energetic flashes of his old enthusiasm and promised to wage a national campaign on behalf of his idea, threatening opponents and praising supporters. But he received almost no backing from any citizen of stature, and he was actually too unsure of the soundness of the scheme to proceed alone. He grumbled in his correspondence, but could find no one who would listen to him, and by the end of 1783 he still stood alone. So many bankers and financiers, among them Morris of Philadelphia, told him the plan was impractical and visionary that he reluctantly abandoned it.

But he was as stubborn now as he had been in his middle years, and until the end of his days he was prepared to argue with anyone who discussed taxation with him that he had found the "only way" to solve America's financial dilemmas. Other men, he maintained, were shortsighted, and he was hurt by their lack of faith in his judgment.

In other spheres he could still make contributions of value, though many of his attitudes revealed his continuing ingenuousness. In one of his rare newspaper pieces, published on April 21, 1783, he declared:

We are now at peace. God be thanked, with all the world; and I hope we shall never intermeddle with the quarrels of other nations. Let the United States continue in peace and union; and in order to do this, let them do justice to each other. Let there no longer be secret journals or secret committees. Let the debates in the Congress be open, and the whole of their transactions published weekly. This will tend to the speedy rectifying of mistakes, and preserving mutual confidence between the people and their representatives, and let care be taken to prevent factions in America, foreign or domestic.

Questions pertaining to matters of national security made it impossible to dispense with all secret proceedings, and not only would political parties appear during Adams's lifetime, but he himself would become the head of one. Some of his other ideas were valid, however, and the *Congressional Record* was the direct result of his ideas.

A portion of his time was now devoted to such matters as arranging the program for Boston's celebration of Independence Day, but he had too long been active on the national scene to think only in strictly local terms, and showed his concern in various ways, among them letters to John Adams urging that the United States arrange a commercial treaty with Great Britain as soon as possible. A prosperous United States would need trade with both Britain and her West Indian dependencies, he declared, and, as usual, he and his cousin were in complete agreement.

Chapter
Thirty-three

With the coming of peace Sam Adams's place on the American scene continued to shrink—because he wanted it that way. In 1783 he again refused to run for governor, and when some of his friends insisted on placing his name in nomination for lieutenant governor, he would not campaign for the office and his old friend, Thomas Cushing, won handily. Adams consented to hold office only as a member of the Massachusetts Senate, and for the third time became president of that body.

He was concerned with public finances, as were all men in public life, and he worked to improve lines of communication between the legislature and the state's delegates to the Congress. The formal end of the war made it imperative that the question of the return of the Loyalists be considered, and Adams, demonstrating that forgiveness was not one of his more prominent characteristics, was unalterably opposed to the return of even those Tories who swore allegiance to the United States. He had himself made chairman of a special committee of both houses of the legislature, and in that capacity he wrote the first official report he had penned since leaving the Continental Congress.

This document was a vituperative, emotional diatribe that does no credit to his reputation, and was but the beginning of a struggle that continued for a number of years.

By 1784 much of the public hostility to the Loyalists had drained away, and by 1785 a number of the younger members of the legislature proposed that the Tories be allowed to return or that they be paid fair compensation for their confiscated property. The continuing opposition of Adams to the idea delayed the passage of new legislation until 1787 and 1788, by which time his opponents mustered the strength to defeat him and permitted the return of those Loyalist refugees who wanted to come home and the payment of compensation to others.

Adams's hatred of Great Britain diminished somewhat after the war, and he acknowledged America's many debts to the former mother country as well the two nations' mutual need for trade. But he never became reconciled to the Tories, and until the time of his death always referred to them as "traitors." In any matter relating to American independence it was impossible for him to consider compromises of any kind, and in his stubborn opinion all issues were either black or white, with no gray areas worthy of consideration.

Yet in other matters he was far in advance of his time. In 1770 and 1771 he and Dr. Samuel Hopkins of Newport, Rhode Island, exchanged a number of letters in which both expressed their hatred of slavery and their particular loathing for the slave trade. The fight for American independence thereafter occupied all of Adams's time and attention, but in 1783 he returned to the subject of slavery. In that year he submitted a bill to the legislature in which he stated that "all human servitude is repugnant to any man who loves freedom." Liberty, he said, was not divisible, and in one realm "it is not possible to house both freeman and slave." The measure would have abolished the slave trade in Massachusetts, but both houses were indifferent, and Adams could not muster enough support for its passage. He persisted, however, and in 1788 he obtained passage of a strong measure that prohibited the slave trade in the commonwealth, making Massachusetts the first state to take such action.

Adams's actions were always consistent with his own personality. In any question relating to American independence, no matter how peripheral, he was always unyielding, but in everything else he was a humanitarian. He sympathized with the slaves and was outraged by the social system that permitted them to be held in bondage, but he was heartless in any matter concerning the Loyalists and believed that their suffering was "the just punishment of the Almighty."

Boston was now the third city of the land in population, having been passed by Philadelphia and New York, but it was still growing rapidly, and new immigrants settled there in large numbers after the war, the majority coming from Scotland and Ireland. But the first city of New England was still America's cultural capital, and Adams unfailingly attended the monthly meetings of the American Academy of Arts and Sciences. He particularly enjoyed commenting on various literary efforts submitted to the organization, but his own writing days were at an end, and he is not known to have prepared any papers for the academy himself.

He was still a simple man who advocated what he called "the ordinary rules of frugality and morality," and he is not known to have deviated from his own standards. He deplored the formation of all secret societies, which he regarded as threats to democracy, and he never lost his faith in the "common man," even advocating the extension of the franchise to all who could read and write, a revolutionary doctrine in an age when only property owners were granted the vote. He was one of the first Americans to believe that education was a panacea, and he was firm in his opinion that every child should be given an education at the expense of the state.

The war and the granting of independence to America did away with whatever traces of hereditary aristocracy existed in the United States, but in 1783 and thereafter many of the wealthier citizens developed an interest in heraldry and coats of arms, and made energetic efforts to trace their ancestry to aristocratic foundations. The very idea outraged Sam Adams, whose family was one of the first in Massachusetts, and in 1784, when someone offered to trace his pedigree, he exploded. "You had better not try," he said. "It is a subject I have not thought much about. On this side of the water, I believe my ancestors were exemplary men and good citizens. But I have never looked much beyond that, not knowing what scoundrels a further research might rake out."

At the close of the war a number of former Continental officers formed an association which they called the Order of the Cincinnati, and it quickly attracted members in every state. Sam Adams was one of the first to oppose it, and was quickly joined by Franklin, John Adams and Jay. Adams realized it was a harmless, fraternal organization founded by men who wanted to maintain the associations they had formed during the long years of the war, but he was afraid it might develop into a pressure group of men with aristocratic tendencies. It was because they were *military* men that they were dangerous, he believed, and he thought they might try to force the country to accept what they considered best for the United States.

He was upset when General Washington joined the Order, and in mid-December 1784, he wrote at length to John Adams, deploring the General's act, though he recognized Washington's right to do as he pleased. He said, in part:

> ... It is a tribute due to the man who serves his country well, to esteem him highly and confide in him. We ought not, however, to think any man incapable of error. But so it is with the bulk of mankind, and even in a free country; they reprobate the idea of implicit faith, and at the same time, while the impression of gratitude is deep in their minds, they will not admit that of a benefactor which must be said of every man— *aliquando dormitat.* I would never inculcate a base and envious suspicion of any man, especially of those who have rendered signal services to their country. But there is a degree of watchfulness over all men possessed of power or influence, upon which the liberties of mankind must depend. It is necessary to guard against the infirmities of the best as well as the wickedness of the worst of men. Such is the weakness of human nature, that tyranny has perhaps oftener sprung from that than any other source. It is this that unravels the mystery of millions being enslaved by the few.

What was it that induced the Cincinnati gentlemen, who have undertaken to deliberate and act upon matters which may essentially concern "the happiness and future dignity of the American empire," to admit foreign military subjects into their society? Was there not danger before that a foreign influence might prevail in America? Do not foreigners wish to have weight in our councils? Can such a junction of the subjects of different nations (and those nations widely differing in their principles of government), to deliberate upon things that relate to the union and national honor, the happiness and future dignity of *one*, consist with sound policy? Are we sure that these two nations will never have separate views, and very national and interested ones, too, because they once united in the same object, and it was accidentally their mutual interest to fight side by side? If we admit that the Cincinnati had the right to erect themselves into an Order for the national purposes of their institution, had they a right to call in foreign aid for those purposes? It appears to me as impolitic, preposterous, and dangerous as it would be for the United States to invite and admit a delegation from that foreign power into their Congress.

Adams's dislike of foreign influence was also seen in his opposition to the granting of citizenship to any man who held a hereditary title. But his hatred of the Cincinnati was based on his suspicion of all military organizations and of the military mind. Tyrants almost always rose to power through military means, and he was determined that the United States always would be ruled by civilians elected by the people. This principle, subsequently accepted as right, normal and natural by following generations, was relatively new in his own day, although it was an outgrowth of America's heritage from Great Britain. It was shared by virtually all of the Founding Fathers, which was one reason for the eventual collapse of the Order of the Cincinnati. Too many people were opposed to it in principle as well as parctice, and it could not survive such scorn.

In 1784 Adams once again was returned to the state Senate and became its president, and later in the year the legislature, still hoping he would become more active in national affairs, unanimously voted him a place in the congressional delegation. Again he declined because of his "very precarious state of health," and no man was more disappointed than his old comrade from Virginia, Richard Henry Lee, who had just been elected president of the Congress.

They still corresponded regularly, and Lee said the Congress suffered from a "wonderful lassitude which only the presence of Samuel Adams could dispel." Adams admitted in a long reply that he often felt a desire to return to the Congress because of his concern for what he called the "national character," which he discussed in thousands of words of high-sounding generalities. But he lacked the stamina for a long journey, and he knew his health would not permit him to survive a life of living in lodging houses and eating in inexpensive taverns.

Both Adams and Lee readily admitted the weakness of the Confederation they had been so active in forming, and both reluctantly concluded that a stronger national government was necessary. But, in their many exchanges of letters, neither of these leaders of the Revolution produced any new, specific ideas that would be helpful in the creation of a federal government. Their time of creativity had come to an end.

But they were still of one mind in virtually all matters relating to the present and future of the United States. Both were anxious to restore trade with Great Britain, but were indignant because the border posts that were to have been handed over to the United States under the terms of the peace treaty were still occupied by the British and were being reinforced. Both wanted fair trade with France, the expansion westward of the American frontier, friendship with Spain "consonant with our national dignity," and above all, a continuing protection of the liberty of the individual. Both were unhappy because America had not yet solved her financial problems, in spite of growing prosperity, but it did not occur to either that the troubles would remain until a new federal government was empowered to raise money on its own authority.

In the winter of 1784–1785 Sam Adams suffered from the ague, an ailment later known as influenza, and refused to become a candidate for any office. Since his only income derived from public office, he had no funds; vague hints in correspondence with his children indicate that they contributed to his support and that of Mrs. Adams throughout the year. Hancock was also in ill health and refused to be a candidate to succeed himself, so the two men who had so long dominated politics in the state were on the sidelines. Popular interest in the election was so badly lacking that no candidate received enough votes for any office to assure his election, and the matter had to be referred to the legislature. Bowdoin became governor, Cushing was made lieutenant governor and Samuel B. Phillips was elected president of the Senate. Both in the public election and in the action taken by the legislature Sam Adams received a smattering of votes for all three offices, but he would have been unable to serve even if he had been elected.

It appeared that his career had come to an end at the age of sixty-three, and the letters exchanged by his wife and daughter indicate they believed he might not live for more than a short time. He was too weak to leave his bed, and Mrs. Adams's favorite word in describing his condition was "wretched."

John Adams, now the United States minister to Great Britain, corresponded with his kinsman during the year, at least one letter being carried to the United States by his son, John Quincy Adams, who was following the family tradition and entering politics. Only two of Sam Adams's letters to his cousin during the year have ever been found, and both dealt with minor matters.

No other letters written by Sam Adams in 1785 have ever been located, and the year is generally regarded as a "lost" period in his life. His convalescence in the autumn and winter was slow, and he sometimes went for a stroll, usually accompanied by Mrs. Adams, but otherwise did not exert himself. He took literally no active part in political affairs on any level during the year, but presumably he kept abreast of matters national and local by reading the newspapers and chatting with the many friends who called on him.

Those who believed he stood at death's door and would never

again be active failed to take into consideration his love of life and recuperative powers. By the spring of 1786 he felt sufficiently recovered to permit his name to be entered as a candidate for the Massachusetts Senate, and won election without difficulty. He also received, without his permission, a number of votes for governor and lieutenant governor. Governor Bowdoin, his protégé, supporter and friend for many years, promptly appointed him to a seat on the Council, a post which had evolved into the equivalent of a Cabinet position on a state level, but Adams declined in a brief letter that offered no explanation. Presumably he believed the duties would be too taxing for one who had not yet completely recovered his health.

But events beyond his control forced him to play a larger role in the affairs of state than he had anticipated. The future of the United States was placed in grave jeopardy in 1786; the initial, unexpected crisis first developed in Massachusetts, and had the problem not been handled with firmness, the new nation well might have destroyed itself. Sam Adams accepted the challenge, and played a major role in the restoration of order and the renewal of public confidence in the United States.

The situation that developed in Massachusetts in 1786 grew out of the continuing muddle in American finances, which the Congress, under the Confederation, lacked the authority to control. In 1781 the exceptionally able Robert Morris of Philadelphia had been made superintendent of finance, and had done what he could to lessen the chaos. He was aided by Jefferson and by Gouverneur Morris and Alexander Hamilton of New York. This group produced the decimal system of coinage, with the Spanish dollar as its base, but the new plan could not be put into effect for some time because metal money was scarce; the United States was not yet in a position to mint coins and paper money issued by the Congress and separately by most of the states was still in use everywhere. These factors, combined with a heavy adverse balance of trade, forced the postponement of the creation of American specie, and the coins of Great Britain, France and Spain continued to circulate for many years.

The Finance Department tried to create a reserve of hard

money to use for the redemption of paper, so in 1781 Morris, aided by Hamilton, formed the Bank of North America in Philadelphia, and it went into business armed with $400,000 in specie. The notes issued by the bank did not fluctuate in value, so merchants, traders and manufacturers were able to function from day to day. But the bank wasn't doing enough, and although these moves were sound, they did nothing to help the debtor class. Prices had fallen, the Continental paper had collapsed, and the farmers were in serious trouble. Their products brought them fewer dollars, but their debts were not reduced, and as they were unwilling to pay in hard money, they demanded that new paper be issued by the states.

These farmers, in the main, had been among the strongest supporters of the Revolution from the beginning, and were supported by the urban workers who had not yet won the right to vote. Between them these two groups constituted the pillars on which Sam Adams had built his entire political career. They had been educated by him, and now they turned what they had learned from him to their own advantage. If a just government was founded on the consent of the governed, did the individual owe obedience—and even allegiance—to a government that failed to provide what the individual regarded as economic justice? Many regarded the state governments and the courts that compelled obedience to the laws made by those governments as instruments of exploitation. In the eyes of these farmers and town laborers, the wealthy and privileged had substituted themselves for the Crown, but the "common man" enjoyed no greater benefits than he had as a British colonial.

To an extent these grievances were justified. Almost everywhere the franchise was still held exclusively by the property-owning class—which did include those who were the proprietors of their own farms to be sure—but most of the less affluent were still unable to vote. This situation enabled the financial conservatives, among them the merchants and moneylenders, the traders and lawyers and judges, to control the various state legislatures.

Attempts were made by the paper money advocates to gain supremacy in the legislatures, but only in Rhode Island were they successful. In Massachusetts they were so badly defeated that they became desperate. In the western part of the state, where the rocky soil made it hard for a farmer to earn his living under the best of circumstances, men banded together under the leadership of Daniel Shays, a stubborn, hard-bitten veteran of Bunker Hill. Before anyone in Boston quite realized what was happening, Shays and his followers broke up the sittings of courts in Worcester and Northampton where debt cases were being heard. Then they attempted to obtain arms from the United States arsenal at Springfield, and when the effort failed they actually placed the town under siege.

The government of Massachusetts overnight discovered that it was required to deal with a full-scale insurrection.

Chapter
Thirty-four

The events that came to be known as Shays's Rebellion won great sympathy for insurrectionists throughout Massachusetts, and Dan Shays overnight became the hero of the debtors class and those who had not yet won the franchise. Men had adapted the simplified philosophy they had learned from Sam Adams to their own use, and believed they were engaging in a holy crusade.

Responsible men throughout the United States recognized the clear threat to organized government. If debtor farmers were allowed to win their rebellion, other pressure groups would feel they had the right to do the same thing, and the authority of a government elected by those citizens entitled to vote would be destroyed. Events in Massachusetts once again were providing a test case for the entire nation, and if the rebels were allowed to have their way there, it was possible that all state governments and the already weak national government under the Confederation would collapse. Shays's Rebellion was the gravest threat the new United States of America had yet faced.

Sam Adams, who had done little of consequence for a long

time, was called into consultation by Governor Bowdoin, who summoned the legislature to a special session in September 1786. Master and pupil were in complete agreement that the rebels could not be allowed to win, but the situation was made ticklish by the fact that the very men who supported Adams and Bowdoin were in complete sympathy with Shays and his followers. Once again Sam Adams represented a minority view, so he reverted to the tactics that had been so successful in the years prior to the outbreak of the Revolution.

His first step was to call a Boston town meeting on September 9, at which he acted as moderator. A committee—with Adams as chairman—was ordered to prepare a petition to the governor which would be "expressive of the public disapprobation of the riotous proceedings in the interior, and of the readiness of the people of this city to assist government in every measure taken for the preservation of the constitutional rights of the people." As soon as this document was prepared, copies of it were sent to every town in the state, precisely as the Boston Committee of Correspondence had done in prewar days.

Shortly thereafter the attack on the Springfield arsenal took place, and Adams agreed to become a member of the Governor's Council for the duration of the crisis. His ill health forgotten, he attended daily meetings, and the situation was so grave that sessions were even held on Sundays, which the last of the Puritans had rarely permitted in earlier times.

Bowdoin sent a firm demand to the rebels, ordering them to surrender without delay, but his stand was weakened by the hesitation of the House and Senate, where support for Shays and his friends was so strong that it became impossible to obtain a majority in favor of the governor's position.

The insurrection gained strength in October, and in some of the western parts of the state, particularly in Hampshire County, the militia was ready to march to the aid of the rebels if Bowdoin sent troops to end the disturbances. As members of the militia on both sides were veterans who had seen long service during the war, the very real possibility existed that a civil war would break out in Massachusetts.

From the outset Sam Adams took a stand from which he never deviated: the rebellion had to be ended without delay, and if necessary force should be used. At his instigation the governor appointed a special committee, with Adams inevitably as chairman, to request that the militia be called out to protect the courts sitting in Taunton and Cambridge, and to prevent the disruption of the activities of the Supreme Court, which was sitting in Middlesex County. These recommendations, on which the governor acted without delay, completed a paradoxical circle, placing Bowdoin and Adams in a position precisely opposite that which they had held prior to the war.

Using all of the political influence he had accumulated over a period of more than twenty turbulent years, Adams persuaded the Senate, in October, to give the governor its unqualified support, and he won a majority vote for the purpose. But the squabbles continued in the House, which could not make up its mind, and Bowdoin, still trying to avert bloodshed, was reluctant to order the militia to disperse the rebels and arrest Shays and his lieutenants.

But Adams argued that the insurrection was reaching alarming proportions and that further delays could not be tolerated. Bowdoin agreed, and in early November he suspended the writ of habeas corpus for eight months. Adams was the chairman of a special committee that prepared a bill authorizing the governor and Council to imprison any persons they regarded as dangerous, and at the same time a pardon was offered to all insurrectionists who would take an oath of allegiance.

The Senate passed the measure without delay, and the House, frightened by the fact that more than two thousand of the insurrectionists were gathered at Springfield, finally did the same. Bowdoin promptly ordered four thousand militiamen, all of them veterans, to report for duty, and placed them under the command of General Benjamin Lincoln, one of the most popular and efficient of the Revolutionary War leaders. Lincoln was ordered to disperse the rebels.

One of his advance columns was attacked by the insurrectionists, and for the first time blood was spilled, with three men being

3 4 9

killed and a number wounded. Shays and his men were dispersed, but they tried to collect their forces for an all-out attack on the arsenal. They were prevented from carrying out their plan by General Lincoln, who followed them to Northampton and Hadley. It was December now and the weather had turned very cold, but Lincoln stayed in the field, and when he learned that the rebels were retreating to Petersham, he made a night-long march of thirty miles in a snowstorm, cut them off and captured one hundred and fifty men.

This broke the back of Shays's Rebellion, and organized resistance to the legal government of Massachusetts came to an end. The "war" was not completely over, however, and for some months small bands of guerrillas made life uncomfortable for the advocates of order in Hampshire County.

Many people still failed to understand what had been at stake in Shays's Rebellion, and Bowdoin's actions were so unpopular that it soon became evident he would not be able to muster the strength to win reelection in the spring. But he had ended the threat to constitutional government in the state, and Sam Adams deliberately risked his own reputation in February 1787, when the legislature reconvened, by writing, sponsoring and forcing both houses to vote the governor a joint resolution of thanks for his vigorous, firm action.

Although the resolution, which was written principally for dissemination, was not one of his more noteworthy efforts, it nevertheless demonstrated that, as he approached his sixty-fifth birthday, Adams had not lost his touch as a propagandist.

The Senate and House of Representatives in General Court assembled have read and duly attended your speech at the opening of this session, and take this earliest opportunity to express their entire satisfaction in the measures you have been pleased to take, pursuant to the powers vested in you by the Constitution, for the subduing a turbulent spirit which has too long insulted the government of this Commonwealth, prostrated the courts of law and justice in divers counties, and threatened even the overthrow of the Constitution itself.

The General Court congratulates your Excellency on the success with which Providence has been pleased hitherto to bless the wise, spirited, and prudent measures which you have taken; and they earnestly entreat your Excellency still to encounter, repel, and resist, by all fitting ways, enterprises, and means, all and every such person and persons as attempt or enterprise in a hostile manner the destruction, detriment, or annoyance of this Commonwealth, and to pursue such further constitutional measures as you may think necessary for extirpating the spirit of rebellion, quieting the minds of the good people of the Commonwealth, and establishing the just authority of government. And in order that your Excellency may be possessed of the *full* power of the Constitution to effect these great purposes, the General Court have thought it highly necessary, after mature deliberation, to declare that a rebellion exists within this Commonwealth.

This Court are fully persuaded that by far the greater part of the citizens of this Commonwealth are warmly attached to our present happy Constitution. They have a high sense of the merit of a respectable body of the militia, who have with readiness attended your Excellency's orders on this pressing emergency, as well as the patriotic zeal of a number of private citizens who have cheerfully advanced their money in aid to government; and you may be assured, sir, that the most speedy and effectual means will be used for the payment of the officers and soldiers who have been, or may be, employed in this necessary and most important service; and for the reimbursement of the moneys generously advanced for its support.

It is to be expected that vigor, decision, and energy, under the direction and blessing of Heaven, will soon terminate this unnatural, unprovoked rebellion, prevent the effusion of blood, and the fatal consequences to be dreaded from a civil war; and it is the determination of this Court to establish a criterion for discriminating between good citizens and others, that each may be regarded according to their characters and deserts.

If it should appear to your Excellency that the time for which the militia under the command of Major General Lincoln are enlisted is too short to effect the great objects in view, it is the request of this Court that you would be pleased to direct the Commanding General to re-enlist the same men, or enlist others for such further time as you may think necessary, or to replace them by detachments from the militia, and, if you should think it expedient, to increase their numbers and continue them in service until those purposes shall be completely accomplished.

The General Court will give the most ready attention to your message of the 3rd instant, and every other communication you shall be pleased to lay before them. They will vigorously pursue every measure that may be calculated to support the Constitution, and will still continue to redress any real grievances, if such shall be found to exist, humbly beseeching Almighty God to preserve union and harmony among the several powers of government, as well as among the honest and virtuous citizens of the Commonwealth, and to restore to us the inestimable blessings of peace and liberty under a wise and righteous administration of government.

The insurrectionist officers offered to negotiate with the state, with their principal condition being the granting of a full pardon to everyone who had taken part in the uprising. But Adams wrote and the legislature passed a resolution that in both tone and intent was reminiscent of the words of George III and Lord North: no compromise would be countenanced.

On March 6 Governor Bowdoin announced that the last of the holdout insurrectionists had been captured, and Adams immediately introduced a bill granting pardons to all but Daniel Shays and three of his lieutenants. Whether his thoughts drifted back to the days when he and John Hancock had been proscribed by the Crown is not known.

The election of state officials was held in April, and when Bowdoin was opposed by Hancock, who had recovered his health but had taken no active part on either side in the rebellion, it was a foregone conclusion that the latter would be elected. He was, with the western part of the state giving him its overwhelming support.

Sam Adams was again returned to the Senate by his Boston constituents, and that body, grateful for the vigor he had shown during Shays's Rebellion, elected him to the office of president. Adams appears to have taken a new lease on life, and had so thoroughly demonstrated his mastery of both the Senate and House that he had emerged as the dominant figure in the legislature. So Hancock deemed it expedient to renew an old alliance, and invited his one-time teacher to dine with him at his Beacon Hill mansion.

They ate alone, and neither man ever divulged any details of their conversation, but it soon became evident that they buried whatever hatchets they were still carrying in their belts. They renewed their old alliance, and Adams, forgetting his ague, fatigue and other ailments, finally accepted a post on the Governor's Council.

By far the most important event to take place since the close of the war was the Constitutional Convention that convened in Philadelphia in May 1787. Men in every state had become convinced that the new nation could not be adequately governed under the Articles of Confederation. It had become obvious that a national government sufficiently strong to direct foreign affairs and financial policy had to be created, and that it required the powers to settle disputes between the states.

Most of the delegates in attendance were men who had been prominent in the direction of American affairs from the early days of the Continental Congress, but a number were missing. John Adams and Thomas Jefferson were abroad, the former in England and the latter in France. Three of the original radicals were also conspicuous by their absence. Patrick Henry refused a place in the Virginia delegation; Sam Adams and John Hancock, both of whom could have been elected, chose not to attend because they entertained serious doubts that a new constitution could protect the personal liberties of individuals, and they made no secret of their feelings.

Adams and Hancock were still the most prestigious men in New England, and their attitude was shared by others in the area. Rhode Island was the only state in the Union that sent no delegates to the Convention, and New Hampshire procrastinated, its delegates delaying their departure for weeks. The

353

leaders of the Massachusetts delegation were Elbridge Gerry, who shared many of Adams's and Hancock's doubts, Rufus King and Nathaniel Gorham, one of the new leaders of the business community.

Dr. Franklin was the Convention's chairman, but usually dozed after eating his main meal of the day at noon, so General Washington became the active presiding officer. A number of plans were submitted, and Madison and Hamilton accepted the task of coordinating and reconciling them. Out of the original chaos and the many conflicts that ensued, none of which have a rightful place in these pages, the Constitution of the United States as it is now known emerged.

The delegates deliberately worked in secret so they would not be subjected to outside pressures, and in view of the enormity of their task they completed it swiftly, adjourning on September 17 after slightly less than four months of labors. The proposed Constitution was submitted to the several states, each of which was asked to call a Constitutional Convention of its own for the purpose.

Everywhere men were divided overnight into two groups. The Federalists, who included most conservatives, men of property and substance who believed a new national government was essential, supported the Constitution. The Anti-Federalists included the Daniel Shayses of every state.

Delaware became the first state to ratify the Constitution, acting on December 7, 1787, and within six weeks was followed by New Jersey, Connecticut and Georgia. It was a foregone conclusion that Pennsylvania, with most of its population clustered in the eastern portion of the state, also would ratify the Constitution.

By the early winter of 1788 the action to be taken by Massachusetts became critical to the acceptance or rejection of the new Constitution. Vermont had not yet been formally admitted to the Union, although her state government was operative on a de facto basis, so she had no voice in the proceedings. But New Hampshire and Rhode Island were ready to follow the lead of Massachusetts. If these three states rejected the Constitution it appeared certain that at least two wavering states would join them, and the proposed new government would be defeated.

From the beginning it appeared that more Anti-Federalists than Federalists were represented in the Massachusetts Convention, but men from other states soon learned that the majority had not yet made up their minds. Overnight the national spotlight once again was turned on the two Patriots whose decision could influence the other members of the Massachusetts Convention, Sam Adams and John Hancock.

Chapter
Thirty-five

Before the Massachusetts Constitutional Convention convened in Boston on January 9, 1788, it was clear that the future course the United States would take was in her hands. James Madison wrote from New York that "the decision of Massachusetts either way will involve the result in this state," and he also admitted that the Massachusetts action would determine the result in Virginia. Maryland was undecided, too, and seemed certain to follow the lead of Virginia.

So everything depended on Massachusetts, and the proponents of the Constitution deluged Adams and Hancock with letters. Sam Adams was able to see both sides of the issue, and was undecided, writing to Arthur Lee on the eve of the Convention, "I confess, as I enter the building, I stumble at the threshold."

Still a maverick and a radical, still dedicated to the cause of the greatest freedom that could be conferred on the people, he was inclined to oppose the Constitution, and although he did not take an adamant stand, he presented cogent arguments:

... I meet with a national government instead of a federal union of sovereign states. I am not able to conceive why the wisdom of the Convention led them to give the preference to the former before the latter. If the several States in the Union are to become one entire nation under one legislature, the powers of which shall extend to every subject of legislation, and its laws be supreme and control the whole, the idea of sovereignty in these States must be lost. Indeed, I think, upon such a supposition, those sovereignties ought to be eradicated from the mind; for they would be *imperia in imperio,* justly deemed a solecism in politics, and they would be highly dangerous and destructive of the peace, union, and safety of the nation.

And can this national legislature be competent to make laws for the *free* internal governments of one people, living in climates so remote, and whose "habits and particular interests" are, and probably always will be, so different? Is it to be expected that general laws can be adapted to the more Eastern and the more Southern parts of so extensive a nation? It appears to me difficult, if practicable. Hence, then, may we not look for discontent, mistrust, disaffection to government, and frequent insurrections, which will require standing armies to suppress them in one place and another, where they may happen to arise. Or, if laws could be made, adapted to the local habits, feelings, views, and interests of those distant parts, would they not cause jealousies of partiality in government which would excite envy and other malignant passions, productive of wars and fighting? But should we continue distinct sovereign States, confederated for the purpose of mutual safety and happiness, each contributing to the Federal head such a part of its sovereignty as would render the government fully adequate to those purposes, and *no more,* the people would govern themselves more easily, the laws of each State being well adapted to its own genius and circumstances, and the liberties of the United States would be more secure than they can be, as I humbly conceive, under the proposed new Constitution.

... The seeds of aristocracy began to spring, even before the conclusion of our struggle for the natural rights of men,— seeds which, like a canker-worm, lie at the root of free governments. So great is the wickedness of some men and the stupid servility of others, that one would be almost inclined to conclude that communities cannot be free. The few haughty families think that they *must* govern; the body of the people tamely consent, and submit to be their slaves . . . .

In spite of these sentiments Adams did not take a conclusive position on the new Constitution, and Hancock, equally uncertain, also hesitated. The merchants and other wealthy men of Boston were Federalists, but their opinions had never been important to Adams. What was of far greater meaning to him was the strong stand taken by the men of his "natural constituency," the Boston artisans. Their fervor for the Constitution was genuine, and he was impressed by their arguments that the entire nation would benefit.

A tragic distraction made him forget the Constitution for a short time when, only a week after the convention opened, Dr. Samuel Adams died at the age of thirty-seven in his father's house. The Convention adjourned as a mark of respect to the grieving Adams, and the members attended the funeral in a body.

But the public had to be served, so he bore his loss in private and went back to work. Bowdoin, a staunch Federalist, was frequently heckled by representatives from the counties that had taken part in Shays's Rebellion, and on two occasions Adams hastily moved an adjournment to prevent fistfights. Then the more virulent Anti-Federalists adopted the tactic of attacking the Constitution paragraph by paragraph, and tried to destroy it piecemeal. Adams sternly rebuked them, and members of both groups applauded him.

The Federalists had worked on Hancock's vanity from the outset, and their influence had elected him President of the Convention, but he still refrained from joining them. It was important, he said, that he find out how Sam Adams intended to vote before he committed himself. But the Federalists told him "the salvation of the nation" was in his hands, and he began to yield.

Hoping to sidestep an early decision he retired to his mansion with a diplomatic illness, but the friends of the Constitution persisted, and finally persuaded him to make a speech advocating the adoption of the new system of government.

Similar pressures were exerted by both sides on Sam Adams, except by men like Bowdoin who knew him best and who realized that neither flattery nor threats would move him. Hancock had succumbed so easily that he was able to persuade no one to join him, and the ultimate decision Massachusetts would make now rested on the word of Adams.

He was conscious of the responsibility he bore, and insisted that the Constitution be studied in depth, that no decision be made, regardless of the expense or time spent, until the entire subject was thoroughly investigated. Gradually he came to the conclusion that the single greatest weakness of the Constitution was the lack of provision for the rights of individuals, and he wrote to Arthur Lee that the absence of amendments that would provide a "bill of rights" made the proposed Constitution a farce. The phrase became common, but Adams may have been the first to call what ultimately became the first ten amendments to the Constitution the Bill of Rights.

It is fascinating to observe, in passing, how closely Adams's activities paralleled those of Patrick Henry at this time, just as they had been similar in the past. Henry was the leading Anti-Federalist in Virginia, but ultimately became reconciled to the Constitution, provided it contained a Bill of Rights. He, even more than Adams, was responsible for the addition of the first ten amendments to the Constitution.

The proponents of the Constitution induced Hancock to try to influence his old mentor, and Adams was invited to Beacon Hill. Some of the other advocates of the new form of government were there, and Adams finally indicated a shift in his position. He might not be averse to voting in favor of the Constitution, he said, if it included guarantees of freedom of assemblage, speech, worship and the press.

This was the signal that Bowdoin and others awaited, and, according to a story told by Daniel Webster in 1833, the "mechanics" of Boston held a meeting at the Green Dragon Inn on Union Street, and after unanimously passing a resolution in favor of the Constitution, they asked that it be presented to Adams.

It was taken to him by Paul Revere, but Adams was dubious. "How many mechanics were at the Green Dragon when the resolution was passed?" he asked.

"More, sir," Revere replied, "than the Green Dragon could hold."

"And where were the rest, Mr. Revere?"

"In the streets, sir."

"And how many were in the streets?" Adams persisted.

"More, sir," Revere said, "than there are stars in the sky."

Sam Adams not only was a prophet of democracy, but practised what he preached. The electorate—*his* followers—had spoken, so he accepted the collective wisdom of the people.

The mechanics' resolution was handed to him on January 30, 1788, and now that he had made up his mind he acted without further delay. He made a bargain with the Federalists, promising to support the new Constitution if they, in turn, pledged that they would stand behind a number of proposed amendments to the Constitution. On January 31 he seconded resolutions for various amendments:

That all powers not expressly delegated to the Congress be reserved to the states.

That the powers of taxation and the granting of commercial monopolies by the Congress be restricted.

That grand jury indictments be provided in capital trials.

That the jurisdiction of federal courts be limited to cases between the citizens of different states, and that the right of trial by jury be prescribed in such cases.

On the same day he made a long, somewhat rambling address in which he announced to the Convention that he had decided to support the Constitution. His principal points were that the decision made by Massachusetts was vital, as she would influence others, and that the unanimity of all states was essential. At the conclusion of his speech he offered a resolution that would embody amendments that, he stressed, were necessary for the preservation of American liberty. That resolution stated:

> And that the said Constitution be never construed to authorize Congress to infringe the just liberty of the press or the rights of conscience; or to prevent the people of the United States who are peaceable citizens from keeping their own arms; or to raise standing armies, unless when necessary for the defence of the United States, or of some one or more of them; or to prevent the people from petitioning, in a peaceable and orderly manner, the Federal Legislature for a redress of grievances; or to subject the people to unreasonable searches and seizures of their persons, papers, or possessions.

This resolution, which the Convention adopted, was subsequently embodied in the Bill of Rights. The ideas were not original with Adams; some had come from the pen of Patrick Henry, and all were being widely reported and discussed in the press. The demand for such amendments was growing daily throughout the country, and Adams could be fairly secure in the knowledge that the entire nation was not only aware of the omission of the guarantees of personal liberty in the Constitution but fully intended to include them. The influence of Massachusetts was so great that all but two of the states whose conventions voted later included similar recommendations for a Bill of Rights when they ratified the Constitution.

But the battle in Boston was not yet ended, in spite of the stand taken by Adams and Hancock. The Anti-Federalists remained strong and were refusing to yield; representatives from the western counties were particularly adamant. As Hancock had played no part in the suppression of Shays's Rebellion, his influence was greater than that of any other leader in western Massachusetts, so Sam Adams found a new way to deal with the matter. He referred to the various proposed amendments as though all had been Hancock's ideas, and others quickly followed his example. The westerners began to waver.

The Convention voted early in February: 187 favored the adoption of the Constitution, while 168 were opposed.

Maryland came next, and her Convention ratified the Constitution by an overwhelming vote of 63 to 11; South Carolina followed by a margin of more than two to one. In June New Hampshire had the honor of being the ninth state to vote for the Constitution, and put the new system of government into effect. Two of the key states were among the last to ratify, and in both the margin was very narrow: the Federalists won by only three votes in New York and by ten in Virginia. Rhode Island continued to refuse to take any action one way or the other, and not until 1790, when the Congress threatened her with a commercial boycott, did she finally consent to ratification.

Sam Adams best expressed his views on the Constitution in a letter he wrote to Richard Henry Lee on August 24, 1789:

> I have always been apprehensive that, through the weakness of the human mind, often discovered in the wisest and best of men, or the perverseness of the interested and designing, in as well as out of government, misconstructions would be given to the Federal Constitution, which would disappoint the views and expectations of the honest among those who acceded to it, and hazard the liberty, independence, and happiness of the people. I was particularly afraid that, unless great care should be taken to prevent it, the Constitution, in the administration of it, would gradually, but swiftly and imperceptibly, run into a consolidated government, pervading and legislating through all the States; not for Federal purposes *only*, as it professes, but in all cases whatsoever. Such a government would soon totally annihilate the sovereignty of the several States, so necessary to the support of the confederated commonwealth, and sink both in despotism. I know these have been called vulgar opinions and prejudices. Be it so. I think it is Lord Shaftesbury who tells us that it is folly to despise the opinions of the vulgar. This aphorism, if indeed it is his, I eagerly caught from a nobleman many years ago whose writings, in some accounts, I never much admired. Should a strong Federalist, as some call themselves, see what has now dropped from my pen, he would say

that I am an Anti-Fed, and amendment-monger, &c. Those are truly vulgar terms, invented and used by some whose feelings would be sorely wounded to be ranked among such kind of men, and invented and used for the mean purpose of deceiving and entrapping others whom *they* call the vulgar. But in this *enlightened* age, one would think there was no such vulgar to be thus amused and ensnared.

I mean, my friend, to let you know how deeply I am impressed with the sense of the importance of amendments; that the good people may clearly see the distinction—for there is a distinction—between the *Federal powers* vested in Congress and the *sovereign authority* belonging to the several States, which is the palladium of the private and personal rights of the citizens. I freely protest to you, that I earnestly wish some amendments may be judiciously and deliberately made, without partial or local considerations, that there may be no uncomfortable jarrings among the several powers; that the whole people may in every State contemplate their own safety on solid grounds, and the Union of the States be perpetual.

The Bill of Rights, which derived from the Magna Carta, the English Bill of Rights, comprised the first ten amendments to the Constitution, and their passage by both houses of the new Congress was one of the first orders of business when the new United States government met in the spring of 1789 in New York City. They were adapted, at least in part, from the Virginia Declaration of Rights written in 1776 by George Mason, who joined Henry in opposing the Constitution unless such guarantees of personal freedom were included.

A total of twelve amendments to the Constitution were written by James Madison, and of these ten were ratified by the states, many of which then included similar bills of rights in their own constitutions. The requisite number of states ratified the amendments in 1791, and they became an integral part of the Constitution at that time.

Sam Adams never failed to act a champion for the Bill of Rights, and frequently expressed the fear that "wicked and selfish men" might try to block their passage. In spite of his apprehensions, however, the amendments were virtually unopposed in all states, whose legislatures ratified them, in accordance with the provisions of the new Constitution, after very little discussion. The United States had won her freedom from Great Britain, and now her people were assured that they would enjoy the most precious of English heritages.

In the wake of the ratification of the Constitution by each of the states, something for which that great document did not provide—political parties—spontaneously came into being. Sam Adams, who disapproved of anything that appeared to him to complicate the democratic process, was dismayed. And the rise of political parties caused him the worst humiliation he had ever suffered since he had become a politician.

Chapter
Thirty-six

When the Massachusetts Constitutional Convention drew to a close, the people of the state found, as did the citizens of other states, that the issue of states' rights had so firmly polarized public opinion that two political parties had been formed, the Federalists and the Anti-Federalists, soon to be called the Democratic Republicans. John Hancock, who had been told by those asking his support for the Constitution that they would favor him for the office of president of the United States, tried to win friends in both camps. But Sam Adams stood aloof, refusing to identify himself with either party and forbidding both to make any use of his name.

Late in 1788 the citizens of Massachusetts went to the polls to elect members to the new United States Senate and House of Representatives. Adams, since 1781 repeatedly adamant in his refusal to return to the Continental Congress from which he had retired, allowed himself to be persuaded by a number of Boston friends that the activities of the first, precedent-making federal Congress were so important that they required his presence. So he agreed to run for a seat in the national House of Representatives.

Under no circumstances, however, would he permit his name to be entered as a candidate on the lists of either the Federalists or the Democratic Republicans. The people of Boston had been electing him to one office or another for twenty-six years, he said, and his constituents knew him as well as he knew them. He failed to realize that he was out of tune with the times, and apparently he had forgotten the first requirement for all who held elective public office—a solid power base. Nothing his friends could say to him changed his mind.

Under the circumstances they did the best they could, and placed his name on the ballot as a candidate of both parties. Unfortunately, each already had a candidate, but his friends believed—and so, presumably, did he—that the magic of the Adams name would carry him to victory, as it had so often in the past.

Adams's supporters stressed the debt that the people of Massachusetts owed him for his past services, and this, too, was a mistake. The other candidates, campaigning actively on their own behalf, talked about the issues of the day that were of vital interest to the electorate, but Adams made no speeches, and his supporters were content to stress his record.

The younger voters, who were now in the majority, knew him, of course, but they felt no special gratitude toward him, and he was soundly defeated by Fisher Ames, the primary Federalist candidate, a lawyer who was only thirty-one years old. Never had Adams been so completely rebuffed.

Yet another insult was an unprecedented incident that took place on the day of the election. Adams went for a turn in his garden before breakfast and found, in a letter that had been dropped over the wall, a warning to the effect that an attempt would be made to assassinate him. He treated the threat with contempt, noting on the envelope in a scribbled hand that there was little to be feared from secret conspirators, and that if they had seriously intended to kill him they would have dared to attack him only after dark.

John Hancock's ambitions had received an even more severe blow. He had made a serious attempt to win the presidency of the United States, and leaflets, possibly printed at his own expense, hailed him as the "Saviour of His Country." But even the voters in his native Massachusetts had refused to take his bid seriously, and General Washington was the unopposed candidate for president in that state, as he was everywhere else. When the members of the Electoral College cast their ballots on the first Wednesday in February 1789, a number of names appeared as the second choice. John Adams received slightly less than half, and was elected vice-president.

Jefferson was named secretary of state, Hamilton became secretary of the treasury, the brilliant but erratic Edmund Randolph of Virginia was appointed attorney general and Henry Knox of Massachusetts was named secretary of war. Knox had held this post throughout the postwar years of the Confederation, and therefore had spent little time at home, so he was not involved in Massachusetts politics.

While the new federal government was being formed in New York City, John Hancock licked his wounds and decided to seek another term as governor. Politicians of every persuasion, including those who had worked against Sam Adams in the congressional race, felt he deserved recognition for his long services, and promoted his candidacy as lieutenant governor. Hancock was delighted, and formally requested his old mentor to appear on the ticket with him, both men avoiding party labels.

The duties of the lieutenant governor, who was also a member of the Governor's Council, were light, and in large part ceremonial. The salary was considerably higher than that paid the president of the Senate, and Adams, no longer sustained by income from his son, needed the money. So he accepted the offer.

The two heroes of the Revolution were formally reunited, and the printers of the ballots were so pleased that the names of the pair appeared in gold, while those of other candidates were printed in black. This was contrary to the law, but no one seemed to mind, except possibly General Lincoln, Adams's opponent.

So, in April 1789, while his cousin was taking the oath of office as vice-president of the United States, Sam Adams became lieutenant governor of Massachusetts.

He served four terms in that office, and other than participating in an occasional ceremonial function, he had few duties to occupy his time. An office was maintained for him in the State House, and he went there daily, but did little except correspond with John Adams and with such old friends as Richard Henry Lee, now a member of the federal House of Representatives.

Adams and his wife lived in an old house they had purchased on Winter Street, and had two servants to attend them. The house had been painted yellow some years earlier, but, as a physician who attended Adams in the latter years of his life wrote, both were a trifle the worse for wear. Adams took a daily walk, weather permitting, and occasionally he dropped in for a chat with an old friend, but he and Mrs. Adams rarely went out and seldom entertained anyone but members of the family. Other men who had been prominent before and after the Revolution were active in the affairs of the nation, but Adams was content to drift. In 1792 he was seventy years of age, and his life appeared to be behind him. In his only activity of significance, the last of the Puritans made a strong public statement upholding Hancock's refusal to permit a theatrical company to present one of William Shakespeare's plays in Boston.

Then, on October 8, 1793, John Hancock died and Sam Adams automatically became governor of Massachusetts. At the age of seventy-one, after living in semiretirement for more than four years, he suddenly found himself thrust into an active role. Many people wondered whether he was physically capable of performing the duties of his new office, for in the huge funeral procession, Governor Adams, who had started out on foot as befitted the principal official mourner, had been compelled to complete the ceremonial journey in a carriage after his strength failed.

The United States was a vastly changed country, and still more change was in the air. There were fifteen states now, Vermont and Kentucky having been admitted to the Union, and Tennessee stood on the threshold of statehood. President Washington and Vice-President John Adams were serving their second terms in office, and America's relations with both Britain and France were complicated by the newest war between those nations, which followed on the heels of the French Revolution.

There were more than four and one-half million people in the United States now, and the population continued to soar, principally because of the continuing migration from the British Isles. Benjamin Franklin had died three years earlier, his Philadelphia funeral drawing a crowd of more than twenty-five thousand mourners, and Noah Webster was now regarded as America's leading author.

The country was still agrarian, and less than a month after Adams took office, Eli Whitney of Mulberry Grove, Georgia, obtained a patent on a device he called a cotton gin, which would increase cotton exports from a meager 140,000 pounds in 1792 to almost 18,000,000 pounds in 1800. Manufacturing plants were springing up in ever-increasing numbers, most of them in New York, Philadelphia, New England and Baltimore, but the day was still far distant when America could boast that she had become self-sufficient.

Her dependence on imported manufactured goods was still her greatest problem, although the dollar was sound now, and her situation was complicated by the interference of both British and French warships with her merchant marine. American ships were stopped regularly on the high seas, and the British made matters even worse by impressing American seamen into the Royal Navy, a practice that infuriated the entire country.

New educational institutions, from primary grade schools to universities, were being built everywhere, and their proliferation was "the glory of America," as Governor Adams called it. More were appearing in Massachusetts than in any other state, and he often said that a literate America was the great hope of the future.

The change in Sam Adams's personal life was startling. He and Mrs. Adams moved out of their modest house on Winter Street and took possession of the handsome governor's mansion facing the Common, where a staff of a dozen servants attended them. Two carriages, one a coach of state, were available for their use, and they were required to entertain and be entertained so frequently that they seldom could spend an evening alone. Sam Adams overnight had more money than he had ever seen, his salary being increased from $600 to $2,500 per year.

There was an immediate shift in his political status, too. President Washington's efforts to mute the activities of the political parties had failed. The leader of the Federalists was Hamilton, whom John Adams had tacitly joined. Jefferson was the acknowledged head of the Democratic Republicans, whose platforms had changed since their Anti-Federalist beginnings.

Sam Adams cast his lot with the Democratic Republicans for a number of reasons. They were anti-British and pro-French, so he and they felt alike. They were zealous in guarding the rights of the states, and he agreed with that attitude, too, although, as he stressed in his address to the legislature on January 17, 1794, he was equally concerned that the states not infringe on the rights of the federal government, either. By joining the Democratic Republicans he swam against the tide in New England, where a strong majority had become Federalists, and because he was governor now, he automatically became the titular head of his party in Massachusetts. For the first time he and John Adams stood on opposite sides of a political fence.

His sudden return to a position of power and eminence brought no change in Sam Adams's habits of mind. His faith in the democratic process was as pure as Jefferson's, and his political philosophy was uncluttered. "In this state of society," he said in his address to the legislature, "the inalienable rights of nature are held sacred, and each member is entitled to an equal share of all the . . . rights." He put on no airs, left his door open to all who wanted to see him and, despising pomp, refused to accept an honor guard on ceremonial occasions.

Those who feared his health could not withstand the strain of his new office quickly learned better. Though nearing his seventy-second birthday, he was so invigorated that he could spend twelve hours or more at his desk without tiring, and his address to the legislature, ninety minutes long, was delivered extemporaneously.

On that occasion he dwelt at length on his favorite subject, the freedom of all Americans and the liberties of the individual. "I should think no man, in the exercise of his reason," he said, "would be inclined in any instance to trespass upon the equal rights of citizens, knowing that if he should do it he would weaken and risk the security of his own. Even different nations, having grounded their respective constitutions upon the afore-mentioned principles, will shortly feel the happy effects of mutual friendship, mutual confidence, and mutual strength. Indeed, I cannot but be of opinion that when those principles shall be rightly understood and universally established, the whole family and brotherhood of man will then nearly approach to, if not fully enjoy, that state of peace and prosperity which ancient philosophers and sages have foretold."

Freedom and democracy, then, remained for Adams the cure-alls for society's ills. Most American leaders were discreet in their references to the French Revolution, but the meaning of discretion was unknown to him, and he devoted an entire section of his address to panegyrics in which he heaped praise on France for her "noble new democracy." On every possible occasion thereafter he unfailingly continued to applaud the French Revolution, going out of his way to offer public toasts to the French consul in Boston.

He was equally lavish in his praise of education, and after quoting Plato—from memory—he declared that the education of youth was "almost sufficient to supply the place both of legislation and administration." He felt certain, he said, that the legislature would "cherish the interest of literature, the sciences, and all their seminaries," and he reminded the members that it was their duty under the Massachusetts Constitution to found, finance and administer enough schools to provide "a sound and sensible education for all."

Although he could be broadminded in some ways, Adams's elevation to the highest office in the state made him no less a bigot in others. Theaters were functioning and drawing large, enthusiastic and enlightened audiences in New York, Philadelphia and throughout the South, but there were no theaters in Massachusetts and, under the law, none could be established. An attempt had been made in 1792 to evade the letter of the law when a group of intellectuals, supported by several wealthy merchants, built what they called an "exhibition hall." But the sheriff had halted the first performance, and had been supported by Governor Hancock.

Now a number of the younger members of the legislature, believing that the Massachusetts stand was hopelessly old-fashioned, initiated a new bill to repeal the old law. Somewhat to their surprise the measure passed both houses and was sent to Governor Adams—who promptly vetoed it, scribbling in his shaking handwriting that the theater was "licentious and immoral." Thereafter a number of the younger men of both parties jocularly referred to him as Oliver Cromwell.

In 1794 Sam Adams was permanently relieved of financial embarrassment for the rest of his life. The claim of his late son, a bachelor, for payment of his wages as a surgeon in the Revolution was finally settled in the courts, and Adams was awarded the sum of five thousand dollars. He invested the better part in an inn in Jamaica Plain called the Peacock Tavern, which included forty acres of land and a number of farm buildings. This was the only financial venture of his life that ever proved profitable: it brought him an income of more than one thousand dollars per year, and at the time of his death was worth sixteen thousand dollars. His daughter inherited it from him, and when she died in 1820, the property was sold by her heirs for more than fifty thousand dollars.

Adams also enjoyed another financial windfall in the spring of 1794, this one completely unexpected. In spite of the new prosperity the United States was enjoying and the relative soundness of the dollar, creeping inflation was making all goods more expensive, and the members of the legislature knew that the governor, unlike his predecessor, had no private funds on which he could draw for the ceremonial entertaining that was one of his duties. So a bill was passed by both the House and Senate increasing his salary to $3,333 dollars per year.

The governor was outraged, considering the appropriation

frivolous. But the legislators had known in advance how the old man would react, and were ready to deal with him. A special committee paid him a call, and after being informed, as they had expected, that he intended to veto the bill, they assured him that they had more than enough votes to override the veto. So he was forced to accept the raise, but he made a public statement attacking extravagance.

He could not accustom himself to any of his new luxuries. He had never used a carriage, and found the coach that was one of the accoutrements of his office an embarrassment. Frequently he and Mrs. Adams would drive to the home of friends, and then, while the ladies went for a drive, the governor and his companion would take a stroll through the streets. When Adams was told by one of the younger members of the legislature that such conduct lowered the dignity of the governor's high office, he replied indignantly, "The Almighty gave me two feet for the purpose of using them, sir! I have been walking through the streets of Boston for seven decades, and shall continue to do so until I can no longer walk!"

When people halted him in the streets, as they frequently did, his manner was formal but cordial, as it had always been. He allowed himself one luxury after becoming governor, a walking stick with a head of embossed gold that, he said, enhanced the dignity of his position. His one vanity was his refusal to wear his glasses in public, except when absolutely necessary, although he could not read or write without them. As a consequence he rarely wrote anything but his signature in the presence of others, and when forced to read from a document he usually held his glasses up to his eyes.

What was truly remarkable was Adams's overall physical and mental rejuvenation. After living in semiretirement for several years and showing little interest in the world around him, his sudden elevation to the governorship brought him to life again, and he was as active as he had been a quarter of a century earlier. The last phase of his public career became one of the most frenzied.

Chapter
Thirty-seven

After Sam Adams had served six months as governor, the time came for the election of Massachusetts' chief executive, and to the surprise of no one he decided to run for a full term. The Democratic Republicans gave him their undivided support, but the Federalists, who were the majority party in the state, put up Judge William Cushing against him and believed he would win handily. Adams's old magic touch had been restored, however, and he swept to a triumph, with Cushing barely receiving a respectable vote.

The interference of both Great Britain and France with American merchantmen on the high seas was bringing the new nation closer to war, but many Democratic Republicans questioned the right of the new federal government to act on behalf of the states in the growing crisis. Adams was not one of them, and his realistic position was far closer to that of the Federalists, as an excerpt from his address to a joint session of the legislature, delivered on May 31, 1794, makes clear:

We are met at a very critical period. The baneful influence of war in Europe has already too far extended itself into this remote region,—a war of kings and nobles against the equal rights of men. The first object was to control the common right of all civil societies, by prostrating the attempt of a magnanimous nation to establish a constitution of government for themselves according to their own mind. More lately the nefarious design has been to crush the new-formed republic in its infancy. But the God of armies, who favors the brave in a righteous cause, has hitherto appeared for its protection, and crowned the astonishing efforts of its defenders with astonishing victories.

Great Britain takes an active part with the mighty combination of kings. Indeed, it does not appear that she has made a demand on our confederate republic to join the league,—a demand which we are well informed she has made on some of the neutral republics of Europe. But whilst we have preserved the most strict neutrality towards the belligerent powers of Europe, in observance of treaties made under the authority of the United States, which are the supreme law of the land, she, for the sake of aiding the cause in which she is so deeply engaged, has employed her naval force in committing depredations on our lawful and unprotected commerce. Thus, in fact, she has commenced hostilities.

The Federal Government, although very solicitous, if possible, to prevent the calamities of war, have meditated measures preparatory for the event. The papers and communications which I have received on this subject shall be laid before you. It was a declared intention of the people of the United States, when they adopted our present Constitution, "to form a more perfect union,"—an important object indeed. The voice of the people ought, therefore, to be attended to. Union formed upon the genuine republican principles and views of our political institutions, by combining our strength, will have a powerful tendency in time of war to reduce an unreasonable enemy to terms of justice and the re-establishment of tranquility, and in peace to secure the blessings of equal liberty to the present and future generations.

Adams's popularity, particularly the support given him by the older generation, undoubtedly derived from his continuing hatred of Great Britain. His attitude toward her had remained unchanged since the days before the Revolution, and those who remembered that stirring period gave him their unqualified support now that he had become active in politics again. But he was unable to carry his party with him: the Federalists had won comfortable majorities in both chambers of the legislature, and in the autumn of 1794 their candidates handily won election to the federal Congress.

Long accustomed to swaying with the winds of political fortune Governor Adams made it his business to work with the legislature, and they showed him equal respect. There were surprisingly few frictions, and no bills were passed which he felt compelled to veto. On a national level he consistently supported the federal government, and late in 1794, when President Washington issued a proclamation of neutrality intended to prevent American involvement in Europe's war, Adams again addressed the legislature on the subject, saying in a key paragraph:

> We have been under apprehensions of being made a party in the desolating contests in Europe. Permit me just to observe, that the first and main principle which urged the combined powers to enter into the contest is, in my opinion, unsupportable by reason and nature, and in violation of the most essential rights of nations and of men. The repeated acts of violence which have been committed on the property of American citizens might, in the opinion of some, have justified reprisals; but the policy of the Federal Government has directed to other measures. The wisdom of our own counsels, with the unexampled successes of our magnanimous ally, the republic of France, afford the strongest ground of hope that, under the continued smiles of Divine Providence, peace and tranquility, so interesting to a rising republic, will in the end be firmly established.

The Federalists could find nothing in Governor Adams's domestic policies to attack, and the worst they could say about his stand on foreign affairs was that he showed too much partiality to France. Inasmuch as too many people remembered French aid to America during the War of Independence and were still grateful for it, criticism of him on that score was muted.

So, when he chose to run for yet another term in the spring of 1795, they put up only token opposition to him, and he was reelected by what was tantamount to a completely unanimous vote. Only the right-wing Federalists even bothered to attack him during the campaign, making the unsubstantiated charge—heard in no other quarter—that he was growing senile. He ignored the accusation and, following his lifelong custom, did not even bother to campaign on his own behalf. His support now, at the age of seventy-five, was even greater than any he enjoyed prior to the Revolution or during the early days of that struggle. He was proving to younger men that he was the most popular politician in the history of Massachusetts and, having been restored to public favor, he could do no wrong in the eyes of the electorate.

This popularity enabled him to function independently, and he sought the support neither of his own Democratic Republicans nor of the Federalists. John Adams, observing him from his own pinnacle as vice-president of the United States, remarked that he comprised "a majority of one." Members of both parties tried to win the governor's support for various pet measures they were bringing before the legislature, but he stood aloof, refusing to make deals with anyone. The days of the Boston Caucus Club were far behind him, and in the twilight of his career, enjoying unique prestige and power, he preferred to rise above partisanship in the conduct of Massachusetts' affairs and in the administration of her government.

In his inaugural address, delivered on June 3, 1795, he continued to proselytize for the type of government for whose establishment in the United States he bore so much responsibility:

> We have a regular exercise of our Federal and State governments; and we owe our unceasing gratitude to the Supreme Ruler of the universe, who safely carried us through our arduous struggle for freedom, for which other nations are now

contending at the expense of their blood and treasure. We cannot but rejoice that the principles for which we contended, and which are constitutionally established in United America, are irresistibly spreading themselves through two mighty nations in Europe. We are now able to embrace those powerful sister republics, and what adds much to our joy on this occasion is, that those nations became allied to us in an hour when we were engaged in our hard conflict with an oppressive tyranny.

He refused to take part in the increasingly sharp conflict between the Federalists and the Democratic Republicans that was causing President Washington so much unhappiness in his second term. In fact, Sam Adams understood the lines of demarcation of the powers of the federal government and the states far more clearly than did men who were becoming emotional on the subject, and in spite of his Democratic Republican label, he accepted that division without cavil. Devoting the final paragraph of his inaugural to the matter, he said:

> Let us, fellow citizens, cultivate a due observance of the laws which are constitutionally made by the authority of this government as well as those of the Federal Government, agreeable to the Constitution of the United States. Let us transmit our liberties, our equal rights, our laws, and our free republican Constitutions, with their various concomitant blessings, to those who are coming upon the stage of action, and hope in God that they will be handed down in purity and energy to the latest posterity.

He returned to the subject again in 1795, when the country was upset by the so-called Whisky Rebellion, an insurrection of Pennsylvania farmers who refused to pay an excise tax imposed on them by federal law, claiming it reminded them of the Crown taxation responsible for the Revolution. They enjoyed the tacit support of Jefferson, who wrote to Madison that the law was "infernal," and would become "the instrument of dismembering the Union."

Washington, acting on the advice of Hamilton, called up fifteen thousand troops from Pennsylvania, Maryland and Virginia, and sent them on the march to western Pennsylvania. The insurrectionists disbanded, so no fighting took place; the leaders were arrested, and two were convicted of conspiracy, but Washington, having established the authority of the federal government, granted them pardons.

Sam Adams was deeply disturbed by the violation of principles, and his address to a special session of the legislature is the clearest and most precise statement he ever made on the subject of federal versus states' rights. Obviously he felt he still needed to pursue his self-appointed campaign of educating the people of Massachusetts and those elsewhere who read his address. He said, in part:

> We have solemnly engaged ourselves, fellow citizens, to support the Constitution of the United States and the Constitution of this Commonwealth. This must be reconcilable in the rights of every man who judiciously considers the sovereign rights of the one as limited to Federal purposes, and the sovereign rights of the other as acting upon and directing the internal concerns of our own republic. . . .
>
> Let those who wish to persuade the world to believe that a free representative republic cannot be supported will no doubt make use of every art to injure, and by degrees to alter, and finally to eradicate, the principles of our free Constitutions. But the virtuous and enlightened citizens of this Commonwealth and of all United America have understanding and firmness sufficient to support those Constitutions of civil government which they have themselves formed, and which have done them so much honor in the estimation of the world.
>
> It is with pain that I mention the insurrection which has lately taken place in a sister State. It was pointed more immediately at an act of the Federal Government. An act of that government as well as of the governments in the Union is constitutionally an act of the people; and our Constitutions provide a safe and easy method to redress any real grievances. No people can be more free than under a Constitution estab-

lished by their voluntary compact, and exercised by men appointed by their own frequent suffrages. If any law shall prove oppressive in its operation, the future deliberations of a freely elective representative will afford a constitutional remedy. But the measures adopted by the President of the United States, supported by the virtue of every citizen of every description in that and the adjacent States, have prevailed, and there is an end to the insurrection . . . .

The sovereignty of a nation always of right resides in the body of the people; and while they have delegated to their freely elected Legislature the power of exercising the sovereignty in their behalf, the executive department, as well as the magistrates who are appointed to render the Constitution efficient by carrying the laws into effect, are no less important to the people. For what avails the making of good and wholesome laws, unless they are duly executed? . . .

The Government of the United States is intrusted solely with such powers as regard our safety as a nation; and all powers not given to Congress by the Constitution remain in the individual States and people. In all good governments the legislative, executive and judiciary powers are confined within the limits of their respective departments. If, therefore, it should be found that the constitutional rights of our Federal and local governments should on either side be infringed, or that either of the departments aforesaid should interfere with another, it will, if continued, essentially alter the Constitution, and may in time, I hope far distant, be productive of such convulsions as may shake the political ground upon which we now happily stand.

Constitutional questions did not bother him as much as did the British seizure and search of American ships on the high seas and the continuing impressment of American merchant seamen in the Royal Navy. He objected strenuously to the new treaty John Jay had just worked out with the British, looking ahead and rightly seeing that the abuses would not end. It was the duty of the United States Senate to ratify or reject the agreement, and as the chief excutive of a state, Adams had no direct voice in the matter. But he was one of the nation's most distinguished elder statesmen, and he was still on intimate terms with some of the most powerful national leaders, so he made his influence felt in his own way. Reviving his career as an indefatigable letter writer, he unleashed fresh barrages of correspondence, writing to Jefferson and John Adams, among others, as well as to Jay himself.

The Democratic Republican minority in the Senate lacked the votes to block the treaty, which was ratified, and Sam Adams became the national spokesman for his party on the issue when he called the agreement "a degrading insult to the American people." There was an immediate flurry within the ranks of the party, and a number of men called for Sam Adams's election as president in the autumn of 1796, but he halted the boom before it could gather momentum, pointing out that he would be in his seventy-fifth year at the time of the election.

Governor Adams responded to the defeat of his party by proposing an amendment to the Constitution that would have given the House of Representatives a voice equal to the Senate's in ratifying all treaties. But the Massachusetts legislature was still dominated by the Federalists, who made no move to act on his recommendation.

Although he was too old to consider serving as president of the United States, Adams was still sufficiently vigorous to run again for governor of Massachusetts in the spring of 1796. He received a plurality of two to one in Boston and the eastern part of the state, although his opponent, Increase Sumner, won in several of the western counties. The Federalists, who increased their hold on the legislature, were gaining such strength that they liked to joke that Sam Adams was the only Democratic Republican in Massachusetts. But they continued to take good care to cooperate with him.

His relations with the legislature remained harmonious throughout the year of what was destined to be his last term in office. That year was quiet, and Adams continued to function as an able administrator, his age proving no handicap. In the presidential election that took place in the autumn of 1796, he was honored when the Electoral College seriously considered him for the presidency of the United States in spite of his protests that he was too old. John Adams received the highest number of votes, and was elected president; Jefferson stood second, and became vice-president. Behind them came Thomas Pinckney, Aaron Burr and Samuel Adams.

Seriously pondering his own retirement, Governor Adams sent warm letters of congratulations to president-elect John Adams and vice-president-elect Jefferson. Both replied in kind. It is presumed that, had he wished a place in his cousin's Cabinet, Sam Adams could have had the appointment. But he had reached the end of the road at last, and wanted neither honors nor fresh responsibility.

At the end of January 1797, a month prior to the inauguration of the new president and vice-president, the governor appeared before the Massachusetts legislature and delivered an exceptionally long address. Speaking for more than two hours, he reviewed the accomplishments of his administration, lectured the members and reminded the citizens of their duties. He had revealed his personal plans to no one, so it was assumed he would again run for reelection, and he created a stir when, at the end of his address, he declared:

> I think it is a duty incumbent upon me to acquaint you and our fellow citizens at large, that, having arrived to a stage of life marked in holy writ and verified by constant experience as a time of labor and sorrow, it is highly proper, both upon my own account and that of the public, to decline the future suffrages of my fellow citizens for the office I now have the honor to sustain. I have had this in contemplation for near a twelvemonth past. The infirmities of age render me an unfit person in my own opinion, and very probably in the opinion of others, to continue in this station; and I mention it now, that those of the electors who may probably be too warmly attached to me may not nullify their own votes by giving them for me.
>
> I have always been convinced that many others might have been found to fill my place with greater advantage to the Commonwealth than is now, or ever has been, in my power. In the civil department, during the times of war and peace, I

have served her in various stations to the best of my ability, and I hope with general approbation; and I can say with truth, that I have not enriched myself in her service. My warmest thanks are justly due to my constituents for the confidence they have repeatedly placed in me. When I shall be released from the burdens of my public station, I shall not forget my country. Her welfare and happiness, her peace and prosperity, her liberty and independence, will always have a great share in the best wishes of my heart.

Chapter
Thirty-eight

Late in May 1797, Sam Adams attended the inaugural of his successor, Judge Sumner, and then, before retiring to private life, he gave to the state a team of horses and carriage that had been presented to him a few years earlier by a group of his admirers. He lived quietly, frequently receiving visits from old friends. Those who knew him best noted that, as he grew older, he tended to remain silent in the company of strangers, but was talkative in the presence of people he knew.

His handwriting, which had greatly worsened in recent years, was now almost illegible, so his two grandsons and his granddaughter took turns writing his letters for him. He still maintained such a heavy correspondence that the task was not inconsiderable. As his eyesight failed his grandchildren also read to him, usually from the many newspapers sent to him regularly from every part of the United States. Everything that happened in the country remained of vital concern to him.

One of Adams's correspondents was Vice-President Jefferson, who usually called him "my very dear and ancient friend." The nature of their continuing discussions is best exemplified, perhaps, by a quotation from a letter written by Jefferson in late February 1800, about a year prior to his own inauguration as president:

> ... A letter from you, my respectable friend, after three-and-twenty years of separation, has given me a pleasure I cannot express. It recalls to my mind the anxious days we then passed in struggling for the cause of mankind. Your principles have been tested in the crucible of time, and have come out pure. You have proved that it was monarchy, and not merely British monarchy, that you opposed. A government by representatives elected by the people at *short* periods was our object, and our maxim at that day was, "Where annual election ends, tyranny begins." Nor have our departures from it been sanctioned by the happiness of their effects. A debt of a hundred millions, growing by usurious interest, and an artificial paper phalanx overruling the agricultural masses of our country, with other *et ceteras,* have a portentous aspect.
>
> I fear our friends on the other side of the water, laboring in the same cause, have yet a great deal of crime and misery to wade through. My confidence has been placed in the head, not in the heart, of Bonaparte. I hoped he would calculate truly the difference between the fame of a Washington and a Cromwell. Whatever his views may be, he has at least transferred the destinies of the republic from the civil to the military arm. Some will use this as a lesson against the practicability of republican governments. I read it as a lesson against the danger of standing armies.

In the spring of 1800 Caleb Strong was elected governor of Massachusetts, and on the day of his inauguration he followed the custom of marching to the State House to take oath of office. Strong, although a Federalist, as were all Massachusetts officials at this time, had nevertheless been a long-time admirer of Sam Adams. As the procession passed the Adams house on Winter Street, the governor-elect saw the old man in the window of his sitting room, watching the parade. He immediately halted and went inside for a word, and the hundreds who were taking part filled the street. The pair came to the door together, and at the sight of Adams the commander of the military escort ordered his men to salute. The whole crowd cheered, and Adams received a public demonstration of affection. It was one of his last public appearances.

On March 29, 1801, three weeks after Thomas Jefferson's inauguration, the new president sent a letter to his old comrade:

> I addressed a letter to you, my very dear and ancient friend, on the 4th of March; not indeed to you by name, but through the medium of my fellow citizens, whom occasion called on me to address. In meditating the matter of that address, I often asked myself, Is this exactly in the spirit of the patriarch Samuel Adams? Will he approve of it? I have felt a great deal for our country in the times we have seen, but individually for no one so much as yourself. When I have been told that you were avoided, insulted, frowned on, I could but ejaculate, "Father, forgive them, for they know not what they do." I confess I felt an indignation for you, which for myself I have been able under every trial to keep entirely passive. However, the storm is over, and we are in port. The ship was not rigged for the service she was put on. She will show the smoothness of her motions on her republican tack. I hope we shall once more see harmony restored among our citizens, and an entire oblivion of past feuds. Some of the leaders, who have most committed themselves, cannot come into this. I hope the great body of our fellow-citizens will do it. I will sacrifice everything but principle to procure it. A few examples of justice on officers who have perverted their functions to the oppression of their fellow-citizens must, in justice to those citizens, be made. But opinion, and the just maintenance of it, shall never be a crime in my view, nor bring injury on the individual. Those whose misconduct in office ought to have procured their removal, even by my predecessor, must not be protected by the delicacy due only to honest men.
>
> How much I lament that time has deprived me of your aid. It would have been a day of glory which should have called you to the first office of the administration. But give us your counsel, my friend, and give us your blessing; and be assured

that there exists not in the heart of man a more faithful esteem than mine to you, and that I shall ever bear you the most affectionate veneration and respect.

Although the health of the seventy-nine-year-old Sam Adams had declined sharply, his mind was still clear and active. He was thoroughly conversant with the issues of the day, and had lost none of his skill with words. In a reply to Jefferson, dated April 24, 1801, dictated to his granddaughter and calling the president "my very dear friend," he said:

Your letter of the 29th of March last came duly to my hand. I sincerely congratulate our country on the arrival of the day of glory which has called you to the first office in the administration of our Federal government. Your warm feelings of friendship most certainly have carried you to a higher tone of expression than my utmost merits will bear. If I have at any time been avoided or frowned upon, your kind ejaculation, in the language of the most perfect friend of man, surpasses every injury.

The storm is over, and we are now in port, and I dare say the ship will be rigged for her proper service. She must also be well manned and very carefully officered. No man should be fit to sustain an office who cannot conform to the principles by which he must be governed. With you I hope we shall once more see harmony restored; but after so severe and long a storm, it will take a proportionate time to still the raging of the waves. The world has been governed by prejudice and passion, which never can be friendly to truth; and while you nobly resolve to retain those principles of candor and justice, resulting from a free elective representative government, such as they have been taught to hate and despise, you must depend upon being hated yourself, because they hate your principles; not a man of them will dare openly to despise you. Your inaugural speech, to say nothing of your eminent services to the acceptance of our country, will secure you from contempt. It may require some time before the great body of our fellow citizens will settle in harmony, good will, and peace. The eyes of the people have too generally been fast closed from the view of their own happiness. Such, alas! has always been the lot of man. But Providence, who rules the world, seems now to be rapidly changing the sentiments of mankind in Europe and America.

May Heaven grant that the principles of liberty and virtue, truth and justice, may pervade the whole earth. When deep prejudices shall be removed in some, the self-interestness of others shall cease, and many honest men, whose minds, for want of better information [. . . ?], shall return to the use of their own understanding, the happy and wished-for time shall come.

It is not in my power, my dear friend, to give you counsel; an old man is apt to flatter himself that he stands upon an equal footing with younger men; he indeed cannot help feeling that the powers of his mind, as well as his body, are weakened, and fondly wishing his young friends to think that he can instruct them by his experience, when in all probability he has forgotten every trace of it that was worth his memory. Be assured that my esteem for you is as cordial, if possible, as yours is to me. Though an old man cannot advise you, he can give you his blessing. You have my blessing and my prayers.

Samuel Adams

P.S.—My dear Mrs. Adams will not suffer me to close this letter till I let you know that she recollects the pleasure and entertainment you afforded us when you were about to embark for France, and she hopes that your administration may be happy to yourself and prosperous to your country.

This letter makes it obvious that Sam Adams had not lost his common sense approach to life. A lesser man might have been tempted to offer advice to President Jefferson, but he was wise enough not to trust his own judgment.

As he grew still older his correspondence diminished, and in his last two years those who were close to him noted his tendency, in his conversation, to dwell increasingly on the dramatic days before and during the War of Independence. Only that period, in which he himself had achieved immortality, seemed to interest him, and he was impatient when relatives or friends tried to change the subject.

But he was neither too old nor too senile to return to battle when principles he regarded as sacred appeared to be at stake. In October 1802, his old comrade and fellow propagandist, Thomas Paine, returned to the United States after spending fourteen stormy years in England and France. Paine had been indicted for treason in Britain, but had escaped across the Channel, and had taken an active role in the French Revolution. In fact, he had been condemned to imprisonment and probable death, and had been set free after spending almost a year in prison only because Robespierre, the would-be French tyrant, had died. Paine was still highly regarded in America, and intended to settle down on a farm of ten thousand acres that the state of New York had given him.

But it came to Sam Adams's attention that his former friend intended to write a major attack on religion in general and on Christianity in particular. This was more than the last of the Puritans could tolerate, and he sent off a long, stern letter, writing it in his own hand. It is the last of his letters that has ever been found.

He opened it on a warm note, recalling his past association with Paine and acknowledging the philosopher's great contribution to the cause of American liberty. Then his tone changed, and he said that "when I heard you had turned your mind to a defence of infidelity, I felt myself much astonished and more grieved."

He referred to Jefferson as a mutual friend, and after saying that the president was trying to heal the nation's wounds, he begged Paine not to make matters worse, reminding him that Jefferson frequently had been attacked, "without the least shadow of proof," as an atheist. What was foremost in the old man's mind was that precious freedom to which he had devoted his life, and he closed by saying that "neither religion nor liberty can long subsist in the tumult of altercation, and amidst the noise and violence of faction."

Paine wrote a long, careful reply in January 1803, defending himself and his position. Eventually the two letters were printed by scores of American newspapers, then republished as pamphlets in defense of organized religion, and Sam Adams was again in the limelight during the last days of his life. Whether he was aware of the publication of his letter is not known; in any event, he did not reply. As the year progressed he became increasingly feeble, and by summer his daily "walks" consisted of taking a few steps in the street outside his house. In September his mind began to wander, and his physicians put him to bed. He was still lucid at times, and knowing he was dying, gave strict instructions that he wanted no ostentatious funeral, no funeral parade and the plainest coffin available. He made out his will, leaving his entire estate, which had become substantial only in recent years, to his wife, daughter and grandchildren.

On the night of October 1 he began to slip, and the family gathered at his bedside. He suffered no pain, and dozed, awakening from time to time and smiling at Mrs. Adams. At seven o'clock in the morning he said something to her, and she leaned forward in an attempt to hear him. Again, he smiled, and was gone.

The entire country joined in mourning for the Grand Incendiary. President Jefferson issued a statement paying tribute to him, and John Randolph delivered a long, stirring eulogy in the Congress. Adams's request for a quiet funeral was ignored, and he was given a burial in state, with an escort of troops. Among the pallbearers were his old comrades, Elbridge Gerry and Major General William Heath. The church bells of Boston tolled, shops were closed, and the guns on Fort Independence in the harbor were fired at sixty-second intervals.

For the rest of the year members of the United States Senate and House of Representatives wore mourning bands on their sleeves, and the Massachusetts legislature quickly followed the example of the Congress. Former President John Adams, afraid he might be seen weeping in public, remained in seclusion for a month.

It was rumored that, a few months prior to his death, Sam Adams had written a last letter to President Jefferson as a legacy to his country, and that it would be published soon thereafter. If Jefferson actually received such a communication he never acknowledged its existence, much less made its contents public.

Assuming that Adams did write the letter, it may be that, composed in his dotage, it was not worthy of him, and for that reason Thomas Jefferson treated it as private.

In the years that followed, the memory of Adams was gradually overshadowed by that of the other giants of his era, and by the time of the Civil War he had become a shadowy figure, remembered principally as the originator of the Boston Tea Party. But the accomplishments of the Father of American Independence continue to speak for themselves, two centuries after his victory in the cause he regarded as sacred.

Select Bibliography

ADAMS, JAMES TRUSLOW. *The Adams Family*. Boston, 1930.

———. *The Founding of New England*. Boston, 1921.

———. *Revolutionary New England, 1691 – 1776*. Boston, 1923.

ADAMS, JOHN. *Works*. Boston, 1819. 5 vols..

ADAMS, SAMUEL. *The Writings of Samuel Adams*. H. A. Cushing, ed. Boston, 1904–1908. 4 vols.

———. *Warren-Adams Letters*. Boston, 1917–1925. 2 vols.

AGAR, HERBERT. *Land of the Free*. Boston, 1935.

AVERY, ELROY. *History of the United States*. Cleveland, 1904–1910. 7 vols.

BANCROFT, GEORGE. *History of the United States*. New York, 1883–1885. 6 vols.

BEARD, CHARLES A. and MARY R. *The Rise of American Civilization*. New York, 1933–1939. 3 vols.

BECKER, CARL L. *The Declaration of Independence*. New York, 1922.

———. *The Eve of the Revolution*. New York, 1920.

BEMIS, SAMUEL F. *The Diplomacy of the American Revolution*. New York, 1935.

BOGART, ERNEST L. *An Economic History of the American People*. New York, 1930.

BULLOCK, CHARLES J. *The Finances of the United States from 1775 to 1789*. Madison, 1895.

CHINARD, GILBERT. *Honest John Adams*. Boston, 1933.

CHITWOOD, OLIVER P. *A History of Colonial America.* New York, 1931.

COMMAGER, HENRY STEELE. *Documents of American History.* New York, 1934. 2 vols.

COUPLAND, REGINALD. *The American Revolution and the British Empire.* New York, 1930.

DOYLE, JOHN A. *English Colonies in America.* New York, 1889–1907. 5 vols.

EARLE, ALICE MORSE. *Customs and Fashions in Old New England.* New York, 1896.

EGERTON, HUGH E. *Causes and Character of the American Revolution.* Oxford, 1923.

FISHER, SYDNEY G. *The Struggle for American Independence.* Philadelphia, 1908. 2 vols.

FRIEDENWALD, HERBERT. *The Declaration of Independence, an Interpretation and an Analysis.* New York, 1904.

GILPIN, H. D. *Samuel Adams.* Boston, 1872.

GREENE, EVARTS B. *The Provincial Governor in the English Colonies of North America.* New York, 1898.

GUEDALLA, PHILIP. *Fathers of the Revolution.* New York, 1926.

HARLOW, RALPH V. *Samuel Adams, Promoter of the American Revolution.* New York, 1923.

HART, ALBERT BUSHNELL. *American History Told by Contemporaries.* New York, 1897–1929. 5 vols.

HOCKETT, HOMER C. *Political and Social Growth of the American People.* New York, 1941.

HOLST, HERMANN VON. *The Constitutional and Political History of the United States.* Chicago, 1876–1892. 8 vols.

LECKY, WILLIAM E. H. *American Revolution, 1763–1783.* New York, 1898.

MCLAUGHLIN, ANDREW C. *A Constitutional History of the United States.* New York, 1935.

MERRIAM, CHARLES E. *History of American Political Theories.* New York, 1903.

MILLER, JOHN C. *Sam Adams, Pioneer in Propaganda.* New York, 1936.

MORISON, SAMUEL ELIOT. *Builders of the Bay Colony.* Boston, 1930.

NEVINS, ALLAN. *The American States During and After the Revolution, 1775–1789.* New York, 1925.

PALFREY, JOHN G. *A Compendious History of New England.* Boston, 1884. 4 vols.

PARKMAN, FRANCIS. *Works.* Boston, 1922. 13 vols.

SCHLESINGER, ARTHUR M. *The Colonial Merchants and the American Revolution.* New York, 1917.

SEELEY, SIR JOHN R. *The Expansion of England.* Boston, 1883.

SMALL, ALBION W. *Beginnings of American Nationality*, Baltimore, 1890.

SPEARS, J. R. *The Story of the American Merchant Marine*. New York, 1918.

TREVELYAN, SIR OTTO G. *The American Revolution*. London, 1905. 3 vols.

TYLER, MOSES C. *Literary History of the American Revolution*. New York, 1940.

VAN TYNE, CLAUDE H. *Causes of the War of Independence*. Boston, 1922.

WEEDEN, WILLIAM B. *Economic and Social History of New England, 1620–1789*. Boston, 1890. 2 vols.

WELLS, WILLIAM V. *The Life and Public Services of Samuel Adams*. Boston, 1865. 3 vols.

WHITTON, F. E. *The American War of Independence*, New York, 1931.

WILSON, WOODROW. *A History of the American People*. New York, 1902. 5 vols.

WINSOR, JUSTIN C. *The Narrative and Critical History of America*. Boston, 1884–1889. 8 vols.

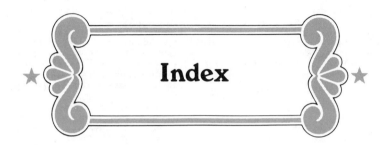

Index

Livingston, Philip, 242
Livingston, Robert R., 276, 277
Locke, John, influence of, 7–10, 14, 19–20, 31, 39, 84, 112, 135, 273
Long Island, Battle of, 287–288, 290
Loyalists ("Tories"), 211, 230, 266; Adams vs., 205, 280, 321, 337–338, 339; and Coercive Acts, 202–203; exile of, 222, 284, 315; leaders of, 213; return of, 338; strongholds of, 220, 224, 226, 231, 251, 299, 325, 329
"Loyalty and Sedition" (essay), 16–18

McKean, Thomas, 330–331
Mackintosh (shoemaker), 47
Madison, James, 119, 378; and Federal Constitution, 332, 354, 356, 363
Malcomb, Captain Daniel, 81, 83
"Manifesto" (Adams & T. Paine), 314
"Marlborough" (pseudonym), 186–187
Maryland: and independence, 275, 276; loyalism in, 299; and Federal Constitution, 362. See also Baltimore
Mason, George, 363
Massachusetts: and Federal Constitution, 354–364 passim; state constitution for, 288, 308, 309, 319–321, 332. See also Boston
Massachusetts Assembly: and Boston Massacre, 111, 112, 114; and Boston Tea Party, 188–189; and Coercive Acts, 200, 201, 220; and Committees of Correspondence, 125, 159–160, 176; radical control of, 104, 121, 122; and Stamp Act, 48, 50, 52; and tea boycott, 117; and Townshend Acts, 70–75, 90–91, 93 (see also Circular letter)
Massachusetts Spy, 112, 116, 117, 139–140, 160, 179, 227
Mein, John, 83
Merchants' Association (Boston), 222
Merchants' Club of Boston, 81, 83, 117
Minutemen (paramilitary organization), 231, 234; and Lexington & Concord, 238–241
Molasses Act (1733), 33, 37
Monmouth, Battle of, 312
Montgomery, General Richard, 253, 262
Morris, Gouverneur, 344, 345
Morris, Robert, 264, 335, 344

Natural rights doctrine, 57–58, 135–138, 139. See also Locke, John
"Natural Rights of Colonists as Men" (report), 135–138, 139, 143, 146
Navy: American, 253, 311 (see also Privateers); Royal, 126, 225, 264
Neutrality Proclamation (1793), 376

Newfoundland fishing banks, 331
New Hampshire: and Federal Constitution, 353, 362; and tea blockade, 183
New Jersey: in Revolutionary War, 290 (see also: Monmouth; Trenton)
Newport, R.I., in Revolutionary War, 313, 321–322
News-Letter. See Boston News-Letter
New York: Assembly dissolved in, 65, 66, 70; and Boston Tea Party, 175, 182, 183, 185–186; British troops in (prewar), 104, 161, 173; and Federal Constitution, 362; and independence, 280, 281; loyalists in, 220, 226; and Quartering Act, 56–57, 65; in Revolutionary War, 265, 271, 282, 284, 319 (see also: Fort Ticonderoga; Saratoga)
Nonimportation agreements. See Boycotts
North, Lord, 115, 127, 153, 170, 216, 352; assessments of, 219–220, 224, 225; blamed by Adams, 258–259; and Boston Tea Party, 164; and Coercive Acts, 205–206, 231; and Revolutionary War, 248, 250, 284–285, 305, 311, 312
North Carolina, Revolutionary War in, 314, 324
Northwest Territory: Quebec Act and, 192; in Revolutionary War, 234

"Observation" (pseudonym), 128, 168
Ohio, formation of, 253
Oliver, Andrew, 13, 43, 44, 45, 106, 159, 216
Oliver, Peter, 189
Order of the Cincinnati, 340–341
Oswald, Richard, 324
Otis, James, 9, 20–21, 26, 27, 58, 62, 78, 79–80, 119, 120–121, 278; and British troops (1768), 102, 103; and Stamp Act, 43, 47, 48, 52, 57, 60–61; and Sugar Act, 35, 36, 38, 39, 42; and Townshend Acts, 81, 83, 89, 94
Ottawa Indians, 234

Paine, Robert Treat, 201, 208, 241, 242
Paine, Thomas, 253–254, 319, 389–390; Common Sense of, 254, 256–257; "Manifesto" of, 314
Paper money bill (1740), 10
Parker, Captain John, 238, 240
Patriots, 79–80, 104, 128, 130, 161, 204, 220, 230; and British troops (1768), 102, 103; and Coercive Acts, 203; in Conn., 210, 241; and Continental Association, 222; and First Continental Congress, 200–201, 211, 214; in Georgia, 231; increase in strength of, 196, 204–205,

Congress, 209, 221; and independence, 227; and Lexington & Concord, 240; and Mass. Committee of Safety, 207; and tea boycott, 116

Washington, George, x, xi, 145, 228; and Adams, 262–263, 323, 340–341; and Constitutional Convention, 354; and First Continental Congress, 211, 212–213, 215, 254; as military commander in chief, 244, 245, 249, 251, 262, 264–265, 273, 282, 286 *(see also* Continental Army); as President, 254, 367, 368, 370, 376, 378–379; Revolutionary War campaigns of, 247, 250, 289, 290, 291, 293–295, 298, 299, 301, 302, 307–308, 310–312, 324, 330

Webster, Daniel, 359–360

Webster, Noah, 369

Wells, Andrew E. (brother-in-law), 231

Wells, Francis (father-in-law), 231, 248

Wells, Hannah Adams (daughter), 23, 40, 66, 76, 101, 149, 150, 190, 206, 209, 248, 250, 287, 289, 306, 315–316, 329, 343, 372, 390

Wells, Captain Thomas (son-in-law), 23, 329

Wells, William V. (great-grandson), 10, 27, 42, 127–128, 138, 175, 240, 266, 269, 270, 326

Wendell, Oliver, 196, 229

Western land claims, 253, 300–301

Whigs (American). *See* Patriots

Whigs (English), 50, 224–225; and Boston Tea Party, 154, 188; and Revolutionary War, 248, 256, 284–285, 305. *See also:* Barré, Isaac; Burke, Edmund; Fox, Charles James; Pitt, William the elder

Whipping-Post Club, 16

Whisky Rebellion (1795), 378–379

Whitney, Eli, 369

Wilkes (Mass. radical), 130

Williams (tax commissioner), 86, 88

Works (John Adams), 78

Writs of assistance, 65

Yard, Mrs., 253

Yorktown, Va., British surrender at, 330

"Z." (pseudonym), 128